Created and Directed by Hans Höfer

INSIGHT GUIDES

The New GERMANY

Edited by Wieland Giebel

Translated by Tony Halliday

Editorial Director: Dieter Vogel

APA PUBLICATIONS

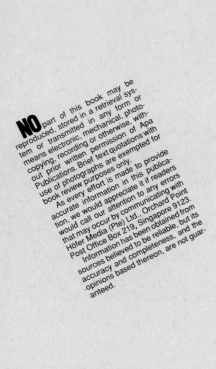
The New Germany

ABOUT THIS BOOK

When Apa Publications launched the first edition of its highly successful *Insight Guide: Germany* in 1987, nobody could have foreseen that, only four years later, a completely new book on the country would be needed. One day, many knew, the Berlin Wall would come down and the German Democratic Republic would unite with the Federal Republic. But even the most cockeyed optimist couldn't have predicted the speed at which the map of Europe changed. With the automatic lifting of all travel restrictions, new doors to new destinations were opened up overnight. Keeping pace with these developments Apa, too, set about integrating the old with the new. The result is *Insight Guide: The New Germany*, published in six languages.

The Authors

Much of the information presented in the original Germany book has been retained and updated, but new chapters on history and culture had to be written and a much wider territory covered. As well as describing the new destinations now accessible to visitors, *The New Germany* aims to show how much the people of the two parts of the country have in common, despite 40 years of forced separation. But it is clear, too, that barriers still exist between the east and the west and that real reunification will be a long process.

The task of bringing the whole of Germany "under one roof", amalgamating the new material with original book which Heinz Vestner edited in 1987, was assigned to project editor **Wieland Giebel**. Born in Thuringia, one of the new federal states, Giebel grew up in Kassel in the state of Hesse. He has worked all the way from the Ruhrgebiet to the heart of Africa, written books about Northern Ireland and the labour market in Germany and has reported on the environment both for radio and the Berlin newspaper *taz*. Giebel himself wrote quite a number of articles for *The New Germany*, mainly dealing with the southern part of the former GDR, describing all the sights between his native Thuringian Forest and the city of Dresden which is commonly referred to as as the "Venice on the Elbe". He also deals with the catastrophic environmental problems in the former GDR, his chapter "The Bitter Taste of Bitterfeld" summing up the legacy of neglect bequeathed by the old regime. Cityguides *Dresden* and the *The New Berlin* are further Apa projects of which Giebel has taken charge.

Apart from clarifying the "Origins of Germany" for the history section, **Roger Jopp**, a former history teacher from Düsseldorf, contributed the features on the "Hanseatic League" and "The Sciences in Germany". He also takes a close look at the romantic city of Heidelberg. Germany's legendary tennis-playing wonders Boris Becker and Steffi Graf were both born near Heidelberg; the feature by **Norbert Thomma** describes their rise to fame and glory. Other legends are followed by **Reinhard Böhme** on "The Trails of the Brothers Grimm".

Horst Kuhley, who has both studied and taught in the US and Britain, contributed the articles "Journey Along the Rhine", "Along the Weser" and the pieces on Hamburg and the North Sea and Baltic coasts. The southern part of Germany was covered by **Joachim Beust**, who wrote about the charms of the Black Forest; **Carla Meyer**, who takes a close look at the Bavarian metropolis of

Giebel   *Jopp*   *Meyer*

Munich and escorts us on a long and winding tour through her homeland of Franconia; and **May Hof**, who leads us along the German Alpine Road and down to Lake Constance.

Augsburg-born **Maja Specht** and Berlin writer **Michael Bienert** take us to all those fabled towns and castles along the "Romantic Road". One of Germany's most celebrated castle builders was "mad" King Ludwig II of Bavaria, whom Bienert describes in his feature "The Fairy Tale King". He also looks at the lives of two of Germany's most famous sons, the poet Goethe and the composer Ludwig van Beethoven, delves into the changing eating habits of the Germans in "The German Cuisines" and relates the life story of the legendary Volkswagen "Beetle".

Further environmental issues are dealt with by **Gerd Rosenkranz** in his features "The Dying Forests" and "Atomic White Elephant". Western Germany's industrial power house, the Ruhrgebiet, is described by local man and *taz* correspondent **Walter Jacobs**.

Martin Clemens, a historian from Munich, takes us through complex story of the rise and fall of the German Empire and **Dietmar Hertl**, who studied German, history, and political and social science in Munich, contributed an informative article on this "Land of poets and Philosophers". **Herbert Ammon**, a Berliner active in a number of political movements in recent years, was responsible for piecing together the postwar developments in both East and West Germany. **Matthias Geis**, the GDR expert for *taz*, experienced the dramatic changes in the East at first hand. Here he describes the final hours of the old GDR.

In the creation of the totally new articles covering Berlin, the editor enlisted the services of *taz* journalist **Petra Dubilski**, who was born and bred in the metropolis on the Spree. Here she looks closely at the city's history, its people and everything else that makes the city tick. Further articles on the former GDR were provided by **Barbara Hinz.** Trained as a photographer in the GDR and now living in Munich, she describes and photographs north-eastern Germany in her article "From the Brandenburg Marches to the Baltic" and looks at the unspoilt wilderness of the "Mecklenburg Lake District".

Responsible for the overall production of the book was **Dieter Vogel**, Apa's editorial director in Munich. Vogel's written contributions to the book include "Along the Moselle", "The Road to Cologne" and "Relaxation in Eastern Bavaria".

The Photographers

Much of the photography was provided by **Erhard Pansegrau**, a trained electronics engineer from Berlin, whose work appears in many of the other Apa titles originated in German. Almost all other photographers represented here also come from Berlin: **David Baltzer**, the Chilean **Victor Barrientos**, **Harald Hauswald**, **Michael Hughes**, **Sabine** and **Karl-Heinz Kraemer**, **Kai-Uwe Müller** and **Stephan Maria Rother**. In addition, **Wolfgang Fritz** from Cologne and **Rainer Kiedrowski** from Düsseldorf provided their usual high-quality contributions.

A comprehensive Travel Tips section was provided for the English-language edition by **Andrew Eames** and **Susanne Pleines**. Additional editing work was done through Apa's London editorial office by **Marcus Brooke** and the book was proof-read and indexed by **Sophia Ollard**.

Bienert

Dubilski

Vogel

Pansegrau

History & Features

Places

Maps

TRAVEL TIPS

THE NEW GERMANY

In the Autumn of 1989 Germany became the focus of world attention. Television pictures told the story. The Brandenburg Gate was opened, the Berlin Wall was dismantled and carried away and within a year the division of Germany was to become a thing of the past. Former enemies would become friends and the Cold War was to be buried once and for all.

What a challenge – to grasp the implications of these remarkable developments. Now, Germany as a travel destination takes on a completely new countenance. One of the first and most poignant symbols of change occurred when thousands of "Trabis" – Trabants, the two-stroke flagship of the automobile industry of the former GDR – began pouring over to the West. The aspiration of the people to travel to the West was one of the most powerful motors of change, and no wall could indefinitely suppress the will of the people to see the world with their own eyes. The people had opened the door by their own account and the Trabi, symbol of economic backwardness, was now at the head of the movement to end the degrading system of 40 years. And when the Trabi broke through the Wall it heralded the free flow of traffic in the other direction.

Worldwide participation: The reunited Germany is naturally something of an unknown quantity. Interest in its history and its people is indeed immense; TV crews and journalists were on the spot when the dramatic changes occurred. The participation of outsiders in these developments is astonishing. Even at the time of writing, in the shops of New York City, Tokyo and Melbourne, fragments of the wall continue to fetch high prices. But behind this facade there hides a very real desire to know more about this country, its people and its history. Who are these Germans, and which road will this new "great power" now take?

For the Germans themselves a new door to new destinations has also been opened up.

And this new Germany offers an inexhaustible supply of extremely varied tourist attractions. People from the East tend to head first to the south, to the Alps and the Romantic Road. They might then go in search of those fabled castles on the Rhine, and then head up north beyond the spires of Cologne Cathedral to Hamburg and to the North Sea coast.

Visitors from the West can rediscover the tracks of Goethe by walking the "Rennsteig" in the Thuringian Forest. They can admire

the Residence of August the Strong in Dresden, or hop from one castle to another via the 600 or so lakes of the Mecklenburg Lake District. And anyone looking for excitement can head for the cities with their wide choice of culture and entertainment, particularly in the former and future capital of Berlin.

In these days of polluted beaches and delayed flights, might it not be a good idea not only for Germans, but for others to enjoy what will be a relatively hassle-free trip right on their doorstep? In conjunction with the Federal Railways many local operators and tourist associations now offer packages which include walking, cycling and boating holidays to what used to be the East. In an attempt to catch up with the West, the authorities in the former GDR have created new nature reserves, wildlife sanctuaries and national parks.

Germany is endowed with an extremely varied landscape: from the North German Plain with its quaint red-brick houses dating from its Hanseatic past, on along the North Sea and Baltic coasts, down to the fortified diocesan and free cities in the central highland areas and on to the picturesque villages in the Alps. In many places the past harmoniously mingles with the present. Ancient buildings remain as symbols of the nation's endurance to change; monuments in stone to a long and eventful German past.

History is made by man: New architectural styles, new ways of life, new ideologies evolve with the times. The restrictions of the Middle Ages were torn asunder by both material and intellectual developments in Germany, the land of poets and philosophers. The German spirit won through against the Pope in Rome and gave birth to Protestantism. The ideas of Socialism were also originally formulated by Germans, but the form that these assumed in the former GDR was ultimately smashed by the influence of those very same Protestant ideologies.

The places of interest in Germany can only be fully appreciated with background knowledge of all those people who composed and wrote, loved and built, ruled and suffered. The extensive history section in this book is devoted to the personalities and events that lay behind the wonderful creations we see, hear and read today. In guiding the reader through the country the book aims to place at the forefront those men and women who have had a positive influence on developments, who have aided progress towards a humane society.

While the travel destinations, the impressive churches and the important museums are all described in this book, their inclusion does not eclipse references to the dark side of Germany's past and present – the memorials and the concentration camps, the uranium contaminated areas around Ronneburg, the pollution of the waterways and the sick or dying forests. It is only possible to appreciate beauty when one is aware of how endangered it is; only then can concrete steps be made towards its preservation. In this regard,

this book is very much "into" conservation.

In September 1990, one year after the collapse of the Wall, the Foreign Ministers of the four victorious powers and the two – still divided – German states affixed their signatures to an agreement recognising the new Germany as a sovereign state. And then the country was reunited. Never before had the dissolution of a state in peacetime been carried out so quickly and radically. With Germany's recognition of the Oder-Neisse border with Poland, this hitherto incomplete chapter of European history was closed once and for all. This book can therefore justifiably claim to be an all-German guide book.

In the heart of Europe: Geographically

speaking, Germany lies at the very centre of Europe. All major trans-European communications paths meet here. In order to cross Germany from north to south, one has to commence the journey at the town of List on the North Sea island of Sylt and finish 876 kilometres (544 miles) away in Oberstdorf in the Allgäu Alps. From Aachen in the west to Görlitz on the Polish border in the east the distance is about 630 kilometres (390 miles) as the crow flies. Germany now has a total area of 357,000 sq. km (137,840 sq. miles) and with almost 80 million inhabitants is the most heavily populated country in Europe. 35 million cars now roll along Germany's roads. By the year 2000 this will have increased to 42 million. The north-south connections in Germany are some of the busiest highways in the world. Despite the good quality of the roads, traffic comes to a complete standstill again and again on both the *autobahns* and the trunk roads. Together with the inland air services, the railways provide for an efficient, comfortable and ecologically sensible means of getting from one major centre to another.

The German economic power and the proverbial thoroughness of the German people engender both respect and a certain amount of dread among European neighbours. However, the historically justified fears concerning any possible designs that this European central power might have are all but dispelled by the fact that Germany is an integral and committed member of the European Community and is keen to play its role in the security of the area.

tantism comes out tops with a total of 30 million adherents. Less than one percent of the population of the former GDR was made up of foreigners, as against 7.6 percent in the old Federal Republic. In the GDR foreigners were isolated and had little influence on society. The barriers for the successful integration of foreigners were thus in place long before the collapse of the Wall. They are barriers that the general population of the five new states still have to overcome.

Five new states for Europe: With 250 people per sq. km (650 sq. miles), the west of Germany is more densely populated than the east, which has only 150. Nevertheless, there are parts in the east that are very densely

Religion: Numbering 27.3 million, the Catholics make up the largest religious minority in the land. While in the old Federal Republic there are actually more Catholics than Protestants (26.3 million to 24.9 million), seen across the whole country Protes-

populated, notably the highly industrialised areas around Halle and Leipzig. However, almost a quarter of the East German population still lives in communities with less than 200 inhabitants; in the west that figure is only 6 percent. Since 3 October 1990 the new Federal Republic has consisted of 16 states: Bavaria, Baden-Württemberg, Saarland, Rhineland-Palatinate, Hesse, North Rhine Westphalia, Lower Saxony, Schleswig-Holstein, and the city states of Hamburg and Bremen, have now been joined by Thuringia, Saxony, Brandenburg, Sachsen-Anhalt, Mecklenburg-Vorpommern and naturally Berlin as its own state and the new capital.

<u>Left</u>, the "Trabbi" breaks through the wall. <u>Above</u>, the symbol of unity – black, red and gold.

It seems that the beauty of the countryside of the Neckar Valley was already appreciated as long ago as the Early Stone Age. Here, near the city of Heidelberg, the earliest known human remains in Germany were discovered: *homo heidelbergiensis* is about half a million years old. Young by comparison are the bones of Neanderthal Man who lived in caves about 50,000 years ago on the River Nahe near the present day city of Düsseldorf.

The reconstructed village settlement at Unteruhldingen on Lake Constance testifies to the advanced construction techniques used by New Stone Age man about 8,000 years ago. Here he built his houses on stilts in the lake to protect them from attack by man and beast. And on the Lüneburg Heath in Northern Germany huge tombstones dating from this era are still standing. The Germans aptly call these megaliths the "graves of the giants" – *Hünengräber* – because surely nobody but a giant could have transported such massive slabs of stone.

The Celts: Although their origins are obscure, it was the Celts who between 800-400 BC developed the first Middle-European period of high culture, known as the *La Tene* Culture. The Celts settled an area from Northern France to the Balkans and lived from agriculture and trade. Unlike the Germans, who had settled north of the River Danube and east of the Rhine, the Celts built cities which the Romans called *oppida*. The largest *oppidum* south of the Danube was located near present-day Malching, a small town near Ingolstadt in Bavaria.

Until the middle of the 1st century BC, the Germans were a continuous thorn in the flesh of the Celts as they pushed south and attempted to subjugate Celtic territory. Then the Romans arrived on the scene and having completed their conquests of Celtic Gaul (58 BC) they then devoted their energy to securing the borders of the empire as far east as the Rhine and as far north as the Danube. It wasn't long before the entire area of Celtic settlement came under Roman control and the Celts became assimilated to Roman culture. The Germans were now therefore the

Left, the minstrel Walther von der Vogelweide.

most immediate neighbours of the Romans.

In AD 60 the Roman historian Tacitus characterised the Germans thus: "They have blue eyes and red hair, and although they have an impressive build and are strong fighters they are not given to hard graft". He was referring to the multitude of tribes living on the vague northern borders of the Roman Empire and partly within Roman conquered territory. These tribes must indeed have appeared unruly and uncultured to the sophisticated Romans. They knew no cities and their agriculture was not developed much beyond subsistence level. The grey skies and rainy weather can have done little to add to the appeal of the country in which they lived, particularly for the Romans, hailing as they did from much warmer climes.

Be that as it may, around the birth of Christ the Romans under Caesar Augustus attempted to expand their empire towards the north. Their legions crossed the Rhine and the Danube in an attempt to annex Germania as part of the Roman Empire. However they came up against stiff opposition and indeed the warriors of the Cheruscan tribe under their commander Arminius so soundly defeated three of their best legions (approx. 20,000 men) at the Battle of Teutoberger Wald in AD 9 that the Romans opted to withdraw and accept the Rhine and the Danube as the frontier of the empire. They secured their territory from the Germans by building a series of fortifications, the *limes,* along a length of 550 kilometres (350 miles).

Along this distant frontier of the empire, cities such as Mainz, Trier and Augsburg were built on the Roman pattern. The "Barbarians" thus came face to face with unimaginable luxury. Theatres, public baths, roads, bridges and villas – everything that the Romans knew from their homeland – were built in order to make life more bearable in remote and hostile Germania.

However, by AD 406 at the latest, when Germanic Vandals poured across the Rhine, the death knell of the Roman Empire which economically, politically and militarily was on its last legs, was rung.

Clovis, king of the Franks: This fate did not befall the Franks. In the middle of the 4th century AD they had settled in present-day Belgium and rather than attempting any major expansion of territory had been content to launch small campaigns into Roman-occupied Gaul. This policy changed when Clovis from the house of Merovingia became king of the Franks in AD 481, at the age of only 15. In the 30 years of his rule he transformed his Frankish warriors into a mighty army and extended his realm eastwards as far as the Rhine, westwards as far as the Atlantic and southwards as far as Spain.

Wherever the Franks advanced, they found the country firmly in the control of bishops, for Christianity had been the state religion of the Roman Empire ever since AD 380. While

the Roman Empire was disintegrating these bishops had taken over the control of important administrative functions. Doing business with the bishops was of mutual advantage. When Clovis had himself baptised in AD 496, he could rely on the support that the bishops gave him and they in turn could reinforce their position through the power and authority of the king. There followed Christianisation of the Franks and Christianity spread as the realm expanded.

With the help of the church the Franks were successful in maintaining their empire, despite the fact that treason, assassinations, division and expansion of territory were all part of the political routine in the ensuing 150 years. It was a period during which one Frankish family in particular was to emerge as the most dominant force within the realm – that of the Carolingians.

Charlemagne's empire: From AD 768 it was Charlemagne who guided the fortunes of the largest empire in the western world. Like his predecessors, he maintained no fixed residence, preferring to travel through the country with his entourage and to live on his various estates. Here he held court, received emissaries and pronounced judgements.

As far as his exploits in Germania are concerned, Charlemagne was extremely successful. His life story could be told around the battles that he waged. Through a long series of bloody and cruel campaigns, it took Charlemagne more than 30 years to bring the Germans to heel, to Christianise them and to annex their territory. Ultimately Charlemagne, the Frankish tribal potentate, became recognised as the supreme leader of the Christian West. Only England, Southern Spain and Southern Italy lay outside his influence. He regarded himself as the legitimate heir of the Roman emperor, and sealed this position by having himself crowned Emperor on Christmas Day AD 800.

Carolingian renaissance: Charlemagne's crowning achievements were the organisation of the empire's administrative structures and the establishment of its cultural base. He standardised the laws of all the tribes within his realm and divided it into states to which he assigned loyal leaders. He also summoned learned intellectuals to his favourite palace in Aachen and established schools in the monasteries throughout his empire in order to raise the standard of education. However, the monasteries were more than just the educational centres of the Carolingian Empire. Beyond the royal possessions, they established model estates on which new crops were grown or new methods of cultivation, such as the three-field system, were tested.

With the help of the clergy and the monastery-trained laymen, Charlemagne succeeded in introducing Latin as the official language of the realm. The monastery and palace schools taught the art of book illustrating, drew up contracts, translated the classics and established libraries. We have these institutions to thank for translations of the writings of Caesar, Tacitus and Juvenal.

The beginnings of German history: Charlemagne was neither a German or a Frenchman: he was a Frank. In his day the division of the empire into an east and west would have been unthinkable. Yet, within 30 years of his death it became reality: in 843 his grandsons divided the empire between them at the Treaty of Verdun and it is this year that marks the actual beginning of German history. The first king of the Eastern Empire, Ludwig the German (843–876), ruled over a land which for the first time can be called "German". Forty years after his death his last male descendant, Ludwig the Child, died, thus ending the Carolingian dynasty in the eastern Empire. Eight years later the right of

danger was presented by over-ambitious princes who threatened the empire with disintegration. However, he mastered this problem through clever personnel policy and the inclusion of the Catholic church in the governing process. The bishops could often advance to important political posts, not only because they were educated and good administrators, but also because they had no heirs to threaten the power of the king.

Thus fortified, Otto, just like Charlemagne, succeeded in capturing the iron crown of the Langobard dynasty and intervened in the political chaos in Rome. He also managed to have the Western Slavic tribes incorporated in the Roman Church, and by doing so was

succession passed to the king of a Germanic tribe whom Charlemagne had so bitterly fought against, the Saxon king Henry.

Otto the Great: It was Otto, Henry's son, whom fate called upon to make one of the most important decisions for the west, namely to pitch himself and his subjects against the advancing Hungarians. In AD 955 Otto and his army which was composed of all-Germanic tribes defeated the invaders at Lechfeld in south-west Germany. The other major

able to secure the realm's eastern borders.

Church and emperor: From AD 906 right up until the fall of the empire in 1806, the title of emperor was inseparably linked to that of the German king. Nobody who had not already been the German king could be crowned emperor. The realm came to be called "The Holy Roman Empire of German Nations". The special status of the German emperor was thereby defined, namely as the ruler over "eternal" Rome with a responsibility to fulfil the functions of both the German king and the Roman emperor.

The Carolingians and the church co-operated on the basis of mutual advantage. Char-

Left, Roman watchtower along the Limes. **Above left**, the German imperial sceptre. **Above right**, a bust of Charlemagne.

lemagne made his conquests in the name of the church and the church expanded its influence. However effective this partnership was, it carried with it a danger which came to the surface in the 11th and 12th centuries and rocked western Christendom. The church had taken on an increasing amount of secular responsibility. The emperor would intervene in the election of the bishop and make sure that only those who were interested in secular power got anywhere in the church. The bishops became prince-bishops, and naturally this secularisation of the church did not find favour with the Pope in Rome.

The open struggle between the Pope and the emperor began in 1076 when, according

position but his ecclesiastical authority was severely shaken.

The powerful princes of the empire no longer recognised the power of the emperor to the extent that they had previously. The title of the king was no longer to be linked to birth, but was to be decided by the nobility. Even the outstanding kings of the Hohenstaufen period, Friedrich Barbarossa (1152–90), Heinrich VI (1169–1197) and Friedrich II (1212–50), ruling in an era regarded by many as the high point of medieval imperial rule, could not achieve a lasting return to the old order.

The Romanesque: These politically turbulent times, from the turn of the millenium to

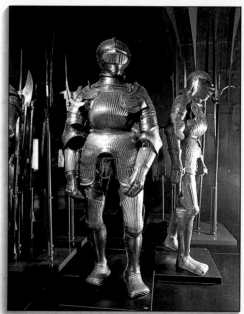

to the traditions of the time, Emperor Henry IV appointed the new Archbishop of Milan. Pope Gregory VII, who demanded that the emperor revoke his decision, was dismissed. The Pope hit back by excommunicating the emperor and forbidding him to rule over the German and Italian kingdoms. The highest Christian authorities had come to blows! Who really had the power?

The emperor, whose position had been weakened by the immediate flare-up of opposition from the nobility, was forced in 1077 to beg the Pope personally for forgiveness in order to release himself from excommunication. He was thus able to win back his

the 14th century, were accompanied by an amazing cultural resurgence. Not only did an independent German literature emerge, but architecture also received fresh impulses. The new building style of the Romanesque which developed around the year 1000 utilised classical motifs such as the rounded arch, but the buildings were plainer, more austere and less perfect than those of the classical age. The Romanesque churches and abbeys, built of massive stone with little space for windows and crowned by defiant towers, were intended to symbolise the power of the church. They were invariably built on a much larger scale than secular buildings.

Medieval literature: The origins of German literature are obscure, although it has its roots in epic songs handed down by word of mouth, in proverbs and in magic chants, such as the famous *Merseburg Spells*. The heathen Germanic epic songs were committed to parchment from the 8th century onwards. While the heros call on the Christian god, as in the *Hildebrandslied*, the traditional Germanic virtues of courage in battle, honour and pride continue to play a central role.

Nevertheless, an independent German literature hardly existed around the turn of the millenium. As was the case with the politics of the day, literature was almost totally oriented towards Italy and Rome where the

Ages. The Middle Age courts became the focal point of literary pursuits: "courtly" became synonymous with "well-bred", "brave", "pure". The medieval knight not only required courage, strength and dexterity, but was also characterised by his inner harmony, self-discipline and pursuance of honour, loyalty and compassion. Only having achieved these virtues through a hard inner struggle with himself could the medieval knight match the ideals demanded by his social standing.

This literature of adventure was accompanied by a further central theme, namely the homage to a pure lady of nobility – Mistress Love, as this courting of such a lady was

language most commonly used was Latin.

Slowly there emerged a secular literature which was based on traditional myths and legends, on reports of travelling minstrels and on oriental legends which had been acquired during the Crusades. The year 1170 ushered in the heyday of German Middle Age literature, whose narratives were primarily based on descriptions and glorifications of German orders of knighthood, for these played a dominant role in the high-Middle

Far left to right, Maria Laach Monastery, the climax of Romanesque architecture in Germany; shining armour; builders at work; at a tournament.

known. The chivalrous bards who composed at the various courts of the empire, expounded the joy, but also the pain, engendered by love. Thus Heinrich von Morungen (*circa* 1200) claimed: "If she were to die, then I too would pass away…all shout that my pain pierces her heart, for she has tormented me for long enough".

The days of chivalry: The literature of chivalry outlined the ideals for which the knight should strive. These same ideals applied to the whole of Christian Europe largely because of the contribution made by the Crusades which, from the 11th-13th centuries, provided a common goal for all Europe's knights in freeing the holy cities and shrines from the Arab infidels. Although the Crusades, which resulted in extreme sacrifice and brutality, were complete disasters from a military point of view, they did succeed in establishing a closer relationship between East and West.

The life of a knight was anything but romantic. Even training was extremely tough. At the age of seven boys born into the nobility would be brought to serve as page boys in another castle. Here they would not only wait on their elders but they would also learn social poise and good table manners. The primitive level of etiquette at the dining table can be surmised from the "etiquette rules"

travelled the country as "poor knights" without estate.

Ulrich von Hutten (1488–1523) described the conditions in the paternal castle: "Surrounded by a tight girdle of walls, cramped by cattle sheds, armouries, powder magazines and gun positions… Everywhere in the building is the stench of powder and the excrement of cattle and dogs…"

It was the invention of firearms that rendered knights' armour useless. The once so proud and distinguished orders of knighthood, with all their ideals and virtues, became impoverished and disintegrated.

Medieval towns and cities: The few towns that existed in Germany before the turn of the

which had to be heeded: "Don't burp whilst eating!", "Don't sneeze on the table-cloth!", "Don't eat with the fingers!"

At the age of 14 the pages became squires and served the knights both in tournament and in battle. They practised jousting, riding and javelin throwing and became fully-fledged knights when they were 20. Reading and writing were not part of the curriculum - these were the domain of the higher ranking clergy and some daughters of the nobility. Just because somebody became a knight did not necessarily mean that he acquired a castle. Many simply became followers of a wealthy knight of the same order or just

millenium, such as Trier, Cologne, Augsburg and Regensburg, had been founded on Roman settlements and fortifications. They could continue to thrive after the Romans left because they were transformed into diocesan centres of the expanding Catholic church. Later on, cities emerged from monastic centres (Munich), castles (Nuremberg), river crossings (Frankfurt) or at the intersections of the few major European trade routes. The princes soon came to recognise the advantages of these settlements. Here they could exact customs and taxes and obtain rare goods, and excellent craftsmen. The towns were also safe havens from which the princes could more effectively control their territory. Between 1100 and 1250 the number of towns in Germany increased tenfold. Whoever arrived in the cities was guaranteed the free right of abode after a prescribed period. As the settlements grew they became more wealthy and with this increasing prosperity the self-confidence of the populace also grew. A simple "town" would have a population of some 2,500 which, in today's terms, is more of a village than a town. But in those days there were also large cities on the scale of Venice and Rome, with more than 100,000 inhabitants.

The towns soon became aware of the important role they played as trading centres

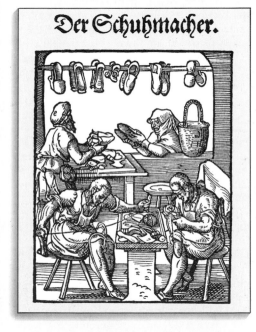

Der Schuhmacher.

and many accrued enough power of their own to be able to limit the powers of their overlords, whether these were bishops or powerful noblemen, or both. Some towns succeeded in becoming vassals of just one ruler who would then guarantee their independence from the greedy designs of the emperor's own princes. These cities proudly called themselves "Free Cities of the Empire" (Nuremberg, Regensburg, *et al.*).

Merchants and craftsmen: While every citizen had a right to a certain freedom, this did

Left, medieval peasants at work. **Above**, at the cobbler's.

not guarantee that people lived as equals in the crowded medieval town. Some were more equal than others! The most important class was that which the town had to thank most for its prosperity, namely the merchants. These organised themselves into associations which virtually controlled the town: only the associations were represented on the council and dealt with matters of government.

Between the 13th and 15th centuries the second most economically important group, the craftsmen, succeeded in gaining their share of the power in many towns. They were organised in guilds, one guild for each trade, which would set the price, quality and amount of manufactured goods. Violations were punished and master craftsmen were either accepted into a guild or rejected. Funds were established to look after the needs of those no longer able to work, as well as widows. The guilds organised uprisings in Augsburg, Nuremberg and many other cities to secure their place on the councils.

The Gothic cathedral: The Gothic cathedrals, soaring heavenwards, became the most potent symbols of a town's prosperity and self-confidence and their rich tracery and sculpture were clear indications of the skills of its artisans. The cathedrals in Freiburg, Strasbourg, Ulm, Cologne and Regensburg were started in the 13th century and took centuries to complete. New techniques, first developed in France, allowed the Gothic to evolve from the Romanesque. Pointed arches, exterior buttresses and vaulting not only enabled buildings to reach ever-increasing heights, but also allowed walls of massive stone to be replaced by walls of stained-glass. The Gothic cathedrals were built to the glorification of God, as symbols of Man's aspirations to reach Heaven.

The lower classes in the towns: But the towns and cities of the Middle Ages were not only dominated by the power of the merchants and the skills of the artisans. Between one-and two-thirds of the urban dwellers, including menial workers, maid servants, domestic servants, bastards, beggars and outcasts as well as those with despised professions such as hangmen and grave diggers, had no civil rights at all. These groups were often dependent on the good will of the church or charities established by wealthy citizens. Only he who gave something to the poor could expect God's mercy. In many German cities hospitals were therefore built, as well as old people's homes or even, as in Augsburg, special housing for the city's poor.

The Jews: The Jews lived as a separate entity. In every Middle Age city there was a Jewish community which was generally detached from the Christian quarters. The Jews, repeatedly the target of pogroms and expulsions, were subject to strict laws laid down by their Christian fellow citizens. The violence against the Jews was only in part based on religion. The Jews were responsible for the murder of Jesus Christ and the ritual murders of children were also laid at their door. But anti-Jewish sentiments were mostly provoked by economic considera-

tions. In many places the Jews were forbidden to carry out "respected" professions, and many were forced to earn their living as money lenders and pawnbrokers. On the other hand, Christians were forbidden to lend money on security or to levy interest. In difficult times many citizens were therefore highly indebted to Jewish creditors, who were often driven out of town or murdered.

During the Middle Ages the Jews were persecuted throughout Europe. During the 15th century in Germany this ultimately led to the disintegration of many Jewish communities (Mainz 1438, Augsburg 1439).

The plague: The plague, the "Black Death", most probably transported to Europe by merchants returning from the East, decimated the urban populations in the 14th century. Trade practically came to a standstill and lines of supply virtually collapsed. Nor did the country dwellers, who still accounted for 90 percent of the population, escape the ravages of the plague. Their plight was not helped by the appalling conditions in which most of them lived.

Originally the Germans were genuinely free men. However, in the centuries of upheaval governed by continuous wars and struggles there was a great deal of newly acquired territory which required to be ruled. A new class of large, mostly noble, landowners emerged. Many small farmers, who got into difficulties by being continuously called up to fight, were forced to hand over their property to the landowners as a means of buying their way out of military service. They got their land back for cultivation, but only in return for dues and fixed services such as building and maintaining tracks and helping with the harvest. They sank into servitude, semi-free peasants who were forbidden to own land. Apart from the odd period of economic upswing, the economic and legal position of most peasants drastically deteriorated in the Middle Ages. Many found it hard to eke out even the barest living.

Religious devotion and superstition: In these difficult times, many people found comfort in the Christian religion, which promised compensation for earthly suffering in the next world. The populations of both the cities and the countryside were imbued with a piety that came to govern their entire existence. This was clearly expressed in the many chapels and pilgrimage churches, the worship of relics and the popular religious tracts of the time. This Christian zeal also had its dark side, however, as in the persecution of witches that spread throughout Europe in the late-Middle ages. In the 16th century, at the height of these persecutions, women lived in constant fear of calumniation and accusation. It is thought that in Germany alone up to 100,000 were persecuted and killed as witches. It wasn't until 1749 that the body of the last German witch was burned on a hill outside Würzburg.

The crisis within the church: Against this background of religious devoutness, the deplorable state of affairs within the church was keenly felt. The moral decline of the papacy, the insatiable greed of the church and the theological ignorance of the clergy were the main objects of criticism. The church exploited the believers' fear of purgatory and damnation to obtain the money required for ambitious building projects and the maintenance of a luxurious lifestyle. For a certain sum anyone could buy his pardon and shorten time spent in purgatory. This sale of indulgences was a highly profitable business for the collectors, the princes and the church.

During the 15th and 16th centuries critical theologians constantly attacked these practices. From 1517 the German Augustinian monk Martin Luther set about reforming the church through a series of damning theses which he displayed for all the public to see. Luther denounced the authority of the Pope, renounced the special status of the clergy as mediators between God and man and instead formulated the idea of having a general priesthood involving all believers.

The peasants' revolt: Luther found support among all levels of society; among the lower nobility, the townsfolk and the impoverished peasant. Luther's campaign for an end to economic and legal discrimination against peasants and his battle against the authority of the church in the countryside, led to an uprising against all authority. In the spring of 1525 the first monasteries and castles went up in flames in southwest Germany and the rebellion, under the leadership of impoverished noblemen like Florian Geyer, spread like wildfire throughout central Europe. But the peasants were poorly equipped and in 1526 the revolt was brutally crushed by the superior forces of the nobility. More than 100,000 peasants either died in battle or were subsequently executed.

The unity of the church was now broken and western Christianity was split between the Catholics and the so-called Protestants. The teachings of Luther were a powerful weapon in the hands of those princes seeking independence from the emperor and the Pope, particularly in northern and central Germany. Religion became a territorial matter, which every lord could settle for himself and his subjects according to his own convictions. The schism within the church was an impor-

tant contributory factor in the fragmentation of Germany into sovereign states.

A new era begins: Luther's successes would not have been possible without a changed world view and the accompanying developments in science, technology and economy. The medieval view that life on earth served merely as a hard test for the eternal life to come changed in the 14th and 15th centuries. People now attempted to interpret the world using logical method and the unravelling of this puzzle became regarded as a service to God. The earth was now round and not flat, Christopher Columbus discovered America and in 1445 Johannes Gutenberg discovered how to print books with moveable letters, so

enabling the population at large to have access to all the new ideas. Education could expand and in the 15th century a large number of universities were founded in Germany (e.g. Leipzig 1409, Freiburg 1455), whose curriculum became increasingly devoted to secular subjects. In the cities reading and writing rooms were established to satisfy the citizens' thirst for knowledge. Primarily out of sound business sense, they were keen to provide their offspring with the best possible education.

The Thirty Years' War: Despite all attempts on the part of the Catholic church to stem the spread of Lutheran Protestantism and to win

Left, medieval bath-time. **Right**, officer cadet in the Thirty Years' War.

back lost territory, by 1600 the new confession had become the most powerful religious-political force in Europe. The religious conflict was further exacerbated by the rivalry between the newly established sovereign states and the struggle between the emperor and his princes.

In 1618 the military confrontations began in Bohemia and soon enveloped the whole of Europe. France and Sweden joined in with the Protestants, England and Spain with the Catholics. The mercenaries, who were not averse to swapping allegiances, were fed and paid from the spoils of war. There was torture and rape and towns were besieged and put to the torch – all in the name of Jesus

Christ. After 30 years of war central Europe was so desolated and exhausted that peace negotiations finally led to an agreement. The "Treaty of Westphalia" brought about recognition for both confessions and the dissolution of the German Empire into some 1,800 separate states. Only the emperor and the common language provided a last vestige of unity. The German population had been reduced by one-third. Epidemics were rife, hunger reigned and the Holy Roman Empire of German Nations had completely lost its influence in Europe.

The rise to a new great power: Germany gradually recovered from the wounds of war and living conditions soon began to improve, promoted by monarchist Absolutism which, following the example set by the French king Louis XIV, found favour among many German princes. The princes saw themselves as the centre of the state, appointed by and only answerable to God. Through the resulting improvement in law and order, agriculture could be reorganised and new citizens settled.

By far the largest states within the empire were the Austrian Hapsburg realm and the Prussian house of Brandenburg, which in the 17th and 18th centuries emerged as the two new great powers in central Europe. Austria expanded to the south-east at the expense of the Turks and Prussia amalgamated a number of fragmented states with the help of its mighty army. In the 18th century rulers emerged in both states who regarded themselves more as "servants of the state" than as absolute rulers. Particularly Friedrich II – Frederick the Great - of Prussia and Emperor Joseph II of Austria were strongly influenced by a new attitude which promised to change the world: Enlightenment.

"Have the courage of your convictions" was the revolutionary appeal of the Age of Enlightenment, which not only influenced the sciences, but all spheres of life. Philosophers such as Locke, Montesquieu and Rousseau formulated their views on liberty and the legitimate exercising of power. Frederick the Great and Joseph II were advocates of the movement and attempted to seek some sort of common ground between the maxims of enlightenment and the power claims of the princes.

Under Frederick the Great the Prussians abolished torture, supported religious tolerance and secured the personal rights of the citizens. But at the same time the Prussian king waged bloody wars of expansion, the nobility maintained all its privileges and the peasants remained totally dependant on the lord of the manor.

In Austria Joseph II went even further than Frederick the Great, but most of his reforms were so rash that they had to be repealed by his successors. In both states, however, the necessary steps were taken to herald the emergence of a modern, centralised state.

<u>Left</u>, Frederick the Great of Prussia. <u>Right</u>, Martin Luther, the great reformer.

In Germany, too, the end of the Middle Ages marked the beginning of the process of disintegration for the old feudal system. The traditional relationship between the nobility and the peasants crumbled as a result of war and the economic changes that came about through innovation. The prime beneficiaries of these changes were the towns and cities. From the simple craftsmen and merchants of the Middle Ages there emerged a self-assured bourgeoisie whose newly acquired freedoms and whose rational thought and behaviour broke down old barriers. These developments resulted in an increased demand for new technologies and goods, so benefitting the artists and artisans.

Artistic developments: With the emergence of the Renaissance and the return to classical notions of art and science, the people were liberated from centuries of religious dogma and indoctrination. A new realism in art emerged. With his precisely calculated effects of colour and light the Würzburg altar painter **Matthias Grünewald** (1460–1528) was one of the first Germans to herald in this new age. But he would undoubtedly have been ostracised had he not conformed to the dictates of the Catholic establishment and taken religious themes for his paintings.

Albrecht Dürer (1471–1528) from Nuremberg, on the other hand, broke totally new ground. During his travels to France and Holland, Dürer acquired the ability and expertise to create works of art that were a bridge between the late-Gothic and the modern trend. This *homo universalis* was a master of goldsmithery, painting and graphic art. He was also a writer and was familiar with the anatomy and the techniques of drawing in perspective, all talents that made him shine above his contemporaries as the most important German contributor to the humanistic ideals of the Renaissance. His portraits set the standard for centuries to come. His most famous works are his *Self-portrait* (1500), his *Portrait of Hieronymus Holzschuher* and his charcoal drawing *The Artist's Mother*. They show human beings

filled with great inner strength, their faces as mirrors to their souls, reflecting erudition, calm and the objectivity of intellect.

Dürer's contemporaries **Hans Holbein the Elder** (1465–1524), who painted *The Altar in the Vineyard* and his son **Hans Holbein the Younger** (1497–1543) were also important exponents of the German Renaissance. The latter became the court painter to King Henry VIII and created celebrated portraits of the English nobility before dying of the plague in London. His woodcut cycle *Danse*

Macabre, a climax of German graphic art, is a revealing example of Renaissance art in Northern Europe.

Dürer's pupil **Hans Baldung** (1485–1545) abandoned the straight course of naturalism and through the deliberately distorted proportions of his figures became an early exponent of the Mannerist style which, precisely through the distortion of the subject, aimed to increase the involvement of the beholder in the work. **Lucas Cranach the Elder** (1472–1553) from Wittenberg painted first in the style of classical Renaissance. The court painter was a friend of the great reformer Martin Luther and often painted portraits of him and his family. He thus became known as the painter of the Reformation, although he also undertook work for the Catholic church.

From mysticism to the Reformation: German mysticism was deeply rooted in the Middle Ages. The Dominican monk Johann Eckart, known as **Master Eckart** (1260–1327), formulated an early profession of direct communication between God and Man with the concept of *unio mystica*, where the soul itself became the intercessor between God and his creations. The union of the soul with God could be achieved by strict self-denial and through God's mercy. Such ideas did not go down well with the Archbishop of Co-

interests of the development of mankind, sought to collect and publish the knowledge that the ancient Greeks and Romans had documented. Humanism was first taught on German soil in Prague by **Cola di Rienzo** and **Petrarca**. Charles IV's chancellor **Johann von Neumarkt** saw a reformed language as the basis for establishing a new German philosophy based on Italian and Greek traditions. **Philipp Melancthon** (1497–1560) began his studies at Heidelberg University when he was only 12 and became professor of Greek in Wittenberg at 21. It was only with Melancthon's guidance that **Martin Luther** (1483–1546) managed to translate the Bible and formulate the ideas of

logne, for where now was the role of the Church? Twenty-eight of Eckart's religious principles were therefore damned as heresy, but that did not stop them having a profound effect on German philosophy and theology for the next 200 years. His work in these areas was continued by **Johannes Tauler** (1300–61), another Dominican from Strasbourg, who wisely decided to have his main work *Theologia Deutsch* published anonymously in Frankfurt. With his anti-papist and anti-imperial demands for German independence, he increased the explosive potential of mysticism.

A humanist was someone who, in the

the Reformation. Other humanists shared the criticism of the reformers concerning the ossification of the papacy and the empire. They included Melancthon's great uncle **Johann Reuchlin** (1455–1522), a renowned Hebrew scholar. As the publisher of a Hebrew grammar, he was of great assistance in helping compare the Greek translations of the Bible with the source text.

With his translation of the Bible, polemic writing, letters, hymns and speeches, Luther created the basis of the modern German language. "Listen to how the common people speak" was his advice to scholars and it was contact with the people that injected life into the stale written German of his contemporaries. German was now written in a form that everybody could understand.

It was precisely because Luther could offer the answer to the German people's craving for a church that spoke their own language that the Reformation was able to spread so quickly in Germany. And here there were enough disenchanted people at all levels of society prepared to see a conflict with the Pope and the emperor through to the end. The ideas of the new enlightened age – the liberation from the rigid view of scholasticism and the dominance of the Church – won through. At last the works of the Greeks, which had been a closely guarded secret for

so long, could now be publicly studied, quoted and translated. At last man could, on his own account, probe the mysteries of the world as it was, and not as it was supposed to be.

With all the divisiveness among the church and nobility created by the Reformation, it was now the common people who set about forging a unity of language and culture. Workingmen and craftsmen established guilds of **Meistersingers** for the cultivation of poetry and music. The competitions for

Left, the Isenheim Altar by Matthias Grünewald. **Above**, a wooden madonna by Tilman Riemenschneider.

the *Meistergesang*, the comedies of Nuremberg shoemaker **Hans Sachs** (1494–1576), the satirical work *Das Narrenschiff* (Ship of Jesters) by **Sebastian Brandt** (1457–1521) and the novels by **Jörg Wickrams** (died *circa* 1562) all contributed to establishing a broad base for German as a language of rhyme and prose.

Whether one found happiness on the edge of an abyss or paid for it through eternal damnation, all was vanity. As the Middle Ages drew to a close the psyche of the Germans became dominated by an attitude of transience and arrogance towards all mortal endeavour. With all the wars, plagues and heretic persecutions, everyone was condemned to a short life, so why not make the best of it?

As humanism spread, this world view transformed into a progressive doctrine. Knowledge was no longer the work of the devil and a life in search of knowledge was no longer followed by the burning fiery furnace. The doctor and alchemist **Paracelsus** (1493–1541) established the first scientific basis for German medicine. And in his *Buch der Deutschen Poeterey* **Martin Opitz** (1596–1639) was the first to formulate fixed norms for spoken and written language. He introduced the professional ruling that only the nobility may appear in tragedy; that comedy be left to the lower classes. Lyric poetry first manifested itself in hymns and sonnets, an exponent of the latter being **Andreas Gryphius** (1616–64), who also wrote comedies and tragedies for a wide public. He also inspired **Daniel Caspar von Lohenstein** (1635–83) to write his dramas in the flowery language of Mannerism. In his first polemic *Cautio Criminalis* the lyrical poet and Jesuit **Friedrich von Spee** (1591–1635) was bold enough to speak his mind about heretic persecution, which he regarded as a cruel deviation from normal behaviour.

The struggle between the princes and the emperor, between the Reformation and the Counter-Reformation ended in a stalemate because Luther had been unable to mould an alliance between the princes and the German people. The end of the Reformation had a decisive effect on German history for the ideas of a politically united nation state were now left to gather dust. In his book *Der abenteuerliche Simplicissimus Teutsch* published in 1669, **Hans Jakob von**

Grimmelshausen (1622–76) described the tumults of the Thirty Years' War. He was carried off to fight at the tender age of 12 and experienced all the destruction at first hand for 14 long years. Caustic irony and pitch-black humour are the author's final weapons against despair at the senselessness of a war which, together with famine and epidemics, decimated Germany's population from 17 to eight million.

The courtly geometry of power: The destruction of the Holy Roman Empire of German Nations resulted in a patchwork quilt of principalities where the power of the emperor was now divided amongst some 300 princes and rulers who jealously guarded the

north of the Alps since the turn of the 17th century, so the rococo, with its rich ornamentation and multiplicity of forms, now became the dominant style in secular buildings. The lightness and playfulness of the rococo banished the severity of the Gothic and Renaissance. Two outstanding examples of this style are the Residence in Würzburg and the Palace of Sansoucci in Potsdam. The Geometric planning of palaces and their gardens gave physical expression to the power and new sense of order that the princes had attained.

However the splendour of the court would not have been complete without the atmosphere created by music. Works such as Bach's

sovereignty of their respective domains.

Meanwhile, beyond the Rhine in the west, a centralised nation state had silently emerged to become governed by the absolute power of the monarch. The "Sun King" Louis XIV was able to exclaim unequivocally: "I am the state!" With its huge dimensions and splendid decor the Palace of Versailles was built as a powerful symbol of the French king's authority. Versailles and the courtly magnificence of imperial France became the shining example that every German potentate now attempted to emulate.

Just as the style of the Baroque had governed the design of religious architecture

Brandenburg Concertos fitted perfectly into the palace setting of neat parks, magnificent courtyards, and mirrored halls. **Johann Sebastian Bach** (1685–1750) was born into a family of musicians in Eisenach in Thuringia. After the death of his parents his elder brother nurtured his musical talents. In 1723 he became the choirmaster-organist of the Church of St Thomas in Leipzig. Alongside his numerous concertos, his *Art of the Fugue* and *Well-tempered Clavier* became very popular, as did his hymns, cantatas and oratorios such as the *St Matthew Passion* which he wrote just before he died.

Bach's contemporary **George Frederick**

Handel (1685–1759) began his musical career playing the violin and the harpsichord. In contrast to Bach, his music was not so much influenced by his family and religious background, but by his travels all over Europe. He became a British citizen and court composer to George III.

Enlightenment: However, it was not only courtly splendour that spread from France at this time, but also revolutionary thinking, as formulated by René Descartes' thesis *Cogito: ergo sum* (I think: therefore I am), which finally released the natural sciences from religious tutelage. Perception became based on tangible experience and science became governed by its own laws. The philosophers

and scientists broke out of the tight straightjacket of the past.

In Germany, **Gottfried Wilhelm Leibnitz** (1646–1716) became an exponent of "Enlightenment" long before this term was actually used to express intellectual emancipation. Extraordinarily gifted even as a young child, he commenced his studies of law, natural sciences and philosophy when he was only 15, attaining his doctorate at the age of 20. A genius in many fields, his particular speciality was mathematics where he dis-

covered both infinitesimal calculus and binary, which enabled him to construct a mechanical calculator. As a philosopher, he believed that a pre-ordained harmony formed the basis of the relationship between Man and God, between the body and the soul. According to Leibnitz, this was the unifying spiritual substance from which the material properties of the universe were derived.

In both his dramas and theoretical writings, **Gotthold Ephraim Lessing** (1729–81) was another advocate of these new ideas. He fought for the release of dramatic art from self-inflicted rigidity and ossified formalism. For his part, the high-born *Minna von Barnhelm* could appear in a comedy while the bourgeois *Miss Sara Sampson* could become a tragic heroine. Fifteen years before the storming of the Bastille, Lessing's *Emilia Galotti* already dealt with the conflict between nobility and hoi polloi, while *Nathan the Wise* with its plea for religious tolerance among Christianity, Judaism and Islam remains as relevant today as it ever was.

While the colonies in North America were fighting for their independence and the first signs of revolution were appearing in France, Germany became a heartland of philosophy. Over 200 philosophical publications with potentially explosive contents were in circulation. Their underlying themes were the tenor of Enlightenment – the coming-of-age of mankind. "Have the courage of your convictions," implored **Immanuel Kant** (1724–1804), philosopher and professor of logic and metaphysics at the university in Königsberg in remotest East Prussia.

Continuing where Leibnitz left off, Kant delved into the possibilities and limits of human perception. In his *Critique of Pure Reason* (1781) he contended that through a synthesis of empiricism and rationalism the discerning individual could isolate the essence of an object amongst countless individual phenomena (thing-in-itself theory). His *Critique of Practical Reason* (1788) dealt with the relationship between the individual and society as a whole. Personal liberty had to be governed by a common denominator of moral behaviour: "Act in such a way that the maxims of your will can at any time be the principle of a general set of rules!"

Weimar classicism: First formulated in England and France, the ideas of Enlightenment and Rationalism were refined and polished by Kant's idealistic philosophy. But whereas in France the Age of Enlightenment had far-reaching political consequences, culminating in the Revolution of 1789, there was no direct knock-on political effect in Germany. Here the orientation of philosophy and literature towards the models of the ancient world resulted in the emergence of Weimar classicism (1780–1830). The description of Germany as a land of poets and philosophers stems from this period.

The little principality of Weimar began its sudden rise to the intellectual centre of Europe when in 1775 Duke Karl August brought together **Johann Wolfgang von Goethe** (1749–1823) and **Friedrich Schiller** (1759–

law. He had the most varied interests, ranging from experiments in alchemy, devotional piety, German architecture to natural sciences and, as part of his professional duties, mining and military affairs. After studying and working in Leipzig, Strasbourg, Frankfurt and Wetzlar, he travelled in Switzerland before being summoned to Weimar in 1775. His journey to Italy (1786–88) provided Goethe, in collaboration with Schiller, with the basis for establishing the literary movement of Weimar classicism.

Inspired by the great thinkers of Classical Antiquity, the movement encouraged each and every individual to use his liberty responsibly. Man was duty-bound to act mor-

1700 n. Chr.

Leibniz in Berlin.

1805), a professor of history in neighbouring Jena. Schiller's abhorrence of any kind of despotism went right back to the days of his youth when he was forced to study theology, law and medicine. As a reaction he turned to writing and submitted *Die Räuber* (1780) to the theatre in Mannheim where it was greeted with outrage and he was banned from publishing any more works. When summoned to the history faculty in Jena in 1790 he only had another 15 years in which to enjoy a fruitful exchange of ideas with Goethe.

Born in Frankfurt, Goethe had the privilege of receiving thorough private tuition before being compelled by his father to study

ally, in moderation and in appreciation of the natural beauty that surrounded him. The harmonious balance of the natural world must be mirrored in Man's own cultural environment. Schiller's *Mary Stuart*, *Don Carlos*, *The Maid of Orleans*, *Wallenstein* and his political treatise *On the Aesthetic Education of Man* were based on these ideals, as were Goethe's *Iphigenie*, *Torquato Tasso*, *Egmont*, and *Faustus*.

Viennese classicism: In the 18th century Vienna emerged as the capital of a new musical movement. The formalised, soulless compositions of the rococo salons and pavilions left little scope for musicians and composers to express their personality. Radical reform of opera through **Christoph Willibald Gluck** (1717–87) paved the way for the blossoming of the German classical music composition soon to embrace such illustrious names as Haydn, Mozart and Beethoven.

The musical abilities of **Joseph Haydn** (1732–1809) were first discovered by the master of the Vienna Boy's Choir. He was brought to Vienna where he learnt the art of composing. His employment by Prince Esterhazy as the choirmaster in Eisenstadt gave him the security he needed in order to devote his energies to completing countless compositions. Returning to Vienna he wrote

choirmaster of the Bishop of Salzburg, who did not recognise his genius, Mozart's financial situation was always precarious. He spent the last 10 years of his life in Vienna, without a fixed income and beset by hunger and illness, a fact which makes his musical achievements even more remarkable. He bequeathed a total of 600 compositions including the operas *Idomeneo*, *Marriage of Figaro*, *Don Giovanni* and *The Magic Flute* as well as scores of symphonies, concertos, sonatas and sacred music, such as his last, unfinished work, the *Requiem*.

The first freelance composer in the history of music was **Ludwig van Beethoven** (1770–1827). Born in Bonn, he learned composi-

The Creation (1789) and *The Seasons* (1804), as well as the imperial anthem for Emperor Franz I – today Germany's national anthem.

His contemporary **Wolfgang Amadeus Mozart** (1756–91), the child genius from Salzburg, performed his first concert at the age of six. Mozart spent his childhood and youth on musical tours throughout Europe, playing before some of the most important personages of his time. But employed as the

Left, philosopher Leibniz gives a lecture at court. **Above left**, Lessing, the guiding light of the Enlightenment. **Above right**, Immanuel Kant, the creator of German Idealism.

tion as a pupil of Haydn and had already become well-known when the pain of love and the signs of growing deafness threw him into deep despair. From 1816 he could only communicate with visitors and guests through "conversation books" in which questions and answers were written. His *Ninth Symphony*, an arrangement to Schiller's *Ode to Joy* displays his strong belief in the ideals of classicism. Beethoven used his music to confront and stir the people with particularly powerful emotions.

The one composer of Viennese classicism actually to have been born in Vienna was **Franz Schubert** (1797–1828). Over a period of only 11 years, he produced an enormous output including chamber and orchestral music, masses and dances and nine complete symphonies. His unique contribution was an opus of over 600 songs and song cycles such as *Die Winterreise* (A Winter's Journey) which heralded the beginnings of the romantic period in German music.

Liberalism and nationalism: After Napoleon's victory over Austria and Prussia in 1806, the Holy Roman Empire of German Nations ceased to exist. In "Prussia's darkest hour", the period of French rule from 1806-13, a new intellectual centre was established at the university in Berlin founded in 1810. The brothers **Wilhelm von Humboldt** (1767–1835), the linguist, and **Alexander von Humboldt** (1769–1859), the geographer and natural scientist, established the core of a group of academics intent on reforming the Prussian state on the basis of humanistic ideals. As Minister of Education, Wilhelm von Humboldt established elementary schools throughout the state to raise the standard of education. Influenced by the ideas of the French Revolution, the far-reaching reforms of Chancellor **Baron von Stein** and **Prince von Hardenburg** transformed what was essentially a feudal society into a modern nation state.

During the years of war-time French occupation the ideas of German liberalism and nationalism fused and ultimately resulted in an open struggle against the occupiers. **Johann Gottlieb Fichte** (1762–1814) made rousing *Addresses to the German Nation*. The poets **Ernst Moritz Arndt** and **Friedrich Jahn** wrote of the "power and upright character" of a free and united German people. But when Napoleon was driven out after the Battle of Nations in 1813 the former masters continued to sit firmly in the saddle. The Congress of Vienna (1815) re-established the old *status quo*, which was not given to fostering the German national and liberal spirit.

The rise of German idealism: Berlin University meanwhile continued where Kant had left off. Fichte formulated a theory that claimed that a "thing-in-itself", in as far as Kant had made this the basis of his theory of perception, did not exist. Philosophy must choose between two paths: materialism – where physical matter is the fundamental reality and all being and processes and phe-

nomena can be explained as manifestations of matter – or idealism, where the ultimate reality lies in a realm transcending basic phenomena, as being the result of subjective reason. Fichte plumped for the latter of the two options.

His successor was **G.W.F Hegel** (1770–1831), who sought to bridge the gap between materialism and idealism through his definition of dialectic in history. Hegel undertook to overcome the dichotomy between spirit and matter, belief and reason, self and society, Man and God. According to Hegel, a concept or its realisation passes over into and is preserved and fulfilled by its opposite. Thus, the worldly spirit relinquishes its real

identity to pass over into its other state, nature, before being recalled from this self-alienation by man. Truth and freedom develop hand in hand with the resulting increase in awareness of the worldly spirit.

Although Hegel saw in the Prussian state a fair realisation of the worldly spirit, his ideas were too revolutionary for the Prussian king Friedrich Wilhelm III. After Hegel died, the king sought to remove his dragon seed from Prussian soil by summoning Hegel's former friend **F.E.J. Schelling** to Berlin. Schelling had a pantheistic view of the world. For him the task of the artist – the writer or the painter – was to satisfy the human soul's craving to be at one with nature. The central idea of romanticism was born.

German romanticism: The German romantics saw that the make-up of mankind could not only be explained by the purely rational and logical notions postulated by Enlightenment and classicism. People were also motivated by irrational and subjective forces.

The aim of early romantics like **Novalis** was the integration of the old German legends and fairytales with medieval mysticism to produce a universal literature. The late romantics, including **Joseph Görres**, **Clemens Brentano** and **Joseph von Eichendorff** attempted to achieve a new synthesis between emotions and reason.

viewpoint, to describe it simply as it appeared to the eyes of the beholder. This view was further radicalised by **Friedrich Nietzsche**: "God is dead" was the creed with which he sought, with all his sarcasm and perception, to tear apart the convictions of generations of philosophers. In his book *Thus Spake Zarathustra* he recognised only the "will to power" as being the fundamental driving force behind all existence.

Another critic of German idealism wrote: "The philosophers might have interpreted the world; the main thing, however, is to change it." In his main work *Das Capital* (1876) **Karl Marx** (1818–83) together with **Friedrich Engels** (1820–95) presented an

E.T.A. Hoffmann (1776–1822) introduced romantic ideas into opera. His natural successor was **Richard Wagner**, whose work represented the finale of the romantic age, a period of some 90 years in which, at last, the German soul could express itself without any inhibitions.

The will to power: Inspired by German idealism, **Arthur Schopenhauer** (1788–1860) was the first German philosopher to see the world from an explicitly non-Christian

Left, the erudite Wilhelm von Humboldt. **Above**, the two principal exponents of German Classicism, Goethe (left) and Schiller.

analysis of the principles of Capitalism and explained how the economic-political base of existing society could be changed. They contended that before mankind could arrive at a classless society the ruling classes of Capitalism would first have to be replaced by a proletarian dictatorship.

Marxism changed the world. Without Marx there would neither have been a Social Democratic reform movement in Germany, nor the Russian Revolution, nor the division of Germany. Only the future will tell whether or not the collapse of the Communist power bloc has rendered his ideology superfluous to the modern world.

Germany at the end of the 18th century was neither an empire nor a united country. Instead, it looked rather like a patchwork quilt of 350 principalities and over 1,000 small states where kings, electors, dukes, counts and knights, monasteries and cities, sat pretty on their limited rights of sovereignty and where bishops came to govern as secular rulers. There were only two powers of any distinction that stood out in the veritable Augean stable that Germany had become: Prussia and Austria. The loose union of states with the grandiose title "Holy Roman Empire of German Nations" had a parliament in Regensburg, but this attempt at achieving stability in an empire without any centralised system of government was futile: no common system of taxation and no common army existed. After 200 years of constant internal strife, Germany had landed right back in the Middle Ages.

Four-fifths of this curious empire's 23 million inhabitants lived tied to the land. In the west the peasants paid their lords in money and in kind, providing services for little or no remuneration. The church demanded its tithe from the yearly harvest. Only a few peasants actually owned the land they worked. For better or for worse, most of them were simple tenants at the mercy of the landowners.

In the extensive Prussian lowlands east of the Elbe, the peasants and their families still lived as inherited subjects of the lords of the manor. Living as serfs they had to do compulsory labour on the knight's or bishop's estate. They were not allowed to marry freely and could not leave the estate without the permission of the landowner. When the stick was the law and the landowner was the judge, there was really nothing very much that the peasant could do.

The peasants' situation was made even worse by the constant wars which were waged by the nobility. Every Prussian peasant was a soldier of the king. They were simply carried off to fight, leaving the farms to decay and the harvest to rot. And the Prussian army wasn't exactly a bed of roses. Conditions were degrading in the extreme and many conscripts died before they even saw the battlefield. The only group that had it good in the army was the nobility.

A free market essential: This structure of hundreds of small states was not conducive to the development of business and industry. Each state and town had its own trading conditions, its own coinage, weights and measures. No wonder, then, that the money from German states was not accepted abroad, and was even ridiculed. Restrictions imposed on the guilds and customs barriers made free competition impossible. Each chief

warden was allotted a certain amount of raw materials which had to be converted into goods with a specified number of craftsmen. Strict local legislation prevented the free movement of people and the resulting immobility of labour made life very hard for entrepreneurs. But things could not stay that way. Particularly after the French Revolution had altered the political and social landscape of Europe, Germany's economic unity became a pressing need.

The empire disintegrates: In 1803, under the auspices of France, there began a radical clean-up in fragmented Germany. Many of the small states lost their independence. Napoleon declared Bavaria and Baden Württemberg to be kingdoms. Sixteen south and west German princes committed open treason and founded the Rhine Confederation under Napoleon's protection. From then on the peasants were required by their princes to serve in the French army.

To all intents and purposes the 900-year-old Holy Roman Empire of German Nations now ceased to exist. It simply fell apart. After Prussia had declared war against revolutionary France, its army's heavy defeat near Jena and Auerstedt in 1806 exposed the extent of its internal weakness. The army dispersed without further ado, the king fled and when Napoleon marched into Berlin

there was no resistance. Europe's mightiest military state, with its 200,000 soldiers and senile officers, collapsed like a house of cards. With the Treaty of Tilsit, Prussia was forced to cede half of its territory and population. It was only thanks to the Russian Czar that Prussia wasn't completely wiped off the map. The foreign rule of the French weighed heavily on Prussia and other German states.

Reforms and War of Liberation: Defeated armies learn quickly and the Prussians learned

Preceding pages: the Proclamation of the 2nd German Empire in Versailles. **Above,** many came to the Hambach Festival of 1832.

too. Reformers came into the fold: men like Baron von Stein and Graf Hardenberg, officers of the calibre of Scharnhorst, Gniesenau and Clausewitz. The peasants were granted their liberty, the guild order was lifted for some trades and the civic administration was restructured. The army was completely reorganised. Mercenaries and the nobles' monopoly of officer posts were abolished and general military conscription introduced.

A national liberation movement grew in Germany. In Berlin the philosopher Fichte made rousing speeches to the German nation. Gniesenau demanded mobilisation and a national uprising against the French and after Napoleon's crushing defeat in Russia in 1812, the time was ripe. The hesitant Prussian king was provided with a *fait accompli* by the patriots when in the spring of 1813 anti-French revolts broke out all over Germany. With the support of Russia, Great Britain and Austria, Prussia finally declared war on France.

The Battle of Nations near Leipzig on 17 October 1813 was a turning point in world history. Napoleon's army was surrounded and defeated, France was forced to withdraw to the west of the Rhine and, after his defeat at Waterloo, Napoleon was forced into exile. Germany's fate was now to be decided at a congress of the victors in 1815 in Vienna.

Triumph of the Restoration: Two emperors, six kings, more than 100 princes, diplomats and countless titled hangers-on, negotiators, imposters, servants, soldiers of fortune and courtesans danced and wasted away about 20 million Gulden in five months. Thousands of peasants were forced to perform compulsory service for the hunting parties of the elegant nobility when Europe's monarchs gathered together at the glittering Congress of Vienna.

By far the most powerful voice at the congress was the political mind behind the Danubian monarchy, Prince von Metternich. And it was largely he who tied together the threads of the new European order. Germany and Italy were once again divided into small states, Poland was made part of Russia and Hungary remained firmly under Austria's thumb. The European reaction was triumphant. The kingdom of God's mercy, the old feudal order and the Catholic Church were reinstalled in their ancestral positions. Finally all those "French ideas" had been removed and the period of the conservative "roll back" could begin. The citizenry was fobbed off with the promise of constitutions and the princes were won over by tempting titbits.

Outside the German sphere Austria's centre of gravity shifted towards the east, while within, Prussia now expanded westwards and became the most important power. At its feet lay 34 principalities and four free imperial cities, combined into a loose confederation without a leader. The result, and indeed the intention, of the Vienna Congress was clear: Germany was to remain divided and powerless. The final agreement of this great congress of princes was fashioned by the

monarchs of Russia, Prussia and Austria. They founded a "Holy Alliance" of the eastern powers, bound together by the ideals of monarchical Absolutism.

In German universities students organised a protest movement against the princes' confederation. Their symbol was a black, red and gold flag. When in 1819 the pro-Russian writer Kotzebue was murdered by a student, Metternich reacted with the Carlsbad Decrees. All opposition was suppressed, the students' societies forbidden and the universities placed under police control. Many democrats landed in jail and even more were forced into exile. A murky dark age of dema-

gogic persecution descended on the land.

Reaction: The overthrow of the French king in Paris in July 1830 was the signal for a general outbreak of unrest throughout Europe. There was an uprising in Leipzig and uproar and the burning of a palace in Brunswick, destruction of the police headquarters in Dresden, followed by open revolt in Brussels and, at the end of the year, revolution in Poland. Although the protests were crushed by the troops of the "Holy Alliance", the bourgeois-democratic opposition movement could not be extinguished. In May 1832, 30,000 people came together at Hambach Castle to demand a free united Germany. The *Hambach Festival* was attended by townsfolk, peasants, craftsmen, academics and students whose leaders held passionate speeches expressing their bitterness at the wretched conditions in which they lived. "Eternal damnation to the kings, the betrayers of the people," they cried. But unfortunately the damned still actually held the reins of power. Metternich's police arrested the ringleaders and the colours of black, red and gold were banned.

Two years later the poet Georg Büchner was to call on the peasants, through the leaflet *Hessischer Landbote*, to rise up against their tyrannical masters. Academics like the Grimm brothers (of fairy tale fame) propagated the idea of spiritual German unity. At meetings of songsters and at sports festivals organised by the German father of gymnastics Jahn, the German national movement gained in popularity.

However, the German bourgeois opposition to the ruling nobility was primarily a liberal movement. The liberals demanded a representative constitution and basic civil rights. In the south German states the monarchs preserved their constitutions, but allowed the citizens a certain amount of participation in government by introducing so-called "second chambers". In Prussia, Austria and many other states, however, gloomy Absolutism – the single-handed rule of the monarchs – continued to dominate the body and the soul of the people. "When I think of Germany at night, then I am robbed of sleep," wrote the poet Heinrich Heine. Radical democrats campaigned for a democratic republic, for the principle of the people's right of sovereignty and for the removal of the monarchies by force. Until its ban in 1843, their most important means of communication with the public at large was the newspaper *Rheinischer Zeitung*. The editor-in-chief was none other than Karl Marx.

Railways and poverty: Literary circles and cultural conformity (*Biedermeier*) characterised the period. Those who could afford it led a cultivated lifestyle. Of course one had to have shares, for the Industrial Revolution was knocking ever-louder on Germany's doors. In Prussia it took only 20 years for the number of steam engines to treble and factories with machines began to force out old manufacturing methods.

The age of the train had arrived and in 1835 the first German steam locomotive chugged

and did not benefit from these developments.

The other side of the economic boom manifested itself in the increasing poverty of the lower classes. Poor peasants were driven to working for a pittance for the rich landowners. There was no more room for all the craftsmen and many landed in the factories. They were forced to work 12 or 16 hours a day for next to nothing, a fact that drove many families to despair and bitterness. In 1844 in Silesia the weavers revolted and smashed all the machinery. Such were the effects of early capitalism in Germany. The appalling social conditions forced many to emigrate, primarily to America. In Switzerland and France secret revolutionary crafts-

its way along the six-kilometre stretch between Nuremberg and Fürth. The nation was entranced. It was with railways, canals and new wide roads, with money and steam, that the up-and-coming citizenry started to undermine the old feudal order. A German customs union including 18 states and 23 million inhabitants was introduced in 1834. This was an important step in achieving a unified internal market. Austria, meanwhile, remained as conservative and feudal as ever

Left, the people took to the barricades in 1848. **Above**, the first German Parliament in St Paul's Church in Frankfurt.

men's unions demanding utopian Communism were established. Karl Marx and Friedrich Engels worked on their theories of revolutionary socialism in Paris, Brussels, London and Manchester. The air was thick with the smell of radical change.

Germany at the barricades: The year 1847 saw a general economic crisis in Europe: failed harvests, inflation, mass starvation, collapse of the banks, falls in production, unemployment and a war over potatoes. It was followed by a hard winter. The first unrest was in the cities, and once again the struggle began in Paris. There, in February 1848, the first barricades were erected and the arsenals stormed. The popular king Louis Philippe was forced to flee with his ministers and the republic was proclaimed. The revolution quickly spread to Germany. The peasants set palaces on fire and withheld their taxes and other dues. Public meetings demanded reforms and a parliament. The rulers were put on the defensive and in order to avoid the worst they were forced to make certain concessions. Common citizens were granted ministerial posts, the *bourgeoisie* was allowed to share in government and to form armed militias.

When an uprising broke out in Vienna, Metternich fled to England dressed as a woman. The emperor promised a constitu-

focused on Frankfurt: people were keen to know which course developments would now take.

The failure of the revolution: Would the French Revolution now be repeated in Germany? Would the National Assembly become a permanent body and would it proclaim the nation's sovereignty and abolish the nobility? Nothing of the sort happened. The German citizens talked and talked, but did not touch the established power centres. The National Assembly allowed the individual states to keep their armies. No powerful people's army was created under its auspices, and nobody could take a governing body without weapons very seriously. The

tion and in Milan, Venice, Hungary and Bohemia the Austrian troops had to give way to the masses. On 18 March the revolt reached Berlin and barricades were erected in the streets. After being forced to order the retreat of his forces, the Prussian king appointed a liberal government. In Poznan the Poles demanded their own state. Parliaments were voted in the member states of the German Confederation and on 18 May 1848 an elected German National Assembly finally came together in the church of St Paul in Frankfurt. Lawyers, professors, civil servants and landowners – a total of 586 delegates – formed the first all-German parliament. All eyes

liberal majority was afraid of the radical demands of the democratic Left, which wanted a republic, and refused to sanction the lifting of feudal dues that the peasantry was still required to pay.

The German revolution ground to a halt. And when the liberals – shocked by the bloody fights in Paris that June – joined the nobility, the train of revolution began to roll backwards. The absolutist overlords knew how to use their power. In Vienna the rebels were shot down by Field Marshal Windischgrätz, and in Berlin the revolution had to contend with General Wrangel. Rebellious Hungary was brought to its knees by the heavy boys acting for the European nobility – the Russian Army. The St Paul's assembly, which had resisted resorting to arms, was dispersed by the sword.

In a last-ditch attempt to force a national constitution, the people took up arms again in the early summer of 1849, but a series of regional uprisings were put down. The princes' forces were not to be defeated without an organised campaign. The town of Rastatt, the last bastion of the revolution, surrendered to the Prussian forces that July. The revolution was lost and the nobility remained in control.

Bismarck and the Second German Empire: Law and order returned to the land. But

A loyal conservative: He was born in 1815, the year of the Vienna Congress, the son of a Brandenburg landowner, a captain in the cavalry. He had a humanistic education, studied law and was given to student pranks and free-thinking. It was only when he married that he discovered his Christian faith. Soon he became a member of the Saxon order of knighthood and made a name for himself in his brave struggle against liberalism in Prussia. During the 1848 revolution we see him on the staff of the pro-Russian and arch-conservative *Kreuzzeitung* newspaper, supporting a counter-revolutionary nation. He spent some time at the court of the Prussian king, who remembered Bismarck.

although the revolution had been crushed, the problems that had caused it remained. The national state had to be created; if not revolutionary or liberal-democratic, then reactionary; if not as a pan-German state (with Austria), then as a single state (without Austria and under the leadership of Prussia). Something had to be done, one way or another. What actually happened will forever be linked with the name Otto von Bismarck. So what kind of man was this Bismarck?

Left, the first German railway line ran between Nuremberg and Fürth. **Above,** the wheels of industry start to turn.

He learned the art of diplomatic intrigue during the eight years he spent as a Prussian delegate at the *Bundestag* in Frankfurt. He recognised that Prussia could only rise if Austria became weak. We see Bismarck travelling often by train, a fat cigar in his mouth, a big eater and drinker. The first bags under the eyes begin to appear. From 1859 to 1862 he was ambassador to the Russian Czar at St Petersburg, a post which reinforced the pro-Russian sentiments he was to keep all his life. After a few months of diplomatic service in Paris, his career really took off. It was October 1862.

First successes: King Wilhelm I summoned

Bismarck to head the Prussian government. His first task was to bring the liberals in parliament into line, which he did, thoroughly. Then, without regard for parliament or the constitution, he pushed through the modernisation of the Prussian army. His first master stroke, however, came a year later when he obtained the support of Austria in winning back the small states of Schleswig and Holstein from Denmark. It was not a people's war, not even a war involving all German states, that put Denmark in its place. No, it was these two conservative dynasties of Prussia and Austria who crowned themselves with the laurels of victory after the successful struggle for the sovereignty of the

into the *Bundestag*. He became a Prussian right-royal revolutionary. Against the will of the small German states he started a deliberately calculated war against the Habsburg monarchy. The decisive battle was near Königgrätz in 1866, where the Prussian army fought with muzzle-loading guns and won. Overnight, Bismarck became Prussia's hero.

His revolution from the top changed the map of Germany. Prussia annexed large areas including Schleswig-Holstein, and France and Austria were forced to agree to this territorial expansion. The German Confederation disintegrated. Prussia forced Austria out of Germany and in the newly-established North German Federation, it achieved un-

German nation. But then they fell out over the spoils. After all, who had the say in Germany? Berlin or Vienna? The Hohenzollerns or the Habsburgs? This question had to be settled, not by discussions and resolutions, but, according to Bismarck, by "blood and iron".

Königgrätz – a German civil war: The years between 1866 and 1870 were the best of Bismarck's life. He cleverly managed to keep all other European powers out of the German Civil War. In 1848 he had cried blue murder against general voting rights. However, now, as a move against Austria, he introduced those very same liberal rights

challenged hegemony. Bismarck had granted the liberals their national wishes at the expense of their democratic ones.

Franco-Prussian War: After the defeat of Austria, for the Prussians there was now only one major competitor in central Europe: France. Bismarck used the deserted Spanish throne as a means of provoking Napoleon III. A Hohenzollern prince should reside in Madrid. The French emperor could not accept having a government loyal to Prussia at his back. The prince finally had to give up his candidature and Bismarck's provocation should really have failed there and then. However, Napoleon III went too far. His demand that Prussia renounce its claims was not accepted by Wilhelm I and, with a little encouragement from Bismarck, the desired war broke out. Led by the old campaigner General von Moltke, the superior German forces triumphed at Sedan on 1 September, 1870. Napoleon III was taken prisoner.

In France he was unanimously deposed by the people, who again proclaimed the Republic. German troops marched into Paris, where in March 1871 the working population had hoisted the red flag of social revolution. Those were the days of the Paris Commune which ended with the bloody crushing of the communards by the troops of the Versailles government – supported by Bis-

marck. France was forced to accept a bitter peace settlement. Germany annexed Alsace Lorraine and received 5,000 million francs in war reparations.

An imperial national state: The new German empire emerged under rather unusual circumstances. It came into being not in Germany, but in France, in the hall of mirrors in the Palace of Versailles. It was not born out of any national democratic movement, but out of diplomatic agreements between German kings and princes. It was not the result

Left, *Weavers' Revolt*, an etching by Käthe Kollwitz. Above, chancellor Otto von Bismarck.

of a victory of the citizens over the nobility, but of the monarchy and nobles over the citizens. It wasn't a republic, but an empire that was proclaimed on 18 January, 1871.

This imperial national state was to last for 47 years, until its disintegration at the hands of the November Revolution of 1918. And it was not only home to Germans. Against their will and oppressed, Poles, Danes and Alsatians also belonged to the German Empire.

Germany the industrial state: If at the beginning of the 19th century four-fifths of the population had lived tied to the land, by the end of the century this figure had been whittled down to barely one-fifth. Germany was transformed from a country of yokels to a nation of industry. Cities like Hamburg, Cologne, Munich, Leipzig and Frankfurt grew many fold. Developments in medicine and hygiene had contributed to the enormous population growth.

The 5,000 million Francs' war reparation helped the German economy to achieve an unparalleled boom. In the so-called "years of promoterism" (1871–74), joint stock companies sprang up like mushrooms. The *Ruhrgebiet* developed into the most important industrial centre in Europe, with the armaments manufacturer *Krupp* in Essen alone employing 50,000 people. The financial influence of the large money institutes – *Deutsche Bank*, *Dresdner Bank* and *Commerzbank* – penetrated the ever-more specialised industry and commerce. Mergers resulted in gigantic monopolies which tended to invest their money abroad. In the 1870s, the gross national product soared past that of France, and by 1900 production had drawn level with England's, and would actually nudge ahead during World War I.

The rise of social democracy: Encouraging and leading a process of industrialisation was not for Bismarck. Both he and his Bonapartist ideology were overtaken by the new age, and he became superfluous to the requirements of the state. The landed class he represented belonged to the land, the whip and the past. Right until the end Bismarck remained an opponent of parliamentary democracy and especially of the social democratic workers. Bismarck's law banning the socialists was in force from 1878–90, but it actually had the opposite of its desired effect. The popularity of the SPD (Social Democratic Party of Germany) increased regardless and by 1912 it had become the strongest political force in the *Reichstag*. The workers accepted improved sick and retirement benefits but gave no thanks. They demanded the eight-hour day, a republic and political power: Bismarck was forced to retire as a failed politician; the young new emperor Wilhelm II had no use for him.

Gunboat politics: On the international front, German tradesmen and troops acquired colonies abroad. In South-west Africa, East Africa, Togo, Cameroon, and in the Tsingtau enclave in China, the black, white and red flag of the German emperor was raised. Krupp, Kirdorf, Hapag, Kaiser Wilhelm and the German Fleet supported German colo-

nial policies. Everybody else had their place in the sun, so why not the Germans?

England, the main competitor, was to be paid back on its own territory – at sea. German imperialism plunged the country into a massive programme of warship building. The Deutsche Bank dealt business with Turkey and in 1902, the Turkish Sultan granted it the concession for a railway to Baghdad. To wrest Morocco (rich in iron ore) from France, the German government ordered the gunboat *Panther* to Agadir. However, Morocco remained French.

All great European powers were arming themselves in preparation for the big show-

down, which was to be fought over the redistribution of colonies and markets. After two Moroccan crises and two Balkan wars the imperial powers had grouped themselves for a war that had been in the air for a long time. Germany and Austro-Hungary against the alliance of France, Russia and England. When Serbian nationalists murdered the Austrian Crown Prince Franz Ferdinand in Sarajevo, the Berlin government exploited its historical chance to rise to a world power by waging a preventive war. The time seemed ripe: the German artillery and infantry were superior and Russia and France did not appear to be ready for war.

The German Empire forced its ally in Vienna into a war against Serbia and threw down the gauntlet to Russia and France. The hostilities wouldn't last for long – only a few weeks or, at the outside, a few months. At least that's what von Moltke and his general staff thought, as indeed did a great many Germans, blinded as they were by patriotic warmongering. They couldn't have been more mistaken. The avalanche of war, once set into motion, buried the old heap of bones, Europe, for a full four years.

German war aims: "I am no longer aware of any parties, I only recognise Germans," announced Kaiser Wilhelm at the outset of hostilities. Applause came from all factions, including the Social Democrats, who agreed to a pact and approved the massive credit required for war. Only Karl Liebknecht, at that time still in the SPD, refused to agree and protested against the capitalist war. Later he and Rosa Luxemburg would together found the Communist Party of Germany.

Chancellor of the Reich von Bethmann Hollweg had outlined the war aims in a secret memorandum: conquering the mining region of Briey, the gradual weakening of France, subjugation of Belgium and Luxembourg and the non-Russian peoples ruled over by Russia, as well as the establishment of a Central European economic and customs union under German leadership. In the end none of these plans came to fruition. As the war raged on, the military and economic inferiority of the Austro-German camp became clear. France could not be defeated in a *Blitzkrieg*. In 1916, over one million people

Above, August Bebel, progenitor of German Social Democracy. **Right**, Albert Einstein.

54

SCIENCE IN GERMANY

For many people, Germany is the land of poets and philosophers. During the course of conversation a number of names will crop up spontaneously – Goethe, Schiller, Kant or Marx. Only a small minority is aware, however, that, for a time at least, Germany was the home of the (natural) sciences.

Virtually everyone has undergone an X-ray examination at some time in his or her life. The discoverer of the process was a German, Wilhelm Conrad Röntgen, who was awarded the first Nobel Prize for Physics in 1901. Immunisations against tetanus and diphtheria developed by Emil von Behring (who won the Nobel Prize for Medicine in 1901) have dispelled the problems caused by these two once feared scourges. Hundreds of thousands of sufferers succumbed to incurable tuberculosis until Robert Koch, a bacteriologist, demonstrated the way effectively to control the disease.

Equal numbers of people today complain of almost drowning in the flood of information with which they are constantly bombarded by the mass media. Whether such knowledge is a benefit or not, our modern communications-based society could not exist in its present form without radio or television, much of the technological basis for which was laid by German researchers such as Heinrich Hertz, Karl Ferdinand Braun and Adolf Slaby. Our knowledge of physical processes has made remarkable progress during the past 100 years, in particular as a result of the trailblazing work of Max Planck (quantum theory), Albert Einstein (theory of relativity), Werner Heisenberg (quantum mechanics), Otto Hahn (atomic fission), and others.

The contribution of technicians and inventors of genius has been almost as significant as that of the theorists. Names that spring to mind include Nikolaus Otto, Carl Benz and Gottlieb Daimler.

Between 1901, the year in which the Nobel Prizes were awarded for the first time, and 1933, when the National Socialists came to power, Germany was the undisputed "Superpower" of the scientific world. During this period, no fewer than 31 Nobel Laureates were German nationals (only six were American). Furthermore, German firms such as Siemens and AEG reigned supreme when it was necessary to adapt new discoveries in the fields of chemistry or electrotechnology to commercial use.

The fundamentals of the high levels of technical and scientific expertise achieved were laid in 1871, at the beginning of the German Reich, when committed scientists such as the mathematician Felix Klein and far-sighted officials such as Friedrich Theodor Althoff founded scientific associations (e.g. for applied mathematics and physics), thus forging closer links between university and industry, between theory and practice. The newly-created technical universities rapidly became an integral part of the German "Scientific Miracle". In order to further its national, military and mercantile interests the state financed promising research projects.

A large number of the scientists responsible for this remarkable series of brilliant discoveries were of the Jewish faith. The racialist persecution unleashed by the National Socialists drove many outstanding thinkers such as Albert Einstein into exile; most fled to the United States. Today, modern German science has still not really recovered from this exodus. Between 1933 and 1990, the USA was awarded 136 Nobel Prizes; Germany received 22.

Some post-war German Nobel Prizes, such as the Physics Prize awarded in 1986, harked back to scientific achievements during the period before 1933. The physicist Ernst Ruska, who was 79 in 1986, received his award for "one of the most important inventions of the 20th century", as stated during the ceremony. He had invented electron microscope in 1930-33.

One invention which failed to be awarded the Nobel Prize was a German development with which Hitler had hoped to win World War II: the V2 rocket and its predecessor, the work of Wernher von Braun and his team. These were the rockets used to bombard London. From 1959 von Braun worked for NASA, developing the *Saturn* launching rocket for the American space programme and making a significant contribution to the first landing on the moon.

lost their lives at Verdun and on the Somme. The switch to an underwater war with U-boats marked the beginning of the end, for this resulted in the Americans entering the war against Germany.

Defeat and revolution: Germany transformed itself into a military dictatorship. A state of siege, censorship and forced labour became part of everyday life, as did the cabbage stalks. The people were starving while gold was swapped for steel. The increasingly detested war was financed by ever-renewed loans. After the Treaty of Brest-Litowsk and the February and October Revolutions in 1917, Russia's part in the hostilities was over. But the war could no longer be won militarily.

At the end of September 1918 Germany's ally Bulgaria capitulated and Germany was now cut off from oil supplies from the Balkans. In such a situation, the quartermaster general Ludendorff made the only sensible suggestion. A monarchist and conservative through and through, he convinced Hindenburg and the emperor that an immediate ceasefire was necessary and that a parliamentary government be formed to "pick up the pieces". The German people thus heard of the entry of the SPD into the new government of Prince Max von Baden at the beginning of October 1918, and of the petition for a ceasefire. The war was lost and the parliamentary monarchy could not be saved. The revolution continued apace.

Councils or national assembly: In the week of 3–10 November 1918 Germany was transformed from a military dictatorship into a republic of committees. Princes and military authorities fell. Armed workers and soldiers formed worker and soldier committees who took over local control. Kaiser Wilhelm fled into exile in Holland. The hour of social democracy and that of its chairman, Friedrich Ebert, had come.

The "council of the people's representatives" – as the six-member social democratic government called itself – was to steer towards the formation of a socialist republic governed by committees, or at least that is what the workers' representatives throughout the country were demanding. But Friedrich Ebert had no intention of allowing this to happen and secretly secured the support of the German army. The Kaiser's generals were prepared to support social democracy in the fight against the workers and Bolshevism.

The first Congress of German Councils met in Berlin in 1918, with the vast majority of the 489 representatives coming from the ranks of the SPD. It was decided to hold elections for a national assembly and the entire political power was entrusted to Ebert's council of people's representatives. The German revolution was thus shunted onto a parliamentary track. "Someone has to be the bloodhound!" exclaimed the Social Democrats' "commander-in-chief" Gustav Noske, and ordered the rebellious workers shot by government troops.

In the capital Berlin, civil war was raging. Rosa Luxemburg and Karl Liebknecht, the leaders of the Communist Party, were assassinated by a group of soldiers from the imperial army. While this bitter internal conflict was in progress, the representatives of the national assembly gathered in peaceful Weimar to elect Friedrich Ebert as president of the first German democratic republic, the Weimar Republic.

Germany after the November Revolution: The Kaiser, kings and princes had fled and the old dynasties had been removed from the European stage. Germany was now a republic with a constitution based on adult suffrage, an eight-hour working day and recognised trade unions. But into the ranks of the conservatives came incorrigible monarchists, old generals, discarded soldiers, east-Elbian nobles, anti-Semites, bankers and influential press barons. These forces created the legend that the war had been lost from within, by a stab in the back.

And then there was Versailles where in July 1919 Germany, as loser of the war, had to sign a humiliating treaty. It lost all its colonies, with Alsace being returned to France, Gdansk to the League of Nations, West Prussia, parts of Pomerania and East Prussia to Poland. German territory on the west bank of the Rhine was occupied by the troops of the victorious powers. The Saar was administered by the League of Nations and its coal fields went to France. There were astronomical sums to be paid for reparations; Paragraph 231 burdened Germany with the exclusive guilt for World War I. A union of Germany and Austria was forbidden.

All these measures provided the ingredients for a new wave of German chauvinism and revanchism. The loudest cries of "war guilt lies" and "interest rate bondage" came from the "brown" supporters of the "National Socialist" movement, whose leader was Adolf Hitler.

Hitler's rise to power: Some Christians believed Hitler to be Satan in human guise. Others believed him to be a psychopath, a confidence trickster, someone with illusions of grandeur, or a criminal. Come what may, he was a product and expression of society at the time: a failed artist with a bourgeois background, stranded in Vienna without skill or trade. It was there that he joined the bandwagon of east European anti-Semitism and pan-German nationalism. He was a cor-

war. He propagated the destruction of Marxism and the Jews, and promised to restore Germany to a world power. And the man and his party, the National Socialist Workers' Party of Germany (NSDAP) became a useful tool in the hands of big business. Steel baron Fritz Thyssen later admitted in a book: "I paid Hitler". Others were to follow: the Berlin industrialist Börsig, the Cologne banker Kurt von Schröder, the Ruhr industrialist Emil Kirdorf, the director of the Deutsche Bank Emil Georg von Strauss, as well as Friedrich Flick. At the height of the economic crisis, when all political differences came to a head and parliamentary government no longer functioned, reactionary circles favoured a

poral in World War I and an informer in the service of the imperial army. Then he became the speech-maker for a small reactionary post-war party in Munich beer taverns, and by 1923 he was a failed *putschist*.

Without Versailles, without the economic crisis in Germany with six million unemployed, without powerful backers in industry and without the army, this unscrupulous demagogue would never have made it to the head of the Weimar state. He organised a chauvinistic mass movement and with the SA he controlled a powerful army of civil

Above, "Heil Hitler!"

transfer of power to the NSDAP. After the cabinets of Brüning, Papen and Schleicher had been worn to shreds, President von Hindenburg appointed Hitler as Chancellor on 30 January 1933.

The Nazis in power: The curtain went up on the barbarous stage of the Third Reich. The brown terror lasted for 12 years in Germany. First of all the Communist Party was banned and its leaders forced into exile or thrown into concentration camps. After the next elections at which the NSDAP acquired 44 percent of the vote, the parties in the Reichstag accepted the Enabling Act, with the exception of the SPD. The NSDAP thus came to power quite legally, without a *putsch*. Then the unions were broken up, and finally all political parties dispersed. The National Socialists called their one party dictatorship the "leadership principle". Factories, offices, schools, universities, radio and the press – almost the entire spectrum of society – was forced into step and regimented.

There were the *Sturmabteilungen* (SA), the *Schutzstaffeln* (SS) (storm and defence brigades), the German Work Front, National Socialist Women's Movement, the German Girls' Association, Hitler Youth, Strength Through Joy and Beauty Through Work. The NSDAP exercised complete control over the body and soul of a whole people. Mass gatherings, torchlight processions and party conferences were the catalysts behind the nation's awakening. The people were given stew once a week and learned to put general well-being before personal advantage.

The fascists made noises about the chosen northern race and began the grisly business of excising all "inferior" life. The Jews were declared second-class citizens, were attacked and robbed in the horrible *Kristallnacht* of 9 November 1938 and from 1941 were led to the "final solution". Millions of European Jews died a gruesome death in the extermination camps of Auschwitz, Treblinka, Madjanek and Buchenwald. It was a holocaust like no other.

World war and capitulation: Shortly after coming to power, Hitler had explained the essence of Germany's future foreign policy to army and navy commanders: "Acquisition by force of new export markets", "acquisition and Germanisation of new land in the east." In order to win future wars against the world powers USA and Soviet Union, fragmented Europe must be combined into a large, unified economic body, under German leadership, of course.

The Nazis embarked on a four-year plan of war preparations and soon tanks were rolling on the new motorways which had been built specially for them, and which still form the basis of contemporary Germany's road network. Within five years Hitler had recouped just about everything that Germany had lost at Versailles. In 1935 the Saar was returned to its "German mother", and one year later the *Wehrmacht* marched into the Rhineland. In March 1938 came the annexation of Austria and after the Munich Conference the Sudetenland in Czechoslovakia became part of the German Empire.

The British and French policy of appeasement at the Munich Conference had failed miserably. After the Soviet-German non-aggression pact of 23 August 1939, Hitler and Stalin divided Europe between them. And in close cooperation German and Russian troops invaded Poland that September, triggering the start of a massive conflict.

With over 50 million dead it was to be the most terrible war ever known in the history of mankind. For two years, the German forces, supported by their allies, marched unstoppably from one victory to another. By 1941 the Fascists controlled Europe and now, in league with Italy, sought to bring Africa under their yoke. From 1942 they embarked on their reign of bloody terror, spreading dissent and opportunism among the people they conquered. Vast numbers were made to do forced labour.

But fortunes began to change when Hitler's advance on the Soviet Union came to a halt before Moscow, and when the Americans entered the war after the Japanese attack on Pearl Harbour, the tide turned. England, the USA and the Soviet Union now presented a militarily superior alliance. The defeat of the 6th Army at Stalingrad and the allied landings in Normandy signalled the end to Germany's aspirations.

While the Allies brought about the end of National Socialism, this isn't to say that there was no resistance within Germany itself. But all attempts by military and civil resistance groups to topple the Nazi regime failed. Hitler's most miraculous escape was on 20 July 1944 when he survived a bomb attack on his headquarters in East Prussia. It was carried out by the young general staff officer and head of the anti-Fascist conspiracy Graf Stauffenberg.

The end of the Third Reich came with its unconditional surrender on 7–9 May 1945. Hitler had wanted to conquer new *Lebensraum* for Germany and to make the nation an invincible world power. But now it lay in ruins, bombed to smithereens, occupied and divided. Apart from this there was also the bitter recognition that Nazi rule had plunged this once so proud nation to the moral low point of its history.

Adolf Hitler in his classic pose.

The end of the Third Reich came with the battle for Berlin. On 30 April 1945 Hitler committed suicide in the bunker of his chancellery and on 1 May the Red Army hoisted the Soviet flag on the ruins of the Reichstag that had been destroyed by fire in 1933. On 7 May 1945 the Wehrmacht commanders signed the unconditional surrender in the allied headquarters in Reims and two days later the capitulation ceremony was repeated in the Soviet headquarters in Berlin-Karlshorst.

The allied plans: Despite mutual distrust, especially between Stalin and Churchill, the war coalition had held together until the victory over Hitler's Germany. The common goal had not only been to defeat the Fascist aggression, but to ensure that Germany would never again become a European great power.

At the end of the war the original plans for the dividing up of the country – apart from the increasingly large cessions of territory – were forgotten. In the post-war European order it was Stalin especially who looked forward to a strengthening of his own position of power through a territorially and economically weakened, but still united, German state.

On 5 June 1945 the Berlin Four Power Conference agreed on a combined administration of the country which had been divided into four zones of occupation. The Soviets obtained the east zone, the Americans the south, the British the north-west and the French the south-west. The erstwhile capital Berlin, as already envisaged by the London protocol of 1944, received a special status and was divided into four sectors.

At the Potsdam Conference (17 July to 1 August 1945), the "Big Three" (Stalin, Truman, Churchill/Attlee) agreed on the principles and aims of the combined occupying regime: demilitarisation, denazification, democratisation and decentralisation of the economy and the state. Economically, Germany should be treated as a complete unit. It was planned to establish central German-run authorities to look after economic and politi-

cal matters. A peace treaty was promised after an unspecified period of occupation. The "resettlement" of refugees from German areas to the east of the Oder-Neisse line should continue in a "controlled and humane manner". That effectively sanctioned the cession of the German-settled areas in the east – notably of Silesia and Pomerania to Poland – until such time as this could be ratified through a peace treaty.

"The idea of ruling Germany together with the Russians is madness", wrote the Ameri-

can diplomat Kennan in 1945 in Moscow. Political and ideological differences were already manifest in the compromise formulas of the Potsdam agreement. There were fundamentally varying interpretations of notions like "peace" and "democracy". However, the disagreements between the superpowers did not immediately ignite into conflict. World peace seemed to have been secured, particularly when, on 26 June 1945, 50 nations affixed their signatures to the United Nations Charter. It was only at the beginning of 1947 that the agenda was set for the division of Germany.

Germany starts again: The Third Reich had

Left, home at last. **Right**, the reconstruction of Germany begins.

transformed Germany into a heap of ruins. Cities like Hamburg, Cologne, Magdeburg, Nuremberg, Würzburg and Dresden had been devastated by bombs. Berlin and many other cities that had been vanquished in the ground war had been reduced to little more than desolate piles of rubble. In the regions west of the Oder-Neisse over one-quarter of all residential buildings had been either completely obliterated or seriously damaged.

The war had destroyed one-fifth of Germany's manufacturing capacity and production sank to one-third of its 1936 level. The collapse of transport systems, the destruction of railways, bridges and tunnels all contributed to this gloomy state of affairs. Not a

tion of the population was afflicted by hunger and illness, particularly during the "hunger winter" of 1946–47. Among the survival techniques were bartering, hoarding, dealing on the black market and theft. City dwellers headed for the country to swap pianos, carpets and jewellery for eggs, ham and potatoes. With the continuing decline in the value of gold the unit of currency on the black market was the American cigarette.

Amongst all this destruction, misery and general demoralisation, the populace set about the organisation of its survival. In the cities the *Trummerfrauen* – "rubble women" extracted the bricks from the ruins for the rebuilding of houses. Railways, bridges and

single major bridge across the Rhine remained intact. In addition, the occupying powers for a long time set limits on industrial output and blocked both foreign trade and trade between the different occupied zones. Only one-quarter of the necessary amount of fuel was available for domestic heating in the big cities.

Between 1945 and 1948 a total of 12 million extra Germans flooded into this destroyed country, whose size had been reduced by one-quarter. Over two million people lost their lives during this period of exodus and forced expulsions from the German-settled areas in the East. A large propor-

machinery were repaired so that the wheels of industry could begin to turn once more. For most Germans, the daily routine was devoted to finding a place to live, procuring food and heating material. The general population took only passive note of what was happening on the political front.

Despite all that they had suffered, it was precisely the anti-Nazis, including many who had survived the concentration camps and prisons, who clung to the right of the Germans for a democratic self-rejuvenation. In many cities the so-called "anti-fascist" committees spontaneously sprang up to organise economic and political development, only then to be dispersed by the occupation authorities. The fate of Germany lay firmly in the hands of the victorious powers.

German writers and artists, including those who had just returned from exile, recognised the scale of the moral catastrophe into which the Fascism of the national socialists had plunged the country. One of the Berlin artist Horst Strempel's triptych paintings was entitled *Night time over Germany*.

The Nuremberg trials and denazification: On 24 November 1945 the Nuremberg trials of the leading representatives of the Nazi regime were opened. Twenty-four politicians, ideologists, military men and industrialists, including Hermann Göring, Alfred

The war crimes trials were continued in 1950, and now the Germans were confronted with the reality of the Nazi atrocities which until this time many had either not wanted or not been able to recognise. While some of the guilty escaped, the denazification process effected the entire population, divided as it was into five categories ranging from "principals" to "exonerated". In the American zone every citizen over 18 years of age had to complete a questionnaire containing 131 questions. Based on the answers given, the "judgement chambers" passed sentences ranging from 10 years in prison to denial of voting rights. In the US zone, the accusation of moral "collective guilt" was vehemently

Rosenberg, Wilhelm Keitel and Gustav Krupp were charged with crimes against the peace and crimes against mankind. The unprecedented arraignment and trial were to set new norms for international law. On 1 October 1946 the International Military Court passed sentence: 12 of the accused (including the absent Bormann) were sentenced to death; three were sentenced to life imprisonment and two to between 10 and 20 years. The remaining three were acquitted.

Left, the accused at the Nuremberg trials. **Above**, "raisin bombers" relieve Berlin with supplies during the 1948 blockade.

dismissed by the German anti-Fascists.

Amongst the majority of "hangers-on" this accusation of guilt engendered a great deal of cynicism, particularly when it became clear that the victors had enlisted the services of some of Nazi Germany's top criminals, including Klaus Barbie who went to work for the American CIA.

In the Soviet zone, the anti-Fascistic cleansing process bore the mark of Stalinist terror from the moment it began. Between 1945 and 1950 in camps like Buchenwald and Sachsenhausen it was not only the functionaries and supporters of the Nazi regime that were killed, but also tens of thousands of randomly arrested people who had been denounced to the authorities, innocent social democrats and Christians.

The policies of occupation: Regardless of the Allied Control Council, the occupation authorities under their respective military governors very much did as they pleased. In the Soviet zone, under the catchphrase "anti-fascistic-democratic reform", a revolution took place from the top aimed at eradicating the "roots of Fascism, militarism and war". This included a comprehensive land reform, the nationalisation of the banks, the expropriation of all "those interested in war", extensive dismantling of industrial plant and the establishment of the "Soviet joint-stock

nationalisation of the Ruhrgebiet and that Saarland become part of the French economic sphere. Nevertheless, many Germans continued to pin their hopes on the "west", and on the Americans in particular. The private relief campaigns and the "care parcels" sent by the American people contributed to this pro-American stance, which was then further reinforced by the events that were being witnessed in the east.

Somewhat later than the Russians, the western military governments allowed parties to indulge in political activities and trades unions to be established in their zones. In the late summer and autumn of 1945 they appointed governments for the newly struc-

company", which took over more than 30 percent of industrial capacity. The uranium mines in Saxony (for the atomic bomb programme), operated by forced labour, also belonged to this combine. After one million people had fled the east zone, not least due to the appalling lack of food, the Soviet Military Administration (SMAD) closed the zone boundary in the summer of 1946.

In the western zones, too, the dismantling of industry was continued right up until 1949, resulting in soaring unemployment. France played a special role in those years. It refused to allow the emergence of any German central authority, demanded the inter-

tured German states. After initial hesitation, the Americans showed interest in promoting economic regeneration in the west zones through private capital.

In summer 1946 the American military governor proposed that the Allied Control Council establish a central economic administration in the four zones. France and the Soviet Union rejected the idea. By the beginning of that September the differences of opinion between the Allies in respect of Germany became pronounced. The Americans and the British agreed on the establishment of the "bizone", a combined economic region for the two zones under their occupation, for 1947. The Soviets and the French protested and on 6 September 1946, the plan was also turned down by the US Secretary of State Byrnes. He proposed the establishment of a combined German government (on state basis) and proposed a revision of the eastern border (Oder-Neisse line) in the peace treaty.

The Cold War: The different policies in the occupied zones reflected the differences in the systems as well as the increasing conflicts of interest between the two superpowers. In 1947–48, the east-west conflict erupted in different venues in Europe and quickly spread to parts of Asia as well. In Eastern Europe – the huge area that had been handed to Stalin at Yalta in February 1945 – the communists

installed dictatorships in their "peoples' democracies". When in Greece the left-wing threatened to emerge victorious in the civil war and when similar tensions began to erupt in Turkey, the Americans announced that they would stamp out the spreading flames of Communism. The Marshall Plan, the American-funded reconstruction of Germany, was also intended to halt Soviet expansion. Under pressure from Stalin, Poland was forced to forego this aid. In February

Left, East Berlin riots in June 1953. **Above**, Konrad Adenauer, the first chancellor of the Federal Republic.

1948 the Communists took over power in Prague. The only Communist country that broke with Stalin was Yugoslavia. While the Iron Curtain divided Europe it was clear to all where the political-strategic centre of conflict of the Cold War lay: in defeated and occupied Germany.

The path to division 1947–49: The decision to divide Germany and to establish a western state was primarily a result of economic considerations on the part of the western powers. The British and the French could only pay for the delivery of foodstuffs to Germany with the financial assistance of the Americans. The military governor Clay made it repeatedly clear in Washington that the Germans would have to pay for their own imports, something that was only possible through an increase in industrial production and exports. As agreement with the Soviets on this issue did not seem to be possible, the establishment of the West German state was organised.

The only real initiative on the part of German postwar politicians to prevent the looming division of the country was thwarted in June 1947. The Bavarian Minister President had called a conference in Munich of Minister Presidents from all zones. However, the representatives from the western zones had been instructed by the occupation authorities to discuss economic questions only, whilst those from the Soviet side of the fence, under the control of the Soviet occupying power, demanded a debate concerning questions of a central government. When their agenda was refused, they left. The front line of the emerging cold war had already been drawn through the middle of Germany.

In the West the CDU chairman Konrad Adenauer supported a course for the strict integration of the west zones into the western family of nations. And the SPD chairman Kurt Schumacher, who had suffered for 10 years in Nazi concentration camps, also turned down any cooperation with the communists. For the time being he accepted the division of Germany. One was comforted by the fact that "opposite poles attract".

The founding of the western state: The final decisions were made at the six power conference on 7 June 1948 in London between the USA, Britain, France and the Benelux countries. It was agreed that Western Germany should be involved in the rebuilding of Europe (OEEC), that the Ruhrgebiet be subject to international control, and that a new West German Federal Republic be created. In protest at these decisions the Russian representative left the Allied Control Council in Berlin on 20 March 1948.

Airlift: On 20 June that same year, the currency reform, that had also been decided upon in London, was carried out. The SMAD responded with its own currency reform in the east zone. The conflict came to a dramatic head when in the continuing argument about the new currency the Soviets reacted with the complete blockade of the western sector of Berlin. The Allies organised an airlift: "raisin bombers" supplied the West

Berlin population with food and coal until the lifting of the blockade on 12 May 1949.

The final division of Berlin came in September 1948. Under the leadership of the ruling Mayor Ernst Reuter (SPD), Berlin changed in the eyes of the world from being the despised centre of the Nazi dictatorship to a potent symbol of the democratic desire for freedom.

A parliamentary council made up of elected representatives of the West German state assemblies was commissioned by the western powers and from 1 September 1948, in King Ludwig's castle of Herrenchiemsee in Bavaria, this set about formulating a provi-

sional constitution, the *Grundgezetz* – the "basic law". After its ratification by the state assemblies this constitution of the "Federal Republic of Germany" was announced. In September 1949 the newly-elected Federal Parliament came together for the first time and Theodor Heuss (FDP) was elected the first president and Konrad Adenauer (CDU) the first chancellor at the head of a civil coalition government. The new state was a parliamentary democracy made up of a number of federal states. But the Western powers made quite sure that they retained control of Berlin, with all the symbolism which that city held for a "united Germany".

The other German state: While the SED (Socialist Unity Party of Germany) attacked the West Germans' "politics of division" with patriotic slogans of unity, as a countermove they set about the foundation of an East German state. On 29 May 1949 the elected People's Congress approved a constitution of the "German Democratic Republic", which was also related to the whole of Germany. On 7 October that same year this was enforced by the provisional People's Chamber, the *Volkskammer*, that had emerged from the Congress. Wilhelm Pieck became the president of the GDR and Otto Grotewohl, formerly a social democrat, acted as Minister President of an SED government of which non-socialist "coalitions" were also a part. However the centre of power lay within the SED politburo and the SED General Secretary Walter Ulbricht occupied the most senior post. In 1952 the declared occupation and nationalisation policies of "anti-fascistic-democratic reform" now became directed towards the "development of Socialism". In addition to the industrial "state-owned companies", collectivisation should also include other branches of production including skilled trades and agriculture.

After the death of Stalin on 6 March 1953, the leading SED functionaries around Rudolf Herrnstadt and the head of security Wilhelm Zaisser attempted to steer towards a new course of "moderation". In cooperation with the Russian ambassador and high commissioner Semjonov they planned to remove Ulbricht from power and to establish the conditions for a reunification of Germany. This was a thoroughly planned manoeuvre aimed at preventing the military integration of the Federal Republic with the West.

Uprising: During this critical period rebellion broke out on 7 June 1953. Construction workers in East Berlin reacted to an increase in work quotas by strike action and mass demonstrations and these quickly developed into an insurgent movement throughout the GDR. The strike slogans developed into outright demands for free elections and the reunification of Germany. The SED reacted sternly, claiming the strike was stirred up by supporters of the West, and used Russian tanks against the protestors. This uprising in the east not only succeeded in securing the political survival of the SED party boss Ulbricht, but it also helped the Bonn Chancellor Adenauer to election victory in 1953 and reinforced his policy of integration with the West. In the Federal Republic 17 July was henceforth to be celebrated as "German Unity Day".

The West German "economic miracle": In Western Germany it took some time for the currency reform to have its desired effect on economic stability. After the currency cut in 1948 the abundance of consumer goods in the shop windows resulted in an increase in production of these goods. A further psychologically important thrust was created by the Marshall Plan of which the Federal Republic became a beneficiary on 15 December 1949. Thereafter, over 3 billion DM was poured into West German production in the form of payments in kind and credits. A veritable boom resulted from the Korean War (1950–53), leading to a sharp increase in demand for German export commodities.

In the 1950s the world came to experience the German "economic miracle" – the *Wirtschaftswunder*: high growth rates of around 8 percent, reduction in unemployment and a steady increase in the standard of living. The economic recovery went hand in hand with the development of a socially-oriented market economy. This concept, introduced by the minister for economic affairs Ludwig Erhard (CDU), was based on the dynamics of the free market and the private ownership of the means of production. The imbalances created by a totally free capitalist system were to be corrected by state-administered control of trade as well as

by a comprehensive social-welfare policy.

The system could only be as successful as it was through the restrained wage policy practised by the West German trades unions. Under their parent organisation, the DGB (German Trades Union Council), the strong unions limited their class struggle to rhetoric and acted as upholders of the economic system – as "social partners". The West German Social Democrats also differentiated between Marxist theory and practice and made Keynesian redistribution concepts the theme of their Godesburg Manifesto in 1959.

By the end of the 1950s the West German economy was producing half of all industrial commodities in the European Economic

Community, which was founded in 1957 as the basis for further economic and political integration within Europe. The VW "beetle" and Mercedes Benz became worldwide symbols of the German economic miracle and "made in Germany" became the trademark of the quality that people now came to expect from German products. Balance of payments figures were in the black from 1952 onwards and by 1969 the Federal Bank had acquired reserves in excess of 30 billion DM. Between 1950 and 1966 real earnings rose by 139 percent.

A primary factor in this success was the availability of a highly-qualified and disci-

Left, Italian guest workers on their way home. **Right**, Rudi Dutschke, a leader of the revolutionary students, speaks during the 1968 demonstrations.

plined workforce, which included the frightened refugees who had fled the former Eastern territories of Germany after the war, as well as the GDR.

The Berlin Wall was built by the GDR leadership on 13 August 1961 as a means of preventing any further exodus from East Germany. Now the Federal Republic became an interesting proposition for unskilled workers from Italy and Southern Europe, whose recruitment had already begun back in 1955. After the 1966–67 recession came a flood of hundreds of thousands of further "guest workers" from Turkey, a migration whose social and cultural implications for the German nation would only be generally

and privately the behaviour of people was governed on the one hand by the realities of the reconstruction of the country and all the hard work which that entailed and on the other by the simple need to settle down and to recover from the years of destruction and regimentation.

East and West firmly divided: During the 1950s the German question was a major political theme for the superpowers. The western powers were concerned with the integration of all the potential within their sphere of influence. NATO was founded in 1949 "to keep the Russians out, to keep the Americans in and to keep the Germans down".

After the Korean War (1950–53), the West-

recognised much later, in the late 1980s.

The Adenauer era: In the middle of the 1950s the Germans waved goodbye to all the ruins and turned to the more pleasant things in life: food, new furniture, holidays in Italy. Much to the disapproval of the older generation, who preferred sentimental films, the youth developed a liking for the rock and roll kings Bill Haley and Elvis Presley. The one unifying ideology of the Adenauer era – understandable enough when one looked to the east – was anti-Communism. While the West Germans had by this time stopped suppressing the past, life became very much geared towards the future. Both politically

ern powers insisted on the rearmament of the West German state. Chancellor Adenauer exploited this military interest in exchange for the acquisition of higher degrees of sovereignty for the Federal Republic. For the conservative Catholic it was hardly a question of reunification, but of gaining an equal footing for the Federal Republic in a united Western Europe. The economic integration of Europe began in 1957 with the establishment of the European Community by the Treaty of Rome.

As far as the Soviets were concerned, a rearmed Western Germany as part of a western alliance represented a provocation of incalculable proportions. In 1952, in order to prevent Germany's integration with the West, Stalin offered a peace treaty for a united, neutral Germany. The Soviet Union was prepared to sacrifice the East German state for a political price and its offers were repeated several times before the Federal Republic's entry into NATO in 1955. The chance for a reunification of Germany had been presented but it was a chance that Adenauer, who rejected neutrality, chose to ignore.

As a power-political alternative to the withdrawal of the Americans the Soviet Union now proceeded with the consolidation and expansion of the area under its control. In 1955 the GDR was equipped with an army

and was incorporated in the newly established military alliance of the Eastern Bloc, the Warsaw Pact. After the formation of the bloc system the four powers displayed no serious interest in solving the German question. However, things came to a head again in 1959 when Khruschev demanded a peace treaty involving both German states and for West Berlin to acquire the status of "free city", without the presence of the Western

Left, Willy Brandt's historic visit to Warsaw in 1970, acknowledging Germany's guilt for the death of the Polish Jews. **Above**, the masses demonstrate in Leipzig.

Allies. The Berlin crisis ended with the building of the Wall on 13 August 1961, an undertaking that was carried out with the prior knowledge and approval of the US government.

The new *Ostpolitik* and the status quo: After the Cuba crisis in 1962, it seemed as though the superpowers had arrived at a situation of détente. This would influence the future foreign policy of the Federal Republic. Willy Brandt, at the head of a social democrat-liberal coalition, geared his new *Ostpolitik* towards the preservation of the unity of the German nation under the prevailing conditions of division. Communication was the basic requirement for the survival of the nation: in Berlin and in Germany as a whole conditions had to be established where people could see and talk to each other again. On the international level, this policy was aimed at forcing a "recognition of reality" – the reality of the post-war borders – and at achieving a relaxation of the bloc system.

Willy Brandt had served for many years as the Mayor of West Berlin. With his election as Federal Chancellor in 1969 there emerged a leader who was, largely for tactical reasons, reviled by his political opponents both for his anti-Fascist stance – involving his emigration to Norway – during the War and for now representing the "other Germany". And it was indeed the East Germans who pinned their hopes on Brandt. They gave him an enthusiastic reception when he arrived in Erfurt for the first negotiations with the GDR Minister President Willi Stoph.

For the world at large, the term *Ostpolitik* was inseparably linked with the gesture of repentance that Brandt, the anti-Fascist, paid the Jewish victims of the Warsaw Ghetto. After the Eastern Bloc treaties with Moscow and Warsaw the Federal Republic signed the "Foundation Treaty" with the GDR, which was aimed at promoting "good neighbourly relations".

Student protest and the 1968 generation: The late 1960s marked a turning point in the development of the Federal Republic. From 1966–67 the West German state experienced its first serious recession, the result of the structural crisis in the coal and steel industries. After the broad coalition of CDU/CSU-SPD had taken measures to intervene and keep the economy afloat the crisis was once more converted into an economic boom.

After years of stability the Federal Republic seemed to be truly rocked by the revolts at the universities, much more so than from any temporary rise in popularity of the right-wing nationalists (NPD). But only a few activists, in particular those belonging to the circle of friends around the West Berlin student leader Rudi Dutschke dreamed that through their protest action aimed at ridding the universities, the state and society in general of all "authoritarian structures" they might also succeed in tearing down the Wall and continuing their socialist revolution in the whole of Germany. The majority protested against the "dirty war" that the USA was waging in Vietnam and in various "Third in Germany that calls itself "The Greens".

In the cause of the fight against Fascism and Imperialism the student uprising left behind an explosive legacy, namely the tradition of political terrorism inspired by the RAF – the Red Army Faction, an organisation that is still at large (the tired RAF veterans found a safe home in the GDR under its veteran leader Honecker). West German politicians and businessmen remain a target.

Conflict and agreement: The long-term perspective of the liberal *Ostpolitik* towards a reunification of the country became rather lost in the 1970s and 1980s. The preservation of two German states came to be defended, especially in German intellectual circles. The

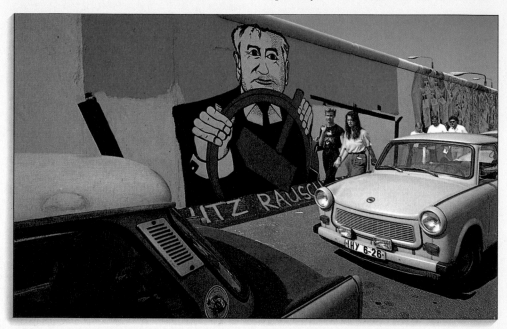

World" movements they sought and discovered the revolutionary subject of global emancipation. The students elected Ho Chi Minh, Mao Zedong and Che Guavara as their idols.

More important in the long run than the expounding of these ideologies was the revolution that took place within German society itself through the "1968 generation". Sexual taboos were cast aside, a new style of education was practised and the new vital consciousness came to be governed by the guiding concepts of "emancipation" and "self-determination". In a round-about way the "68" philosophy of life lead to the emergence of the ecological movement so strong two states had gone their own separate ways for so long that many felt that reunification no longer belonged on the political agenda. Only occasionally, as for example when the SED expelled the poet and singer Wolf Biermann in 1976 (he had sung anti-Honecker songs), were any doubts cast on this ideology of division.

At the beginning of the 1980s definite signals of broad dissatisfaction with the status quo emerged from the peace movement, the protest against a new heat in the arms race on German soil – East and West. The pacifist GDR opposition, which was embodied in the Protestant Church, began to develop into a considerable protest movement, which finally manifested itself in the dramatic revolution year of 1989.

The Wall collapses: German unity came about very suddenly, when nobody really expected it would happen at all. The massive arms race of the 1970s and 1980s had over-extended the capacity of the Soviet economic and technological resources. A "rethink" was the order of the day for the new Soviet leadership under Mikhail Gorbachev. While the opposition to the GDR pinned its hopes on the Soviet leader and reformer, the Stalinist and aged GDR leadership missed their opportunity to liberalise and modernise the regime to make it more sympathetic.

In September 1987 when Honecker went to Bonn on a state visit and was received by Chancellor Kohl with all the honours accorded an equal head of an almost sovereign state, he probably felt that he had reached the zenith of his career: after all, did not this visit demonstrate the existence of two equal-ranking German states? The political agenda was governed by the establishment of the European domestic market in 1992 – and the perpetuation of the division of Germany.

Only a small number of people in the west

Left and above, who knows how long the Wall would have stood without President Gorbachev?

recognised the fact that the increasing number of GDR citizens applying to travel indicated that revolution was imminent. When in Hungary in 1989 the reform Communists, who did not want to miss their chance of joining the West European process of integration, opened the border to Austria, refugees from the GDR poured across the "Green Line". The SED leadership responded to this mass-escape with obstinate gestures demonstrating its sovereignty. The trains carrying the fugitives from Prague had to cross GDR territory on their way to West Germany. At the station in Dresden the scenes were reminiscent of a civil war.

The reunification that the German people themselves achieved did not exactly meet with rapturous approval from the country's European neighbours. In the early phases of the peaceful revolution certain of Bonn's allies had attempted in vain to slow down the pace of the developments. But neither of the two superpowers either wanted or was able to prevent the revolution from going the full distance, and this fact ultimately proved decisive. The formalities of a rapid unification were completed in 1990.

A peace treaty with Germany had never been signed and so Foreign Minister Genscher had suggested instead tabling a discussion on the issue of European security involving the governments of the two Germanys and the four victorious powers. In July 1990 Gorbachev accepted the membership of a reunited but militarily disarmed Germany in NATO - the American condition for the reunification of the country. On 3 October 1990 the Germans celebrated their reunification. The Cold War and the post-war era was finally at an end.

Future challenges: In the favourable circumstances of autumn 1989 the Germans succeeded in achieving a peaceful revolution. At the end of the 20th century Germany, which plunged to the low point of its history with the National Socialists, has now won the chance for a historic new beginning as a united country. What about the danger of a return to national hubris and power-political arrogance? Does not the danger of German hegemony in Europe now threaten? The answer was possibly provided by Vaclav Havel, Czechoslovakia's poet and president who insisted that nobody need have any worries about a democratic Germany.

It was one of the ironies of history: on 7 October 1989, East Germany celebrated its fortieth birthday with the slogan, "The development of the German Democratic Republic will continue to be the work of all the people." This motto would prove to be true – but in a very different way than the SED (Socialist Unity Party) regime of old men had hoped.

In the following weeks, millions of East German citizens shouting "We are the people" marched through the streets demanding democratic rights, free elections, the freedom to travel, and better material conditions. Neither repression nor reformist concessions enabled the Party to stop or to co-opt the protest movement. On 18 October the 77-year-old Party boss, Erich Honecker, was removed from power. On 9 November, under pressure from the ever-more confident mass movement, the Wall in Berlin fell. The Party's claim to leadership was eliminated from the constitution; in December, a Round Table was established in Berlin, and the opposition began to negotiate with the Party on the future of the country.

Free elections, unthinkable until then, were set for 1990. Yet even before the first freely-elected parliament in East German history could assemble, its actual responsibilities were already clear: liquidation of East Germany as an independent state and establishment of German unity. East Germany's fortieth birthday would turn out to be its last.

The initial sparks: Even as the leaders of the socialist world met at a festive banquet in East Berlin on the eve of the fortieth anniversary of the country's founding, several thousand East Germans, crying "We are the people," gathered in nearby Alexanderplatz in a spontaneous demonstration.

Before the eyes of journalists from around the world, the demonstrators made their way to the site of the official celebrations. Shouting "Gorbi, Gorbi," they demanded reform of East Germany's inflexible and old-fashioned socialism. Surprised at first, the police and the infamous State Security Service

(Stasi) began harassing and then beating the peaceful demonstrators indiscriminately. In Berlin and other large cities around the country, several thousand people were arrested, interrogated and held for days. Anger and bitterness among the people produced by this unprecedented brutality would develop in the coming weeks into a decisive impulse for revolution.

Life will punish those who come too late: For months, thousands of resigned citizens had been leaving the country daily across the

Hungarian border, which had been opened in June, 1989. Before the eyes of the world, these refugees presented the inflexible regime in East Berlin with the spectacular bill for its anti-reform line. For, from the moment Gorbachev came to power in 1985, the Socialist Unity Party of Germany (SED) left no room for doubt that it would continue on its dogmatic course, if necessary against the will of the reformer in the Kremlin.

The East German economy might have been the most productive among the socialist countries, but material living conditions remained extremely humble in comparison to Western standards. It no longer satisfied

Left, border guards are now redundant. **Above**, the "wall-peckers" out for souvenirs.

citizens, especially the young, that no homelessness and no unemployment existed in East Germany. As Western television beamed pictures of the apparently inexhaustible stream of refugees into East German living rooms each evening, the SED leadership continued its propaganda. Production and services worsened as a result of the exodus of skilled labour. What Mikhail Gorbachev wrote in the guest-book of the anti-reform SED leadership would soon prove to be a historical verdict: "Life will punish those who come too late."

The opposition forms: Under the pressure of the emigration crisis, the face of the East German opposition also changed. Until mid-

founding of a "New Forum". The appeal was perfectly tailored to the popular mood. It called for a broad dialogue on acute problems and a common search for solutions. In only a few weeks, some hundred thousand citizens had joined the New Forum.

At first, the state took no repressive action against the new opposition, though in the past repression even of many unspectacular activities had been the norm. The East German leadership, with its international reputation already sinking as a result of the wave of emigration, did not wish to cause any more negative headlines by undertaking harsh domestic measures immediately before the birthday of the Republic.

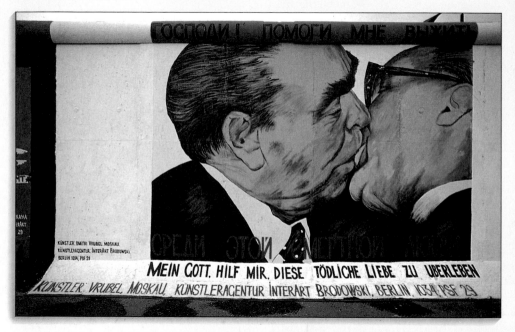

1989, this opposition consisted of a few scattered environmental, peace and human rights initiatives working under the umbrella of the Protestant Church. In comparison with countries such as Poland and Hungary, their influence was insignificant. In the course of the local elections in May, in which the regime once again claimed that they had won almost 100 percent of the votes, country-wide protests against the rigged election results occurred for the first time. However, a broad movement did not develop until September, when an initiating group of 100 people, impressed by the wave of emigration, published an "Appeal 1989" for the

The people force change: Prior to that fateful Monday demonstration in Leipzig on 9 October 1989 – these demonstrations had been occurring each week for months – the situation became critical. Task forces were placed on the alert and local hospitals prepared blood supplies. The press announced that "counter-revolutionary activities" would be stopped for good, if necessary "with weapons in hand." But on that evening, with 70,000 participants Leipzig experienced the largest demonstration since the uprising on 17 June, 1953. The state held back. In the afternoon, the head of the Gewandthaus orchestra, Kurt Masur, together with three secretaries from the Leipzig district leadership of the SED, made an appeal for calm that was subsequently broadcast on local radio. The participation of the Party's district secretaries was a sensation. The Party headquarters in Berlin could no longer push through its hard line. Radical change could no longer be prevented; the Liberals, until then strictly obedient to the SED, openly supported the demonstrators' demands; more and more artists and theatre people were taking part in Church-organised protests, workers were leaving the party-run union. While on the following Monday, 16 October, 120,000 people were taking to the streets of Leipzig, Honecker's downfall had already been sealed

mittee, the following Monday 300,000 people took to the streets of Leipzig. A day later, Egon Krenz had himself elected head of state, thus signalling that the party intended to hold on to its monopoly of power. The Party leadership in Berlin had not recognised the changing times. Instead of entering into negotiations with opposition groups, it attempted to save itself with non-committal announcements of reform once things had quietened down. But this was not to be. On 4 November, Berlin experienced its largest demonstration by far since the November revolution of 1918, with over a million participants. The demonstration was broadcast live on East German television. The tenor:

in Berlin. On Wednesday, 18 October, the Head of Party and State resigned. His closest confidantes went with him – the absolute ruler of the East German economy, Günter Mittag, and the country's top censor, Joachim Herrmann. Honecker's successor was Egon Krenz, who had been spoken of as Crown Prince for years, and until then had been responsible for security questions in the Politburo.

Despite these changes in the Central Committee

demands for a pluralist democracy that guaranteed GDR citizens all the freedoms known in Western societies.

When, two days after the historic demonstration, the government published a new travel law that still required an application before each trip, popular indignation knew no bounds. "Visa-free as far as Hawaii" was the people's motto. Two days later, the entire cabinet handed in its resignation. On 9 November, almost the entire remaining Honecker Politburo resigned. Although its replacements were still not decisive advocates of reform, yet Dresden's Party chief, Hans Modrow, the only prominent SED

Left, comrades of the old school, Brezhnev and Honecker. **Above**, *Deutschland, einig Vaterland* – Germany, one Fatherland.

FLOODS OF REFUGEES

The so-called "voting with the feet" that took place during the summer and autumn of 1989 and ultimately led to the collapse of the Wall was not the first and not even the last time that the people of the GDR expressed their dissatisfaction. Between the collapse of the Wall and reunification on 3 October 1990, no less than 300,000 people left the GDR for the West.

Since the end of World War II the Federal Republic has provided a home for 16 million refugees, emigrés and persons resettled. Altogether they made up one-quarter of the population of the old Federal Republic. Towards the end of, and immediately after World War II, seven million ethnic Germans arrived after being driven out of their homeland of Silesia, which is today part of Poland. From the Sudetenland and the north of Czechoslovakia came a further three million Germans while another 1.8 million fled from Hungary, Rumania and Yugoslavia.

More precise figures are available for those resettlers from the GDR and for emigrants from other countries who arrived after 1950. Until 1988, 1.6 million people trickled in from Eastern Europe and the Soviet Union.

Because of the change in the political climate the flood gates were opened for the mass exodus of those ethnic Germans who wished to return to their motherland in 1988. In that year about 140,000 people arrived from Poland, and something like double that figure followed in 1989. From the Soviet Union came 47,500 in 1988 and 100,000 the following year.

Prior to the building of the Wall on 13 August 1961, 2.7 million GDR citizens had been officially registered as having crossed into the Federal Republic. In addition to this figure a further one million or so who had been immediately taken in by relatives or friends were not listed on this register. With the Wall in place, the numbers naturally dropped, although up until 1988 a further 616,000 people did manage to make it out, either with official exit permits or by escaping. In 1989 no less than 340,000 left the country via Budapest, Prague and Warsaw.

Apart from the political situation it was economic backwardness and the resultant lack of consumer goods, including foodstuffs, that caused so many people to abandon the GDR. While for every 100 households in the Federal Republic there were 152 cars, in the GDR there were only 52. In the West, 94 households possessed a colour TV, only 52 in the GDR did. Nine out of every 100 GDR households could telephone from home, while in the Federal Republic that figure was 98.

Every new influx of refugees immediately puts a great strain on communal budgets. In the long term, however, the work motivation of the new arrivals not only provides a boost to industry, but also causes an increase in the demand for goods, and thus the whole of the national economy is given a shot in the arm. The fact that most of these new arrivals are young also means that once they have found employment they will start to contribute to the state pension fund. According to financial experts, the country will as a result be much better off with the new settlers than without them.

Germany is a country of immigrants with 4.5 million foreign workers, making up 7.6 percent of the population of the former Federal Republic. Until 1973 they were actively recruited directly from their countries of origin, primarily Turkey and Yugoslavia. Seventy percent of these foreign workers have lived in Germany for more than eight years, but only 460,000 of them have acquired the highest residence status – the "right of residence".

The numbers of people who have been granted political asylum in the Federal Republic is small by comparison, although high when compared to the rest of Europe. Of the 150,000 people granted asylum since 1953, 80,000 still live in the Federal Republic. A further 300,000 have been allowed to stay for humanitarian reasons and will not be sent back. Half of these refugees hail from countries of the former Eastern Bloc, and have enjoyed a general amnesty from deportation since 1966.

They are fortunate in comparison to the Tamil, Iranian and Kurdish refugees, and to many others who must first prove that they are victims of political persecution before being allowed to stay. Deportation orders are served on those that can't provide such proof, even if this means they might be tortured when they return to their home country.

member to enjoy the aura of an upright reformer, became Minister President.

The Wall falls: At the end of a press conference, Günter Schabowski, the Politburo member responsible for the press, announced in qualified terms that travel laws were no longer in force. In plain English: The Wall was finally open to those people who wanted to cross it.

A few hours later, indescribable scenes of joy took place at the intra-city border crossings in Berlin. East German border guards, armed to the teeth, had protected socialism here for 29 years; yet, on this evening hundreds of thousands crossed to the western side of the city without hindrance. In the

was expelled from the Party. Ex-Stasi boss Mielke, former Minister-President Stoph, Günter Mittag and many senior SED politicians who had determined East German policy for years were arrested for abuse of office and corruption.

The Party had hit rock bottom in the estimation of the people. Not even its new name, the PDS – "Party of Democratic Socialism" – could change that. In the course of a few months, it lost two-thirds of its former 2.3 million members. The Round Table decision to hold free elections on 18 March 1990 signalled the end of the SED era.

The opening of the border on 9 November not only doomed to failure all the SED's

following weeks, all the Party's efforts to place itself at the head of the reform movement failed. Even the election of Hans Modrow to head the government could not bring the party off the defensive. With the help of the media, the full extent of corruption and privilege in the SED state came to light. Under pressure from the Party grassroots, Egon Krenz resigned from the office of Party leader on 3 December 1989. Almost the entire leadership around Erich Honecker

Beaming with pleasure, East Berliners cross the breached Wall on the 9 November and mingle with West Berliners.

attempts to salvage at least some of its power; it also pulled the rug out from under the opposition's ideal of democratic socialism in East Germany. The population's autumn slogan, "We are the people," soon turned into "We are one people." In the elections of 18 March, the parties that consistently supported unification of the two states received well over 70 percent of the votes. In the first parliamentary elections in a unified Germany on 2 December, 1990, this tendency was confirmed, with 55 percent for Chancellor Helmut Kohl and the governing coalition of the Christian Democratic Union and the Free Democrats.

It was something no one in the world expected of them: tears of emotion and joy, cheering crowds falling into one another's arms. On this night of 9 November, 1989, inner walls broke down, ideologies collapsed. What is the matter with the "Huns," the "Teutons," the "Krauts"? Will this unexpected reunification go to their heads? Will arrogance follow sentimentality? Will they try once again to set themselves up as an example to the world?

It has not been as bad as the rest of the some threatening gestures, did not resort to violence. And in the West, as well, conscientious objectors and the peace movement have gained more public support during the past 10 years than have cold warriors. An attempt to introduce military instruction in schools failed. War toys are frowned upon and rarely sold. Even comics do not contain racist or warlike sentiments. The allies in the United States, Great Britain and France even worried about the reliability and defensive capabilities of the old Federal Republic.

world had feared. The wave of national enthusiasm released by unification did not get out of hand. Yes, German flags waved, but this time not as chauvinistic symbols of German superiority: they expressed a desire to belong together.

Although Germany's size and strength inevitably give her neighbours cause for concern, there is no sign of a re-emergence of the nationalist ideologies that led to two world wars. Pacifism seems to be the predominant tendency in both parts of Germany. The East German revolution was completely peaceful. The demonstrators reached neither for stones nor for weapons: even the state, after

What is "the German" really like? Is it possible to describe the national character? For a long time, the Bavarian and, in contrast, the Prussian were held up as representing the typical characteristics of the different regions. The Prussian state is a thing of the past, as is the Prussian himself. Nevertheless, preconceived notions about the inhabitants of the various regions persist.

The Bavarian goes about in *lederhosen*, wears a chamois hat and empties tankards of beer. The Swabian builds his little cottage and makes sure to take good care of the Mercedes he keeps in the garage. The man from the pits of the Ruhrgebiet breaks coal and keeps carrier pigeons on the roof of the colliery, and the farmer from Lower Saxony breeds cattle and drinks small glasses of clear but potent schnapps.

And the cliché continues: "one German makes a philosopher, three Germans make a club" runs the old saying, which comes close to the truth. Each of the afore-mentioned Germans belongs to at least one society or club – a sport, hometown, folk or small animal breeders society, a club for gardeners, stamp collectors, bowlers or savers. They elect a governing committee, a speaker, a treasurer; they are non-partisan, non-denominational and non-profit-making.

These societies are the links that hold the

Germans together. The Germans? In East Germany, such societies could not assert themselves against bureaucracy. Initiative, power and voluntary commitment were not encouraged.

It turns out that North and South have more in common than one might have suspected at first. For example, grass-roots movements became active at the beginning of the 1970s in both halves of the country. Bavarians fought against the new airfield in Munich-Erding and against the atomic reprocessing

Left, crowds assemble at the Brandenburg Gate. **Above**, "welcome to West Berlin".

plant at Wackersdorf. Farmers organised demonstrations against the Mercedes test track at Boxberg; the men from the pits prevented the construction of a new highway through the Ruhrgebiet.

In the former GDR, any independent organisation was suspect. In the West, grass-roots movements and self-help groups have for years been an integral part of every dispute over nuclear power plants, highways and day-care centres – in fact, over anything and everything. In East Germany, "self-help" was considered a dubious concept, as it was not necessary for East German citizens to help themselves. It was up to the state to take care of that.

In his work, the psychiatrist Hans-Joachim Maaz got to know East German citizens as they really are. For 10 years he directed the psychotherapeutic clinic of the Protestant social welfare centre in Halle, which treated well over 5,000 patients who could not cope with East German reality. His thorough and sensitive work, *Gefühlsstau* (Emotional Barriers), is a unique analysis of how the inhuman East German system tried to deform its citizens; how it hindered all personal initiative, thereby stifling further development of the society. Thus, over the past 45 years, Germans have been more influenced by whether they grew up on the eastern or western side of the Wall than by the historic tribe to which they belonged.

While people in the West had to use their elbows to the point of ruthlessness to achieve success, those in the East were expected to distinguish themselves through subservience. Few could escape the latter system without being harmed. The government continually extorted declarations of approval and loyalty; hypocrisy was necessary for survival. In Hans-Joachim Maaz's opinion, this all became second nature.

In the West, following the anti-authoritarian revolt of the late 1960s, independence, creativity, and responsibility became the decisive educational goals. Parents who were dissatisfied with traditional day-care centres founded self-administered children's centres, whose educational methods rubbed off on conventional day-care.

In East Germany, the situation was different. The repressive norm was imposed above all in schools and day-care centres; it also determined family relations. Education in hypocrisy, deceit, and dishonesty was the rule. Many people never felt truly accepted and understood in childhood. In this way, the East German state hoped to create a chronic deficiency syndrome that would leave people weak and dependent.

As negative as the balance may seem from a Western and critical Eastern point of view, East Germans should not be disqualified. The humiliating system that took all joy out of life survived for many years, but in the end it failed and collapsed. The regime's attempt to cripple citizens in all areas of life disappeared into thin air as if by magic. With the slogan "We are the people," the citizens of the former GDR clearly and successfully

demonstrated their long-submerged, newly-awakened confidence.

It is obvious that the Germans, within their respective social systems, were extraordinarily successful. What characteristics allowed the Federal Republic to become the strongest trading power in the West and East Germany the most successful economic power in the East? The German virtues are industry, punctuality and honesty, so-called "secondary" virtues that can lead to evil as well as to good. But the most important German virtue is thoroughness. The German cannot stand shoddy work. He must have order. He must have structure. He cannot

bear creative chaos like that found in the Mediterranean countries. The Protestant work ethic predominates in East and West. A German cannot stand it if a job is incomplete, sloppy or not on time. Inefficiency is an abomination to him – and to her.

Even the "alternatives", who have had enough of the noise and smog of the city, who want to run farms on a small scale, to set up new lifestyles and to have little to do with bourgeois society, cannot shake off these German virtues. Ecology freaks join together in societies and associations; enthusiastic communes fall apart in battles over who washes the dishes; the Greens lose sight of their common goals and wear themselves out in struggles over principle. Long ago, Lenin, the cynic, heartily ridiculed his German comrades: "When they want to make revolution, they buy a platform ticket first."

However, at some point, even the German has to relax from his overwhelming thoroughness. Once a year he flies off on holiday, and, in accordance with the English saying "My home is my castle," builds a tidy sand castle on Gran Canaria which he feels very proud of. To relax in Germany, the Wessi goes to his garden plot, the Ossi to his "dacha." German *gemütlichkeit* is no longer simply an oak-veneer wall cabinet and a cuckoo clock on the wall, but is also a closeness to nature. Sowing, planting, watching things grow, harvesting and turning the soil and the summer house in the garden, where grandfather keeps his rabbits and grandson has his first romantic adventures.

Garden parties and garden gnomes. As a rule, the garden gnome works. After all, he is a German, East or West. Sometimes he takes out his guitar or has a barbecue. However, the garden gnome is never armed. He wasn't in the West, nor in the East was he required to take part in paramilitary exercises. Contemporary garden gnomes are true examples of peaceful coexistence.

Some things divide, but many things unite the Germans in East and West. Developments since the collapse of the Wall have made one thing abundantly clear: the Germans have enough in common to be able to make the most of a promising future.

Left, another national symbol. **Right**, "in memory of our beloved dead": banners of army associations in Lower Bavaria.

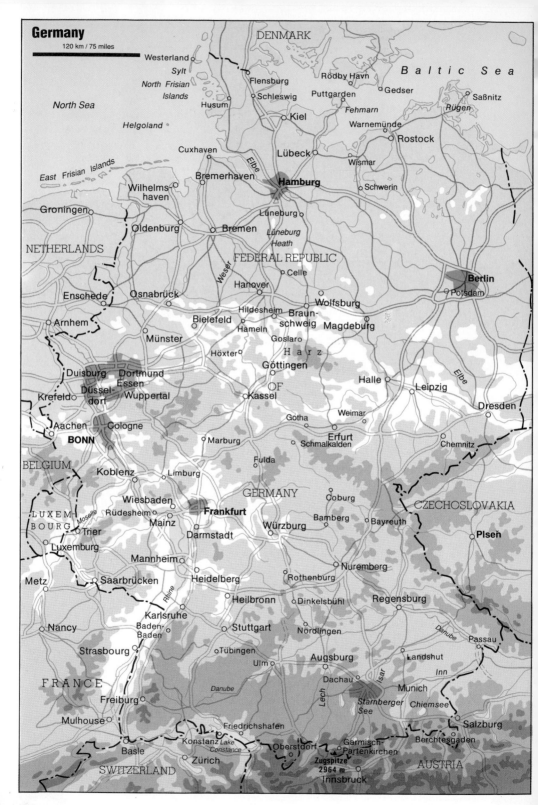

DISCOVER THE NEW GERMANY

The new Germany: five new states, and Berlin within its old borders. That is the new Germany from a Western perspective. For the citizens of what used to be East Germany, the situation is exactly the reverse. Their new country stretches from Flensburg to Füssen.

The starting point for this voyage of discovery is the very German Rhine. Past castles and fortresses, through wine-producing villages to the Loreley, romantic Germany opens up before you. Following a visit to Bonn, increase your knowledge of Roman history in Cologne's museums and its many preserved and excavated buildings. A separate chapter is dedicated to the Ruhrgebiet.

From what city can you better explore the South of Germany than from Heidelberg? Throngs of tourists prove that Heidelberg remains the undisputed leader on the hit parade of romantic German cities. Yet the industrial centres around Mannheim and Ludwigshafen, the state capital of Stuttgart, and many small towns give the state of Baden-Württemberg a leading role in German technology.

Several trips, described in detail, help introduce the south of Germany. Outside the larger cities lie Franconia's ancient settlements. On the romantic road from Würzburg to the fairytale castle of Neuschwanstein you will discover one of the most charming parts of the republic. The tour around Lake Constance and to the Black Forest purposely avoids major roads. The most southern part of the trip takes us to the magnificent paths through the German Alps. After visiting Munich, we suggest that you visit the old cities and deep woods of eastern Bavaria.

On the way to the north, we begin in the banking metropolis of Frankfurt and follow the trail of the Brothers Grimm through Hesse and the Weser Mountain area. Along the coasts of the North and Baltic Seas, large individual farmsteads, wide expanses, mud flats and beach chairs make up the scenery. The trading city of Hamburg combines cosmopolitan atmosphere with Hanseatic understatement.

We introduce classical culture in Kassel, and then travel through the green heart of Germany, the Thuringian Forest, to Weimar. Curving baroque characterises rebuilt Dresden. The road to Berlin, once again designated the capital, leads north along the Polish border. Become acquainted with the central part of the former GDR: Magdeburg, the Harz and the industrial centre of East Germany around Halle and Leipzig on a trip that will take you back to Germany's most ancient and most recent history. From Berlin, two tours take you to the Baltic Sea and the Mecklenburg Lake District, the most sparsely populated area in the country.

Preceding pages: a day out on the mud flats; Germany has many fine half-timbered buildings.

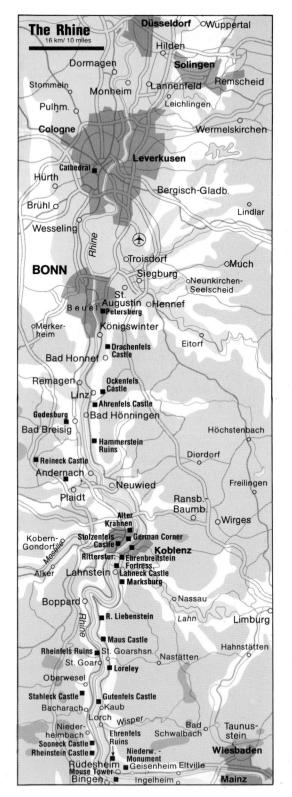

The Rhine
16 km/ 10 miles

Düsseldorf · Wuppertal
Hilden
Dormagen
Solingen
Stommeln · Lannenfeld · Remscheid
Monheim
Pulhm.
Leichlingen
Cologne · Wermelskirchen
Cathedral
Leverkusen
Hürth
Bergisch-Gladb.
Brühl
Lindlar
Wesseling
Rhine
Troisdorf · Much
BONN
Siegburg
Neunkirchen-Seelscheid
St. Augustin · Hennef
Beuel · Petersberg
Merker-heim · Königswinter
Eitorf
Drachenfels Castle
Bad Honnef
Remagen · Ockenfels Castle
Linz
Ahrenfels Castle
Godesburg · Bad Hönningen
Bad Breisig
Höchstenbach
Hammerstein Ruins
Diordorf
Reineck Castle
Andernach
Freilingen
Plaidt · Neuwied
Ransb.-Baumb.
Alter Krahnen
Wirges
Kobern-Gondorf · Stolzenfels Castle · German Corner
Mosel · Ritterstur. · Ehrenbreitstein Koblenz
Alken · Lahnstein · Fortress.
Lahneck Castle
Marksburg
Boppard · Nassau
R. Liebenstein · Lahn · Limburg
Maus Castle
Hahnstätten
Rheinfels Ruins · St. Goarshsn.
St. Goar · Nastätten
Loreley
Oberwesel
Stahleck Castle · Gutenfels Castle
Bacharach · Kaub
Lorch · Wisper
Nieder-heimbach · Ehrenfels · Bad Schwalbach · Taunus-stein
Sooneck Castle · Ruins
Rheinstein Castle · Niederw.-Monument · Wiesbaden
Rüdesheim · Geisenheim Eltville
Mouse Tower
Bingen · Ingelheim · Mainz

JOURNEY ALONG THE RHINE

The Rhine has been Germany's "river of destiny" since time immemorial. Before AD 55, when Julius Caesar had the first bridge built across the river near Andernach north of Koblenz, the Rhine formed the last frontier between the Roman Empire and the unruly territory of the Germanic tribes. But when the Romans crossed this river the Germans were irrevocably drawn into the process of world history.

Countless vineyards and castles, idyllic towns and sombre legends have for centuries symbolised the conflicting traits of the German national character: a zest for living and sentimentality on the one hand, broodiness and haughtiness on the other. The belligerent and the romantic, the bustling and the idyllic are all encapsulated in the landscape of this river.

With a total length of 1,320 km (820 miles, of which 539 flow in Germany), the Rhine is the third-longest river in Europe, after the Volga and the Danube. It has its source at the base of the Gotthard Massif in the Swiss Alps and flows into the North Sea near Rotterdam. For the last 883 km (552 miles) from Rheinfelden near Basle to its estuary, the Rhine is the busiest waterway in Europe. Its waters are daily enriched by a cocktail of some 60,000 different chemicals which are released quite legally from the giant chemical plants strewn along its banks.

Nevertheless, the Rhine appears to have lost none of its romantic appeal, and for the millions of tourists from all over the world who come here every year it remains a symbol of both German history and the German spirit. The symbolism of the Rhine was reinforced by the German, and indeed the English, Romantic poets. Lord Byron described the river in *Childe Harolde*: "The castled crag of Drachenfels/Frowns o'er the wide and winding Rhine/Whose breast of waters broadly swells/Between the banks which bear the vine/And hills all rich with blossomed trees/And fields which promise corn and wine/And scattered cities crowning these/Whose far white walls along them shine/Have strewed a scene, which I should see/With double joy wert thou with me."

Johannes Gutenberg's workshop: Not far from the confluence of the River Main and the Rhine lies the city of **Mainz** (population 187,000), which was founded as "Mongotiacum" in the year 38 BC. After several hundred years of decline, the former capital of the Roman province *Germania superior* embarked on a long period of prosperity in AD 747 when St Boniface, the "German Apostle", made it the seat of an archbishop. The city thereby became the centre of Germanic Christendom. The archbishops of Mainz were not only spiritual shepherds, but in simultaneously performing the role of chancellor to the *Reich* and elector of the emperor, they became one of the strongest secular powers in the Roman Empire of German Nations, quite capable of standing up against the emperor or the king. Back in the Middle Ages, Mainz was one of those cities that was able to wrest certain freedoms from the bondage of feudalism. A leading member of the Rhenish League of Cities from 1254, Mainz succeeded in releasing the Rhine from the grip of the robber knights, who during the Great Interregnum (1250–73) had gained a hold on most of Germany.

Mainz's extensive trade contacts and the financial resources of the merchant Johann Fust were undoubtedly factors that in 1445 enabled the meticulous Johannes Gutenberg to make one of the most important of all inventions: printing with moveable letters. The **Gutenberg Museum**, which contains a replica of the master's workshop, is in the **Market Square**. Along with the old printing apparatus, the most valuable object on display is one of the 47 extant 42-page bibles, testimony to the amazing revolution that Gutenberg began.

The mighty Romanesque **Cathedral** (975) stands opposite the museum and with its six red sandstone towers remains the dominant feature of a city that practically had to be rebuilt after the

Preceding pages: the Rhine Valley at Bingen; Cheers! Below, the historic city of Mainz.

devastation of World War II. Mainz is the capital of the federal state of Rhineland-Palatinate, founded in 1949. The **Electoral Palace** was also completely restored. It is a late-Renaissance building and today houses the **Roman-Germanic Central Museum** as well as the banqueting halls in which the famous annual carnival performances are held. From the palace there is a good view of Mainz's sister city of **Wiesbaden** (population 280,000), the capital of the state of Hesse, on the other side of the river.

It isn't only during carnival time that a stroll through the streets of the **Old City** is an absolute must. In one of the many wine bars you can savour the light white wines of Rhine Hesse and round off the experience with *"Handkäs mit Musik"* – curd cheese garnished with vinegar, oil and diced onions.

A glass of wine in Rüdesheim: From Mainz the Rhine begins to meander its way through the steep valley separating the Taunus and the Hunsrück mountains. In addition to the barges, there are now countless pleasure steamers plying up and down this "romantic" stretch of the river, which is accompanied by ever-changing vistas of quaint villages with pointed church spires and golden weather cocks, and steep vineyards.

Following the poets downstream towards Koblenz, the traveller soon arrives in **Eltville**, the *alta villa* of Roman days, seat of the electors of Mainz for 150 years. The **Wohnturm** (living tower) of the electoral castle recalls the days when the archbishops of Mainz sought refuge here in times of war and rebellion. Countless town houses and former residences of the landed gentry are worth seeing, as indeed is the **Parish Church of St Peter and Paul** (12th-century). The historic Rhine promenade which at one time was going to have to make way for a road and railway has been saved by the efforts of a local action group. In the north of Eltville, a narrow road branches off to the wine village of **Kiedrich** with the ruins of **Scharfenstein Castle** and **Eberbach Monastery**. Here, in 1116, Augustin-

Below, in Rüdesheim. Right, Katz Castle, near Loreley.

ian monks first started cultivating their Rheingau vines.

The town of **Rüdesheim**, with its famous **Drosselgasse**, has somehow managed to market itself to millions of visitors as your typical, quaint wine "village". Despite the **Brömersburg** (the oldest castle on the Rhine built in the 9th century), there is very little to distinguish Rüdesheim from other settlements along this stretch of the river. All have typical half-timbered houses and all have narrow back alleys and *Weinstuben* (wine bars). The visitor would be advised to steer clear of the crowds on the Drosselgasse itself and head for less busy pubs and eateries, where the atmosphere can still be enjoyed – and at reasonable prices.

Germania, a Valkyrie: From Rüdesheim a cable car climbs to the 37-metre high (121-ft) **Niederwald Monument** (unveiled in 1883), whose scale and position high above the Rhine are breathtaking indeed. Created as an expression of Wilhelmenian aspirations of power after the Franco-German war (1870–71), the statue they call **Germania**, symbolically depicted as a sword brandishing Valkyrie, gazes defiantly across the river. But the top dignitaries of the *Reich*, who had gathered together for the inaugural celebrations, would all have gone up in smoke had the two anarchists Reinsdorf and Küchler been prepared to pay an extra 50 pfennigs for waterproof fuses. Due to torrential rain the night before the charge of 16 pounds of dynamite failed to detonate, the nobility was spared and the two would-be assassins ended up paying with their lives.

There is a ferry from Rüdesheim across to **Bingen** at the confluence of the Rhine and River Nahe. Together with the **Mäuseturm**, perched on a rock in the middle of the river, **Castle Klopp** controlled the Rhine at this point for Bishop Hatto of Mainz, who was thus able to derive considerable income from taxation of the commercial traffic both along and on the river. The Mäuseturm served as a customs-post and later as a signal tower to warn the passing traffic of **Bingen Hole** and its treacherous reef.

The Mäuseturm near Bingen.

The reef was cleared some years ago.

A string of castles: The next 16 km (10 miles) after Bingen Hole will make any visitor appreciate why the Rhine has played such a central role in so many fairytales and fables, legends and songs. The majestic Rhine, with its steep valley sides, forested slopes, vineyards and castles, not only holds those of a romantic disposition in its spell. The castles recall the days when the robber knights, having rendered the land routes impassable, blocked the river with iron chains in order then to demand tolls from the lowly merchants. At some time or other every one of these castles has been besieged and levelled to the ground, particularly during recurring Franco-German wars.

A short distance before the town of **Assmannshausen** (famous for its fine red wine) **Ehrenfels** stands sentinel above the right bank of the river. In former times the treasures of Mainz cathedral were stored in this fortress which glares directly across at **Rheinstein Castle** on the opposite bank.

Soon after Assmannshausen comes **Drachenstein Castle** and the neighbouring fortress of **Sooneck**, which is made accessible by the ferry from Assmannshausen. The journey back can be made via **Lorch** and **Bacharach** on the right bank.

Napoleon's defeat: A few kilometres beyond Bacharach, the middle of the river is dominated by the picturesque **Pfalzgrafenstein** island and its castle, which was erected as a customs post in the 14th century. It was at this point that Marshal Blücher crossed the Rhine on New Year's Eve 1813–14 with the help of a pontoon bridge. He was in pursuit of Napoleon's forces who had just suffered a heavy defeat at the Battle of Nations near Leipzig. Opposite stands the small town of **Kaub** and **Gutenfels Fortress** which was built in the 13th century. A little further on, the ruins of **Schönburg** come into view above the left bank of the river near Oberwesel.

Loreley and other maidens: Immediately beyond Oberwesel the smooth flow of the Rhine is disturbed by seven un-

The "Pfalz" at Kaub.

derwater rocks, the **Seven Maidens**. According to legend seven girls were turned to stone because they were so prudish. And local lads still tell this tale – particularly when the response to their approach has been shy and hesitant.

By contrast, the **Loreley** was the downfall of many a man. Dreamed up by the Romantic poet Clemens Brentano in 1801, the story of that particular maiden was enacted here above the perilous rapids on the protruding cliffs of the "Lurlei". The mythical seductive blonde mermaid would sing and comb her hair on the cliff top, diverting the attention of passing boatmen from the dangers lurking in the river. In 1823, Heinrich Heine immortalised the "femme fatale" in his famous poem, which was set to music in 1832 by Friedrich Silcher: "I cannot divine what it meaneth…" is the beginning of Mark Twain's translation.

A few minutes' drive further on, three castles appear simultaneously: **Katz** (cat) **Castle** and **Maus Castle** above the right bank and **Rheinfels Castle** on the left bank of the river near **St Goar**. This is the location of the annual September firework display on the river, the **"Rhine in Flames"**. Not far away, castles **Sterrenberg** and **Liebenstein**, the two "hostile brothers", are separated from each other by a high wall.

Endless vineyards: The white towers of the **Church of St Severin** indicate the approach of **Boppard**, the centre of the largest wine-producing region on the Middle Rhine. On the **Bopparder Hang** alone, there are no fewer than 1½ million vines. A cable car climbs to **Gedeons Eck** (302 metres/991 ft). From here a 30-minute walk leads to one of the best vantage points of the Rhine valley known as the **Vier-Seen-Blick** (Four Lakes View), from where the meandering Rhine looks like a series of lakes.

Castles for sale: The Rhine stops its meandering shortly before **Braubach**. The town is dominated by the mighty **Marksburg Castle** (13th-century) which now houses the **Museum of Castles**, the largest such museum in Central Europe, as well as the German Castle

The epitome of Rhine romance: Sooneck Castle.

Association. This is where those who wish to buy a castle come to sort out the necessary formalities. Diagonally opposite lies the small town of **Rhens**, founded in the 7th century. Back in the Middle Ages this was one of the main centres of power of the German realm and it was here, at the **Kings' Chair**, that the seven electors assembled to choose their kings and emperors. A little further downstream near **Lahnstein**, at the confluence of the Lahn, stands the **Wirtshaus an der Lahn**. The popularity of this inn has less to do with the two castles of **Lahneck** (right bank) and **Stolzenfels** (left bank) than with the fact that Goethe used to come here and mentioned the place in his writings.

Where the Rhine and Moselle meet: The traveller will know that he has almost reached **Koblenz** (population 120,000) when the first bridge across the River since Mainz comes into view. Koblenz is situated at the confluence of the Rhine and Moselle. From the fortress of **Erhrenbreitstein** above the right bank, there are excellent views of the city with the towers of the **Church of our Dear Lady** (12th–15th centuries) and the **Church of St Castor** (9th–12th centuries). The fortress not only houses the largest youth hostel in Germany but also the interesting **Museum of the Rhine**. The other side of the river can be reached via the Pfaffendorf Bridge which leads to the **Electoral Palace**, built in the 18th century on the site of the ancient *castrum ad confluences*.

The **German Corner** (Deutsche Eck) is the promontory between the Rhine and the Moselle. A memorial to Kaiser Wilhelm stood here until 1945. In 1953 the surviving pedestal was renamed the **Monument to German Unity**. Above the Pfaffendorf Bridge, with the Moselle on the left and the Rhine on the right, is the famous **Wine Village**. It was built in 1925 as a replica of a wine-producing village complete with authentic vineyards and typical half-timbered houses from the most celebrated German wine-growing regions. Here one can enjoy a quarter litre of either Rhine or Moselle wine.

Boppard by night.

ALONG THE MOSELLE

In summer 1986 the Moselle between Koblenz and Trier – the classic destination of all who follow the trail of romantic Germany – made headlines. Thousands of dead fish were found in the river. The city brought suit against a French nuclear power company that hoped to build another plant near Cattenom – one that would dump its wastes into the already-polluted river.

But not only the river is suffering. Between 1979 and 1990, every fifth wine-grower on the Moselle went out of business. Many growers who cultivate vineyards of between one and 20 hectares (50 acres) find themselves in tough competition with the other twenty quality wine-growing areas in the European Community, all of whom are fighting for their share of the European market. Many of the well-known, picturesque vineyards on the Moselle, upon whose slate banks the famous fruity white wine thrives, are no longer being cultivated.

Tourism on the Moselle does not seem to have been affected by this development. The people here remain proud of their "Moselle romanticism". True, Moselle pike has vanished from restaurant menus, but trout and carp can still be caught in the river.

A trip on the Moselle from Trier to Koblenz is a wonderful holiday experience, for, like Goethe in 1792, you too will experience "that glorious feeling of well-being that is unique to the wine-growing region and that is passed on to the visitor."

The Moselle Valley is not only wine country. Few regions north of the Alps can boast such a multitude of historical monuments and important sights.

Moselle Wine Gladdens the Heart: The main attraction of the Moselle trip is of course wine, and travel organisers foot the bill: tourist offices, wine-growers' estates and wine-tasters all offer tours of wine cellars, where you can learn everything about how wine is made. Eight wine-teaching paths familiarise the wine lover with wine-growing. Wine seminars and open-cellar days are offered, where anyone can come and taste the wine. From April until the end of November, there is a wine festival somewhere almost every weekend. You can even spend your holiday with a vintner and go fishing in the Moselle.

You can get to the Moselle Valley from Koblenz most easily on the B 416. **Winningen** is the first of many typical Moselle villages, with steep, slate-coloured hills, castles, old churches, narrow streets and market squares, hemmed in by half-timbered houses, old wine vaults and new wine cellars that are found only on the Moselle. Take a look into the back courtyards and try some delicious cake in one of the charming cafés. In addition, no Moselle trip can be complete without at least one visit to a castle.

Eltz Castle: One of Germany's most beautiful castles, 6 km (4 miles) from the railway station Moselkern, it is surrounded on three sides by the Eltz River. The castle was first mentioned in documents in 1150, and since then has be-

Preceding pages: the meandering Moselle near Brem. Below, typical architecture at Bernkastel.

100

longed to the family of the Count of Elce. The castle was spared by the wars of the Middle Ages and escaped destruction by the French, who destroyed almost all the castles in this area nearly 300 years ago. Thousands of visitors have been inspired by its towers, high gables and rich ornamentation. The treasures that the counts collected in the course of centuries can be admired in the weapons hall, the painting collection and the expensively-appointed rooms. Eltz Castle is pictured on 500-DM bank-notes.

The **Imperial Castle** at **Cochem**, 13 km (8 miles) from Eltz Castle, was not built until 1027, and the Cochem Krampen is the first of many idyllic bends in the river that are typical of the Moselle. The market place is adorned by the Baroque **Town Hall** from the year 1739, the Martin fountain, and half-timbered houses with attractive ornaments. At the Moselle bridge, one turns right and soon comes to the entrance to the longest railway tunnel in Germany, 4,203 metres (13,789 ft) long. The Mo-

selle Promenade, with its numerous wine bars, cafés and restaurants, entices the visitor to take a stroll. From the Moselle bridge leading to **Kond** one has a lovely view of the river landscape.

The next stop is **Beilstein**, also called the "Mini-Rothenburg," where a number of well-known sentimental films have been made. Continue to **Marienburg** whose ruined Augustinian monastery (it is today the site of a restaurant) stands in a glorious setting adjoining the **Zell Bend**, from where there are superb views of the valley and its vineyards.

Next comes **Zell**, with its famous fountain and equally famous **"Zeller Schwarze Katz"**. Thirty-seven km (23 miles) from Cochem lies **Traben-Trarbach**, a spa and wine-centre in one. An international motor-boat race takes place here once a year. From here you can also take an excursion to **Mont Royal**, one of the largest European fortresses under the French King Louis XI, and to the ruins of **Grevenburg** (14th century), from where there is a wonderful view of the Moselle Valley.

Remnant from a Roman past: Porta Negra in Trier.

After another 22 km (14 miles) you arrive in **Bernkastel-Kues** (population 7,500), in the heart of the central Moselle, one of the region's best-known wine areas. The romantic market place with the ruined castle of Landshut rising over it has become a symbol of the Moselle. Sixty-five million litres of wine, the product of 5,000 wine growers, are stored in its central wine cellars. Bernkastel is world-famous for its half-timbered houses, the filigreed fountain railing in the market square and the artistic weathervanes on the gables of the houses – an incomparable picture that has long decorated calendars. The traditional Moselle wine festival at the beginning of September, complete with the wine princess "Mosella", attracts more than 200,000 visitors.

The **Cusanusstift** is an over 500-year-old hospital and hospice named after the famous cardinal and philosopher Nikolaus von Kues (in Latin, Cusanus, 1401–64). Kues was an important supporter of German humanism who spoke out for religious tolerance.

The house in which he was born is now a museum dedicated to Kues' life and work at the transition from the Middle Ages to the modern era.

The trip continues along the winding course of the Moselle from Bernkastel-Kues to Trier, past vineyards and through idyllic wine villages such as **Piesport** and **Neumagen**. Wine has been cultivated here since Roman times, as is recalled by the Neumagen wine boat from the 3rd century.

Germany's Oldest City: Founded in the year 16 BC by Emperor Augustus, **Trier** (population 100,000) is considered Germany's oldest city. It has the most impressive Roman constructions north of the Alps. Trier was the residence of Diocletian, Constantine the Great and other Roman emperors. In the 9th century, Charlemagne made it the site of the diocese. An elector resided in Trier from the 12th to the 18th centuries.

Evidence of this impressive history can be seen throughout the city. The **Porta Nigra** (2nd-century), which was once the gate of a Roman fortress and is

Harvest time in the vineyard.

36 metres (118 ft) wide and 30 metres (98 ft) high, is considered the best-preserved construction of its kind north of the Alps. It was converted into a church in 1040, but later returned to its original condition under Napoleon's rule. It was originally built without mortar. The Porta Nigra gets its name from the dark patina that has built up on the limestone blocks.

The **Aula Palatina**, a basilica built in the 4th century as Constantine the Great's coronation chamber, and the **Imperial Baths**, begun but not completed under Constantine, also date back to Roman times, as does the **Roman Bridge**. It is only a short distance from the baths to the ruins of the antique amphitheatre, where 25,000 spectators once attended theatre presentations and bloody gladiatorial battles.

The fortress-like **Cathedral**, one of Germany's oldest churches in the early Romanesque style (11th–12th centuries), bears witness to the Christian Middle Ages. The foundations date from the 4th century. Its treasure contains many precious works including the 10th century gold Portable Altar of St Andrew. Immediately next to the cathedral is the **Church of Our Dear Lady**, one of the oldest purely Gothic churches in Germany. South of the Cathedral is the **Rhineland Archaeological Museum**, which contains the largest collection of Roman antiquities in Germany. Note especially the 3rd-century relief of a Roman ship transporting immense barrels of wine.

From the church it is only a few steps to the **Main Market**, an impressive, picturesque square surrounded by Gothic, Renaissance and rococo buildings, the square is a living art-history textbook. Here is the **Steipe**, an old 15th-century mansion which bears the proud inscription *Ante Roman Treveris stetit annis mille trecentis* ("Trier stood 1,300 years before Rome"). From here it is only a few minutes to Brückenstrasse 10, the house where Karl Marx was born in 1818. The house is now a museum and the destination of pilgrimages from all over the world.

The ancient wine ship of Neumagen.

THE ROAD TO COLOGNE

Having completed the detour along the Moselle, continue following the Rhine northwards from Koblenz to Cologne along the B 42. The low-lying Neuwied Basin, which marks a sudden change in the character of the landscape of the Rhine Valley, is soon reached.

Opposite **Leutesdorf**, an old wine village with charming half-timbered houses, lies the town of **Andernach**. This former Roman settlement of *Antunnacum* can be reached by ferry and is well worth visiting on account of its attractive old town with its 16th-century town hall. To the west rises the fascinating **Eifel massif**, a range of volcanic hills averaging 600 metres (2,000 ft) in height. Its austere beauty makes the Eifel a popular tourist attraction, whose appeal is increased still further by the presence of a real jewel of Romanesque architecture nestled among the hills. On the shores of a crater lake stands the Benedictine monastery and church of **Maria Laach Abbey** (1093–1220). The complex, whose monks have long since become experienced tour guides, marks the very apogee of Romanesque architecture in Germany.

Back on the right bank of the river, continue along the B 42 from Leutesdorf. Above the small village of **Hammerstein** tower the ruins of the 10th-century **Ley Castle**, where Count Otto von Hammerstein managed to defend himself and his wife Irmgard for three long months against the emperor Henry II. Henry did not approve of the match, and when the siege ended the couple were close to starvation.

The Remagen Bridge: The prime attractions of **Linz** are the city gate towers, the late-Gothic town hall and the excellent local wine. From the **Imperial Castle** (Kaiserberg) there are wonderful views across the river to the Eifel massif and the valley of the River Ahr can be enjoyed. From Linz it is possible to take a ferry to the bridge at **Remagen**. At the end of the war the Nazis bombed

Preceding pages: contrasting styles in Cologne. Below, Beethoven witnesses yet another demonstration in Bonn.

all the bridges across the Rhine in order to slow down the allied advance. Miraculously though, the bridge at Remagen remained standing long enough for the Americans to cross it, so shortening the war by several days. The dramatic events are recalled by the **Peace Museum** which is located in the only surviving tower of the former railway bridge.

From the town of **Unkel** it is possible to make a detour to **Arenfels** and **Ochsenfels** castles. The road leads through the picturesque **Siebengebirge** (seven mountains) hills, said to have been created by seven giants who dug a channel for the Rhine and left seven mounds of earth. Atop the Drachenfels (Dragon Rock) stand the ruins of the 12th-century **Drachenfels Castle**. It was named after Siegfried, hero of the *Nibelungen Saga*, who slew the dragon and bathed in its blood to make himself invulnerable to attack.

Provisional capital: Prior to 1949 the major claim to fame the sleepy electoral residence city and university town of Bonn (population 295,000) was as the birthplace of Ludwig van Beethoven (1770–1827). Then, however, it was chosen as the provisional seat of the new Federal Government and transformed into a modern capital, with thousands of officials moving into the stately old buildings and innumerable new high-rise blocks built to house the various ministries and administrative bodies. When the Wall collapsed, the authorities were in the process of investing billions in still more governmental buildings. Highly-paid government officials and civil servants have been dismayed to learn that Bonn is to lose its capital status, which is being transferred to Berlin. Property prices in Bonn, once about the highest in Germany, will fall dramatically.

Almost all of Bonn's attractions are to be found in the old city which is easily explored on foot. There is the **Marketplace** from whose town hall steps President John F. Kennedy addressed the citizenry in 1963. To the southwest on **Münsterplatz** stands the venerable

Picnic on the lawn of the Hofgarten.

BEETHOVEN: THE SOUL OF GERMANY

Germany, the Land of Beethoven. How much truth is contained in that hackneyed phrase? Is Beethoven's music German music? Ludwig van Beethoven was born in 1770 in Bonn on the Rhine. As a young man he travelled to Vienna to study composition under Haydn and Mozart; he remained there until his death in 1827. Beethoven was well-read; he was fully at home in the intellectual tradition for which his contemporary, Goethe, coined the phrase "world literature". He idolised Shakespeare and admired Napoleon until the latter had himself crowned Emperor of the French. All his life he subscribed to the ideals of the French Revolution. He exhibited no interest in the nationalist trends in art frequently pursued by 19th-century composers. He saw himself as a world citizen. His intention was to make the world comprehend through his music a supranational concept of reconciliation:

"O ye millions, I embrace ye!/ Here's a joyful kiss for all!/ Brothers, o'er yon starry sphere,/ Sure there dwells a loving Father."

Beethoven's Ninth Symphony, which sets to music Schiller's "Ode to Joy", is the composer's philosophical legacy. It weaves into a powerful unity a wide range of musical elements: harshly dissonant chord patterns, a main theme with the primal simplicity of a folk song, spirited marches, and monumental choral movements which stretch the human voice to its very limits. It is music of which Friedrich Nietzsche wrote that it made the heart of the philosopher heavy, for the freethinker, having finally liberated his mind from faith, will end up "feeling himself floating above the earth in the starry firmament of heaven, with the dream of immortality in his heart and all the stars twinkling around him as the earth sinks ever further away below."

Beethoven's tonality was so revolutionary that many contemporaries were wont to put their hands over their ears when they first heard his music. From harmony to rhythm and instrumentation there is no musical dimension in which he did not overstep the prescribed limits. He intensified emotional expression whilst creating space for an increased rationality in music. "Beethoven turned on the emotions of fear, of horror, of terror, of anguish, arousing thereby the endless longing which is the very essence of Romanticism," wrote the poet and composer E.T.A. Hoffmann. Taking as an example the legendary Fifth Symphony, he also showed that Beethoven, who in everyday life was often a slave to his emotions, "separated in his compositions his own ego from the inner realm of sounds, in which he was absolute king."

Beethoven's musical structures were so built up that every detail bears a carefully thought-out relationship to the whole. He possessed the genius of reconciling an expressivity which exceeded the traditional framework of the period with an austere formalism; for this reason, Beethoven is surely the most "classical" of all musicians. He has remained the role model for post-Romantic composers, who made their own his comment that "music should appeal to the soul, but should be heard with the intellect."

More characteristic of the German soul than Beethoven himself was the cult of his genius which arose after his death. His methodical approach to composition became stylised as a "struggle for expression"; he himself became a "fighter", a "hero", a "superman". Deaf to his music, the public worshipped Beethoven for his own deafness, his enforced loneliness. He was idolised as the prototype of the German artist, accepting failure in life in order to struggle on in an attempt to achieve a world of perfection in art.

The Beethoven legend has lost something of its magic. Diminished, too, is the belief in the perfectability of man, to which Beethoven clung all his life. The ideas which inspired him have been questioned by a more modern age. The adulation of his tragic genius has been replaced by a more sober appreciation. The Germans no longer honour Beethoven as a national symbol, but revel in his music, of which, on the occasion of his 200th birthday, the French composer, Pierre Boulez, wrote: "Twist and turn this diamond with its thousands facets – in it you will see a thousand suns."

Romanesque **Minster** with its 12th-century cloister. North-east of the marketplace, at Bonngasse 20, is the **Beethovenhaus**, where the great composer was born and grew up. Since 1889 the 16th-century building has housed the world's most important Beethoven museum, whose exhibits include the piano made specially for Beethoven in Vienna. Nearby, the **Beethovenhalle** on the Rhine promenade is today the setting for concerts and festivals.

The Adenauerallee leads through the **Hofgarten** (former palace gardens) and the Stadtgarten. Further to the south, between the Adenauerallee and the Rhine promenade, is the heart of political power in Germany, with **Villa Hammerschmidt**, the official residence of the German president; **Palais Schaumberg**, the site of state receptions, and the **Federal Chancellery** with its adjoining residence of the German Chancellor. The **Bundeshaus** (Parliament building) on the left bank of the Rhine nestles in the shadow of the 30-storey **Langer Eugen**, the chamber of representatives. It is now uncertain whether the new parliament building on the Rhine will ever be occupied.

The suburb of **Bad Godesburg** is home to more than 70 diplomatic missions and various federal ministries. The **Godesburger Redoute**, a rococo electoral palace built in 1791–92, where Beethoven once performed concerts, is now used for state receptions.

The Cathedral city: The most rewarding way to enter the cathedral city of **Cologne** is by train. Looking out of the window from the **Hohenzollernbrücke** you can enjoy one of the world's most spectacular city panoramas: the Rhine embankment with its colourful facades and pointed gabled-roofs above which tower the mighty spires of **Cologne Cathedral**. The most ambitious building project ever undertaken on German soil comes closer and closer until the train draws to a halt in the main station, barely 200 metres (650 ft) from the main portal. With its awesome dimensions – 142 metres (472 ft) long by 43 metres (143 ft) high – the cathedral is the unmistakeable landmark of this city

of one million inhabitants. It was built as a new repository for the **Shrine of the Magi** which had been housed in the old cathedral since 1164. When in 1248, the Archbishop Konrad von Hochstaden gave his blessing to the commencement of construction work, Cologne was Germany's largest city and the third largest city in Europe after Paris and Constantinople. In the Middle Ages it became one of the most powerful members of the Hanseatic League and one of the richest cities in the world. After the university was founded in 1388, the city became, both from an intellectual and an artistic point of view, the enlightened focal point of the Rhine Valley.

In 1560 work on the cathedral, which was modelled on the French Gothic masterpieces of Chartres, Reims and Amiens, ceased. The building would never have been completed if the spirit of historicism and wave of enthusiasm for the Middle Ages had not spread across Europe in the 19th century and fuelled the revival of the Gothic style. In 1842 the Prussian King Friedrich Wilhelm IV laid the foundation stone for the resumption of work and by 1880 the cathedral was completed, the most perfect example of "French" high-Gothic architecture.

The Shrine of the Three Magi, the largest gold sarcophagus in the western world, is positioned at the high altar. The **Treasury**, which contains gold, precious stones and ivory work as well as liturgical raiments and documents from many centuries, testifies to the extraordinary wealth of the Catholic Church. The **Cross of Gero** (around 971) is the oldest wood-carved crucifixion work north of the Alps.

Those who have enough stamina to climb the 509 steps to the top of the cathedral tower are rewarded by a magnificent view of the city. On the opposite side of the river, the eyes come to rest on the tower of the famous **4711 Eau de Cologne** factory, established in the city in 1709 by the Italian chemist Giovanni-Maria Farina. Directly adjacent are the exhibition halls of the Cologne trade fair. The other side of the tower offers views of the inner city, including the main shopping drag, the pedestrian precinct **Breite Strasse**.

Ancient metropolis: The heart of Cologne can be explored on foot and the visitor will constantly be reminded of the city's Roman past. Ancient cobbled streets and an intact thermal bath have been excavated and the **Roman-Germanic Museum** contains priceless treasures and offers a fascinating glimpse into life as it was some 2,000 years ago after the Romans had established their camp of *Colonnia* here on the Rhine. The museum was built over the world-famous **Dionysos Mosaic** which was discovered during construction work on an air raid shelter. The 2nd-century masterpiece covers an area of 70 square metres (84 sq yards) and consists of over one million ceramic and glass components. Next door, the modern **Wallraf-Richartz Museum** is considered to contain one of the most comprehensive collections of European painting, including works by Rembrandt, Renoir and Manet. The building also contains the **Ludwig Museum**, named after the well-known German art collector and sponsor who bequeathed his collection of contemporary art. Although the interiors of the museum building (also housing the Philharmonie concert hall) are architecturally impressive, the exterior has aroused a good deal of controversy.

Not far to the south-west of the cathedral is the Romanesque **Church of St Martin**, surrounded by the squat houses of the **Old City**. While the bombs of World War II missed the cathedral, they showed this church no mercy. However, since being rebuilt in 1963 it has resumed its role as the outstanding landmark of the old city.

When walking through the old city, take the time to pop into one of the old pubs and drink a glass of the traditional *Kolsch* ale. The people of Cologne are friendly and cheerful, a fact that becomes particularly evident during the merry proceedings of the **Cologne Carnival**, when the entire population pours out onto the streets.

Fashion capital: Lying 40 km (25 miles)

Mother and daughter at Carnival.

to the north of Cologne, the city of **Düsseldorf** (population 600,000) is the capital of Germany's most populated federal state of North Rhine Westphalia. The city rose to importance from being a *Dorf* (village) on the river Dussel (a tributary of the Rhine) because of its elevation to the seat of the local Dukes of Berg back in the 14th century. Although it was never as important as Cologne, Düsseldorf's royal patronage nevertheless resulted in it becoming a centre that attracted artists, writers and musicians. The Art Academy, founded in 1777, developed into one of the most respected such institutions in the country. The German writer and francophile Heinrich Heine (1797–1856) was born in Düsseldorf. He was an admirer of Napoleon whom he celebrated in his book *Le Grand*. Napoleon referred to Düsseldorf as "mon petit Paris".

The development of the city really took off with the arrival of the industrial revolution. Situated on the Rhine and within easy reach of the Ruhrgebiet, the city was well placed to become the administrative centre of Germany's industrial power house. Düsseldorf has maintained this position to this day; the headquarters of numerous industrial concerns are located here. The city's importance for trade is reflected in the numerous trade fairs, the best known of which are the **Modemessen** – the fashion fairs. Düsseldorf's role as Germany's No.1 city of fashion is acted out on its world-famous boulevard, the elegant **Königsallee**, where just about everything that money can buy is available – at a price. If you don't want to be seen among all the chic people strolling up and down the "Kö", then a better bet is the **Old City** which, despite being severely damaged during World War II, offers an atmosphere of *Gemütlichkeit* that is hard to beat anywhere. This may partly be explained by the city's long beer brewing tradition. A glass of the renowned top-fermented *Altbier* can be savoured in any one of the numerous pubs, institutions which all make up what is commonly known as "the longest bar in the world".

Kite-flying on the Rhine meadows.

THE RUHRGEBIET

To the north-east of Cologne lies Germany's largest industrial region, the *Ruhrgebiet*, the district of the Ruhr. The River Ruhr gave this tract of land its name, for it was there that the first coal mines were sunk. Irishmen and Silesians were the first to go underground in the Ruhrgebiet and many East Europeans followed in their footsteps, arriving decades ago. From the 1960s onwards came guest workers from Italy, Spain, Portugal, Greece and Turkey. They all made the country between Duisburg (population 575,000) in the west and Dortmund (population 620,000) in the east a unique melting pot of European peoples. Back in 1820 the entire region had a population of only 274,000.

Visitors to the Ruhrgebiet will find it hard to believe that over 60 percent of its 4,432 square km (1,711 sq miles) is open country. The most immediate impression gained will be of the rows and rows of blocks of flats and the endless network of roads which make it very easy for someone not familiar with the place to lose his sense of orientation. If you miss the signs there is often no way of telling that you've passed from one place to another.

During the course of the region's development, small villages have grown into towns which have then fused to produce the gigantic conurbation that the Ruhrgebiet is today. From the air it looks like one single city with dozens of sub-centres.

The green Ruhr: Five large parks in Dortmund, Duisburg, Herne, Gelsenkirchen and Oberhausen/Bottrop provide oases for recreation for the population. In the south, the River Ruhr itself with its dammed lakes offers windsurfing and fishing. By contrast the River Emscher in the north remains the same sewer that it has been ever since the turn of the century and continues to transport its filth right through the district to a treatment plant on the Rhine. The region is due for a massive face-lift, however, as the "International Building Trade Exhibition of Emscher Park" is developed over the coming decades.

Miners and steel men: In 1958 the German writer Heinrich Böll described the Ruhrgebiet as the region where "white is only a dream". This was an accurate description of those days, for in the largest industrial conurbation in Europe the soot from all the coking plants and the reddy-brown filth that the foundries spewed unfiltered into the air all came back down to earth. It settled as a fine layer of dark dust and the whites hanging out to dry turned to grey.

Right up until the 1980s the picture of the Ruhrgebiet was characterised by toil and sweat. Men in protective clothing standing before the furnaces, silhouetted by the bright glow of the molten iron; miners, their faces blackened by the coal dust appearing at the surface after a day underground. This "romantic" vision of the Ruhr no longer holds, no longer reflects the ever-changing world of the 5.2 million people who live and work here today. No, it is modern research projects and high-flying tech-

Left, a future in steel. **Right**, coal is still mined in the Ruhr.

nology that increasingly governs the lives of the people. In 1957 the mining industry employed half a million people but by 1986 this had dropped to 20,000. In the steel industry jobs have also declined, from 230,000 in 1974 to around 140,000 in 1991. While in the 1950s, 80 percent of the region's industrial output was accounted for by the coal and steel industries, today that figure has sunk to 30 percent.

Mining settlements: The days when the Ruhrgebiet's pioneer barons of industry ruled the roost are also over. Instead of Alfred Krupp, August Thyssen and Hugo Stinnes, the administration of the joint stock companies has now been passed on to professional managers.

The organisation of labour in the factories and the mines, as well as the labour disputes, demanded a solidarity among the working people which influenced all aspects of life. It wasn't only in their places of work that the people here stuck together; home life also became strongly influenced by the common cause. If a stranger gains access to

the mining settlements and the living areas of the steel workers, he will still be able to sense this special bond that the people possess. They are governed by a different spirit to that which one normally associates with blocks of flats and housing estates. In the settlements in the Ruhr there is emotional security, conviviality and a quality of life which the inhabitants of the 2,400 or so workers' settlements vigorously defend. There is now a long list of rebellious settlements which were assigned to the demolition experts, but which still stand.

Unqualified proletarians: In the days of the German Empire the Ruhrgebiet was assigned the role of the work house. Kaiser Wilhelm II wanted "neither barracks nor universities" in the region and the elder Krupp said "we need workers, not intellectuals". The most important group of German workers should be kept in ignorance and immobilised, a policy which survived the demise of the empire, and was continued - albeit not quite so strictly – right up until the 1950s. It wasn't until 1965 in Bochum

Duisburg: Germany's car makers start young; high-tech comes later.

that the Ruhrgebiet acquired its first university (today over 25,000 students). There followed further polytechnics and universities in Dortmund, Essen and Duisburg. Today, the region provides higher education to 123,000 people and no fewer than 8,000 scientists teach and carry out research here. Nowhere else in Europe can such a closely packed potential be found – the most important driving force behind the structural changes that are now occurring. There are opportunities, too: exhibitions, six-day bicycle races, classical and rock concerts all take place in centres such as the massive **Grugahalle** in Essen and the **Westfalenhalle** in Dortmund which can seat 23,000 people.

Duisburg: Founded at the confluence of the Ruhr and the Rhine in the ninth century, Duisburg (population 500,000) had already developed into an important trading centre by the beginning of the 12th century when it received its city charter. Because of the need to ship out the coal, the Ruhr was made navigable in 1780, thus greatly adding to the city's

importance. Work on the harbour facilities began in 1831 and these have since been developed to make **Duisburg-Ruhrort** the largest river port in the world, providing an outlet for all the products of the Ruhrgebiet.

Apart from the cruise around the harbour, Duisburg today has other attractions. It has become a major cultural centre. Together with Düsseldorf, it is the home city of the "German Opera on the Rhine" as well as the **Wilhelm Lehmbruck Museum** in which the works of the famous German sculptor (1881–1919) are displayed.

Duisburg also provided the setting for the book by the German journalist Günther Wallraf entitled *Ganz Unten* ("at the bottom of the pile") a truly revealing work of investigative journalism where Wallraf, disguised as a Turk, set out to discover exactly how exploited many Turkish guestworkers were.

Essen: Once known as the "armourer of the nation", **Essen** (population 600,000) no longer produces any steel. None of the original 22 collieries now operate. But it was in Essen that the gigantic industrialisation of the Ruhrgebiet actually began back in 1837, largely thanks to the innovative ability of one man, the pioneer of industry Franz Haniel. He developed a way of getting the miners to the previously inaccessible bituminous coal, which enabled the furnaces to produce pig iron extremely competitively. The steel boom began.

Today many an international industrial combine has its headquarters in Essen, such as *Ruhrkohle AG*, the largest German producer of coal, and *RWE*, the biggest power company in Europe. With a height of 106 metres (348 ft), the glass Town Hall is the tallest such building in Europe. The **Grillo Theatre** and the new **Aalto Opera** and especially the **Folkwang Museum** draw large numbers of people to Essen. The large shopping precinct makes Essen the number one shopping centre of the Ruhrgebiet.

Bochum: In the middle of the Ruhrgebiet, Bochum (population 420,000) is indicative of the developments in the region as a whole. **The**

Museum of Mines is the most popular technical museum in Germany. With replicas of mining villages, mines and real machinery, the museum guides the visitor through the history of industrialisation in Germany and examines its social consequences. The climax of the visit – great fun for children – is a trip down the demonstration mine.

From the "winding tower" of the museum it is possible to see the two Bochum Krupp steelworks, out towards **Wattenscheid**. To the north lies **Gelsenkirchen** home to the area's most famous football team, Schalke 04, where the crowd attendance achieved and indeed the spirit of the fans are consistently high, which is more than can be said for many of the more famous German clubs. To the north-west lies **Wanne-Eichel**, where the largest popular fair in Germany, the *Cranger Kirmes*, takes place every autumn.

Herne (population 187,000) forms the northern extremity of Bochum. One of the first mines in the Ruhrgebiet was located here and its remains can still be visited. It is called **Shamrock** and was founded by Irishmen. **Opel Cars**, a subsidiary company of General Motors, settled in Bochum when the big decline in mining began. Today, its three factories employ 20,000 people working around the clock.

Cultural centre: What makes Bochum and its surroundings so interesting is the combination of industry, university and culture. The theatre puts on an internationally acclaimed programme and in addition the Ruhrgebiet's "young scene" is establishing an increasing number of clubs and pubs, so bringing colour to the once drab region. The international culture scene, too, is acquiring an ever more important profile in the Ruhrgebiet.

Of the 100 or so museums in the region, particularly worth mentioning are the **Folkwang Museum** in Essen, which contains one of the most important collections of 19th-century European painting and sculpture; the **Iconograpy Museum** in Reklinghausen, the only museum of its kind in Europe; the **Open-air Museum** in **Mäckingerbachtal** near Hagen, which reconstructs and practically demonstrates 100 years of local handicrafts history.

Exhausted coal fields in the centre of the region forced the mining industry to move northwards in the last few decades, towards Münsterland. While the coal and steel industry declined, new industries grew – although nowhere near quickly enough. As a result, unemployment in the Ruhrgebiet had risen to 15 percent by the middle of the 1980s. Particularly badly hit was **Dortmund** lying on the eastern fringes of the region. At the time numerous demonstrations organised by the steel workers marched through the city to protest at the mass lay-offs. However, the picture has now changed dramatically. Since 1986 more new jobs have been created than old jobs lost. Now over 60 percent of the working population works in the service sector.

Apart from Regensburg and Cologne, no other city in Germany possesses more medieval churches than Dortmund. The city was granted the right to hold a market way back in AD 990, and much more important, in 1293 it was given leave to start brewing beer. While its coal and steel industries have declined, Dortmund remains at the top of the German brewing league. Indeed, more brewing goes on in Dortmund than in any other city in Europe.

Only four of the region's major centres have been introduced here, but there are many other places where similar structural changes are taking place. Taken as a whole, the Ruhrgebiet promises to continue its role in the future as one of Europe's most important and productive industrial areas.

Münsterland: The northern fringes of the Ruhrgebiet give way to the Münsterland, the so-called "green belt of Germany". Between large isolated farms and flat fields, surrounded by streams and canals, hundreds of moated castles, many of which are open to the visitor, lie hidden in the clearings in the woods. One of the best ways of discovering them is by bicycle and these are available for hire in the towns and villages. The region is well-equipped with cycling paths and is therefore ideal for a family outing.

Münsterland also faces environmental and economic problems. Large pig-fattening farms and over-fertilised fields have resulted in a disturbingly high concentration of nitrates in the ground water. At the same time, particularly since the area was at the centre of a scandal involving hormones in calves, the consumer has become wary of buying locally produced meat, so accelerating the decline of the farms.

Münster: After suffering severe damage during World War II, the historic buildings of this geographic and commercial centre of the Münsterland have been rebuilt. **Münster** (population 270,000) was granted its city charter in the 12th century and it soon became a member of the Hanseatic League. The Treaty of Westphalia, which marked the end of the Thirty Years War in 1648, was signed in Münster.

The ceremony took place in the Gothic **Town Hall** (14th-century) on the large main market square. The wonderfully restored square is dominated by the **Cathedral** (1225–65), the largest church building in Westphalia. In the tower of the **Church of St Lambert** (14th–15th centuries) hang the three iron cages in which the corpses of the leaders of the reformist Anabaptists, who were executed in 1536, were displayed. The authorities here never had much time for deviationists. The Baroque **castle**, now part of the university, and the **Fine Arts Museum** with magnificent altarpieces and Luca Cranach paintings of Luther and his wife, should be visited.

Typical for the merchants guild in this conservative-run city, the time-honoured **Café Schucan**, an establishment steeped in tradition, was saved from the claws of local business. Neither shoe shop nor supermarket was allowed to take over the premises. Equally conservative is the method of transport used here. Many people get from one place to another by bicycle, taking the bicycle "promenade" which runs round the old city walls. Rush-hour traffic may remind one of Peking.

Pigeon racing – poor men's horse-racing – is a popular hobby in the Ruhrgebiet.

Southern Germany

48 km/30 miles

CZECHOSLOVAKIA

AUSTRIA

FRANCE

SWITZERLAND

LUXEM-
BOURG

LIECHTEN-
STEIN

Hof
Selb
Marktredwitz
Bayreuth
Kulmbach
Lichtenfels
Coburg
Bamberg
Schweinfurt
Würzburg
Aschaffenburg
Fulda
Frankfurt
Darmstadt
Mannheim
Heidelberg
Mainz
Wiesbaden
Koblenz
Worms
Ludwigshafen
Speyer
Kaiserslautern
Pirmasens
Saarbrücken
Trier
Metz
Nancy
Karlsruhe
Bruchsal
Pforzheim
Baden-Baden
Strasbourg
Offenburg
Breisach
Freiburg
Lörrach
Basle
Mulhouse
Colmar

Weiden
Amberg
Erlangen
Fürth
Nuremberg
Rothenburg o.d.T.
Dinkelsbühl
Nördlingen
Schwäb. Hall
Bad Mergentheim
Tauberbischofsheim
Heilbronn
Stuttgart
Aalen
Tübingen
Reutlingen
Freudenstadt
Schwenningen
Villingen
Donau-eschingen
Singen

Furth i.W.
Cham
Regensburg
Straubing
Deggendorf
Passau
Landshut
Freising
Ingolstadt
Weißenburg
Augsburg
Landsberg
Memmingen
Kempten
Ulm
Biberach
Ravensburg
Riedlingen
Friedrichs-hafen
Meersburg
Lindau
Bregenz
Konstanz
St. Gallen
Zürich

Munich
Bad Tölz
Wasserburg
Rosenheim
Traunstein
Neu-Ötting
Alt-Ötting
Salzburg
Berchtes-gaden
Königssee
Garmisch-Partenkirchen
Innsbruck
Füssen
Kaufbeuren
Bad Tölz

Rhine
Moselle
Main
Neckar
Jagst
Kocher
Tauber
Rhine
Saar
Mosel
Regen
Naab
Danube
Altmühl
Regnitz
Amper
Lech
Isar
Inn
Salzach
Ammer-see
Starnberger-see
Kochelsee
Walchensee
Tegernsee
Achensee
Chiemsee
Lake Constance

122

What springs to mind when Southern Germany is mentioned? *Dirndls* and *lederhosen*? BMW and Mercedes? The Black Forest and its cuckoo clocks? On a journey through the south of the country the traveller will always be confronted by the living traditions of the past and the products of highly-developed modern technology. The federal states of Baden-Württemberg and Bavaria, which constitute the region, are both conservative and innovative.

Baden-Württemberg has a population of 9.2 million and covers 35,751 square km (13,803 sq miles). The capital city is Stuttgart. Here, the fertile soils of the Rhine plain give way to expansive areas of high ground, notably the Black Forest, the Odenwald and the Alpine foothills. Less well-known but equally appealing is the limestone *karst* region of the Swabian Highlands. The state has the warmest climate and longest periods of sunshine of any state in Germany, enabling agriculture to flourish, with excellent grapes growing on the slopes above the Rhine and even tobacco on the Rhine Plain.

Despite the fact that it possesses few mineral resources of its own, Baden-Württemberg has developed into a highly industrialised area. Trades became specialised at a relatively early date. The textile industry flourished in the Swabian Highlands; the manufacture of clocks and precision instruments was centred in the south of the Black Forest and Pforzheim became a centre of jewellery making. Mercedes and Porsche manufacture their cars in Stuttgart. The Swabians have a motto: "Produce, save and then build your house".

With an area of 70,553 square km (27,240 sq miles), Bavaria is the largest state in Germany and has a population of 11 million. It is separated from Austria in the south by the impressive limestone peaks and ridges of the Northern Alps. Here, just as in the Bavarian Forest to the north-east, many places are dependant on tourism for their livelihood. But barley and hops for the production of "liquid bread" remain the basis of existence for the three "tribes" living in the state, especially the Bavarians, but also the Swabians and the Franconians. In addition to beer, porcelain, glass and metal articles are the mainstay of the economy in Upper Franconia, while the electronics industry has established itself around Munich and Erlangen. Ingolstadt has become a centre of the petroleum and petro-chemical industries.

In the 6th century the Bavarians settled in the land between the Lech, the Danube and the Alps. Their present borders are but a pale reflection of the massive and powerful Bavarian realm which existed back in the 14th century, when Ludwig the Elder acquired not only Brandenburg and the Tyrol, but also the Netherlands.

Preceding pages: revival of past traditions is important to the people of the south; Sunday best in Bavaria.

HEIDELBERG

Both at home and abroad Heidelberg has come to be regarded as *the* symbol of German Romanticism. In 1990 alone, more than 3½ million visitors in search of that special romantic atmosphere which has been the subject of so many songs and poems, flocked to the city. Few can have gone away disappointed and many may even have been moved to exclaim "I lost my heart in Heidelberg".

Even the situation of the city, at the edge of the Odenwald Forest where the River Neckar reaches the Rhine Plain, justifies these lavish praises. Nestled against the hillside which drops down to the river and dominated by the famous castle, the city retains the same romantic beauty it always has.

Homo heidelbergiensis: Man must have been attracted to this place 500,000 years ago. For that is the age of the jaw bone of *homo heidelbergiensis* – the oldest human bone ever discovered in Europe – which was dug up in the vicinity. Much later the Celts came and settled here and the Romans constructed a fort. The city was first officially mentioned in 1196 as "Heidelberch" and from 1214 it came to be ruled by the powerful counts of the Palatinate. For almost 500 years the Electoral College, the body responsible for electing the German kings, was controlled by these counts. And the city bears their unmistakeable mark to this very day: its major landmarks are the castle, the university and the church of the Holy Ghost.

Like everywhere else, the city suffered enormously during the Thirty Years' War. It was occupied and plundered by the troops of the Catholic General Tilly. The famous library, which had been built by the counts, did not escape the pillage. Its priceless books were sent as spoils of war to the Vatican and only a small proportion was ever returned.

The castle: The main thoroughfare of the old city centre is the "High Street" which, today, together with the surrounding alleys and lanes, is a pedestrian precinct linking Bismarckplatz in the west with the **Market Square** and the **Kornmarkt** (corn market) in the east. Here begins the 15-minute climb up the northern slopes of the Königstuhl to the **Castle**. Alternatively, take the funicular which stops at the castle before continuing to the Königstuhl Heights (558 metres/1,860 ft).

Arriving in the courtyard, take a close look at those walls of sandstone that have dominated the valley for so long. It took 400 years before the whole complex, with its fortifications, domestic quarters and palaces, was complete. From 1300 onwards, building styles evolved all the way from Gothic to Baroque. The castle is a testimony in stone not only to the power but also to the artistic taste of its creators.

To the left of the massive gate tower, the simple **Gothic House** is the oldest part of the complex. Here lived the Elector Ruprecht I, who was also responsible for the **Church of the Holy Ghost** in the city. The northern side of the courtyard is occupied by the

Left, a view over romantic Heidelberg. *Right*, typical Heidelberg back streets.

Friedrichs Building (1601–07) with its impressive Renaissance facade decorated with statues of the German kings.

The most fascinating part of the entire castle is the **Ottheinrichs Building** at the eastern side of the courtyard. Its facade is one of the finest examples of German Renaissance architecture. The composition of statues and ornamentation presents a picture of utter harmony and balance. In addition to the Christian saints, Roman gods are also depicted: Jupiter and Mars as well as the five virtues – strength, faith, love, hope and justice. The richly-decorated doorway resembles a classical triumphal arch and above it stands Count Ottheinrich of the Palatinate who had the building constructed between 1556–66. Passing the Friedrichs Building, the visitor arrives at the Castle Terrace, which provides a wonderful view over the city.

Guided tours of the castle take about an hour. Visitors are shown the famous **Heidelberg Vat**, the largest wine vat in the world with a capacity of 250,000 litres (55,000 gallons). It was guarded by Perkeo, the court jester, who was known for his legendary thirst. It is said that he died after being persuaded to drink a cup of water after the wine to which he was accustomed.

Some buildings are now only ruins. Others have been restored and serve today as venues for banquets, concerts and theatrical performances. The Ottheinrichs Building houses the **German Apothecary Museum** which has an impressive collection of furniture, books, medical instruments and bottles of all shapes and sizes.

The Old City: Heidelberg is a typical medieval Gothic town complete with narrow lanes lined by slim houses. Magnificent Renaissance palaces were added in the course of time. During the Palatine War of Succession (1688–97) which, due to the unacceptable claims of the French King Louis XIV, involved half of Europe, Heidelberg was devastated by French troops in 1689 and again in 1693. On the second occasion even the fortifications were razed to the ground. The castle remained in ruins for

Graffiti in the students' lock-up.

many years until the populace decided it was safe enough to commence reconstruction. In the town, new houses in 18th-century Baroque style were built on the medieval foundations.

The tour through the old city begins at the **University**. This world-famous institution was founded in 1386 by Ruprecht I and is thus the oldest university in Germany. During the wars of the 17th century it lost much of its importance and only revived after its reinauguration by Karl Friedrich of Baden in 1805.

Today, the university has more than 28,000 students (about one-fifth of the town's population). In 1930, to cope with the increasing numbers of students a new university complex was built behind Universitätsplatz with the help of donations from America. The establishment later expanded to the other side of the Neckar. Student life today does not quite compare with the glorious student days of yore. A reminder of the riotous past is the former **Studentenkarzer** (student lock-up) in Augustinerstrasse

which, until 1914, served as a jail for students who were guilty of particularly indecorous behaviour in public – mostly through drunkenness. The walls of the cells are covered with humorous drawings and graffiti.

Merianstrasse and Ingrimmstrasse lead back to the market square and the Kornmarkt, the oldest part of the city, where you can visit "**Zum Sepp'l**" (Sepp's Place) and "**Roter Ochsen**" (The Red Cow) – two traditional students' pubs. Traditional student pubs such as these remain the haunts of various student fraternities, whose customs are not only perpetuated by hard-drinking contests, but also by the "duels" where the aim is, as in the 19th century, to have a permanent facial scar inflicted by an opponent! Happily, the number of adherents to this form of masochism is dwindling.

The fact that the times are changing is reflected by the many modern pubs, restaurants and cafés which are packed into the old quarter of town. In the narrow alleys away from the High Street

Student life at the turn of the century.

the facades may not be as magnificent, but the atmosphere of the old Heidelberg is every bit as authentic.

The **Church of the Holy Ghost** stands to the north of the Kornmarkt. The mighty late-Gothic edifice is the largest church in the Palatinate. Its founder, Ruprecht III of the Palatinate who later became king of Germany, lies buried within. His tomb and the rooms of the former Palatinate Library arc worth closer inspection. On the opposite side of the street is the **Hotel Ritter** with its fine facade. It survived the depradations of 1693 unscathed because the French commander chose it as his headquarters. It was built in 1952 by a Frenchman, Charles Bélier, and it remains one of the most beautiful Renaissance facades in Germany. Equally worth seeing is the adjacent former **Court Apothecary**, a Baroque building.

From the church Steingasse leads down to the river. The **Old Bridge**, which crosses the Neckar at this point, is one of the city's symbols: the other is the castle. Goethe considered it to be one of the wonders of the world. His opinion was not so much based on the technical brilliance of the bridge, but on the wonderful view afforded the visitor who walks across it. Upstream looms the **Benedictine Monastery of Neuburg** and downstream the river gradually widens out into the Rhine Plain. And looking back, the city is perfectly framed by the archway of the bridge gate.

Across the river, a steep path winds its way up the Heiligenberg. In the peace of the so-called **Philosophenweg** (philosopher's path), one soon forgets the hustle and bustle of the city. Barges chug slowly up and down the river. The Philosophenweg leads to Bergstrasse which runs down to the new **Theodor Heuss Bridge**. Back on the other side of the river the visitor arrives at **Bismarckplatz**, the western end of the pedestrian precinct.

Modern Heidelberg: Thanks to its students, Heidelberg is a young city, yet life here doesn't only revolve around the university. The city is the headquar-

Ultra-conservative members of a student society.

ters of the German Cancer Research Society and the Academy of Sciences. A Heidelberg printing machine factory is worldwide the largest exporter of the most modern offset-printing equipment. Germany's largest publisher of scientific literature, annually publishing more than 8,000 scientific publications and 190 specialist magazines, is also based in Heidelberg. Countless smaller, though no less successful, companies are evidence that Heidelberg's development did not end in the 19th century and that the city remains as vital as it ever was. But its spirit is also very much geared to the present and future. Incidentally, the tennis star Boris Becker was born in the nearby town of Leimen (see box).

To Speyer Cathedral: Heidelberg is an ideal base from which to explore this historically important region of the Palatinate. To the south-west lies Schwetzingen, with its summer palace of the kings surrounded by one of the most beautiful Baroque gardens in Germany. From there, the journey continues towards the west, to the Rhine and the old imperial city of **Speyer** (population 45,000). Pause on the bridge over the Rhine before entering the city itself and marvel at the panorama, which is dominated by the massive Romanesque cathedral.

Speyer was founded in Roman times around AD 50 and was first mentioned as a bishopric in AD 343. Between 1294 and 1797, it was one of the seven free Imperial Cities of the Holy Roman Empire of German Nations and was subject only to the Emperor himself. More than 50 imperial diets were held within its walls, the most important being that of 1529 when the later "Protestant" princes and estates forwarded their protest against the anti-Reformation resolutions of the majority. However the history of the city was not a fortunate one. While Speyer survived the Thirty Years' War unscathed, in 1689, during the Palatine War of Succession, it was completely destroyed, its medieval heritage annihilated. As a result, only a few historical buildings remain to recall the glorious past.

The Heidelberg Vat, the largest in the world.

TALES OF TENNIS

When Boris and Stefanie were born somewhere in the south of Germany nobody made a fuss about it. Special announcements did not appear in the newspapers or on television for, at that time, nobody knew that they would grow up to be national heroes. In fact they seemed to be no different from any other blonde-haired children of the same age.

Big boys do not normally like playing with little girls and Boris was two years older than Steffi, so it may come as something of a surprise to learn that the two met while they were playing. The truth is that Boris was no "wunderkind" with a racket and ball and other boys of the same age could not be bothered to play with him. So he was sent to play with the girls, where he had to make do with Steffi, who was already showing her great potential on the court.

If life had followed its normal course, Boris and Steffi might have grown up together, fallen in love, married and had little blonde-haired children of their own. But fate, or rather their parents, had different plans for them. They went their separate ways, their talents on the tennis court were developed and nurtured in each case by their ambitious fathers, and later they were both to achieve international fame as tennis players – but of an entirely different kind.

Boris did not stop growing until he reached the proportions of a giant. He also developed a giant's strength, and, in England, his powerful service earned him the nickname "Boom-Boom" Becker. Every time he served he gave the impression that he was gaining his revenge for being sent to play with the girls. He usually left the court as the winner and, in 1985 at the age of 17, he became the youngest player ever to win the men's singles at Wimbledon. He retained his title the following year and his reputation grew along with his bank account.

In spite of a deep-seated anger which sometimes surfaced on the tennis court, Boris began to enjoy life. He loved good food, was not averse to exploiting his popularity with the girls, and was always good for a printable quote. In Germany he became something of a national hero, especially when the German president set him up as a role model for others of his generation. His reputation suffered a little when he moved to Monaco taking his bank account with him, but, on the whole, he was treated kindly by the press. And who would dare to criticise him? Abroad he was more famous than his country's president. And the name of Germany had become associated with the boom-boom of Boris's service.

Stefanie was a quite different tennis player. She darted across the court as nimbly as a fawn, and her passing shots left her poor opponents on the other side of the net with hardly any time to raise their rackets. Her personality was different, too. Whenever she was on court making the other girls look like beginners, she pulled a face as if she had just lost her pet dog, Bennie. Not of a carefree nature, she often made a sullen and sulky impression and the only man in her life remained her father. But she too went relentlessly from one victory to the next, winning the Grand Slam (all four major titles) and the Olympic gold medal in 1988.

Now Germany had two tennis champions and a whole nation went tennis crazy. Tennis schools boomed and ambitious parents invested large amounts of money in lessons for their children hoping to repeat the success of the Grafs and the Beckers. People who had shown no previous interest in the sport became experts themselves, glued to the TV screen whenever major tournaments were shown.

Boris always had to struggle a little bit harder than Steffi to maintain his position at the top. When he wasn't winning he still made the headlines. When the role model of Germany's youth was asked about military service he said that the money spent on defence would be put to better use feeding the poor of the world. Bully for Boris!

Facing increasing competition from up-and-coming young players Steffi was ultimately toppled from her pedestal as well. But this extraordinary pair remain Germany's number one sporting heroes and people continue to watch when Boris's service goes boom-boom and Steffi's passing shot leaves her opponent helpless.

Above everything else rises the Romanesque **Cathedral**, with its six spires. The basilica, built during the Salier period between 1030 and 1125, set new standards for both scale and design. At a first glance the exterior seems plain and austere; only after very close inspection do the open dwarf galleries and their numerous columns and beautifully carved capitals catch the eye. Nor do the large decorative windows in the transept do very much to alter first impressions. This severity corresponds perfectly with the solemn mood within the building. The whole structure is supported by relatively slim columns with heavy Corinthian capitals and pilasters carved with geometric designs.

With a length of 134 metres (440 ft) and a height of 32 metres (105 ft) high (east spires 72 metres/236 ft), Speyer Cathedral is the largest Romanesque church in Europe. In the impressive nave are the statues of eight German Emperors who all found their final resting place here. Their tombs and those of their wives are located in the **Imperial Vault**. The crypt is not only the largest in Germany, but with its painted groin vaulting is also considered to be the most beautiful.

Just to the south of the cathedral is the **Museum of History**, which contains a number of interesting collections as well as a department devoted to the history of wine. Other sights include the **Jewish Baths**, the **Altpörtel**, one of the old city gates from the 13th century from where there is a good view of the city, and the **Church of the Holy Trinity** (1701–17) with its marvellous ceiling frescoes.

Industrial centre on the Rhine: situated at the confluence of the Rhine and the Neckar, the city of **Mannheim** (population 310,000) lies to the north of Speyer. Together with its sister city of **Ludwigshafen** (population 160,000) it is one of the most important industrial centres in Germany, particularly for the chemicals industry (BASF). Nevertheless, it does possess some fine artistic and cultural monuments. The city is marked by the sharp contrast between the busy port and the stylish and elegant

Left, Germany's dynamic duo, Steffi Graf and Boris Becker. Below, impressions of two imperial towns, Speyer (left) and Worms.

Baroque architecture in the centre.

Mannheim was also founded by the counts of the Palatinate. In 1606 the Elector Friedrich IV ordered the place to be fortified. However, this did not prevent it from being destroyed during the Palatine War of Succession. It was subsequently rebuilt by the elector Johann Wilhelm on a grid pattern that still characterises the city centre.

The city flourished after the elector Carl Philipp moved his residence here from Heidelberg, but the glorious days were over when Karl Theodor chose Munich as his electoral seat. In the 19th century the Rhine was developed as a major industrial waterway, and Mannheim gradually became an important river port. But in World War II the city was almost completely destroyed and now Mannheim has a modern character, although enough old buildings remain to be seen.

The most important historical sight in Mannheim is the **Electors' Palace**. Built between 1720 and 1760, it is one of the largest Baroque palace complexes in all Europe. After suffering severe damage in the war, the main stairwell, the palace church and the Knights' Hall were all rebuilt. Today, the palace is part of the university.

Opposite the palace stands the **Jesuit Church**, completely rebuilt after 1945. The splendid interior decoration is true to the original. A few blocks towards the centre is the **Reiss Museum**, housed in the former arsenal. It provides a comprehensive insight into the history of the city and contains a number of collections, including some exquisite porcelain. Here also is the first bicycle made by Baron von Drais in 1817 and a replica of the world's first car invented by Carl Benz in 1886. All who are interested in art should visit the **Municipal Art Gallery**, which houses a collection of wonderful works from the 19th and 20th centuries.

The other side of Mannheim is also worth visiting. It is possible to take cruises through the port area – after Duisburg-Ruhrort this is the second largest inland river port in Europe. The **Early industry on the Rhine.**

point of departure is near the Kurpfalz Bridge, on the left bank of the Neckar.

Only 20 km (12 miles) to the north of Mannheim lies the old imperial city of **Worms** (population 75,000), whose history goes back some 5,000 years. During the time of the Migration of Peoples Worms was the capital of the Burgundian realm which was destroyed by the Huns in AD 437. These events provided the basis for the *Nibelungen Saga* with its blond hero Siegfried and grim villain Hagen.

Numerous imperial diets were held in Worms, including that of 1521 when Martin Luther had to defend his theses against Rome and the Emperor. The visitor can learn more about the city's past in the extensive **Municipal Museum**. Equally worth visiting is the **Town Hall**, as well as the restored **Church of the Holy Trinity** (1709–25) and the so-called **"Red House"**, a fine Renaissance building on Römerstrasse dating from 1624.

The principal attraction of the city is the centrally situated **Cathedral** (12th–13th century). Particularly fine is the Gothic south door, whose "pictorial bible" reliefs have impressed believers and non-believers for more than 700 years. The interior of the building contains a number of Romanesque and Gothic statues and the east choir of this double-choir church is dominated by the Baroque **High Altar** created by Balthasar Neumann in 1741. The red-sandstone church is regarded as the very model of late-Romanesque ecclesiastical architecture. The heaviness of the walls is reduced by the use of glass, including the magnificent rose window.

To the west of the cathedral lies the oldest (11th century) and largest **Jewish Cemetery** in Europe, which fortunately escaped the destructive venom of the Nazis. Not so the **Jewish Quarter**, on the other side of town, which has been the subject of a comprehensive rehabilitation scheme since 1970. Here stands the 11th-century **Synagogue**, the oldest in the country, which has been rebuilt using as much of the original masonry as possible.

The Rhine bridge at Ludwigshafen.

Hotel zum Riesen

A JOURNEY TO FRANCONIA

Before heading for the next major destination on this particular itinerary, Würzburg, the traveller might consider relaxing aboard one of the steamers of the White Fleet which ply their way along the beautiful Neckar and Main valleys, past picturesque little towns, with medieval castles perched high above the river.

Alternatively, by following the B 37 from Heidelberg along the banks of the Neckar via Neckargemünd and Hirschhorn one can reach the charming health resort of **Eberbach**. The journey takes you along the Romantic Road through the Neckar Valley and presents one of the most beautiful of all German river landscapes. The Neckar has its source in the Black Forest and flows for almost 400 km (250 miles) before joining the Rhine at Mannheim. The river is famous for its densely forested shores which rise up to 400 metres (1,300 ft) on

either side. It is a 30-minute walk up from Eberbach to the ruins of **Eberbach Castle** which was built between the 11th and 13th centuries and used to be the largest fortress of the Hohenstaufen emperors.

Castles around Mosbach: Before continuing north from Eberbach through the Odenwald, you might consider taking a detour further along the Neckar to the south for 24 km (15 miles) to Mosbach. Beyond the ruins of **Stolzeneck Castle**, high above the left bank of the river, lies **Zwingenberg**, a health resort with a beautiful castle dating from the 13th century. The picturesque little town of **Mosbach**, with its many half-timbered buildings, dates back to the 8th century, when a Benedictine monastery was founded here. There are two noteworthy fortresses in the vicinity of the town. **Hornberg Castle** dates from 1148 and remains one of the most interesting castles on the Neckar. For 45 years it was the possession of Götz von Berlichingen (1480–1562), the intrepid knight who is im-

Preceding pages: Germany's oldest hotel in Miltenberg.

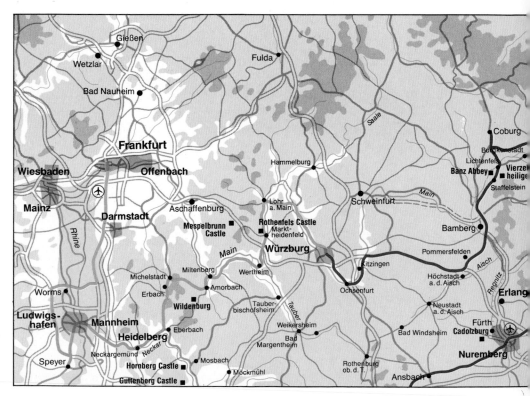

mortalised in Goethe's drama of the same name. A museum was installed in the tower and dedicated to the heroic deeds of this leading figure of the Peasants' Revolt. A little further to the south near Hassmersheim, **Guttenberg Castle** is not only one of the oldest but also one of the best preserved castles in the entire valley. It is a splendid example of medieval castle design and clearly demonstrates the development from castles constructed purely for defence to those built also for residential purposes.

Through the Odenwald Forest: From Eberbach the B 45 cuts right through the heart of the **Odenwald Forest**, one of the most scenic of the German central highland regions, to the picturesque towns of Erbach and Michelstadt. **Erbach**, a health resort and erstwhile residence of the counts of Erbach, has a well-preserved old town dissected by narrow alleys. Parts of the old city wall remain standing. The Town Church from 1748 and the **Town Hall**, a 16th-century half-timbered building, are also worth visiting.

Not far away is the health resort town of **Michelstadt** with its half-timbered houses and romantic nooks. Its completely intact **Market Place** with the town hall is a real jewel of medieval civic architecture planned in 1484. The fountain in the market place dates from 1541. The late-Gothic **Church of St Michael and St Kilian** was built between 1461–1507. Also worth close inspection is the **Odenwald Museum** with artifacts from Celtic and Roman times.

The old Franconian town of **Amorbach** in the Odenwald is famous for its 8th-century monastery. The monastery church, originally built in the Romanesque style and then rebuilt in Baroque between 1742–47, is a unique example of the German rococo. The church still contains the wrought-iron trellis which separated the monks from the laymen and the organ, which with no less than 3,000 pipes, 63 stops and three manuals is the second largest Baroque organ in Germany.

Ten km (6 miles) to the north lies **Miltenberg** which is dominated by the castle of the same name built in 1210. Lying in the shadow of the old castle, the architectural composition of the buildings has made the town world famous. The fountain and the old timber-framed houses as well as the former wine cellars from 1541, the tavern "Zur Gülden Cron" from 1623, and the "Weinhaus am alten Markt" are all part of the ensemble.

The cosy wine taverns and pubs in the Odenwald are not only interesting from an architectural point of view: they offer such regional specialities as *Handkäs mit Musik* (curd cheese garnished with oil, vinegar and onions), apple wine, and excellent home-made sausage served with home-baked bread.

Moated castles and robbers' nests: From Miltenberg continue to follow the Romantic Road to Grossheubach and then on via Eschau and Hobbach to the little town of **Mespelbrunn**. Before the gates of the town, in a clearing in the forest, stands the handsome moated **Mespelbrunn Castle**. Completed in 1564 in the Renaissance style, it remains the property of the family of the counts of

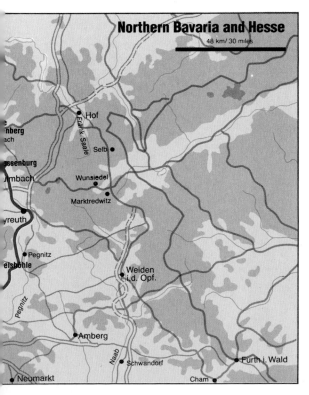

Northern Bavaria and Hesse

48 km/ 30 miles

Hof

Frank Saale

Selb

Wunsiedel

Marktredwitz

Bayreuth

Pegnitz

Weiden i.d. Opf.

Pegnitz

Amberg

Naab

Schwandorf

Furth i. Wald

Neumarkt

Cham

Ingelheim. Because the interior of the castle has been preserved in its original state, the visitor can gain a clear insight into how the nobility once used to live.

The castle is situated in the **Spessart**, an upland region of thick forest which is one of the largest nature reserves in Europe. The River Main flows around it in a U-shape. The beauty of the Spessart becomes apparent when you wander through the extensive oak forests and across the idyllic meadows.

From Mespelbrunn take the motorway A 3 going south to **Wertheim**, the old Franconian town at the confluence of the Tauber and Main rivers. The Main-Franconian character of the town is determined by its narrow alleys and the pointed gables of the buildings around the market place.

Further to the north, the journey continues along the course of the Main to **Marktheidenfeld** with another attractive market square surrounded by half-timbered houses. Nearby, **Rothenfels Castle** towers 224 metres (735 ft) above the river. The earthworks, the dungeon

and the lower storey of the castle date from the 12th–13th centuries.

City of bishops and wine: The city of **Würzburg** (population 127,000) has been a bishopric since the 8th century and most of the sights that appeal to the visitor stem from the heyday of the prince-bishops. This despite the fact that the city was practically annihilated by a massive allied bombing raid just before the end of World War II, on 16 March 1945.

During that fateful night the populace sought refuge in one of the few buildings that escaped the bombing, the old **Marienberg Fortress**, founded in 1201. Surrounded by the vineyards for which Würzburg is famous, the fortress towers above the city on the opposite side of the River Main. The massive rectangular building encloses a courtyard and the 13th-century keep as well as the Renaissance fountain and the Church of St Mary. From 1253–1719 the fortress served as the residence of the prince-bishops, who used it as a stronghold to keep the ever-more powerful townsfolk

Below left, Michelstadt marketplace. Below right, the serene moated castle at Mespelbrunn.

at bay. In 1631, after the city was taken by Gustav Adolf of Sweden during the Thirty Years' War, the fortress was extended and converted and began to take the form of the building we see today, with its Baroque facades and the Fürstengarten (princes' garden).

The palace of all palaces: While the city experienced its heyday in the 18th century under the rule of the House of Schönborn, it was a flourishing place long before that. In 1575, Prince-Bishop Julius Echter founded the **Juliusspital** (hospital) and, in 1582, the old **University**. It was here some 300 years later that Wilhelm Conrad Röntgen discovered the X-ray. In 1719 Johann Philipp Franz of Schönborn became prince-bishop and moved his residence from the Marienberg to the city. The famous master builder of the Baroque, Balthasar Neumann, was summoned to the court. Franz had recognised his genius and commissioned him to plan his new residence. The palace of all palaces, the **Würzburg Residence**, was thus completed between 1720–44. It was built in the style of the south German Baroque and is ranked as one of the finest Baroque palaces in Europe.

Neumann created his own memorial within the palace by designing what is undoubtedly one of the most beautiful staircases of the baroque-rococo era. The stair well extends right up the two-storey building and is crowned by a single concave vault 30 metres (100 ft) long by 18 metres (59 ft) wide. More renowned than the vault itself is the **Ceiling Fresco** painted by the Italian artist Giovanni Battista Tiepolo who was summoned to Würzburg in 1750 to create the largest painting in the world. Tiepolo depicted the Gods of Olympus and allegories of the four continents known at the time – Europe, Asia, Africa and America. The painting also alludes to the marriage between Friedrich Barbarossa and Beatrix of Burgundy in the year 1156. Miraculously, the fresco survived the allied bombs unscathed.

Tragedy of an artist: Many people visit Würzburg in order to admire the works

Window box displays denote civic pride.

of the world-famous woodcarver and sculptor Tilman Riemenschneider, who came to the city in 1483. In his workshop he carved altars from limestone, made tombstones from sandstone and supplied the whole of Main-Franconia with splendid sculptures. The distinguished citizen became a member of the city council in 1509 and served as mayor from 1520-21. During the Peasants' Revolt, Riemenschneider supported the oppressed peasants against the prince-bishop Konrad von Thingen. After the peasants had been defeated at the Marienberg fortress, he was imprisoned and tortured for eight weeks. His hands were cut off and he died a broken man in 1531. His name only became of interest to later generations after his grave was found during road excavations. The world-famous works of Tilman Riemenschneider are now displayed in the **Main-Franconian Museum** in the Marienberg, along with a splendid collection of other Franconian works of art.

A city walk: More Riemenschneider creations can be seen on a walk through Würzburg, starting at the **Hofgarten** (court gardens) behind the Residence, with its impressive wrought-iron gates and beautiful Baroque group of figures. The University is only a stone's throw away. The nearby early-Gothic **Franciscan Church** (1221) contains a *pietà* by Riemenschneider.

Domschulstrasse leads to the Romanesque **Cathedral**. Dedicated to St Kilian, the apostle of the Franks and the patron saint of the city who was murdered in AD 689, the building had to be rebuilt after its complete destruction in 1945. The **Schönborn Chapel**, one of Balthasar Neumann's most important works, is built onto the cathedral transept and contains the shrine of the Prince-Bishops of Schönborn. St Kilian lies buried in the crypt of the adjacent **Neumünsterkirche** (new cathedral).

From here **Domstrasse** leads down to the **River Main**. Just before the **Old Main Bridge** is the **Vierröhren-brunnen** Baroque fountain and the **Old Town Hall** originally dating from the 13th century, although many extensions

Tiepolo's masterpiece in the Würzburg Residence.

have been added since. One of them is the imposing late-Renaissance town hall tower, the **Grafenackhart**, erected in 1659. The nearby **Carmelite Monastery** (1712) has been part of the town hall since the last century. Across the bridge on a hill to the south of the Marienberg stands the *Käpelle*, the votive **Chapel of St Mary**, an important shrine for Catholic pilgrims. The 12 small shrines on the long flight of steps leading up to the chapel represent the 12 Stations of the Cross.

The centre of Franconian wine: One of the statues on the old Main bridge is that of St Kilian, who is also the vintners' patron saint. Wine growing in Franconia goes back more than 1,200 years and Würzburg has always been the centre of its production and marketing. There are many places where one can sample the predominantly white wine from the distinctive *bocksbeutel* bottles, including the old **Burgerspital Wine Tavern**, where it is traditionally accompanied with a type of crispbread known locally as *Weinbeiser*. The Burgerspital itself is

Rococo statue at Amorbach.

in fact an old people's home founded in 1319 by the patrician Johannes von Steren. The establishment is still funded by revenues from the vineyards belonging to the estate.

October, the month of the wine harvest, is the best time to explore the vineyards and villages of the Franconian wine district, most of which lie to the south of the city. Every weekend a wine festival is held in one or other of the villages – in Volkach, Frikkenhausen and Eisenheim.

The Bamberg horsemen: The journey through Franconia continues towards the medieval jewel of **Bamberg**, an old imperial and episcopal city first mentioned in AD 902. The **Cathedral** is the historical and spiritual centre of the city. It not only contains the tomb of its founder Emperor Heinrich II who elevated Bamberg to a bishopric in 1007, but also the only Papal tomb north of the Alps, that of Pope Clement II who had been bishop of the city.

The cathedral was consecrated in 1012, burned down twice and rebuilt in 1237 in the transition period from Romanesque to early-Gothic. Particularly impressive is the **Fürstenportal** (Prince's Door) with its deep niches containing the statues of the apostles standing on the shoulders of the prophets. The statues in the cathedral's interior are also masterpieces of medieval sculpture. The most famous is the **Bamberg Horsemen**, an idealised portrait of Christian kings and knights in the Middle Ages. On the left of the cathedral, in the former chapter house erected by Balthasar Neumann in 1730, is the **Diocesan Museum** with its cathedral treasury of unique exhibits including Heinrich II's cloak.

A tour through the **Old City** reveals the two distinct historical districts of Bamberg: the ecclesiastical half on the "seven hills" and the secular half occupying the island between the two arms of the River Regnitz. From the **Guard House** (1744) the road leads through to Maxplatz with the Baroque **New Town Hall** designed by Balthasar Neumann. The Baroque style can also be recognised at the **Grüner Markt** (Green

Market Place). Nearby, on the right side, is the beautiful facade of the **Church of St Martin** (17th century), and on the left the fine Baroque **Raulino House**.

On the border between the two halves of the city, stands the **Old Town Hall** on an island in the River Regnitz, linked to the banks by a bridge. From here there is a good view of Bamberg's **Little Venice**, with fishermen's old houses on the right bank of the river. The old town hall's unusual location is due to the necessity, in former times, to reconcile the needs of the religious overlords and the burghers. The most distinctive feature is the **Rottenmeisterhäusen**, a half-timbered house balanced on the bridge's central pier. From here wend your way back to the cathedral square through a maze of narrow alleys, passing the erstwhile **Dominican Church** with its attractive cloisters from the 14th century. Today it houses the famous **Bamberg Symphony Orchestra**. At the top of the picturesque steps of the katzenberg is the **Schlenkerle**, one of the best *Rauchbier* (smoked malt beer) inns. Bamberg is famous for its *Rauchbier*.

Back at the cathedral square, the **Alte Hofhaltung** (old residence) is separated from the cathedral by a narrow street. This magnificent Renaissance building completed in 1569 was once the imperial and episcopal palace. It is now the **Museum of Local History**.

The **Church of St Michael** on Michaelsberg is part of the former Benedictine Abbey, founded at the request of Heinrich II in 1015. Both the exterior and interior are now composed of Romanesque, Gothic and Baroque elements. The famous facade above the broad staircase leading up to the entrance (1677) is the work of L. Dientzenhofer. Maternstrasse leads back into the city and to the **Carmelite Monastery** founded in the 12th century. The late-Romanesque cloisters are the largest in Germany.

Neumann's masterpiece: The journey through Franconia continues northwards parallel to the course of the River Main. Between the idyllically situated little towns of Staffelstein and Lichtenfels, two veritable jewels of the Baroque await the traveller. Here the Main Valley is guarded on the left side by the fortress-like **Banz Abbey**, from 1069–1803 a Benedictine abbey and later a castle belonging to the ruling Wittelsbach family. If this building is regarded as one of the greatest achievements of the German Baroque, then the edifice that stands on the opposite side of the valley marks the absolute zenith of the era – the **Vierzehnheiligen** (the Church of the Fourteen Saints) by Balthasar Neumann, built between 1734 and 1751. While the rich rococo ornamentation and frescos are all magnificent, here Neumann's real achievement was in defining the interior space of the building in a series of interlocking ovals. The oval pattern, so typical of the Baroque, is thus an integral part of the design both on a two- and three-dimensional plain. For this alone, the building is an absolute masterpiece.

Grilled sausages: The market place in **Coburg** is a fine place to spend a few hours, though exactly how long you remain will depend on how hungry you are. For, apart from visiting the residence of the Princes of Saxe-Coburg, the prime reason for being here must be to savour the legendary Coburg sausages, relatives of the more common Thuringian variety. The air is redolent with the aroma of glowing pine cones over which the sausages are grilled 365 days a year, as from the town hall (1580) the statue of the *Bratwurstmännle* (Sausage Man) observes the scene. A memorial to Albert, consort of Queen Victoria, stands in the market place.

Another reason for visiting Coburg might be to visit the **Coburg Veste**, the fortress on the hill above the town which, with its triple ring of fortifications, is one of the largest and most impregnable of all German castles. Built in 1200, it provided refuge for Martin Luther during the celebrated Augsburg Imperial Diet in 1530. The fortress houses a large collection of paintings and copper engravings by Luther's artist friend Lucas Cranach (1472–1553), as well as a fine display of hunting weapons.

Strongest beer in the world: Lucas Cranach was born in the town of

Kronach on the B 303. The town, dominated by the 12th-century **Rosenberg Fortress,** is an idyllic place, with narrow alleys, attractive houses and a well-preserved medieval town wall with towers and gates.

More beer is drunk in Germany than in any other country in the world – and the "beer town" of **Kulmbach** 20 km (13 miles) south of Coburg is said to produce the best beer. This is where *Kulminator*, the world's strongest beer, is brewed. The breweries use the local spring water from the nearby Fichtel Mountains and Franconian Forest.

Wagner's town: The town of **Bayreuth** (population 70,000) is first and foremost associated with the composer Richard Wagner. But the poet Jean Paul also lived here from 1804–1825 and Franz Liszt died here in 1886. The cultured Margravine Wilhelmina, Frederick the Great's favourite sister, commissioned the architect Saint Pierre to design the first Bayreuth **Opera House,** which is today regarded as the best-preserved German Baroque theatre.

Saint Pierre was also responsible for the **New Palace** which was designed in the more austere French Baroque style. Built in 1753, it consists of an octagonal sun temple with two curved wings. There are beautiful fountains outside. Richard Wagner and his wife Cosima, Liszt's daughter, lie buried in the park close to Liszt himself.

The **Hermitage Palace** is another famous building in the east of Bayreuth, as is the **Old Palace** which was built in 1718 and extended according to Wilhemina's plans in 1736. North of Bayreuth is the **Green Hill**, where Wagner had the **Festival Theatre** built in 1872–76.

The Franconian **"Little Switzerland"** acquired this name in the last century, because at that time the German Romantics believed this was exactly how Switzerland must look. There are indeed some impressive looking crags such as those that tower above the romantic hill village of **Tüchersfeld**. The high point of a tour through this beautiful national park on the way to

Franconian market stallholder.

Nuremberg is the one-kilometre long limestone cave, the **Devil's Cave** near **Pottenstein**, a fascinating underground world of caverns and grottos full of stalagmites and stalactites.

Free imperial city: To the south is the old free imperial city of **Nuremberg** (population 500,000), the second largest city in Bavaria and an important industrial and commercial centre. Devastated by bombs in World War II, it was rebuilt practically as it had been and thus retains much of its historical charm.

Nuremberg was founded in the 11th century by Emperor Heinrich III as a base for his campaigns in Bohemia and the settlement rapidly developed into an important trading centre. Elevated to a free imperial city by Emperor Friedrich III it retained this status until 1806 when it was annexed by the Kingdom of Bavaria. From 1050 to the 16th century nearly all the emperors maintained their residence in the Kaiserburg (castle), and held their imperial diets (meetings) here. At that time, Nuremberg was regarded as the unofficial capital of the Holy Roman Empire of German Nations.

During the 15th–17th centuries the rich city attracted artists and scientists such as Albrecht Dürer, Adam Krafft and Veit Stoss. In 1600 the political and economic importance of the city declined and real prosperity only returned when the first German railway between Nuremberg and Fürth was inaugurated in 1835. Splendid specimens of the first German steam engines can be viewed in the **Transport Museum**.

One hundred years later another less celebrated chapter in Germany's history was written in Nuremberg. The Nazis wanted to revive the city's tradition as the old capital of the *Reich* and so they built a massive stadium in which they held their rallies between 1933 and 1938. This was the stage on which Hitler made his demagogic speeches. Parts of the stadium are still standing. From 1945 to 1949 Nuremberg once again became the focus of world attention when Nazi war criminals were put on trial by the victorious allied powers.

Back to the Middle Ages: Nuremberg's

Festive evening in Bayreuth.

Old City is surrounded by a sturdy 13th-century defensive wall with 46 fortified towers – the landmarks of the city – and five main gates: the Spittlertor, the Königstor, the Frauentor, the Laufertor and the Neutor. The **Emperor's Castle**, built on sandstone crags high above the old city, consists of three architectural components, each from a different historical period. The western crags provide the foundations for the Kaiserburg which was erected in the 12th century during the reign of the Hohenstaufen Emperor Friedrich Barbarossa. Then there is the **Burggrafenburg**, the first royal castle built by the Salier rulers in the 11th century. The **Kaiserstallung** (imperial stables), originally built by the city fathers as a granary in 1485, is now a hostel.

In the 16th century the castle had to be vigorously defended and battlements were incorporated. Employees of the court were accommodated in half-timbered houses in the outer bailey. In his legendary attempt to escape from his captors who had condemned him to death, the robber knight Eppelein von Gailingen drove his mount over the ramparts of the Kaiserburg . Today one can enjoy a plate of sausages and a glass of beer in a number of cosy little pubs around the castle.

Near the castle, the Tiergartnertor leads to the **Albrecht Dürer House**. This 15th-century building where the famous artist once lived is now a museum. On the **Town Hall Square** stands the **Church of St Sebald**, a late-Romanesque columned basilica from 1256. St Sebald's tomb inside the church is a masterpiece of the German iron founder's art and was cast by Vischer at the beginning of the 16th century. The moving Crucifixion group by Veit Stoss dates from the same period. Opposite the church is the **Fembo Municipal Museum**, housed in a splendid late-Renaissance patrician house from around 1600.

Across the Pegnitz: Crossing the narrow Pegnitz River we come to the **Main Market**, the site of Nuremberg's famous annual **Christmas Market**. The

The old town hall on the Regnitz river in Bamberg.

richly carved **Schöne Brunnen**, a beautiful 19-metre (62-ft) high fountain, stands before the **Church of Our Lady** (1349). The church has an interesting facade with the famous **Männleinlaufen**, a clock which at noon every day re-enacts the homage of the Seven Electors to Emperor Charles IV. The interior contains the **Tucher Altar** (*circa* 1400). The **Town Hall**, whose oldest part is the hall with stepped gables, dates from 1340. In the basement are medieval dungeons with gruesome torture chambers. Nearby is the well-known **Gänsemännchen** (1555), a figure of a peasant with two geese spouting water.

Situated on the picturesque Pegnitz, the **Heilig Geist Spital** (Holy Ghost Hospital) was founded in the 14th century. The German emperor's imperial insignia were kept here until 1796. The inner courtyard has an impressive Crucifixion group by Adam Krafft, and the 14th-century Hansel Fountain.

Beyond this is the **Church of St Laurence**, built in the 13th–14th centuries. Particularly impressive is the chancel with its wonderful star vaulting, suspended from which is the beautifully carved Annunciation created by Veit Stoss in 1517. Another work by the same artist is the Crucifix which can be seen at the high altar together with Adam Krafft's world-famous Tabernacle.

Königstrasse, the shopping street, extends from St Laurence's past the **Mauthalle**, which was built as a granary around 1500 and is now an inn with a beautiful old vaulted cellar. The **German National Museum** at the Kornmarkt, founded in 1852 "to save the German cultural heritage" displays folklore items, artifacts from pre- and early history and copper engravings. No other museum offers such a comprehensive insight into the cultural development of the German-speaking world.

On past the early-Gothic **Church of St Clare**, we come to the **Old Nuremberg** craftsmen's yard **Handwerkerhof**, a model town illustrating medieval handicrafts, gold and precious metal forging, and also the manufacture of the famous Nuremberg gingerbread.

Nuremberg rooftops and the Kaiserburg.

GERMAN CUISINES

For some time now one has come to expect more of the German cuisine than a buffet consisting solely of regional specialities such as knuckle of pork, thick frankfurters, fried sausages, sauerkraut and bread dumplings, smoked eel and Swabian raviolis, Berlin doughnuts and Black Forest gâteaux. "Menus of the world unite!" would now be a suitable motto to have printed at the top of German menu cards. The choice is truly international, from the five-star hotel to the factory canteen, from the small town vegetable market to the deep freezes in the supermarkets.

Traditional German fare is now only one among many specialities and nowadays it is more likely to be encountered in a gourmet restaurant than on the kitchen table at home. While the German populace still baulks at accepting the fact of a multicultural society, German stomachs have long been dependant on international cuisine. After all, which upright German citizen can do without his pizza, his chips and the family outing to the "Balkan grill", and which German kid doesn't demand American fast-food?

It was only with the arrival of the Turks that the German capital acquired a culinary trademark of its own: the kebab. And the kebab has rescued many a hectic hungry soul from having to make the terrible choice between a soggy hamburger and a curry sausage oozing with fat.

The history of culinary culture in the Federal Republic really began with the eating spree that followed decades of ration cards, malnutrition and hunger. The emaciated figures of the first postwar years soon began to expand into overweight gluttons. In the 1950s it was primarily high-calorie traditional fare that arrived at the table. Slowly, however, as a result of their travels to foreign lands, the Germans acquired a taste for other food. Guest workers brought their cuisine with them. Spaghetti became an indispensible "quick meal". Pizza, appearing with an ever-increasing number of toppings, pizza developed into the German national dish and the Balkan spit roast became the very epitome of culinary indulgence. Evenings in front of the TV were spent munching peanuts and crisps, and guzzling demijohns full of Chianti.

The Germans didn't get over their trauma of hunger until the beginning of the 1970s. They then developed a taste for diets and more refined cuisine. The influence of French *nouvelle cuisine* – the trend towards refined simplicity based on first class produce – and the harking back to regional German specialities united to produce the German "kitchen miracle". Since then the representative German cuisine has been rated as among the best in the world.

The refinement of tastes was not restricted to the cooks in gourmet restaurants. Through television and widely-published cookery magazines the developments soon found their way into average German kitchens and dining rooms. The general prosperity made it

The kebab is here to stay.

148

possible, at least to a certain degree, for the democratisation of good taste in the German cuisine.

This first became apparent in the high-class eating spree at the end of the 1970s. This involved the consumption of vast quantities of German truffles, lobster, caviar, mussels, salmon and partridge.

Today there is no real eating culture in Germany. Many an office worker now gorges himself like a medieval baron. Businessmen cook for their business partners. There are children who live mainly from cola, chips and chocolate bars and singles whose primary source of nourishment is ready-made meals. And then there are vegetarians and people who only eat "biological" food. Everybody who isn't totally impoverished can choose what, when, where and how he eats, whether he celebrates his meals as entertainment or stuffs something down during a spare moment at the office.

Rich variety at the baker's.

Matters developed rather differently in the former GDR. The populace was often fobbed off with poor quality produce. Over-eating was widespread in the socialist GDR, where there was cheap food in abundance. However everything necessary for the creation of refined cuisine was either in very short supply or not available at all. When good quality fresh produce made its appearance in the shops it was immediately snapped up and hoarded in deep freezes where it would not infrequently have to survive a number of power cuts before finding its way to the oven.

The gastronomy sector went into rapid decline as a result of the supply problems created by the planned economy. Only the most primitive specialities of the regional cuisine managed to survive those 40 years. Such delights as the famous Thuringian sausage were simplified beyond recognition. The GDR became a culinary desert. Its former inhabitants will require some considerable time before they can munch their way through the West German land of milk and honey. The first thing that is likely to weigh heavily in their stomachs are the extraordinarily high cost.

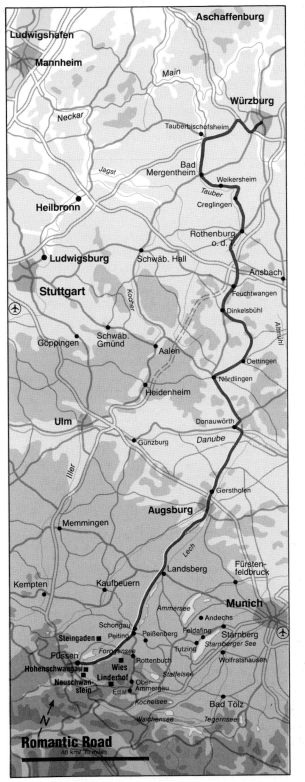

Romantic Road

48 km/ 30 miles

ALONG THE ROMANTIC ROAD

To travel along the Romantic road is to experience the panoply of a historical drama playing from Roman times all the way up to the present day. The principals are emperors, kings and countless nobles as well as burghers and lowly peasants who fought for their territorial and civil rights. The stages they performed upon are fascinating medieval towns, magnificent palaces, castles, churches and monasteries set in the most varied landscapes between Würzburg on the River Main and Füssen at the northern rim of the Alps. Modern times have changed former country lanes into busy roads, yet innumerable places – a narrow alley in Rothenburg, a palace in Augsburg, the Neuschwanstein castle – justify the term "romantic" often given to this route. The jewels of the "Romantic Road" are strung together like the pearls of an exquisite necklace.

The Tauber Valley: After a splendid start in Würzburg (*see page 143*), the Romantic Road wends its way along the picturesque Tauber Valley, a tributary of the River Main. Walking from the bridge along the pedestrian precinct lined with half-timbered houses, the entrance to the **Tauberbischofsheim** marketplace is guarded on the one side by **Haus Mackert**, the Baroque residence of a wealthy wine merchant and on the other by the **Stern Apothecary**.

The square features the neo-Gothic **Town Hall** and, on its southern side, the small Baroque **Church of St Lioba**. A relative of the missionary bishop St Boniface, Lioba governed one of the first convents in Germany here in the middle of the 8th century. The settlement was of Merovingian origin and when it came into Boniface's possession in 725, it acquired the name "Bischofsheim". From the 13th to the 19th centuries Tauberbischofsheim was controlled by the powerful prince-bishops of Mainz, a fact recalled by the wheel in the coat of arms and the **Electoral Castle** (14th–16th centuries) which contains the **Folklore Museum**.

The watch-tower affords a fine view over the town and the Tauber Valley.

Along the valley upstream, the B 290 passes Distelhausen and Gerlachsheim which both boast impressive Baroque churches. Occasional shrines stand by the side of the road, which is the reason why this area is sometimes referred to as "God's country" or "Madonna's district". **Lauda** has for centuries been a centre of wine growing. A 16th-century vintner's house has been converted into a wine and local museum. The prosperity that the wine brought to the locals is clearly demonstrated by the fine medieval half-timbered buildings in the centre of the town.

Bad Mergentheim is famous for its waters. When, in 1826, a medicinal spring was discovered by a local shepherd and the properties were recognised as having a curative effect for kidney and bladder complaints, the small town experienced a veritable boom. It has been officially recognised as a spa town since 1926. However, the town was an important place long before that.

Founded by the Franks in the 8th century, in 1525 the Teutonic Order of Knighthood moved its headquarters to Mergentheim. Successive Grand Masters, invariably kings or dukes, were responsible for the order's imposing **Castle** which was built between the 13th and 17th centuries. It now houses a fascinating folklore museum. Adjacent is the 18th-century Baroque church designed by Balthasar Neumann, with its famous spiral staircase.

While still an unknown musician the young Ludwig van Beethoven performed here on the square in front of the castle, from where Burgstrasse leads to the **Marketplace** which is surrounded by an impressive collection of half-timbered buildings. The **Milching Fountain** in front of the 16th-century town hall sports a statue of Wilhelm Schutzbar, otherwise known as Milching, the knight responsible for bringing the order's headquarters to Mergentheim. Tombs of the order's members are contained within **St John's** and **St Mary's** churches.

Preceding pages: Neuschwanstein Castle in winter; keeping in step. Below, the castle square in Tauberbishofsheim.

A master of painting: Eleven km (7 miles) to the south-west, the village of **Stuppach** owes its fame to a painting of the Virgin and Child that the priest Balthasar Blumhofer acquired from the estate of the Order of Knighthood in 1812. At first it was thought to have been painted by Rubens and only in 1908 was it identified as the work of Matthias Grünewald. The picture (1519) is remarkable not only for its complex symbolism but also for the transparency and luminous power achieved by the casein colours.

Pioneers of architecture: Further up the valley beyond Markelsheim (excellent white wine) is **Weikersheim**. With an elegant curve the erstwhile servant's houses mark the western extremity of the village square and at the same time the entrance to the **Palace** of the counts of Hohenlohe. The major part of the building was constructed between the 16th and 18th centuries. In 1598, the architect in charge experimented with a suspended coffered ceiling which he hung on chains from the rafters, thereby

spanning the magnificent **Knights' Hall**, thus occupying a space of 35 by 12 metres (115 by 39 ft).

However, the greatest luxury of all were the toilets, facilities that were lacking even in the later Palace of Versailles. The garden with its elegant orangery at the far end and its fountains, obelisks and statues of antique mythology, expresses the Baroque love for curves, voluptuousness and allegory. Characters from the court of Count Ludwig (1713–14) were models for the dwarf gallery along the moat.

A few miles to the east, **Röttingen** celebrates its wine festival every October. It is called the *Bremserfest* after the local name for young wine.

Wood-carving to perfection: The **Church of Our Lord** in **Creglingen**, our next destination, has attracted pilgrims ever since the 14th century. Legend has it that while out in the fields ploughing a local farmer found some eucharistic bread, which subsequently became the object of great veneration. In 1500 the Count of Hohenlohe had a church built

on the site and in 1505 he commissioned Tilman Riemenschneider to create the altar which was then dedicated to the Virgin Mary. The wood-carving is regarded as one of his greatest achievements. Only a stone's throw away is the amazing **Thimble Museum** containing over one thousand specimens of varying age and origin.

Living past: One of Riemenschneider's last works was the Holy Cross Altar which can be found in the Romanesque church of **St Peter and Paul** in **Detwang**. Beyond this tranquil town the road winds its way out of the Tauber Valley and there on the western fringe of the plateau rise the walls and towers of Germany's medieval jewel **Rothenburg ob der Tauber**. The town, whose name is derived from the "red castle" in the shady Burggarten park, has become the quintessence of the romantic German past, a fact amply demonstrated by the 1.5 million annual daytrippers who throng the streets. It is precisely for this reason that one should leave enough time to spend the night

here, so as to be able to experience the town once the hordes have departed. Time then to relax and enjoy Franconian specialities in one of the excellent restaurants such as the **Baumeisterhaus** (1596), or be entertained by puppets at **Trexlers Figurentheater**.

Like the spokes of a wheel, all roads lead from the town gates to the marketplace and the **Town Hall**. The Gothic and Renaissance building is crowned by a 55-metre (180-ft) tower from the top of which there is a superb view over the historic town and line of the walls that surround it. Its landmarks include in the south the church of St John and in the east St Mark's with its white tower. Under the protection of its castle, Rothenburg was made a free imperial city in 1274 and this special status contributed to the prosperity of the inhabitants. The main items of trade were wine, cattle and wool and soon the settlement had grown so much that new walls needed to be built. They are well preserved and restored and the walk around them takes about 30 minutes.

Left, detail of the Riemen-schneider altar in Creglingen. **Below**, the "Meistertrunk" or "mighty gulp".

You might begin at the **Klingenbastei** (bastion) in the north after visiting the adjacent **Church of St Jacob** (14th–15th centuries). The **Altar of the Blood of Christ** includes a masterful depiction of Christ's Passion (1501–05) also by Tilman Riemenschneider.

Following the wall round to the east and south, stop at the **Spitlabastei** and follow the Spitalgasse to the **Plönlein**, the most-photographed square in Rothenburg. Particularly worth seeing is the **Museum of Crime** adjacent to the church of St John. Alongside the goodly collection of instruments of punishment, the museum also describes the horrors suffered by Rothenburg during the Thirty Years War. To this very day the salvation of the town from General Tilly's troops is recalled by the play *Meistertrunk* ("mighty gulp") depicted on the clock of the former town hall tavern, as well as enacted on stage during certain annual festivals. The general was prepared to grant mercy to the town if any inhabitant could down a jug of wine (3.5 litres) in one go. The ex-mayor Nusch managed to achieve the impossible and the town was duly saved.

The wit, slyness, but also the ignorance of the local farmers are the central theme of the famous *Hans Sachs Plays* which, like the traditional *Shepherds' Dances*, form part of the summer festival in September.

Back on the Romantic Road (B 25), the market square at **Feuchtwangen** is dominated by its **Collegiate Church** whose altar (1484) is the work of Michael Wolgemut, the teacher of Albrecht Dürer. Further back is the Romanesque **Church of St John** and the so-called **Kasten** (16th century) where the tithes used to be collected. The half-timbered house of the **Café am Kreuzgang** (cloister café) gives access to another of Feuchtwangen's treasures, the Romanesque **Cloister** which, from June to late August, is the stage for the **Kreuzgangspiele** featuring top-grade theatrical performances.

Twelve km (7 miles) to the south of Feuchtwangen, lies **Dinkelsbühl**, a town whose architecture and planning indi-

Rothenburg is a popular tourist destination.

cate a close relationship between the rulers and the peasant culture. The houses here are less stately and the streets are narrower. Even within the town walls a good deal of space is given over to individual vegetable gardens and orchards. Beyond the remains of the old moat there are fish ponds and fields. Dinkelsbühl gets its name from the *Dinkel* (a species of wheat called spelt) which used to be extensively cultivated in the Tauber Valley.

The town can only be entered through one of its four main gates. Strolling through the quaint streets lined with steep-gabled half-timbered buildings the steeple of the parish **Church of St George** points the way to the town centre. The **Marketplace** has always been the place where the merchants and farmers came to trade, leaving their carts and waggons in the Weinmarkt (wine market) and delivering their goods to the **Schranne**. Opposite the church stands the 15th-century **Deutsche Haus** (German house) with its exquisite timber framing.

Every year in July the festival of the *Kinderzeche* begins with the re-enactment of a council meeting that was held during the Thirty Years War. In 1632 the Swedish army stood before the gates of the town and the situation appeared to be hopeless. At least until the watchman's daughter Lore mustered all the other children of the city. Together they bravely marched out of the gates to beg the Swedish colonel Sperreuth to spare the town. Their pleas were heard and the town was saved. Ever since then, a band of children in historical costumes has paraded from the Schranne to the old town hall to confront the "Swedes". The climax is the appearance of the little colonel, a boy in red and white rococo uniform who announces the salvation of the town. His uniform conforms to that of the **Dinkelsbühl Boys' Band**, whose 80 drummers and trumpeters became the symbol of the town.

A crater for astronauts: 15 million years ago a meteorite with a diameter of 1,200 metres (4,000 ft) and a speed of 60,000 mph crashed to earth forming a crater some 26 km (16 miles) wide, known as the **Ries**. Because the landscape here resembles that of the moon, it was an ideal place for training the astronauts of the 1970 Apollo 14 space mission.

The crater is best viewed from above, from the *Daniel*, the 90 metre (300 ft) high steeple of the late-Gothic **Church of St George** in **Nördlingen**. First recorded as *Nordlinga* in 898, Nordlingen became a free imperial town in 1215 and then flourished as a trading centre, its Whitsun fair drawing tradesmen from all over Europe. The 3.5 kilometre (2 mile) long town wall was constructed between the 14th and 17th centuries. With its 11 towers and five gates it remains perfectly intact. Walking along it the visitor will discover the old tanning houses complete with the balconies on which the hides were aired, almshouses and elegant Renaissance town houses. A Renaissance flight of steps leads up to the town hall.

Seventeen km (10 miles) to the east the mighty **Harburg Castle** (12th–18th century) stands sentinel above the Wörnitz Valley. For hundreds of years, Germany's largest castle guarded the important trade route between Augsburg and Nuremberg. Shortly before its confluence with the Danube, there is an island in the River Wörnitz which is called Werth. In medieval times the erstwhile fishing village at the foot of the Swabian Highlands developed into the important free imperial town of **Donauwörth** (Donau = Danube). Most of its historical monuments, some of them completely rebuilt after the disastrous bombing of World War II, are to be found along the main **Reichsstrasse**, a section of the old "Imperial Road" which once linked Nuremberg to Italy. Between the Fuggerhaus (1536) in the west and the Town Hall in the east is the parish **Church of Our Lady** which contains the largest bell in Swabia, the *Pummerin* weighing 6.5 tons.

Balloons and other flying machines: Just outside Augsburg, the little town of **Gersthofen** is a centre of ballooning, and has been so ever since the intrepid Baron von Lütgendorf first succeeded in taking to the air in 1786. The **Balloon Museum** in the old municipal water

Sword dance in the town of Dinkelsbühl.

tower documents the long history of man's non-motorised attempts to conquer the skies.

The so-called "tailor of Ulm" Albrecht Berblinger also attempted to defy gravity by becoming the first hang-glider pilot in history to fly over the Danube, back in 1811. Unfortunately he stalled and plummeted into the river. The master builders of **Ulm** were also great pioneers. With a height of 161 metres (528 ft) the 16th-century spire of **Ulm Cathedral** is the tallest church spire in the world. The spire, the cathedral's magnificent interior and Ulm's picturesque old city, are well-worth the detour along the A 8 motorway.

Imperial centre: Few cities of comparable size can have so many historical monuments as **Augsburg** (population 250,000). The city, at the confluence of the Lech and the Wertach, can look back on an eventful 2,000-year history. From the Roman encampment established here in 15 BC there developed a thriving trading centre and bishopric, strategically located at the junction of important trade routes between Italy and the centres of power of the Frankish-Carolingian realm. By 1500 Augsburg was the largest city in Germany and the local noble Fugger family became one of the richest in Europe. So rich that the Emperors Maximilian I and Charles V came to them for credit, thereby mortgaging their trading and mining rights.

However, the rich banking and merchant family also had a social conscience; the Fuggers were responsible for the unique welfare housing scheme in the craftsmen's quarter, the **Fuggerei** established in 1516. One Rhenish Florin was all it cost to live here, and in accordance with the founder Jakob Fugger's wishes, that is what it still costs today - one DM a year is all that poor elderly Catholic citizens have to pay for a small flat here.

The Fuggerei is only a 10-minute walk from the imposing Renaissance **Town Hall** (1615–20) and the adjacent 78 metre (257 ft) high **Perlachturm** tower, both the work of the city architect Elias Holl. Crowned by its two onion domes, the town hall was built as an unmistakeable symbol of the city's wealth. The **Goldener Saal** (Golden Hall) was restored to its original splendour for the celebrations of the city's 2,000 years of existence in 1985.

The fountains in **Maximilianstrasse** are also testimony to Augsburg's former prosperity. Passing the church of St Moritz, we come to the building which was once the financial centre of the world, the 16th-century **Fuggerhaus**. Opposite the Hercules fountain the **Schaezlerpalais** is probably the most extravagant of all Augsburg merchant residences, and there could not be a more suitable building for housing the **German Baroque Gallery**.

The city's landmark is **St Ulrich's Minster**, which contains the tomb of Bishop Ulrich of Augsburg, whose army was responsible for the final defeat of the Hungarians at the Battle of Lechfeld in AD 995. From here it is worth walking to the old fortifications around the **Rote Tor** (red gate) where an open-air stage is erected in the summer. Return to the city centre by following the city canals past the old tanners' houses and blacksmiths', with perhaps a short detour to the **Handicrafts Museum** or **Roman Museum**.

The oldest part of Augsburg is around the Romanesque-Gothic **Cathedral**, which contains an amazing collection of art treasures including the 11th-century bronze south doors depicting biblical scenes. In the nave the oldest framed glass windows in the world feature the five prophets of the Old Testament. A plaque on the **Roman Wall** south of the cathedral recalls the meetings held between Luther's followers and representatives of the emperor which culminated in the Imperial Diet of 1555, where the right of the citizens to choose their own faith was finally established. Luther's battle had been won, but the nation was plunged into conflict.

Wonderful artistic creations are found throughout Augsburg. Once all the churches have been exhausted, including the chapel of St Ann housing the Fugger family tomb, many more treasures remain to be seen in the **Maximilianmuseum** on Philippine-

THE FAIRY TALE KING

"He is unfortunately so handsome and sophisticated, so soulful and so sincere that I am afraid his life will just fade away like some divine dream", wrote Richard Wagner after his first meeting with the young Bavarian king Ludwig II., who was just 18 years old when he came to the throne in 1864. The king greatly admired Wagner and one of his first official acts was to summon the great composer to Munich and to settle his debts.

Ludwig was appreciative of the fine arts, and he especially loved music and the theatre. Tall, handsome and someone who obviously commanded respect, he was in his youth the very picture of a fairy-tale prince. However, although his subjects adored him, he had little idea of how to respond to their affections. He could not bear to be looked at and soon he would not even receive anyone in audience.

For the first year after his coronation he eagerly involved himself with the task of ruling his kingdom. But it was a job to which he was neither suited nor equipped and as time went on he withdrew deeper and deeper into the solitude of the Bavarian forests and mountains. He preferred to leave the affairs of state to his ministers, to have them rule in his name.

Revolted by the real world, disappointed by people and tormented by a homophile disposition that he could not suppress, Ludwig fled into a world of dreams and aesthetic illusion. He had castles resembling opera stages built just for himself, where the noble company that he kept was but a figment of his imagination.

Ludwig was convinced that he was the successor and equal to the Sun King, Louis XIV of France: he built Herrenchiemsee Castle as a replica of Versailles. Neuschwanstein Castle was his romanticised vision of the medieval world. His castles had no function, they were totally unsuited for living in, and were not designed to cater for nobles and matters of government. They were just petrified realisations of his dreams.

Nowadays a stream of millions of tourists annually come to Ludwig's castles, to wander through the state rooms and suites and marvel at the work of this lonely and unhappy king who hid himself away from the world.

Ludwig and his creations were the last great monument to the myth of royalty as embodied in age-old legends and fairytales, at a time when the decline of monarchy had long set in. By Ludwig's day Bavaria already had a parliament and the business of government lay in the hands of professional party politicians. The industrial revolution was rapidly changing the face of the country and society and the degree of sovereignty that Ludwig had was further reduced by the founding of the German Reich in 1871.

Only a political genius could have prevented the disintegration of royal power, and for the idealist and aesthete Ludwig there was only one way to continue living out his fantasies and to secure for himself some kind of immortality: he plunged deeper and deeper into his own insane world. Ludwig indeed became a legendary figure and he continues to be revered by Bavarians, many of whom won't have a bad thing said about him. Another memorial to the king was recently unveiled in a Munich park.

Initially, Ludwig's castle mania was harmless enough because he funded it from his own pocket. And Bismarck, who corresponded with Ludwig right up to his death, contributed millions of Deutschmarks towards his projects. The Bavarian ministers only became concerned when he went over his budget and threatened to dismiss them if they didn't come up with the necessary funds. In 1885 one of the construction companies sued the king for 100,000 Marks. Ludwig's castles were threatened with confiscation by the state.

In June 1886 the government had the king declared insane by four psychiatrists who had never even seen him. Ludwig was deposed and forcibly brought to Berg Castle on Lake Starnberg. And there, on the evening of 13 June 1886 he and his physician were found drowned in the lake. The exact circumstances of the tragedy have never been clarified. The official version, that the king committed suicide and dragged his doctor down with him, has been the subject of repeated dispute. Many maintain that he was murdered.

Welser Strasse. Then there is the birthplace of the famous German playwright Berthold Brecht (Auf dem Rain 7) and the house of the family of Leopold Mozart (Frauentorstrasse 30). Both are now museums. Out by the MAN truck and bus factory another museum is dedicated to Rudolf Diesel and his epoch-making invention.

Rococo treasure chest: The Romantic Road continues to the south of Augsburg along the B 17 and the River Lech towards the alpine foothills. In **Klosterlechfeld** the pilgrimage church recalls the above-mentioned Battle of Lechfeld. The small town of **Landsberg** has a historic centre which has been wonderfully restored in recent years. Founded by Henry the Lion, it derives its name from the old castle of the Bavarian kings and dukes, the *Landespurch,* which guarded the border between Bavaria and Swabia. Possessing the only bridge between Augsburg and Schongau, the town was strategically located to derive a great deal of wealth from the salt coming from Reichenhall. The town is smothered in rococo architecture, including the Town Hall which was the work of Dominikus Zimmermann, mayor of the town from 1749 to 1754. He also worked on the Church of the Dominicans and the Church of St John and summoned other Rococo masters to the town.

After his failed Munich *putsch,* Hitler was imprisoned in the forbidding **Landsberg Fortress** from 1923 to 1924. This is where he penned his *Mein Kampf* (My Struggle).

The countryside gets more hilly as we approach the Allgäu Alps. There is a splendid view of the mountains from the top of the 988-metre (3,260-ft) **Hohenpeisenberg** near Schongau. The villages are usually dominated by rich churches, such as that in **Rottenbuch**, where, from 1737-47, painters, sculptors and stucco artists from the Wessobrunn School devoted their manifold skills to transforming the Gothic basilica into a flamboyant model of Baroque and rococo Catholicism.

Even more remarkable is the

Romanesque simplicity (left) and Baroque extravagance.

Wieskirche (church in the meadow) which stands alone amidst the rolling hills. Dominikus Zimmermann and his brother Johann Baptist needed just nine years to build this Baroque jewel from scratch (1745–54). It was built as a pilgrimage church to house the statue of Christ that a local farmer's wife had discovered with tears in its eyes while sorting out her old junk. Hundreds of pilgrims came to the tiny chapel she erected on the meadow and this prompted the Abbot of Steingaden to commission the church. Johann B. Zimmermann was responsible for the ceiling fresco which gives the illusion of a high vaulted ceiling but which in reality is almost flat. The **Steingaden Monastery**, in which Dominikus Zimmermann lies buried, is very plain when compared to the magnificent church in the meadow, a true masterpiece of south German Baroque.

Even though there is some debate as to their artistic value, no one can deny that there can be no more dramatic climax to the Romantic Road than the castles of **Hohenschwangau** and **Neuschwanstein**. Hohenschwangau dates back to a medieval castle which crown prince Maximilian had rebuilt in neo-Gothic style in 1833. It was here that King Ludwig II spent his youth and acquired the romantic fantasy that he later converted into stone in Neuschwanstein Castle. An "eagle's nest" high above the Pöllat Gorge was the spot Ludwig chose for the realisation of his dreams. In the **Sängersaal** (bard's hall), the focal point of the Neuschwanstein, he had scenes from Richard Wagner's opera Tannhäuser depicted, while other rooms were designed to look like the interiors of exotic palaces. Even after 17 years of construction, Neuschwanstein was still not completed when the king died in 1886.

From both castles there are fine views over **Forggensee Lake**, the Allgäu Alps and the town of **Füssen** dominated by a 16th-century castle, once the summer residence of the bishops of Augsburg. Today Füssen is the most popular summer and winter resort in the Allgäu.

A bird's eye view of Nördlingen.

THE GERMAN ALPINE ROAD

Wending its way through the Alps from Lindau on Lake Constance in the west to Königsee near Berchtesgaden in the east, the German Alpine Road is the oldest tourist route in Germany. In most road atlases, the serpentine course of the route is marked by additional colouring.

Our description starts just after **Füssen**, from where the route crosses into Austrian territory and follows the Ammer Mountains for some 30 km (18 miles) before passing the German border again on its way to Oberammergau. In the solitude of the Graswang Valley, the fairy-tale king Ludwig II had yet another of his dreams come true. **Castle Linderhof** was built between 1870-79 according to the plans of Georg Dollman. The building contains powerful Baroque and rococo elements: its 10 relatively small rooms are richly adorned with almost stifling pomp.

The two most interesting rooms are probably the bedroom and the dining hall. In the latter, the table was designed as a "Magic Table" straight out of *Grimms Fairy Tales*, which would appear from a trap door in the floor. Then there are the artificial caves out in the park, as well as the Moorish pavilion and the "Hundinghaus", a kind of hunting lodge that the Wagner admirer Ludwig had modelled on the stage set of the opera *Valkyrie*.

Following the Graswang Valley, it is only another 10 km (6 miles) to **Oberammergau**, a town made world-famous by its Passion Plays. After an epidemic of the Plague in 1633, to which every tenth inhabitant succumbed, the survivors vowed to perform Christ's Passion every 10 years thereafter as thanksgiving for their deliverance. The first performance was staged in 1634 and the next one is due in the year 2000. The auditorium of the Passion Play theatre has a seating capacity of 4,800 and looks onto the world's largest open-air stage (45 metres/148 ft across, 30 metres/98 ft deep).

Oberammergau is also famous for the fine frescoes on the facades of its typical Upper Bavarian houses, which is not surprising when one considers that Franz Zwinck, the "inventor" of this technique of *Luftlmalerei* influenced by fresco techniques used in Italy, lived and worked in the town in the 18th century.

In the shadow of the steep slopes of the 1,633 metre (5,358 ft) Ettaler Mandl lies the Baroque Benedictine abbey **Ettal Monastery**. The massive fresco under the dome depicts no less than 431 figures on a total painted area of 1,300 sq metres (13,993 sq ft). Ettal liqueur, distilled on the premises and available for sale, is said to have curative properties.

A steep mountain road leads down to **Garmisch-Partenkirchen**, nestled beneath the mighty ramparts of the **Wetterstein Range**. It was on the occasion of the Olympic Games in 1936 that the then separate communities of Garmisch and Partenkirchen were fused. In the district of Garmisch the central **Marienplatz** is surrounded by a number of especially attractive buildings, in-

Preceding pages: the Alps from the summit of the Zugspitze. Left, Linderhof, another fairytale castle. Below, a Bavarian beauty.

cluding the **Old Apothecary** with its black and white scratchwork facade.

The summit of Germany's highest mountain, the **Zugspitze** (2,966 metres/ 9,731 ft) is the eastern-most peak of the Wetterstein Range and can be reached either by taking the rack railway from Partenkirchen, or the faster cable car from nearby Eibsee. When the weather is clear, the visitor is greeted by a spellbinding panorama arching all the way across the mountains of Austria past the Grossglockner and to the ridgeline of the Bohemian Forest far away to the east. The high corrie of the **Zugspitzplatt** to the south-west of the Schneefernhaus (Germany's highest hotel) is the highest skiing area in the country, with snow guaranteed for most of the year.

For hikers, the approaches to the Zugspitze ascent are guarded by the **Partnachklamm**, a deep mountain gorge where the track leads under overhangs with waterfalls cascading down. During the winter months, when the water has turned to ice, torch-lit walks are organised through this unique creation of nature.

The two **Olympic Stadiums** – the ice-skating and skiing stadiums – are located in Partenkirchen. Off the beaten track, a flight of steps on the western slopes of the **Wank** mountain leads to the late-Baroque votive **Chapel of St Anton** (18th-century). The dome fresco by the South Tyrolean painter Johannes Holzer is a true masterpiece.

A detour to Mittenwald: Mittenwald lies in the valley that separates the Wetterstein Range from the towering summits of the Karwendel Range in the east. Despite the fact that it lies just off the main through road from Austria, the village character of this small town has been largely preserved.

Mittenwald developed into a worldfamous centre of violin-making after Matthias Klotz, who had learned this difficult art in Italy with the Grand Master Stradivari, returned to his home village. Six violin makers continue to produce the instruments today, and visitors can learn more about this rare skill at the **Violin-Making Museum** at Ballenhausgasse 3. Mittenwald's outstanding landmark is the Baroque tower of the **Church of St Peter and Paul**, one of the finest church towers in Upper Bavaria.

The detour to Mittenwald can be continued by skirting via Wallgau around to the north of the Karwendel Mountains to **Walchensee**, which, at 802 metres (2,631 ft), is Germany's highest mountain lake. To the immediate west of the lake, a chair lift leads up to the 1,731 metre (5,679 ft) high **Herzogstand**, which provides another stunning view of the Alps. To the north, the road leads down in a series of hairpin bends to Kochelsee. The main claim to fame of the village of **Kochel** is the **Franz Marc Museum** containing mementos of this most important exponent of German Expressionist painting. Another 5 km (3 miles) along the B 11, is the impressive Benedictine monastery complex of **Benediktbeuren**, which is overshadowed by the 1,801 metre (5,909 ft) high Benediktenwand, and provides a popular excursion for hikers.

If you decide you wish to remain in

Another Bavarian beauty.

the Bavarian Alps proper, then the Alpine route follows the toll road which branches off to the right just after Wallgau and penetrates the **Karwendel National Park**, following the **River Isar**. The road runs for 15 km (9 miles) to **Vorderriss**. From here, hikers can turn south to the village of **Hinterriss** and the Eng Valley which provides direct access to the impressive northern limestone walls of the Karwendel, a paradise for trekkers and climbers alike.

Continuing in an easterly direction, the route passes the **Sylvensteinsee**, where the river has been dammed, and continues to the **Achen Pass** (944 metres/3,097 ft) before dropping down to the town of **Kreuth**, which has developed into a centre for winter sports. A short distance further on you can take the cable car to the summit of the **Wallberg** (1,722 metres/5,650 ft). In the summer this is a favourite launching pad for hang-gliders and in the winter alpine skiers make their descent.

In the midst of a picture postcard landscape of gently sloping meadows lies **Lake Tegernsee**. First to arrive here were the monks; then came the Wittelsbachs, the Bavarian royal family, followed by a host of famous artists. After the war, Tegernsee became a haven for politicians and super-rich businessmen and their families all of whom secured their expensive plot of land down by the lake shore. Practically all the shore is in private hands. At the southern end of the lake is the twin community of **Rottach-Eggern**. The writer Ludwig Thoma, the poet Ludwig Ganghofer and the celebrated tenor Leo Slezak lie buried in the graveyard of the **Church of St Laurence**.

Worth seeing in the picturesque town of **Tegernsee** is the **Monastery Church of St Quirin**, whose Baroque doorway gives access to a triple-naved basilica with a ceiling fresco by Johann Georg Asam. Beautiful examples of Upper Bavarian domestic architecture can be found off the busy main road. Those who like raucous merriment can pop into the "Herzoglich Braustuberl" to sample the beer.

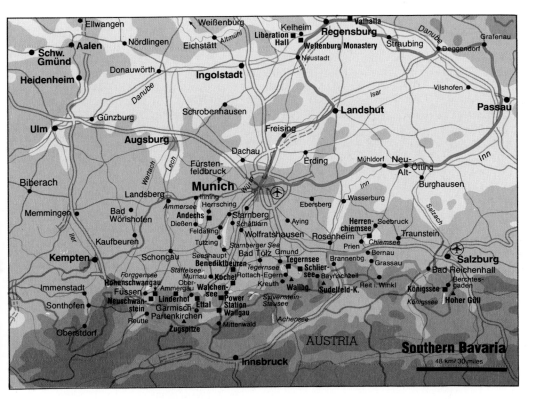

Less hectic in the summer is nearby **Lake Schliersee** to the east. The village of the same name remains an oasis centred around the **Parish Church of St Sixtus**, whose stucco and frescos are the early works of Johann Baptist Zimmermann. The route continues through hilly pastureland past the unmistakeable **Wendelstein** (1,838 metres/6,030 ft), to **Bayerischzell** and on through the dark gorge of the Tatzelwurm (toll road), where one is inclined to believe the medieval legend about a dragon barring the way.

Beyond **Brannenburg-Degerndorf** the route crosses the motorway on the German side of the Austrian border and winds its way via Bernau and Grassau to **Reit im Winkl**, the famous ski resort which is also a good setting-off point for hiking excursions in the summer time. Then on past idyllic villages such as **Inzell**, inviting country inns with beer gardens shaded by chestnut trees to the spa town of **Bad Reichenhall**. While the periphery is not particularly attractive, the fine houses around the spa garden are testimony to the prosperity of the town at the turn of the century and visitors with respiratory problems continue to come here literally to inhale the brine: in the **Gradierhaus** 400,000 litres of saline water daily drop onto the brushwood grating where evaporation increases the salt content in the air.

The last section of the German Alpine Road is without doubt one of the most beautiful stretches in the entire Alps. As the road climbs to the south, new views of the spectacular mountain world of the **Berchtesgadener Land** lurk behind every bend, with the **Watzmann** (2,713 metres/8,901 ft), one of Germany's highest mountains, dominating the scene. The basis of the wealth of the present mountain spa of **Berchtesgaden** was established by Emperor Frederick Barbarossa when he granted the local Augustinian monks the prospecting rights for salt and ore.

The salt mine is still in operation and a visit is highly recommended. Dressed as a miner, you will travel on the "Hunte" about 500 metres (1,650 ft) into the depths of the mine. Sights within the town itself are the high-Gothic collegiate **Church of St Peter and John** and the **Castle**, a former abbey, with Romanesque, Gothic and Renaissance architectural elements. This was the home of the popular Bavarian Crown Prince Rupert until 1938.

To the east of the town, well out of harm's way on the **Obersalzberg**, Hitler erected his "Eagle's Nest", his official hideaway in the mountains. The high point of the trip is the scenic **Rossfeld High Road** which snakes its way up the mountainside and provides wonderful views, to the south-west the sheer east face of the Watzman dropping almost 2,000 metres (6,500 ft) into the dark waters of the **Königsee**.

During the summer it is possible to take a boat trip on this lake, past the picturesque **Chapel of St Bartholomew**. Those with the time and the energy may even consider an ascent of the Watzmann itself, or a trek up to the **Steinerne Meer** (the sea of rocks), a high plateau to the south of the lake which divides Germany from Austria.

Left, Saint Bartholomew's chapel on Königsee. **Right**, Bavarian tradition: both horses and riders receive the blessing.

MUNICH: CAPITAL OF BAVARIA

With a population of 1.3 million, the Bavarian capital ranks as Germany's third largest city after Berlin and Hamburg. Lying on the banks of the Isar River, with the majestic Alps and several scenic Bavarian lakes just a short drive away, Munich offers a wealth of recreational activities in addition to its wide palette of cultural attractions. The city draws visitors from all over Germany and indeed from around the world.

The large number of museums and art collections as well as the variety of music and theatre events make Munich a cultural metropolis of international rank. Here, too, Germany's largest university with almost 100,000 students is located. More publishers have their headquarters in Munich than in any other German city. In recent decades, the city has developed into a centre for high tech, with a number of well-known international companies having their headquarters here.

Despite copious amounts of international seasoning, Munich has managed to retain an almost provincial flavour. The true natives, having found a way to ignore all the hustle and bustle around them, retain a serenity and lust for life which is unmatched. They take pride in their Bavarian customs and traditions thus ensuring their continuation in this otherwise cosmopolitan city.

A settlement for monks: A monastery named *Munichen* (meaning "monks" in High German) is known to have existed here from the 8th century. In 1158, Duke Henry the Lion had the bridge over the Isar which belonged to the Bishop of Freising (north of Munich) removed and had another built at Munich, so diverting the salt trade route between Bad Reichenhall and Augsburg and enabling Munich to prosper from the taxes levied on this valuable commodity. Emperor Friedrich Barbarossa legalised Henry's action by awarding the rapidly growing settlement the right to hold markets and to mint coins. The foundations were thus laid for the politi-cal and economic development of the city. In 1180 the Palatinate Duke Otto von Wittelsbach was awarded the imperial state of Bavaria and it was his house that guided the fate of Bavaria for almost 750 years, until 1918.

Duke Wilhelm IV (1493–1550) chose Munich as his residence and the capital of Bavaria. The growth of the city now began to accelerate, particularly under Maximilian the Great (1573–1651) who was appointed Elector in 1623. However, the city did not escape the ravages of the Thirty Years' War (1618–48), during which it was sacked and occupied by the Swedes. After the war, the erection of the Column of St Mary in front of the Town Hall marked the beginning of a new building boom and under the Elector Max II Emanuel (1679–1726) Munich attained the rank of a European city.

In the following century, the city once more became involved in the tumults of war and occupation. Famine and poverty struck. At the beginning of the 19th century the French occupied Munich

Preceding pages: the English Gardens, an oasis of green in the heart of Munich. Below, the Glockenspiel in Munich's town hall.

for one year, and then the Austrians followed. After the alliance with Napoleon in 1806, which made Bavaria a kingdom, the city entered a new period of prosperity. Napoleon dissolved the monasteries and had their estates nationalised. Through the administrative reforms that he introduced Bavaria and Munich entered a new age of political, economic and cultural prosperity. In 1819 the first Bavarian parliament assembled in Munich. King Ludwig I (1825–48) is considered to be the second founder of Munich, having had a great influence on shaping the present face of the city.

Capital of The Movement: After the death of the fairy-tale King Ludwig II Munich developed into a large modern city under the government of the Prince Regent Luitpold (1886–1912), and by the turn of this century had a population of about half a million. But the hunger, poverty and economic collapse brought about by World War I did not pass Munich by. Under revolutionary "pressure from the streets" Ludwig III, the last king of Bavaria, was forced to abdicate in November 1918. Soon after proclaiming the Socialist Republic of Bavaria, the leader of the revolution Kurt Eisner was assassinated and there ensued bloody street battles which were waged for six months and left some 600 dead. The revolution was crushed and a new, tragic chapter of German history, whose first lines were written in Munich, began.

It was in Munich that the Austrian Adolf Hitler rose from being a simple party member to the chairman of the NSDAP. On 8 November 1923 he believed himself to be in a strong enough position to topple the national government. However, after his rally on 9 November 1923 at the Feldherrnhalle was forcibly dispersed, his attempted coup failed. With the Munich Agreement in 1938 the city continued its key role in the events leading up to World War II. But the war brought catastrophe to the Bavarian capital; 70 bombing raids reduced it to little more than a pile of rubble. Although some buildings sur-

Marienplatz from the Glockenspiel.

vived, a great deal had to be restored or rebuilt.

First orientations: A stone's throw from the **Main Station** is one of the busiest squares in the city, **Karlsplatz**, which is known by the locals as Stacchus. At the end of the 18th century, the square and its imposing gate, the **Karlstor**, were part of the city walls. Only the gate now remains to mark the beginning of Munich's pedestrian precinct leading though to Marienplatz and the town hall. In the summer time the precinct, which is busy at any time of year, really comes to life with musicians, buskers and clowns, all vying for the attentions of shoppers and tourists. There are a number of sights which are worthy of attention, including the **Richard Strauss Fountain**, the **German Hunting Museum** and the **Church of St Michael**, one of the most famous Renaissance churches in Germany where Ludwig II, the doomed Dream King of Bavaria, is buried. Munich's main landmark the **Church of Our Lady** is a late-Gothic edifice built of red brick and conse-

crated in 1494. The discerning eye will notice that one of the two domed towers is slightly lower than the other. The building represents the pride and the prosperity of the city's population in the late-Middle Ages. The crypt contains the tombs of 46 Wittelsbach princes as well as those of a number of cardinals of the Freising, the diocesan centre north of Munich. The south tower affords a wonderful view over the city and the Alps in the south, which look deceptively near when there is *Föhn*, a warm, dry wind from the south which tends to cause headaches and irritability in many people.

Marienplatz marks the centre of Munich. In summer the restaurants put chairs outside and the square is a great place in which to while away an hour or two. Particularly large crowds gather in the late-morning (11 a.m.) to see the world-famous **Glockenspiel** in the tower of the **Town Hall**. The carillon depicts two episodes from Munich's history: a tournament held on Marienplatz in 1568 and the *Schäfflertanz* (dance of the coop-

Left, resting weary legs at the statue of Juliette. **Right, vegetables galore at the Viktualien-markt.**

ers) commemorating the end of the plague in Munich in 1517. The town hall itself (built 1807–1908) is an ornately decorated neo-Gothic building. The **Old Town Hall** (1470–74) dominates the east of the square. The building was almost completely destroyed in the war, but its tower has been reconstructed to look like the original. The building now contains the **Munich Toy Museum**.

Behind the old town hall and across the road is the **Church of the Holy Ghost**. It was originally built in the 14th century, but fully restored in baroque style between 1724 and 1730. The church contains the famous **Hammertal Virgin**, a wooden sculpture from the 15th century. Immediately next door is the **Viktualienmarkt**, Munich's very special open-air food market (*Viktualien* =victuals), where it is possible to buy just about everything: radishes and *Weisswurst*, venison, local produce from around Munich and Bavarian beer. Fine wines and international fish, fruit, vegetable and cheese specialities. The at-

mosphere is maintained by the market women with their ready wit and a few local old boys who have long since been accepted as part of the scenery.

On the opposite side of the street a path leads up to the *Alter Peter*, as the **Church of St Peter**, the oldest parish church in Munich is popularly known. Steps lead all the way to the top, providing another view over the city and a bird's eye view of Marienplatz.

The **Rindermarkt** (cattle market) leads to Sendlinger Strasse with the **Asamkirche**, which was mercifully spared the bombing of the war. This famous church was built by the Asam brothers between 1733 and 1746 and its magnificent interior makes it a real jewel of the South German ecclesiastical baroque, where the use of light and rich colours produces a theatrical, almost mystical atmosphere.

The **Munich City Museum** is only a short walk from Sendlinger Strasse. It was built as an arsenal and livery stable in the 15th century and now houses permanent and special exhibitions de-

Beer maiden and beer garden; beer is the "bread of Bavaria".

voted to the history of the city. It also contains a fascinating **Puppet Museum**.

Cultural metropolis: Beyond the Isator, another of the old city gates, cross the bridge over the Isar and arrive at what is probably the most famous museum in Germany, the **Deutsches Museum**, situated on an island between two branches of the river. Opened in 1925, this is the world's largest museum for science and technology. It contains more than 15,000 exhibits of all shapes and sizes, from sailing boats to aeroplanes and from steam engines to micro-chips. Coal and salt mines record the development of the mining industry from the simple pick and shovel to the hi-tech drills of the present day. Days, if not weeks, are required to see everything.

From the museum cross the road and stroll along the right bank of the Isar to the **Maximilianeum** (1857–74), the seat of the Bavarian Parliament, which rises proudly above the river. It stands at the end of **Maximilianstrasse** which was conceived as and remains an elegant avenue, nowadays because of innumer-

able noble shops and cafés, boutiques and private galleries strung along much of its length. Here too is the **Museum of Anthropology** with its ethnological collection and the **Munich Kammerspiele**, one of Germany's most renowned theatres.

Wittelsbach residence: A few steps further and Maximilianstrasse opens out into broad **Max Joseph Platz**, whose northern edge is occupied by the **Residenz** (Royal Palace), which both from a historical and artistic point of view is the most important complex of buildings in the city. The original edifice dates from 1385, and this was continuously added to and enlarged right up to 1835, with masterful Renaissance, baroque and neoclassical elements. The Wittelsbach family, which guided Munich's fortunes for 750 years, resided here until the abdication of the last king of Bavaria in 1918. Since 1920 the Residenz has been open to the public. The Residenz's museum is housed within the **Königsaal** which is on Max Joseph Platz. Next to this building is the Opera House which dominates the eastern side of the square, and behind it are all the other residence buildings including the Old Palace, the All Saints Church, the Ballroom, the Palace Theatre and, perhaps the most exquisite building of all, the **Cuvilliés Theatre**, whose interior is a rococo jewel.

Prior to the building of the Old Palace, the Bavarian dukes' centre of power had been the **Alter Hof** between Max Joseph Platz and Marienplatz. Despite modernisation, the essential character of the inner courtyard has been preserved.

A visit to Schwabing: From Max Joseph Platz, Residenzstrasse leads to **Odeonsplatz** which is dominated by the **Feldherrenhalle**. Built in 1844 by F. von Gärtner, it was designed as an imitation of the Loggia dei Lanzi in Florence. Another building which evinces Italian influence is the 17th-century **Theatiner Church** to the left of the Feldherrenhalle. With its twin towers and imposing 71-metre (236-ft) high dome the ochre-coloured baroque building is an imposing sight. Its interior has

a magnificent high altar and more Wittelsbach tombs. Odeonsplatz marks the beginning of the elegant **Ludwigstrasse**, which leads out to the north of the city centre towards Schwabing. It was conceived by Ludwig I, and the architects F. von Gärtner and Leo von Klenze designed impressive neoclassical buildings to run along both sides, including the **Bavarian State Library**, one of the largest libraries in the world, and the **University** which is situated shortly before the **Siegestor**, the "Victory Gate". Standing exactly one kilometre from the Feldherrenhalle, the latter was erected in 1850 to commemorate the Bavarian soldiers who fell during the Napoleonic wars.

At the Siegestor, Ludwigstrasse gives way to **Leopoldstrasse**, once the bustling heart of the legendary artists' district of Schwabing. But the pulse of both Schwabing and its boulevard no longer beats to quite the same rhythm, although this is still the area to come to for those in search of nightlife, with bars and clubs open until all hours. The street is lined with poplar trees and cafés, pizzerias and discos.

Pleasure gardens: The **English Gardens** lie to the east of Leopoldstrasse. With an area of 364 hectares (900 acres) they form part of the expansive green belt that runs parallel to the River Isar practically all the way through Munich. Although nobody really knows where they end in the north – they just merge with the river meadows – in the south their beginning is defined by Prinzregentenstrasse and the **Haus der Kunst** (Museum of Modern Art). This massive building dating from the Nazi era contains works of 20th-century masters, including Picasso, Matisse, Dali, Klee and Warhol. For those on foot it is most easily reached from Odeonsplatz via the **Hofgarten**. The **Bavarian National Museum** on Prinzregentenstrasse is one of the best-known museums in the city, providing an insight into the history of European art, particularly Bavarian art and culture from the early Middle Ages to the present.

Laid out between 1781 and 1785, the

Two attractions of Munich: its art galleries (left) and its football (below).

English Gardens are more than just a pleasant "English-style" park containing the **Monopterous** (a Greek temple), the **Chinese Tower**, three beer gardens and the **Kleinhesseloher Lake**. There is something for everybody here: vast lawns for playing frisbee and football, the *Eisbach*, a side-channel of the river, for those who dare brave the cold. The whole park is a stage for acrobats, Zen Buddhists, musicians, organ grinders and African drummers. This is where Munich unites with students taking the afternoon off, old ladies taking their poodles for walks and joggers and cyclists dodging out of each other's way on the gravel paths. When the sun shines the park is strewn with hippies, ex-hippies, bronzed gods and goddesses, all lying in one naked mass on the grass.

Non-sunworshippers can continue exploring Munich's art world. The densest concentration of the city's art treasures is to be found to the west of the city centre, in the so-called *Maxvorstadt*. Surrounded by neoclassical buildings, **Königsplatz** is probably the most im-pressive square in Munich. The **Propylaea**, the **Glyptothek** and the **Antikensammlung** are of considerable architectural significance. Commissioned by Ludwig I, they earned Munich the nickname "Athens on the Isar". The Antikensammlung contains collections of world-famous Greek vases, Roman and Etruscan statues and artifacts made of glass and terra cotta, while the Glyptothek is devoted to Greek and Roman sculpture. Behind the Propylaea, which is a neoclassical archway, the **Lenbach Villa** is situated in a beautiful garden; it was built in 1890 for the celebrated Munich painter Franz von Lenbach. A copy of a Tuscan villa with balconies and courtyards, today it houses the **Municipal Art Gallery** with the works of Munich artists from the 15th to the 20th centuries. From Königsplatz it is only a short walk to **Karolinenplatz** with its obelisk erected in 1812 as a memorial to Bavarians killed in Napoleon's Russian campaign. On the left, Barerstrasse leads to the **Alte Pinakothek**, one of the most important art

The "church on the meadow" in the Alpine foothills.

galleries in Europe, exhibiting works of European masters from the 14th-18th century. After its destruction in the war, the adjacent **Neue Pinakothek** was housed in a new complex designed by Alexander von Branca, opened in 1981. About 400 paintings and sculptures provide a survey of European art from the antique period, impressionism, symbolism and art nouveau.

A summer residence: To celebrate the birth of the heir Max Emanuel, Prince Ferdinand Maria of Bavaria presented his wife Henrietta of Savoy with a large estate just outside the gates of Munich in the northwest. **Nymphenburg Palace**, the summer palace of Bavarian princes and kings, was built by the Italian master Agostino Barelli and is regarded as one of the most important late-baroque palace estates in Germany, complete with pavilions, galleries and out-buildings (including the orangery and the livery stables and the famous Nymphenburg porcelain factory). The main building, with its marble hall and the Wittelsbachs' living and reception rooms in the north and south wings should all be visited, as should the **Gallery of Beauties**, commissioned by Ludwig I, and the **Stables Museum** which contains a fine collection of coaches, sleighs and ceremonial vehicles used by royalty. The park was laid out on the French pattern and contains a number of smaller buildings, including the **Badenburg** built in 1721 (containing baroque baths), the **Pagodenburg** (1719), the **Magdalenenklause** (1725) and the **Amalienburg**, completed in 1739 by Franz Cuvilliés the Elder and a masterpiece of European rococo.

Around the ring road to the north is the impressive **Olympic Park**, built for the Olympic Games in 1972 and now Europe's largest sport and recreation centre. The main attractions are the Olympic Stadium (the football team Bayern München's home ground), the Olympic Hall, the Swimming Pool and the 290-metre (960-ft) high TV Tower, whose revolving restaurant offers magnificent views of the Alps, 100 km (60 miles) away to the south. The distin-

guishing feature of the complex is the tent roof which spans the whole site in a series of giant "spider's webs", covering a total surface area of 75,000 sq. metres (18.5 acres). On the other side of the ring road is the equally futuristic looking **BMW Museum** building, a cup-shaped edifice in front of the main BMW office tower.

Beer gardens: Particularly in the summer time, many people in Munich tend to spend their evenings and weekends either cycling north or south along the Isar, driving out to the Bavarian lakes and mountains or simply staying put and savouring the *gemütlichkeit* of the city's beer gardens. Beer gardens are a Bavarian institution and they are to be found in plenty dotted around the city, in the parks and by the side of the Isar: over 100 in all.

There are small beer gardens with seating for only 50 or 60 people, and those which have a capacity of 5,000 or 6,000. Often you have to walk or cycle to get to them, as is the case with the **Chinese Tower** in the English Gardens and **Flaucher Beer Garden** in the south of Munich on the Isar, where the cool waters of the river take the sting out of the heat of the day.

However large or small the beer garden is, you generally have to fetch your own beer, usually served in one-litre *Mass* glasses, and your own food, which varies in quality but is always the same typical Bavarian fare: knuckle of pork (*Schweinehax'n*), grilled chicken (*Händl*), varieties of sausages with sauerkraut and the ubiquitous *Brezen* (pretzels). Alternatively, you can always take your own food along and set up a picnic on the table.

Munich's beer-drinking culture is divided into special seasons, starting with the strong beer festival just after carnival time and winding up with the world-famous *Oktoberfest* on the Theresienwiese, which starts at the end of September and goes on for two raucous weeks.

Bavarian Lakes: To the south of Munich lies a paradise for swimmers and sailors, climbers and hikers and, in the winter time, skiers. One of the most popular destinations is **Lake Starnberg**, some 30 km (24 miles) to the southeast of the city. The main centre is the town of Starnberg itself, from where it is possible to board the steamer for a number of attractive destinations, including Pöcking and **Possenhofen Castle** or **Feldafing**, a beautiful lake shore community with a Pompei-style villa where the Austrian empress Sissy secretly met Ludwig II. The health resort **Tutzing** is well-known for its evangelical academy and the 728-metre (2,400-ft) high **Ilka Heights** provides a splendid view of the lake. The eastern shore is the more peaceful side of the lake. At the village of **Berg** a cross in the lake, marks the spot where Ludwig II drowned in mysterious circumstances in 1886.

To the west of Lake Starnberg, **Ammersee** is somewhat smaller and not so crowded. Again, there are steamers plying up and down the lake and when the weather is clear there are superb views of the Wetterstein Range and the Zugspitze to the south. From **Herrsching** a path leads up to the **Andechs**, one of the most famous of all the Bavarian monasteries whose reputation is very largely based on the outstanding "Andechs" beer brewed by the monks.

Chiemsee, to the south-east of Munich at the base of the beautiful Alpine foothills of the Chiemgau is another popular outing. On the island of **Herrenchiemsee** stands Ludwig II's imitation of the palace of Versailles, completed in 1878. It was intended as the highest expression of princely splendour and regal might of the Bavarian throne. During summer concerts are held in the stately hall of mirrors. The King Ludwig Museum offers a fascinating insight into the king's life and his close association with music and theatre. Also accessible by boat from Prien is the smaller **Fraueninsel**, which is visited because of the Benedictine **Abbey of St Mary**. This convent has been standing since AD 766 and its harmonious combination of Romanesque, Gothic and baroque styles make it a very significant document of central European architectural history.

The magnificent hall of mirrors in Ludwig's palace on Herren-chiemsee.

RELAXATION IN EASTERN BAVARIA

With most visitors tending to head south from Munich to the Alps, the eastern part of Bavaria has remained largely off the beaten track. But it is a region well worth exploring, not only on account of its rich past recalled by such jewels as the towns of Regensburg and Passau, but also for its vast expanses of rolling countryside, including the scenic Bavarian Forest which runs along the eastern border to Czechoslovakia.

Thirty km (19 miles) to the north of Munich, **Freising,** one of the oldest towns in Bavaria, was for centuries one of the most powerful diocesan centres in central Europe. Apart from the diocesan **Museum of Religious Art,** the principal attraction is the **Weihenstephan Brewery.** Founded around 1050, it is considered to be the oldest brewery in the world. It is situated on a hill overlooking the town and visitors can relax in the beer garden.

To the north of Freising, the B 301, the German "hop road", penetrates the heart of the **Holledau,** the largest area of hop cultivation in the world. In mid-September, the strong hop aroma wafts over the town of **Wolznach,** the scene of a large festival where the Hop Queen is crowned. Within a period of three weeks 12 percent of the total world production of hops is harvested in and around the small villages of the Holledau.

Where the past comes alive: Landshut lies 30 km (19 miles) to the northeast of Freising on the River Isar and is well worth visiting on account of its beautifully preserved old town and the bustle of its streets which have retained the same essential character as they had back in 1475. That was the year in which the Archbishop of Salzburg married the princess Hedwig of Poland to the Duke's son George in **St Martin's Minster.** The event is celebrated to this day: the *Landshüter Fürstenhochzeit* (Landshut Royal Wedding) is Germany's most famous historical pageant and is performed every five years.

Landshut is dominated by **Trausnitz Castle** which was founded in 1204. In the 16th century the building was converted into a Renaissance palace and served as the Lower Bavarian seat of the Wittelsbachs. In addition to the shady gardens there is a café terrace from which the visitor can enjoy the view over the city.

From the Isar to the Danube: Neustadt is 45 km (28 miles) along the B 299 from Landshut. From here it is only another 18 km (11 miles) along the Danube to **Kehlheim,** a town at the confluence of the Danube and the Altmühl. The monument perched high above the river is the **Befreiungshalle** (liberation hall) which was built by Ludwig I to commemorate the Wars of Liberation (1813–15). Kehlheim has become a popular place to visit since the **Archaeological Museum** was opened. Here it is possible to see how mammoths were hunted by our forefathers 80,000 years ago. In 1983 the museum received the European Museum of the Year Award.

From Kelheim, stroll along the right

Left, getting away from it all – the Bavarian Forest. **Right,** like father like son.

bank of the Danube through the deepest and narrowest stretch of the river, the **Danube Gap**, and on to the famous **Weltenburg Monastery**. Built during 1715–34, the monastery church is a South German baroque masterpiece of the Asam brothers. Most visitors, however, take the boat (every 30 minutes). The trip along this stretch, where the river cuts through the Jurassic limestone, is one of the highlights of a tour through Eastern Bavaria.

It is worth making a detour through the **Altmühltal**, a picturesque river valley, watched over by the **Prunn Castle** perched on a high cliff 100 metres (330 ft) above the river. However the valley, a popular recreation area, will never be quite the same since the construction of the controversial Main-Danube Canal.

Where history is fun: After a 15-km (9-mile) drive from Kehlheim along the B16, the 2,000-year-old city of **Regensburg** (population 131,000) comes into view. The former Roman legionary camp *castra regina* was founded by the emperor Marcus Aurelius and has been a bishopric ever since the days of the Irish missionary St Boniface (739). After becoming a free imperial city in 1245, Regensburg developed into a medieval metropolis of Germany and a hub of European commerce, trading mainly with Italy. It was the regular seat of the *Reichstag* from 1663 until the disintegration of the old Empire in 1806.

This gem of an ancient German city lies at the northernmost point of the Danube, which is navigable from here all the way down to the Black Sea. The city suffered no damage during World War II and is a veritable treasure trove of Roman and medieval buildings and monuments. Wandering through the old streets, there is something interesting to see whichever way you look; decorations, staircases, courtyards and pubs that are centuries old.

The best view of the town can be had from the **Stone Bridge**, a masterpiece of medieval engineering (12th century) that spans the Danube with 16 arches over a total length of 310 metres (1,017 ft). The river is lined by stately man-

The largest organ in the world is in Passau.

sions above which tower the 105-metre (345-ft) spires of the **Cathedral**, the most impressive Gothic structure in Bavaria (1250–1525). Its treasury contains exquisite reliquaries, crosses, chalices and vestments. The cathedral is also the home of the world-famous boys' choir, the *Domspatzen* (cathedral sparrows).

Near the cathedral is the **Bischofshof** (bishop's palace), the bishop's residence from the 11th century and now a hotel and restaurant. From here it is only a short walk to the arches and tower of the *Porta Praetoria* with its ruins from Roman times. Pass the bishop's palace and turn right at the Niedermünster Church with its fascinating excavations and arrive at the picturesque **Alter Kornmarkt** (old corn market) with the **Herzogshof** (ducal palace), the residence of the Bavarian Dukes from AD 988, whose Ducal Hall has a magnificent ceiling.

Also worth seeing is the **Old Town Hall** with its large Gothic hall in which the *Reichstag* once assembled. The cellars of the **Reichstagsmuseum** contain one of the last examples of a medieval torture chamber. German law in those days demanded that any criminal who did not confess be released once he survived three days of torture, even if he were found guilty by the court. You can sit in the very seat of the doctor who had to decide when to stop the torturing.

Follow Bachgasse to the Benedictine **Monastery of St Emmeran**, which was founded in the 7th century and became a centre of monastic culture. Nearby is the residence of the Princes of Thurn and Taxis who, in 1504, introduced the first postal service in Europe.

Many hotels in Regensburg not only have pleasant-sounding names and well-appointed guest rooms, but also famous local specialities on their menus, including *Wels* (a Danube fish) and *Tafelspitz* (boiled beef) at moderate prices. Near the Stone Bridge, the historic **Würstküche** is said to be the oldest cooked sausage house in Germany.

German hall of fame: Some regard the **Valhalla**, 11 km (7 miles) east of

Bavarian beer tent.

Regensburg, as the quintessential monument of the 19th century or even the most important artistic creation in Bavaria since the Middle Ages. The Valhalla is modelled after the Greek Parthenon and was built in 1830–42 according to the plans of Leo von Klenze. It is the result of a competition ordered by King Ludwig I of Bavaria for a German *Ruhmeshalle* (hall of fame) to be built in honour of famous men and women of the German tongue.

Twenty-five km (16 miles) to the north of Regensburg is **Weiden**, famous for its fine china, ceramics, lead crystal vases, candlestands and ashtrays produced by world-famous companies. Some of them cater mainly to foreign customers, offering "factory sales" and even mail order services.

Those who wish to experience the *Oktoberfest* atmosphere yet are visiting Germany in August, might wish to settle for a day in **Straubing**, 45 km (28 miles) southeast of Regensburg on the B 8 towards Passau. Straubing's **Gäuboden Fair** is Bavaria's second largest *Volksfest* and its seven beer tents and giant amusement park attract almost a million visitors each year.

The Bavarian Forest: North of Straubing, cross the Danube and travel through the fertile district of **Gäuboden**, Bavaria's granary, where wheat, corn, potato and other vegetable fields are separated by lines of poplars and adlers. You then arrive at the natural woodlands of the hilly **Bavarian Forest**, a region with a number of moderately high peaks, including **Lusen** (1,371 metres/4,498 ft), **Dreisessel** (1,378 metres/4,521 ft), **Rachel** (1,452 metres/ 4,764 ft) and **Grosser Arber** (1,457 metres/4,780 ft) with its idyllic lake. The forest extends along the border with Czechoslovakia and in the northeast merges with the Bohemian Forest, thus forming the largest continuous area of forest in central Europe. It is a landscape with a beauty all of its own, depicted in the works of the well-known 19th-century novelist Adalbert Stifter.

This is a great place to come for those wishing to get away from it all and enjoy the wide open spaces. The local economy revolves around forestry and the widespread glass industry – the Bavarian Forest is the leading centre of glass production in Europe. Tourism also makes an important contribution. Traditional resorts offer a wide variety of accommodation and a multitude of recreational activities.

Countless museums illustrate the history and economy of the region: the **Glass Museum** in **Frauenau**, the **Silver Mine** at **Bodenmais** and the **Forest Museum** in **Zwiesel**. The 120-sq. km (46 sq. miles) **Bavarian Forest National Park** around Grafenau is not only a unique sanctuary of primeval flora and fauna, but through its well-maintained 200-km (120-mile) long network of footpaths also provides refuge for those who want to be close to nature.

City of the three rivers: On account of its unique situation at the confluence of the rivers Danube, Inn and Ilz, **Passau** (population 51,000) was ranked by the geographer Alexander von Humboldt as among "the seven most beautifully situated towns in the world". The city itself is situated on the promontory formed at the confluence of the Danube and the Inn. The **Church of St Mary** stands on the opposite bank of the Inn. The **Oberhaus Fortress** towers high above the old city where the town's Italianate churches and houses are huddled together.

The visitor can spend hours here strolling through the old streets and popping in at the elegant delicatessens or the 600-year-old **Apothecary** on Residenzplatz. Here there are the old and new **Bishop's Palaces**, as well as a number of fine houses rebuilt in the 17th century in the local baroque style. At around 11.45 am tickets are sold on nearby **Domplatz** (cathedral square) for the organ concert in the **Cathedral**. The building was founded in the 8th century, expanded in baroque style in 1662, destroyed but then built anew.

Between May and September almost all visitors to Passau assemble here at noon to listen to the music resounding from the 17,300 pipes of the world's largest church organ.

NUCLEAR PROTEST WINS IN WACKERSDORF

Situated in the north-eastern corner of Bavaria between Nuremberg and the forested border to Czechoslovakia, the Oberpfalz (Upper Palatinate) is a peaceful tourists' paradise far from the madding crowd. Here is lots of broad open country dotted with historically interesting cities and attractive health resorts, numerous lakes and ponds. There are country pubs, small hotels and holiday homes. What could be more idyllic? Hiking and swimming, fishing, rowing, riding and tennis, and holidays on ice in the winter. Whatever your tastes, here is a region for the holiday connoisseur.

However, in 1981 this romantic idyll came under threat. The German nuclear industry planned to construct a reprocessing plant just outside the tiny town of Wackersdorf with its 3,800 souls. Bavaria's deceased Minister President Franz Josef Strauss had succeeded in having the mammoth project brought to Bavaria and thereby achieved something nobody could have dreamed of in this politically conservative backwater: teachers, postmen, foresters, farmers, town councillors and neighbours marched through the streets of their home towns with banners declaring: "he who sows this seed will harvest resistance".

Lo and behold: 15 years after the first protests and demonstrations the designs for Wackersdorf were finally abandoned: in the spring of 1989 the energy barons silently waved goodbye to their reprocessor, a project that had previously been declared "indispensible" by a whole generation of politicians and nuclear industrialists.

What had been planned was a giant plant to reprocess spent atomic fuel rods from power stations in a complex process involving their mechanical breakdown and chemical dissolution. This dangerous procedure would isolate uranium and plutonium from the highly radioactive solution and permit them to be used again.

In the end, however, after 2.6 billion DM had been pumped into the planning and building of Wackersdorf, the German operators left the politicians out in the cold and decided to have their fuel rods reprocessed elsewhere, namely in La Hague in France and Sellafield in England – plants that have been reprocessing spent fuel rods for years.

The bitter opposition of the mostly conservative populace of the Upper Palatinate was a major factor in bringing about this "escape from Wackersdorf".

From 1981, when the already hotly-disputed name of Wackersdorf became widely known, there developed a dispute of unbelievable proportions: the regional action committee called massive demonstrations involving tens of thousands of people. In the Taxölderner Forest, which was due to make way for the plant, the protesters erected so-called hut villages. No sooner had these been completed than they were pulled down by the police. The authorities set about fortifying the site: they built a 4,850-metre (5,300-ft) long perimeter fence made of concrete and steel and costing 28 million DM. This became the venue for regular pitched battles between demonstrators and police, which resulted in the deaths of three people. During the huge Whitsuntide demonstration in 1986 almost 1,000 people were injured on both sides.

Politically conservative-minded people, who for so many years invested so much of their energy in fighting the project, now maintain that the struggle has given them a new outlook on life.

Even in the summer of 1988 nobody could possibly have imagined that only a year later other industrial concerns would be casting lots for the prime site that the reprocessing plant had left behind. The region, structurally weak before the nuclear industry came marching in, has now, paradoxically, been given a new lease of life.

Although some forest has been destroyed, the worst has been averted. No longer is there risk to generations of people, and the countryside remains largely intact – the much feared sell-out of the natural environment has not taken place. So what remains? Lots of broad open country dotted with historically interesting cities and attractive health resorts, numerous lakes and ponds. Here are country pubs, small hotels and holiday homes; hiking, swimming, fishing, rowing, riding…

LAKE CONSTANCE

With a surface area of 538 sq. km (208 sq. miles), Lake Constance is the largest lake in Germany, although its waters are shared by Switzerland and Austria. The climate here is so mild that orchards of apples, pears and plums flourish. Long hours of sunshine ensure that the grapes in the vineyards ripen at the same time as those in Mediterranean countries.

The silent lion: A tour of the lake commences in **Lindau,** an island town on German soil connected to the mainland by a road and rail causeway. In 15 BC the Romans established a military base on the island and fishermen subsequently came to settle in the area. In the 13th century, Lindau became a free imperial city, whose economic prosperity was closely linked to the Lindau Messengers. This courier service – at that time a complete novelty – operated all the way between Italy and northern Europe. The climax of the town's importance came in 1496 when the Imperial Diet assembled in the town hall. In 1803, Lindau lost its free imperial city status and in 1806 became integrated with Bavaria, to which it has belonged ever since.

With its broad promenade, the **Seehafen** (harbour) is flanked by a number of hotels and inviting cafés. The harbour entrance is guarded on one side by a 33-metre (108-ft) high lighthouse and on the other by the symbol of Bavaria, a stone lion. The lion has never been able to roar because the sculptor forgot its tongue.

The **Mangturm** tower which is all that remains of the old fortifications stands in the middle of the promenade. From here it isn't far to the **Reichsplatz,** the main square, with its **Lindavia Fountain** and the Gothic **Old Town Hall.** Both the back and the front of the building are richly decorated with frescoes depicting events from the Imperial Diet.

The **Brigand's Tower** (Diebesturm) stands to the northwest of Maximilianstrasse, adjacent to the Romanesque **Church of St Peter.** Within, the frescoes depicting the Passion are attributed to Hans Holbein the Elder. Apart from the Church of St Mary of the Assumption and St Stephen's, another interesting sight on the **Marketplace** is the baroque painting on the facade of the **Haus zum Cavazzan** (No. 6). Today a museum, the art exhibition it contains is one of the largest in the Lake Constance region.

The Austrian side: From Lindau it is only 10 km (6 miles) to **Bregenz,** the capital of the Austrian province of Vorarlberg. The town comes to life during July and August when the Bregenz Opera Festival is performed on the largest floating stage in the world. At the weekends, the inhabitants tend to stroll along the promenade, although better views of the lake itself can be enjoyed from the summit of the **Pfander** mountain (1,064 metres/3,491 ft) which can be reached by cable car.

The Swiss side: The Swiss border lies immediately to the west of Bregenz. The former prosperity of the town of **Rorschach** (corn market and weavery) is reflected in the fine facades of the patrician houses on the Marienberg and lining the high street. A museum of local crafts has been established in the baroque corn exchange.

Fifteen km (9 miles) to the west, **Romanshorn** is the terminal for ferries to **Friedrichshafen** on the German side of the lake. On the way it is well worth making a detour south to **St Gallen.** Founded in AD 612, the Benedictine abbey was one of the first education centres in Christian Europe and contains a magnificent library with documents dating back to the era of the Carolingians and King Otto.

Lakeside university town: Between the Unter- and Ober-See lies **Konstanz** (population 80,000), the largest town on Lake Constance. The Romans erected a camp here and named it after the emperor Constantinus Chlorus. Konstanz became a bishopric in 540. The most important event in the town's history was the Reform Council of 1414–18, during which the only election ever of a Pope on German soil took place. The prince-bishops also sentenced the reformer Johannes Hus to death. He was burned at the stake before the town gates in 1415. The Council met in the **Council Building** in the old town, which was built in 1388 as a corn and wine warehouse. Other buildings worth closer inspection are the Romanesque-Gothic **Minster** and the town hall.

The oldest quarter of the town is **Niederburg**, with its maze of narrow streets extending between the **Rhine Tower** and Münsterplatz. Also worth seeing is the replica of the Holy Sepulchre in the **Mauritius Rotunda**. Historians from all over the world come to the Kunkel Haus to view the fine **Weber Frescos** (late 13th century) which depict the individual stages in the manufacture of silk and linen.

The Rhine Falls: Strongly recommended is the journey along the Rhine to the west of Lake Constance to the **Rhine Falls** near Schaffhausen in Switzerland. The impressive spectacle of the Rhine plunging 21 metres (69 ft) along a length of 150 metres (450 ft) is best enjoyed from below. There is also a boat which goes right up underneath the falls.

Fruits and flowers: To the south-east of Radolfzell, the island of **Reichenau** in the Ober-See is connected to the mainland by a man-made causeway. It is the most important centre of market gardening in Germany, with 15 percent of the 5-km (3-mile) long and 2-km wide island being taken up by huge glasshouses. The **Benedictine Abbey** on Reichenau was a major spiritual centre of western European culture for 300 years (AD 724–1000). Charlemagne's sons were educated here.

On the other side of the Bodenrücken peninsula in Überlinger See lies the famous flower island of **Mainau**. This sub-tropical paradise is in full bloom between March and October and can be reached by ferry from the mainland.

Back to the Stone Age: Opposite Mainau on the northern lakeshore lies **Überlingen**, a picturesque little town with much of its medieval fortifications still intact. The best view over the roof tops may be enjoyed from the tower of the Gothic **Minster of St Nicholas**, the

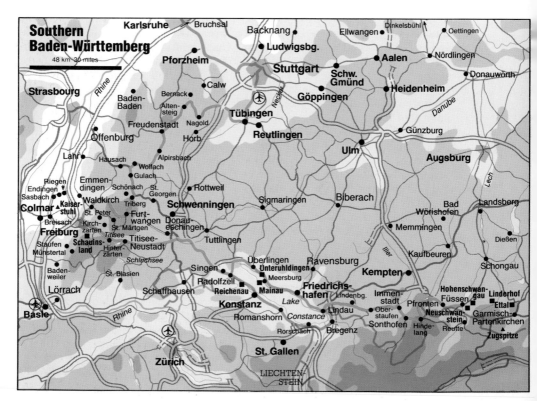

largest church in the Lake Constance region. The town hall contains the splendid **Council Chamber** created by Jacob Russ in 1490 with its wonderful wood-carved frieze of statuettes representing the 41 medieval trades.

Five km (3 miles) from Überlingen on the road to Meersburg, the lake is dominated by the pilgrimage church of **Birnau** with its magnificent rococo decor. Its main attraction is a life-size roguish putto, *The Honey Sucker*. Nearby, at **Unteruhldingen**, is the fascinating reconstruction of a Stone Age village, an open-air museum. Here, man ensured protection from his enemies by constructing his houses on stilts in the lake.

Magic of the Middle Ages: Meersburg is considered to be one of the best preserved medieval towns in Germany. The magic of the place, which was never once destroyed, is best appreciated in the evening after most of the tourists have gone. Time then to admire the half-timbered houses in peace, accompanied by the melody of bubbling fountains and church bells. The historical centre is marked by the **Old Castle**, one of the oldest castles in Germany dating from Merovingian times. In the **New Castle**, the erstwhile summer residence of the prince-bishops of Konstanz, classical concerts are now performed. The imposing staircases, built according to plans of Balthasar Neumann are the showpiece of the building.

The **Fürstenhausen** formerly belonged to Annette von Droste-Hülshoff (1797–1848), one of the most revered poetesses of her time. Her novella "Judenbuche" is still compulsory reading in German schools. Her statue stands before the bridge to the Old Castle.

Friedrichshafen (population 52,000), the second largest town on Lake Constance, rose to fame at the end of the 19th century when shiny silver airships were built here. Their inventor, Graf Ferdinand von Zepellin (1838–1917) came from Konstanz. The museum, located in the north wing of the town hall, has an entire department devoted to Zepellin's achievement.

Count Zeppelin built his airship on Lake Constance.

THE BLACK FOREST

While the Romans described the Black Forest as an impenetrable wilderness inhabited only by wild beasts and barbarians, much has changed since their day and there is now little danger of being set upon by a wild boar. The region has been gradually tamed and developed and made accessible by road, rail and an extended network of walking trails. There is little left of the dense pine forest as it existed in ancient times. For decades the trees have been felled in their tens of thousands and their trunks shipped on huge rafts down the Rhine to Holland.

While isolated farmsteads existed here from the end of the dark ages, major changes began to occur from the 16th century onwards, particularly along the navigable river valleys where the land was cleared and agriculture established. Small industries, notably glass and watch making, came to settle here, and together with forestry and tourism these remain the backbone of the Black Forest economy.

Tourists have been drawn to the Black Forest ever since the 18th century, attracted by the contrast of the Rhine Plain and the mountains rising some 1,200 metres (4,000 ft) above it. In the lowlands the summer days are hot, the evenings warm and one tends to sit outside to enjoy a meal and a glass of good wine. The forested slopes rising above the picture postcard valleys provide extensive possibilities for walking. Heathcocks and pheasant, buzzards and hawks, deer, foxes and hundreds of different species of butterfly populate the more remote areas, where the mountain folk still cling to their traditions, on public holidays wearing their beautifully embroidered costumes.

University town: A journey through the Black Forest can begin in **Freiburg** (population 171,000), the gateway to the south of the region. Who wouldn't envy anyone having the good fortune to study here, a city at the edge of the forest with wonderful Gothic architecture, fine wine and countless pubs and bars where discussions can continue until the early hours of the morning?

The development of Freiburg and its university has always been closely linked to the Catholic Church. Immediately after its founding in 1457 the **University** was famous throughout Europe as a centre of liberal humanism. It then became a Jesuit bastion of the Counter-Reformation and remained true to this strict Catholic tradition right up until the 1920s.

The city centre around **Münsterplatz** is characterised by narrow cobbled streets and the fast-flowing rivulets called *Bächle* which are perfectly clean now but in medieval times acted as sluices for carrying away sewage. It would require a whole book to describe adequately the architectural and artistic refinements of the **Minster**. Only 80 years after the city's founding, in 1120, the populace set about the construction of a parish church which soon grew into one of the most magnificent minsters of medieval Germany. Many regard its 116-metre (380-ft) high steeple as being the finest in Christendom.

Around the minster is one of the most picturesque open-air markets in Germany. On a bright Saturday morning in the summer the minster seems to float like a giant ship in a sea of stalls, vendors, housewives, musicians, tourists, preachers, flowers, bread, vegetables, fruits and grilled sausages.

The visitor can commence his exploration of the old city by walking eastwards from Münsterplatz to the **Swabian Gate**, the old city gate tower, housing a museum of miniature figures. **Gasthaus Bären** (Bear Inn), which claims to be the oldest inn in Germany, is not far away. To the south the **Gewerbebach Canal** was once the main artery of the city's medieval economy and to the west is the Rathausplatz featuring Freiburg's early-Renaissance **Town Hall**. An example of late-Gothic architecture is the **Haus zum Walfisch** on the corner of Franziskanerstrasse. Behind the town hall in Turmstrasse the old **Guild Hall** displays collections of carnival masks and *Häs* (jester's cos-

Left, a hidden creek in the **Black Forest**.

tumes) which lend the *Fasnet* (Alemanic for carnival) an air of wild, untethered ritual.

Up and away: Only five minutes from Münsterplatz, the **Schlossberg** is an area of lush parkland which is ideal for taking a stroll. Alternatively, the visitor can escape the city altogether and take the car or bus to the top of Freiburg's very own mountain, the 1,284-metre (4,210-ft) high **Schauinsland**. On clear days there is a magnificent view from the top, from the Black Forest across the Rhine Plain to the Vosges over to the west in France.

The Baden cuisine is held by many to be the best in Germany, and one should certainly not miss the opportunity to savour it (together with a glass or two of the region's full-bodied wine) in one of the many inns in and around Freiburg. A local speciality are the *Hechtklösschen* (pike balls).

Dallas in Germany: Just a 10-minute drive to the north of Freiburg on the B 3/ B 294 is one of the most beautiful valleys in the Black Forest, the **Glottertal**, an idyll of lush green slopes giving way to forest, which is, however, rather ruined by the endless array of restaurants, hotels and other tourist facilities lining the road. Tranquil by comparison is the **Föhrental**, a side valley of the Glottertal. It is here that the TV serial *Black Forest Hospital* was made, a kind of poor man's *Dallas*, which actually made it onto British television screens.

The road continues to climb until the towers of the **Abbey of St Peter** come into view. It was founded by Benedictine monks in 1093. On All Saints Day and Good Friday there are processions to its opulent baroque church.

St Märgen, dominated by its Augustinian monastery, is 7 km (4 miles) further on, the journey accompanied at every turn by wonderful views of the hills and valleys. The roofs of the typical Black Forest farmhouses almost touch the ground. The area around St Märgen offers a perfect compromise between remote, natural beauty and the needs of modern-day tourism.

From heaven to hell: When venturing east of Freiburg to Lake Titisee, forget your car and take the train. The half-hour journey, along tracks that were laid in 1887, is spectacular. The stretch runs from the station at **Himmelsreich** (realm of heaven) to **Höllental** (valley of hell), climbing about 625 metres (2,050 ft) as it does so, a record for German railways. The journey up the gorge can be broken at the hill resort of **Hinterzarten** where a meal at the Parkhotel Adler is recommended. The restaurant is well-known for its fine cuisine and the fact that Queen Marie Antoinette once dined here.

At weekends the road leading down to **Lake Titisee** is choc-a-bloc with visitors. It is a popular destination, with many shops selling souvenirs such as walking sticks and cuckoo clocks. The walking sticks may come in useful for the ascent of the **Feldberg** (1,493 metres/4,900 ft), the highest mountain in the Black Forest, at the head of the scenic **Bärental**. The pleasant stroll around the lake takes about two hours.

The Tuscany of Germany: The maritime winds blowing through the Rhine Valley result in the mild climate that has made the western part of the Black Forest an important region for the cultivation of fruit. The vineyards among the foothills of the **Markgräflerland**, dropping gently down to the plain to the south of Freiburg, are reminiscent of more southern climes.

The picturesque little town of **Staufen**, 20 km (12 miles) to the south-west of Freiburg, became famous in 1539 when the magician Dr Faustus was murdered in the **Gasthaus Löwen** by one of the higher-ranking devils. The alchemist Faustus, who probably blew himself up while making "gold" for the local baron, was later immortalised by Goethe's famous drama. Today, the "devil" waits in the form of Markgräfler wine and the powerful Black Forest fruit schnapps which can be drunk at any of the inns lining the streets of Staufen's centre.

Situated on a rounded hill, **Badenweiler** has been a health resort ever since AD 100. In the spa gardens are the remains of old Roman Baths, the best preserved example of Roman spa culture north of the Alps. There are also giant Californian Redwooods in the gardens. On account of people convalescing, cars are barred from the town.

The Emperor's seat: Rising from the plain west of Freiburg, the **Kaiserstuhl** (Emperor's seat), is of volcanic origin. This creates a unique micro-climate with temperatures reaching almost tropical levels. Wild orchids, unusual butterflies, lizards and other exotic plants and animals abound. The climate is also perfect for the cultivation of fruit and wine. Despite the fact that the vineyards were reorganised in the 1970s – small wine growing villages such as **Oberbergen** have retained their traditional character. And the wine itself does not seem to have suffered, as you will notice when tasting the full-bodied *Sylvaner* in **Achkarren**, the aromatic *Gewürztraminer* in **Bickensol** and the velvet-red *Late Burgundy* in **Oberrotweil**.

The town of **Breisach** is situated on the Rhine to the southwest of the Kaiserstuhl, perched on basalt cliffs rising above the river. It is dominated by the **Minster** which was built between the 12th and 16th centuries and contains a huge wooden carved altar by the unknown master "H.L.", rated as one of the most beautiful examples of German wood carving. The town is a lively place in summer with art festivals, open-air theatre and, in July, one of the best known wine festivals – the "Hock Festival". Railway fanatics can enjoy the scenery from a wooden carriage of the "Rebenbummler" train to **Riegel**, pulled by a vintage steam engine.

Time machines: Vintage machines of a different kind can be admired in the **Clock Museum** in **Furtwangen**. Clocks of all shapes and sizes are on display. One particularly fine piece is the one with the tailor who, every hour on the hour, has a shoe banged on his head by his wife. In **Schonach** is the largest cuckoo clock in the world. Nearly 7 metres (23 ft) high, the cuckoo itself measures nearly 1 metre from beak to tail. The visitor will come across a great deal of *kitsch* in the countless clock shops lining the streets of Furtwangen, **Schönwald** and **Triberg**, but may also

Black Forest woodcarvings.

be able to pick out a piece of real value.

A relaxing break from shopping is a visit to the **Triberg Falls**, with a height of 103 metres (338 ft), the highest waterfall in Germany. From Triberg or the nearby St Georgen, the Black Forest Railway runs to **Hausach** and provides one of the most scenic railway journeys in the land.

Three km (2 miles) to the south of Hausach the **Vogtsbauernhof Museum** is well worth a visit. It is an open-air museum consisting of houses and farmhouses from the different regions of the Black Forest, complete with old furniture and agricultural implements. It gives a vivid impression of what life used to be like here and also traces the development of agriculture and forestry in the region.

Another must for the Black Forest visitor lies 20 km (12 miles) to the northwest of Hausach in the Kinzig Valley. The former **Benedictine Monastery Church** in **Alpirsbach** is one of the most beautiful Romanesque basilicas in Germany and has hardly been altered since it was built in 1095–99. A pew inside is one of the last remaining examples of Romanesque church furniture in Europe.

Thirty-eight km (24 miles) east of Freudenstadt is **Nagold**, a town beautifully situated in the river valley of the same name. The 1,000-year-old **Church of St Remigius** contains some beautiful frescoes and an unusual statue of the Holy Mary holding the Christ-child in her hand.

"The most beautiful place I know on the Nagold is Calw" wrote the famous writer Hermann Hesse who was born here in 1877. **Calw** still exudes that feeling of youthfulness and vivacity that the author so masterfully captured in his novels. There is a **Hermann Hesse Memorial** in the local museum. In nearby **Hirsau** stand the ruins of a monastery and two churches which once belonged to one of the most powerful abbeys in Europe which controlled more than 100 monasteries in the area.

Athens on the Neckar: If Germany indeed ever was the "land of poets and philosophers", then **Tübingen** can at least partly lay claim to this title for itself. Many brilliant minds lived and studied in Tübingen. There was Johannes Keppler (1571–1630), the first man to calculate the elliptical orbit of the planets, and Wilhelm Schickhardt who, in 1623, invented the world's first mechanical calculator. The philosophers Hegel and Schelling also lived in the "Athens on the Neckar", as did such writers as Hölderlin, Mörike, Uhland and Hauff. All were students at the **Tubingen Foundation**, an evangelical theological seminary established in 1536.

Tübingen is built on two hills overlooking the Neckar and Ammer rivers. Its medieval attractions all survived World War II intact. Particularly worth seeing are the 15th-century Gothic **Collegiate Church**, and behind it the oldest parts of the **University** founded in 1477, where the reformer Philipp Melancthon lectured from 1514–18. Down on the Neckar is the **Hölderlin Tower** where the insane poet Hölderlin lived from 1807 until his death in 1843. From there the Bursagasse leads to the **Town Hall**, a half-timbered building dating from 1435. It stands on the old marketplace, where on market days farmers in rural costume come to sell their products. Above, the **Burgsteige** path climbs to the 16th-century **Hohentübongen Castle** which at 373 metres (1,220 ft) offers a splendid view over the roof tops and down to the Neckar.

City of the "bright star": Capital of the federal state of Baden Württemberg, **Stuttgart** (population 600,000), has the highest per capita income of any city in Germany. Since 1926, the silver Mercedes star, the "shining star of the roads", has shone over Stuttgart's skies.

The city dates back to a stud farm that was founded in AD 950. This developed and came to be known as *Stutkarten*, literally "stud garden". The city lies in a bowl-shaped depression surrounded by wooded hills with orchards and vineyards. There are a number of interesting buildings to see in the centre, including the 16th-century **Old Palace** on Schillerplatz. Opposite, across the

THE DYING FORESTS

When the sorry state of Germany's trees became apparent at the beginning of the 1980s, the appalling vision of the seemingly unstoppable destruction of vast tracts of verdant German woodland became one of the most important issues and topics of public and political debate. Many Germans have an almost mystical bond with their forests. Forests were always more than just a useful source of revenue, more than a playground for recreation and more than simply a life-giving ecological system.

Forest still accounts for some 30 percent of the land area of Germany. Although for over a century the "German Forest" managed to survive the effects of industrialisation, there had to come a time when its capacity to cope with ever-increasing pollution would be exhausted. When the damage started to become visible, the culprits were searched out. They were a complex cocktail of poisonous gases from the chimneys of industry and from the exhaust pipes of millions of cars and trucks that had been plaguing the leaves and the needles for decades. The rain, once the lifeblood of the forest had become its number one enemy; it had been transformed into a deadly shower of acid.

Both the national and state governments initially invested hundreds of millions of Deutschmarks in tracing the precise cause of the destruction of the firs, the pines, the poplars and the beech, and ultimately the most German of all trees, the oak. But the forest didn't respond to all this fuss about its lingering illness – it simply continued to die. By the end of the 1980s, half of all trees in the old Federal Republic were either seriously sick or dead.

And things weren't any better in the territory of the former GDR. Although favourable climactic conditions have brought a certain amount of respite over the past year or so, the damage to the deciduous forest has increased dramatically. There is now nothing much left to save in the higher areas of the Black Forest, the Bavarian Forest, the Harz, the Fichtel or the Erz Mountains.

Large areas have already been transformed into steppe. Reforestation is not considered to be a lasting solution. Any such attempts are doomed to failure because of the increasingly high acid content of the soil.

In the winter and spring of 1990 a series of freak hurricanes swept over central Europe, and in southern Germany in particular the sick trees could no longer resist such high velocity winds. Millions of trees simply snapped like matchsticks. Storm damage on such a massive scale had never before been registered in Germany.

Successes to date in reducing air pollution have been mainly limited to one single component: the burden created by sulphur dioxide has been largely eradicated by the use of filters in the chimneys of coal-fired power stations. However, the emission levels of nitrogen oxide and other polluting agents have not been reduced. Although many private cars are now equipped with catalytic converters, this has little effect on air pollution as a whole because the number of cars on the road is also increasing at an astonishing rate, thus cancelling out any improvement that may have been possible.

The Federal Republic remains the only western industrialised nation with no general speed limit in effect on its dense network of motorways. In full agreement with the car manufacturers, the politicians continue to support "free driving for free citizens". There is as yet no strategy for the salvation of the forests, and it now almost seems as if the general population has begun to accept the dead trees, the brown needles and the bare hillsides as a fact of life.

Of late, government has tended to concentrate more on curing the symptoms of this plague rather than attacking the root causes. For example, in order to counteract the increasing acidity of the soil, chalk is widely used in areas where forest is not yet completely destroyed in order to give afforestation some chance of success. More exotic "solutions" are also becoming increasingly popular – such as the attempt in the former GDR to breed acid-resistant trees. In 1988, in West Germany, the first seed bank for the German forest was established and the seeds of indigenous trees and shrubs await better days in cold storage.

Planie, stands the **New Palace** (1746–1807) which houses the Ministries of Culture and Finance. Behind the palace the state Parliament building is surrounded by the **Academy Gardens**. The **State Theatre**, the domicile of the world-famous **John Cranko Ballet**, stands opposite the palace gardens and the **State Art Gallery,** containing one of southern Germany's leading art collections, now occupies a new building behind the theatre. Situated near the main station, the **Linden Museum** is one of the best museums of anthropology in Germany.

In the district of Untertürkheim automobile fans will find the fascinating **Daimler Benz Museum**. On the right bank of the Neckar, in the district of Bad Cannstatt, Gottfried Daimler demonstrated the world's first petrol-driven car in 1886. This is also where the **Cannstatter Wasen**, the Swabian equivalent of Munich's Oktoberfest, is held every autumn. The massive **Neckar Stadium**, home ground of the very successful "Stuttgarter Kickers" football team, is also located in Bad Cannstatt.

Gold city: Travelling westwards in the direction of Karlsruhe, all those who crave valuable jewellery should make a point of stopping in **Pforzheim** which lies on the northern flanks of the Black Forest at the confluence of the Enz, Nagold and Würm rivers. The reputation of Pforzheim's goldsmiths can be compared with that of the diamond cutters of Amsterdam. Around 80 percent of all German jewellery is manufactured here, most of it hand-crafted in small workshops. The visitor should not miss the unusual **Museum of Jewellery** in the Reuchlinhaus.

Eighteen km (11 miles) to the northwest in **Maulbronn**, the well-known 12th-century **Cistercian Monastery** is the best-preserved medieval building of its kind in Germany.

Karlsruhe: Reliable reports maintain that Margrave Karl Wilhelm of Baden one day decided he'd had enough of his prude wife and had a new palace built where he could live in peace with his nubile female bodyguards. Initially, in

Rooftops in the university town of Tübingen.

200

1715, there was only the palace in the middle of nowhere. But by 1805 **Karlsruhe** (Karl's rest) had become the capital of the Grand Duchy of Baden, the city spreading like a fan around the palace and its gardens.

Most of the city's attractions are found around the palace, which is today the Baden State Museum. There is the **State Majolica Manufactory** which has a fine display of faience and the **State Art Gallery** which contains one of the best displays of European painting in southern Germany. The **Botanical Gardens** and the orangery are also nearby. So too is the **Federal Constitutional Court** which was established as the custodian of the German constitution and the last arbiter in the major issues of German politics. The **Federal High Court** is responsible for protecting the rights of the individual.

European summer capital: The unique combination of German *Gemütlichkeit* and French *savoir-vivre*, enchanting landscape, spa-springs and the most beautiful casino on earth were the foundations on which **Baden-Baden** built its claim to be Europe's summer capital.

Although Baden-Baden has only been officially categorised as a spa since 1507, the town's spa tradition actually goes back to Roman times. But the imperial spirit of the 2nd century only returned in 1838 when Jaques Benazet opened his luxurious *salles de jeu* in the Kurhaus. It suddenly became fashionable to visit Baden-Baden. In the summer, in addition to the European aristocracy came writers and musicians and a regular flow of heads of state. The Prussian king, Russian princes, Queen Victoria and Johannes Brahms all appeared here, as did the notorious gambler Dostoevsky.

However, there is more to Baden-Baden than just spas and casinos. At the foot of the **Neues Schloss**, a romantic Renaissance castle, the narrow lanes of the old town, and the **Lichtentaler Strasse** along the River Oos, are incentives for long walks.

The **Iffezheimer Races** on the outskirts of the town are the highlight of the German horse-racing calendar.

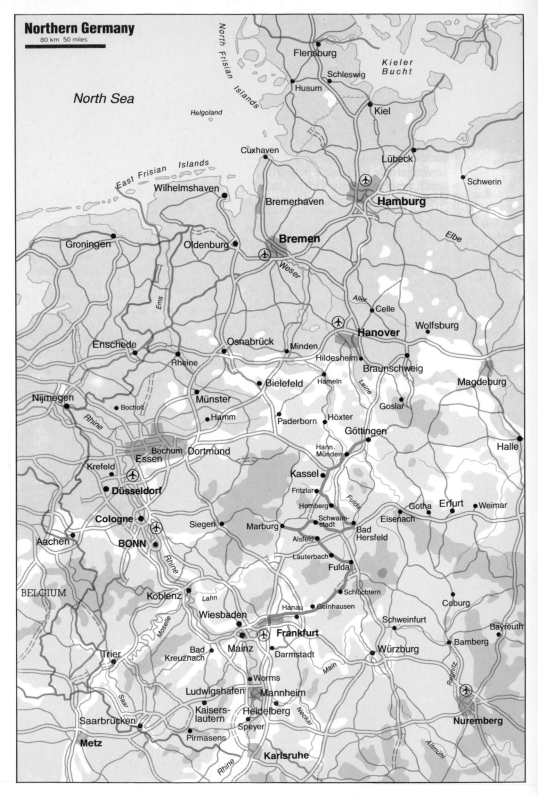

Northern Germany

80 km 50 miles

North Sea

North Frisian Islands

Kieler Bucht

Flensburg
Schleswig
Husum
Helgoland
Kiel
Lübeck
Schwerin

East Frisian Islands

Cuxhaven
Wilhelmshaven
Bremerhaven
Hamburg
Elbe

Groningen
Oldenburg
Bremen
Weser

Aller
Celle
Wolfsburg

Enschede
Osnabrück
Minden
Hildesheim
Hanover
Braunschweig
Magdeburg

Rheine
Bielefeld
Hameln
Leine

Nijmegen
Bocholt
Münster
Hamm
Paderborn
Höxter
Göttingen
Halle

Rhine

Bochum
Dortmund
Hann. Münden

Krefeld
Essen
Kassel
Goslar

Düsseldorf
Fritzlar
Homberg
Gotha
Erfurt
Weimar

Cologne
Siegen
Marburg
Schwalm-stadt
Eisenach

Aachen
BONN
Alsfeld
Bad Hersfeld

BELGIUM
Koblenz
Lauterbach
Fulda

Lahn
Schlüchtern
Coburg

Moselle
Wiesbaden
Hanau
Gelnhausen
Schweinfurt
Bayreuth

Trier
Bad Kreuznach
Mainz
Frankfurt
Darmstadt
Würzburg
Bamberg

Saar
Worms
Main

Ludwigshafen
Mannheim
Regnitz

Saarbrücken
Kaiserslautern
Heidelberg
Neckar
Nuremberg

Metz
Speyer
Pirmasens
Altmühl

Karlsruhe

Rhine

Fulda

However unlikely the term "Weisswurst Equator" ("White Sausage Equator") might sound, the fact remains that an invisible border that divides the south of Germany from the north runs along the River Main. As the landscape changes so does the character of the population. North of the Main is Protestant country, and even if not everyone votes SPD, attitudes tend to be more liberal.

The state of Hesse with its capital city Wiesbaden covers an area of 21,115 sq. km (8,150 sq. miles) and has a population of 5.5 million. It is characterised by a number of upland regions and is the most forested state of the old Federal Republic. Thirty percent of the population live in the Rhine-Main area where many industries including chemicals, electronics and car manufacturing have settled.

Lower Saxony completes the transition from the Central Highlands and the Harz to the lowlands and mud flats of the North Sea Coast. The state covers an area of 47,450 sq. km (18,320 sq. miles), has 7.2 million inhabitants and its capital city is Hanover. Lower Saxony is dissected by the River Weser, and the River Elbe forms its natural boundary with the new state of Mecklenburg Vorpommern in the east. The state is rich in mineral resources. The production of steel is centred around Salzgitter and Peine, Volkswagen cars are manufactured in Wolfsburg and confectionery is produced in Hanover. Other than fish processing, the main source of income for the people on the coast and the East Friesian islands is tourism.

The city state of Bremen lies within the borders of Lower Saxony. Of a total of 677,000 inhabitants, 140,000 live in the port city of Bremerhaven 60 km (37 miles) to the north. Founded in 1827, it has been the embarkation point of the first trans-Atlantic steamer service between the European mainland and America since 1847. Bremen lives from its port which imports wool, tobacco, cereals and rice from all over the world.

In the city state of Hamburg which, with 1.6 million inhabitants is the second largest city in Germany, the port facilities and warehousing are continuously expanding. Alongside shipbuilding, the city's main industries are petroleum, chemicals and electronics. Hamburg is also Germany's most important press centre

Situated between the North Sea and the Baltic, the state of Schleswig-Holstein covers an area of 15,725 sq. km (6,070 sq. miles) and has 2.6 million inhabitants, 245,000 of whom live in the capital, Kiel. There is little industry here and three-quarters of the land is devoted to agriculture.

Preceding pages: Northern German pastures; across the sands of the North Coast.

ON THE TRAIL OF THE BROTHERS GRIMM

Nowhere else in Germany is there an urban metropolis where the new has detached itself quite so much from the old as in **Frankfurt**. Not without cause the locals have disparagingly labelled this city on the Main with the term "Mainhattan". The new cathedrals of big business, the skyscrapers in which all the world's largest banks and financial consortia reside, have created a city whose pulse now beats to the whims of the money markets. The Bundesbank, the Stock Exchange and sundry leading German and European financial institutions are now situated cheek to cheek in the heart of Frankfurt City.

The power of money is causing the traditional infrastructure of the city to collapse. Old established shops and lowly burghers can no longer cope with the staggering rents and are forced to move out into other districts or even leave the city altogether. And even the oldest business in the world has had to move away from its established site on Kaiserstrasse at the main station: it now must make do with alternative accommodation in other districts far from the city centre.

The still somewhat grimy station area which once had a decidedly seedy reputation is now destined to become *the* address of post-modern Frankfurt, as already symbolised by the new **Messeturm** which at 257 metres (843 ft) is the tallest building in Europe. The position of Frankfurt and its resultant emergence as a nodal point of motorway and rail connections make the city today a hive of quick money and rapid careers, as well as disastrous failures. Unfortunately, much of the old has become irretrievably lost, including many of the traditional newspaper stands, cosy pubs and their beer gardens, and the corner shops in which the parlance always used to be the local Frankfurt dialect. And yet, some of the old Frankfurt has managed to remain intact. Romantic nooks can still be found, evidence of a 1,000-year-old tradition and

Left, the new Messeturm in Frankfurt is the tallest building in continental Europe. **Right**, handling gold bullion in "Bankfurt".

the locals remain as open-minded as ever. For those who care to take a little time, there is much to discover in Frankfurt.

A glorious past: Frankfurt has played an important role in German history ever since it was first mentioned in the 8th century. From 855 to 1792, no fewer than 36 rulers were elected here, and from 1502 onwards the emperor was crowned in the city's cathedral. The most important medieval buildings can be best appreciated by strolling through the old city. The glorious past is recalled by the **Römer**, the town hall, with its Emperor's Hall in which the coronation ceremonies were once held. The **Römer Square** in front of the building is home to the **Fountain of Justice**, as well as the **Haus Wertheim**, a richly decorated half-timbered building from the 16th century which contains a cosy little pub where you can rest your legs.

Beforehand, however, it would be well worth taking a closer look at the **Ostzeile**, the row of superbly restored half-timbered buildings directly oppo-

site the Römer. The **Museum of History**, the oldest building in the city, the **Church of St Nicholas** (1290) and the **Cathedral** are situated immediately adjacent. Not far away is the **Church of St Paul** which had to be rebuilt after the severe damage it incurred during World War II. Here was the seat of the first elected German parliament of 1848–49. Ceremonies which take place here today include the awarding of the Goethe Prize and the Peace Prize of the German book trade. The **Goethehaus**, where the great poet was born and where he spent his childhood, is just around the corner. Nowadays it is a museum.

Shopping: Shopping expeditions are best begun at the **Hauptwache** (1792) right in the city centre. From here the visitor can take a stroll along the **Zeil**, the longest shopping street in Germany and the **Fressgass**, a pedestrian precinct which gets its name from the multitude of delicatessens and restaurants strung out along its length (*fressen* = to eat). The **Old Opera House** which has been restored to its former glory stands at the end of the Fressgass. Here you can find the famous *Jazzkeller* which made valuable contributions in establishing Frankfurt's reputation as a metropolis of European Jazz.

Frankfurt's museums alone provide enough reason to visit the city. One of the most interesting is the **Senckenberg Museum of Natural History** with its world-famous collection of fossils and dinosaur skeletons. No fewer than eight museums occupy the south bank of the Main river, the **Museum Bank**. They include the **German Film Museum**, the **Museum of Architecture** and the **Museum of Arts and Crafts**.

This is the district of **Sachsenhausen** whose pedestrian precinct, centred around the *Klappergass*, is lined with charming old taverns, some with their own beer gardens. Here visitors and locals sit and drink *Ebbelwoi* (apple wine) until late in the evening. You can also try the local favourite *Handkäs mit Musik* (curd cheese garnished with vinegar, oil and onions).

Other places of interest in Frankfurt

Frankfurt is Europe's second-largest airport.

are the **Zoo**, the **Palmengarten** (botanical gardens) the **Mainpromenade** (the promenade along the River Main) and the **Stadtwald**, the largest area of municipal woodland of any city in Germany. Frankfurt is also the city of trade fairs, including the famous **International Book Fair**.

Excursions from Frankfurt: The romantic countryside around Frankfurt provides for a number of interesting excursions. Situated only 25 km (16 miles) away in the rolling foothills of the **Taunus Mountains, Bad Homburg** is a world-famous spa resort. Emperors and czars, kings and dukes all came here to seek cures for their ailments. And English visitors came and built the first tennis courts on the continent and then later returned to provide Germany with its first golf course. A **Siamese Temple**, a **Russian Chapel** and the world's oldest **Casino** can be found in the spa park.

There is a bus connection from Bad Homburg to nearby **Saalburg**, a reconstructed Roman fort which existed here from AD 83 to AD 260 to protect the border of the Roman Empire. The **Saalburg Museum** contains a unique collection of artifacts that were found during the excavation.

From the centre of Frankfurt it only takes 25 minutes by *S-Bahn* to reach the town of **Kronberg**, which is dominated by the castle of the same name (built in 1230). The Middle Age town centre is well worth a visit, as indeed is the nearby **Opel Zoo**, which will be a hit with the children.

Oberursel, the gateway to the Taunus, can also be reached in 25 minutes, by taking the underground train (U 3) from the city centre. The best starting point for expeditions into the Taunus is at the foot of the **Feldberg**. Marked trails and footpaths take you through the Taunus from the underground station at Hohenmark. More relaxing is the bus ride to the summit of the **Grosser Feldberg** which, at 890 metres (2,920 ft), is the highest mountain in the Taunus. There is an observation tower and a famous falconry at the summit.

Fairy Tale Road: The two brothers Jakob

The historical centre of Frankfurt was built anew after World War II.

(1785–1863) and Wilhelm Grimm (1786–1856) became famous for their *Grimms Fairy Tales* even during their own lifetime and their collection of traditional folk tales and legends from the land of Hesse has since been translated into over 140 languages. The two brothers were also outstanding linguists who developed the basic principals of German grammar and worked on a German dictionary. Last, but not least, the brothers were champions of civil liberties and democracy, a stance which often landed them in trouble with the authorities.

The Grimms lived and worked in Hesse and the Weser Hills and it is thanks to them that these regions have maintained such a rich tradition of folklore, which was originally handed down from generation to generation by the ordinary people. Reason enough to begin our travels along the "German Fairy Tale Road" at the place where they were born, at **Hanau** on the River Main. Our journey begins at the memorial to the two brothers on the market place and ends 595 km (370 miles) away in the free Hanse city of Bremen.

Worth visiting in Hanau are the **German Goldsmith House** (built 1537–38), on the old market place, the **Philippsruhe Palace** with its interesting museum, and the health resort of **Wilhelmsbad** with its attractive park. Many visitors are also attracted by the **Hesse Dolls Museum**.

Our next port of call 20 km (12 miles) to the north is **Gelnhausen**. Here are the remains of the **Imperial Palace** commissioned by Emperor Friedrich Barbarossa. This was an important junction of routes running through his empire, and in 1170 he united the three small settlements in the area to create the "imperial city" of Gelnhausen. The first imperial diet was held here in 1180 and the town maintained its strategic importance all through the Middle Ages.

The route continues from Gelnhausen through the delightful **Kinzig Valley** via Wächtersbach, which has retained the magic of a small royal town nestling between the national parks of the

Left, the brothers Grimm at their birthplace in Hanau. **Right,** in Marburg the houses huddle around the castle.

Vogelsberg and the Spessart Mountains. As in many other towns and villages along the route, the road is lined by quaint medieval half-timbered houses. A little further on, **Bad Orb** and **Bad Soden** are idyllic health resorts. Continuing to follow the old trading route between Frankfurt and Leipzig, the traveller arrives in **Steinau**, a small, romantic town at the heart of the "Bergwinkel" (mountain nook), one of the most picturesque regions in all Germany. Jakob and Wilhelm Grimm spent their childhood here in the old **Amtshaus**.

Schlüchtern, 8 km (5 miles) further on, is an old monastery town nestled in the rolling hills. The **Bergwinkel Museum** recalls the lives of the Grimm brothers as well as Ulrich von Hutten (1488–1523), a humanistically inclined knight who fought for a strong and united German Empire.

St Boniface: In Schlüchtern the traveller should consider leaving the Fairy Tale Road and making a detour to the cathedral city of **Fulda** (population 60,000), lying on the river of the same name between the Rhön Mountains and the Vogelsberg. The history of the city goes back to the year 744 when St Boniface gave the Benedictine monk Sturmius the task of establishing a monastery on the ruins of the old Merovingian castle. It became a centre of religion and science in the Frankish kingdom. After Boniface had died his martyr's death in Friesland on 5 June 754, his mortal remains were brought here and laid to rest in the Church of our Saviour in the monastery. The tomb of St Boniface, the "Apostle of Germany", became a place of pilgrimage. Under Rabanus Maurus (educator of the German people), the monastery school acquired a high reputation in the 9th century, for it was here that German first evolved as a literary language.

For its general situation Fulda's baroque quarter is unique. The **Palace** dates from the beginning of the 17th century when the prince bishops of Fulda had the former Renaissance palace remodelled and extended according to the plans of Johann Dientzenhofer, who also drew up the plans for the **Cathedral** which was built on the foundations of the old basilica. This had been erected at the beginning of the 9th century after the old sepulchral church of St Boniface could no longer accommodate the ever-increasing stream of pilgrims. Today, the **Tomb of St Boniface** lies in the cathedral crypt. A baroque alabaster relief framed with black marble depicts the martyrdom of the saint.

A few minutes' drive from Fulda is the **Fasanerie**, a baroque pleasure palace. Another sight worth seeing outside the city is the **Benedictine Abbey** on the **Petersburg**, an outstanding example of ecclesiastical architecture, with some of the oldest frescoes in Germany. The crypt contains the remains of St Lioba.

In the **Open Air Museum** in **Tann** visitors are introduced to the bygone lifestyles and customs of the mountain peasants of the Rhön. The **Rhön Mountains** are the remains of a volcanic massif consisting of high moorland and bleak plateaux rising to nearly 1,000 metres (3,500 ft). They extend from Fulda in the northwest to **Bad Kissingen** in the south, a spa town which has become one of the most popular health resorts in Bavaria, lying as it does in the picturesque valley of the River Saale. Much of the Rhön has been declared a national park.

On the summit of the **Wasserkuppe** (950 metres/3,120 ft) is a centre for gliding and related activities, which in the winter becomes a mecca for skiing enthusiasts. On the way to the Wasserkuppe the visitor will see the impressive remains of a Celtic hill fort atop the **Milseburg** (835 metres/2,240 ft).

Back to the Road: The Fairy Tale Road can be rejoined at the town of **Lauterbach**, 25 km (16 miles) northeast of Fulda. This is the centre of Germany's garden gnome industry: hundreds of thousands of the little men are produced here annually. A more worthwhile reason for visiting are the fine medieval half-timbered houses clustered around the **Ankerturm**. There are many additional attractions, including **Riedesel Castle**, **Eisenbach Castle** and the

Hohaus Palace, which has a museum.

More medieval architecture can be found in **Alsfeld**, about 20 km (12 miles) further up the road. The town is well-known for its half-timbered and stone houses mostly dating from the 14th century. In recent years many of the facades have been stripped to reveal the original structure. Fine old oak beams, carved corner posts and inscribed lintels testify to the high degree of craftsmanship that the medieval artisans of Alsfeld achieved. The focal point of the town is the market place with its impressive **Town Hall** (1512–16), the **Wine House** (1538) and the **Wedding House** (1564–71).

Approximately 40 km (25 miles) to the west is the university town of **Marburg**, the cradle of German Romanticism. It was here that the Grimm brothers began their research into German folk tales and stories. The old town, with its winding alleys and picturesque market square, climbs up the slopes of the Schlossberg above the River Lahn. Marburg's most beautiful building, the **Church of St Elizabeth**, is a masterpiece of early-Gothic architecture and a perfect example of a hall church. The **Landgraves' Castle** (13th–15th century), which contains the largest knights' hall in Germany, was the scene of the famous "Marburg disputation" between Martin Luther and Zwingli in 1529. Marburg's atmosphere is still very much dominated by the **University**. Founded in 1527, this was the world's first Protestant university.

Little Red Riding Hood Country: The region to the north of Alsfeld and to the east of Marburg is Little Red Riding Hood country, for the well-known fairy tale originates from these parts. In the towns and villages at the weekends and during festivals the locals still don their traditional costumes and headgear. The focal point of the region is **Schwalmstadt**, which is an amalgamation of the two little towns of **Ziegenhain** and **Treysa** and a number of other small communities. The parades during the *Salatkirmes* (salad fair) in Ziegenhain and the *Hutzelkirmes* (dried fruit fair) in

Waterfall at the Wilhelmshöhe Park in Kassel.

Treysa are among the most colourful in Germany, with authentic costumes and accurate portrayals of old customs.

Back on the Fairy Tale Road, the route passes through the two health resorts of **Neukirchen** and **Oberaula** on the southern slopes of the **Knöll Hills**. These resorts offer facilities for sports and hiking trails lead through the hills. Nineteen km (12 miles) to the east of Oberaula lies the spa town of Bad Hersfeld. The town is famous for its festivals which take place amongst the ruins of the **Abbey**, the largest Romanesque church ruin north of the Alps. Apart from its healthy climate, Bad Hersfeld possesses two popular mineral springs, the **Lullusbrunnen** and the **Vitalisbrunnen**. The Lullus Festival is held every October to commemorate the founder of the town which celebrated its 1250th anniversary in 1986.

Just off the A 7 between Bad Hersfeld and Kassel are two particularly attractive little towns: Homberg and Fritzlar. The district town of **Homberg** is famous for its many well-preserved half-timbered houses. Especially attractive is the market square with the imposing **Church of St Mary** surrounded by old town houses. The historic **Krone Inn** is, after the "Riesen" in Miltenberg, the oldest such establishment in Germany. It was founded in 1480.

In **Fritzlar**, some 15 km (9 miles) to the north, St Boniface cut down an oak tree which the heathen Germans had dedicated to their God of Thunder. Thor did not strike back and Boniface could proceed with establishing his Benedictine monastery on the site in 724. By the 9th century Fritzlar had become an important imperial city. The visitor will be impressed by the medieval town centre, the city walls, towers and the half-timbered houses surrounding the market square. For centuries Fritzlar was the property of the prince bishops from Mainz and its 1,250-year history is inseparably bound with the Catholic tradition. By far the most dominant building is the **Cathedral** which was built between the 11th and 14th centuries.

City of the Documenta: The city of

Kassel lies 25 km to the north of Fritzlar, precisely at the geographical centre of the new Germany. With a population of 200,000 it is the seat of the Federal Labour Court and the Federal Social Court. On 22 October 1943, 78 percent of the city was destroyed by bombs. The reconstruction work obliterated Kassel's heritage still further as the city planners decided to restore only very few of the damaged buildings. The sleepy residence city has now developed into the main centre of the region between Frankfurt and Hanover, Dortmund and Erfurt. The main landmark of the city is the **Hercules Monument**, standing in the splendid **Bergpark Wilhelmshöhe** which was laid out on the English pattern between 1701 and 1707, with the **Great Fountain** and its waterfalls and cascades. **Wilhelmshöhe Palace** (built 1786–1802) stands in the middle of this baroque hillside park and contains an outstanding collection of Dutch and Flemish masters.

Kassel is the city of museums. Both in Wilhelmshöhe and the summer palace Wilhelmstal the visitor can gain an insight into the lives of the electors. A rarity is the **Museum of Tapestry** whose prize exhibit is a panorama tapestry dating from 1814 depicting the Battle of Austerlitz.

Since 1955 Kassel has become a meeting place of artists and art lovers from all over the world. The *Documenta*, Kassel's exhibition of contemporary art, is held every five years (1992), lasts for 100 days and is considered to be the world's largest art exhibition. Despite drops in the numbers of visitors to modern art exhibitions generally, interest in the *Documenta* has grown. The exhibition is held at a number of venues including Europe's oldest museum building, the **Fredericianum Museum**, and the **Orangery** in the baroque park of Karlsaue.

The Grimm brothers lived for more than 30 years in Kassel and compiled most of their fairy tales here. The **Brothers Grimm Museum** illustrates their life and works.

Kissing a goose girl: Taking the new Intercity connection, **Göttingen** (population 135,000), another historical domain of the Grimm brothers, is only a few minutes away from Kassel. Between 1351 and 1572 Göttingen was a prosperous member of the Hanseatic League. The once thriving trading centre was badly hit by the Thirty Years' War and its fortunes started to improve only in 1734 when the elector Georg August of Hanover set up the university.

By 1777 Göttingen university, with no less than 30,000 students, had become the largest centre of learning in Germany. At least 30 Nobel Prize winners studied or taught in Göttingen. The city's special atmosphere has always been derived from its medieval quaintness and its Hanseatic splendour, as evinced by its Gothic churches and the **Old Town Hall** (1369–1443). In front of the building stands the "most kissed girl in the world", the attractive **Goose Girl** on the fountain in the market place. By tradition every post-graduate student who receives his doctorate is required to kiss the cool bronze mouth of this beauty.

Left and **right**, the Documenta in Kassel, the world's most important exhibition of contemporary art.

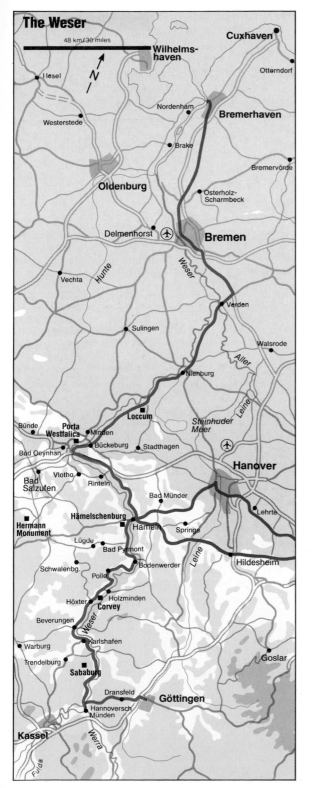

ALONG THE WESER

The Werra and the Fulda join together in Münden to form the River Weser. From here the river snakes along, twisting around countless bends on its 440-km (273-mile) journey through picturesque landscape. Virgin riverside meadows, spruced up towns and villages, castle ruins and Renaissance palaces lead one to believe that, just as in the fairy tale of Sleeping Beauty, time actually could stand still here. The concept that "life is like a long smooth river" is not merely the conclusion of the post modern era. Along the Weser, this has been an irrefutable piece of wisdom for thousands of years. And the people here are quick to remind one of this wisdom in discussions at the local pub or in conversation in one of the village shops. The Grimm Brothers' fairy tales, collected mainly along the Weser, also serve as a constant reminder.

Green rolling hills, some reaching a height of 500 metres (1,640 ft), stretch along both sides of the river. The *Wesertalstrasse* runs along the right side. From here the panoramic views of the fishermen and rowing boats, freighters and excursion boats are equally as lovely as those from the "German Fairy Tale Road" along the left bank.

Today there is little remaining evidence that this romantic region, with its time-honoured villages, narrow streets, crooked half-timbered houses and palaces built in the style of the **Weser-Renaissance** (a mixture of renovated Gothic facades and distinct Renaissance elements) was once the centre of the Holy Roman Empire's German nation. At the end of the 16th century the Weser valley served as one of central Europe's granaries. The wealth of the area's rulers and residents can still be seen in the beautiful palaces, town halls and patrician buildings.

Münden: This picturesque town was founded in the year 1170 by Henry the Lion. It lies, according to the inscription on a 19th-century monument, "where the Werra and the Fulda join in a kiss, thereby sacrificing their names. And out of this kiss is born the Weser, which flows through Germany all the way to the sea." Münden boasts nearly 500 well-preserved half-timbered houses from the 16th and 17th centuries. The **Town Hall**, a Renaissance structure, is worth a visit as is the **Welfen Palace** from the 16th–17th centuries and the **Ägidien Church** containing the grave of the notorious Dr Eisenbarth (1661–1727). During the summer, a play about his radical methods of healing is performed every second Sunday. His house still stands in Langen Strasse.

A ferry crosses the river in the lovely village of **Veckerhagen**, 13 km (8 miles) north of Münden. This ferry, though relatively old, is modern from an ecological point of view – its energy comes solely from the river current. Further north lies **Burgfelde** with its 12th-century Benedictine monastery where one can marvel at the medieval mural paintings and a bell dating from the 14th century. Across the river, just a few kilometres past Veckerhagen, is the vil-

lage of **Gottstreu**. Here members of the Protestant sect of the *Waldenser* were granted asylum by the Hessian aristocracy in 1722 when they were forced to flee the French and Italian Inquisitions.

Travelling in a westerly direction through the **Reinhards Woods**, one reaches the Sleeping Beauty's castle, **Sababurg**, perched on a high plateau. Although half of the castle lies in ruins, the other half has been turned into a hotel with modern comforts where guests can spend the night in a fairy-tale setting. Nearby, in the middle of the primeval forest surrounding the castle, is a zoo which has specialised in the preservation of native species of animals and the reintroduction and breeding of those which have become extinct, for example the bison.

Returning to the river, the rafting village of **Gieselwerder** is not far away. And shortly past that is another *Waldenser* settlement called **Gewissensruh** (peace of conscience). The "white city" of **Bad Karlshafen** was founded by the aristocrat Karl von Hessen-Kassel

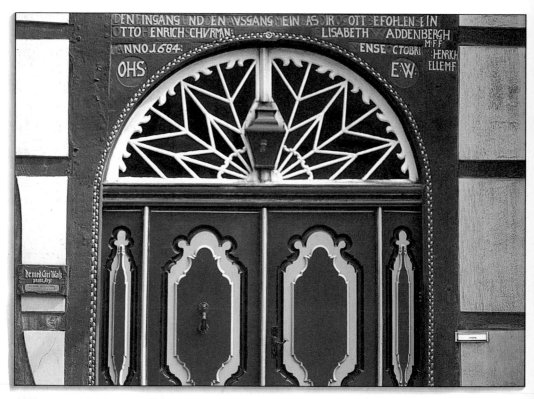

as "Sieburg" in order to link the Weser and the Diemel via a canal. When it became obvious that his plan was impracticable, he turned the area over to his fellow believers, the Huguenots, who had fled religious persecution in France. The appreciative settlers named their village after their benefactor. The many well-preserved relics in the **German Huguenot Museum** provide an insight into the history and culture which these refugees brought with them. The discovery of a salt-water spring here turned the town into a health spa starting in 1730, resulting in revenues which made possible the construction of a multi-storied "white" baroque building which gave the town its nickname.

The 15th-century **Trendelburg**, southwest of Karlshafen and on the opposite side of the Diemel is the site of a hotel, a perfect place from which to set out on explorations of the region. Not far from here is the "wet cloudburst", a 12-metre (40-ft) deep crater lake with a 1,000-year-old oak on the shoreline.

Journeying up the river from Bad Karlshafen, the road crosses over the river in **Beverungen** and turns into a smaller route leading north to **Fürstenberg**. Here is the oldest porcelain factory in the country (founded in 1747) after Meissen. Nearby is **Höxter** with its ancient city walls, half-timbered houses and noteworthy Town Hall. To the northeast is the former *Reich* Abbey of **Corvey**, built in 822. In medieval times this was a cultural centre of European-wide importance and in the 12th century the parliament of the German Empire often met here. Following along the Weser, passing by **Holzminden** on the right bank, one arrives at the Weser-Renaissance palace of **Bevern**.

Lying Baron: Baron von Münchhausen, better known as the "Baron of Lies" (*Lügenbaron*), was born in **Bodenwerder**, a town of well-preserved city walls and half-timbered houses. A monument in front of the Town Hall was built in memory of the baron's "ride on half a horse". Passing by the huge concrete cooling towers, the symbol of the atomic

The Pied-Piper of Hamlin.

power plant **Grohnde**, one reaches **Emmern**. The **Castle of Hämelschenburg**, located somewhat off the beaten track, is the most important example of a Weser-Renaissance castle. Constructed between 1588 and 1610, the entire building, including the oriels and octagonal towers, is extremely well-preserved.

The city of the Pied Piper: Hameln, which grew out of a monastery in the 8th century, proudly and rightfully calls itself "the city of the Weser-Renaissance". It contains many old structures which have been built in this style since the 17th century as a sign of affluence. The city became world renowned, however, through the delightful story of the *Pied Piper of Hamlin*.

In the year 1284 the city was suffering a plague of rats. A fancifully dressed man named Bundtig who happened to be passing through town promised to end the plague and was hired by the city fathers. He lured the rats out of the city by playing his flute, but the city fathers refused to pay him his due reward. One Sunday, when all the adults were in church, he earned his revenge by once again playing on his flute, this time luring away the children. Every Sunday from July to October, a play depicting this legend is performed in front of the **Hochzeithaus** (wedding house). This building is noteworthy for its rat-catcher clock with its mechanical figures.

An excursion to Hanover: From Hameln one can easily journey to **Hanover** (population 514,000), the capital of Lower Saxony. This city, which is the state's centre of trade and industry, is also well known as the location of the **Hanover Messe**, the world's largest industrial fair which is held annually in April. Founded in the year 1163, Hanover soon thereafter became a member of the Hanseatic League. Hanover and Great Britain were governed by the same ruler from 1714 to 1837, at which time the city came under Prussian jurisdiction.

Because of the devastation suffered during World War II, this city has only a few remaining noteworthy structures. However, the 14th-century Ägidien Church, the old Town Hall and the market place merit a visit. The grave of the famous philosopher G.W. Leibniz (1646–1716) is in the Neustädter Church which is located near the 17th-century **Leine Castle**. The **Kestner Museum** displays ancient Greek, Roman and Egyptian art. The **Lower Saxonian State Museum** has an impressive collection of German impressionist paintings. The geometrically laid out **Grosse Garten**, a beautiful baroque garden, is located in the western part of Hanover along the Herrenhäuser Allee, a street lined with four rows of linden trees.

Braunschweig, northeast of Hanover, has a population of 260,000, making it Lower Saxony's second largest city. Destroyed in World War II, it was quick to regain its position of economic significance. Henry the Lion, Duke of Bavaria and Saxony, lived here from 1166 onward. The Dankwarderode Castle with its **Braunschweiger lions**, located in the centre of the old city, serves as a reminder of this ruler. His gravestone, a splendid example of Romanesque stone-masonry, lies in the middle nave of the Romanesque **Cathedral** (1173–95).

A half hour's drive north of Braunschweig is **Wolfsburg** where a company sprang up in 1938 which is today Europe's largest automobile manufacturer: **Volkswagen**. The tiny village of 150 souls quickly became a modern city. Returning to the Weser near Hameln, only a short distance away, the picturesque village of Hildesheim is the next destination. In this bishop's city (in existence since 815), the Romanesque cathedral with its **1,000-year-old rosebush** climbing several metres up the outer wall is well-preserved. An Egyptian collection is found in the **Roman Pelizäus Museum**.

On the way to Bremen: North of **Rinteln** on the Weser, the **Schaumburg Castle** offers a delightful view of the valley. Travelling through **Vahrenhold** (another jewel of Weser-Renaissance) and **Vlotho**, one reaches **Bad Oeyhnausen**, a well-known health resort with one of the world's largest thermal springs. The famous **Jordansprudel** spouts its water 52 metres (170 ft) into the air every

THE VW BEETLE

The customs officers at New York's LaGuardia airport could not believe their eyes. They had asked a businessman from Germany to open his baggage and were presented with blueprints and plans for a four-wheeled hunchbacked thingumajig. The man insisted that the drawings were of a car, a car that he intended to sell in America. But the officials were not the slightest bit impressed and told him he wouldn't be able to pass his "thing" off as a car anywhere in the world. The documents were declared as "graphic art" on which the German had to pay $30 import duty.

The incident is supposed to have occurred around Easter time in 1949. The businessman was none other than Heinrich Nordhoff, head of Volkswagen, Inc. His deft marketing skills turned this car into an overnight sensation and it became a German best-seller even in the heart of Chevrolet and Cadillac country.

No fewer than five million Beetles were eventually sold in the States. By 1972, Volkswagen had surpassed the sales record set by Henry Ford's "Tin Lizzy". Ford's car, the first to be manufactured by mass production, had sold 15 million. In the end more than 20 million Beetles which were exported to 147 countries were produced, a world record that still stands.

"Volkswagen" literally translates as the "people's car". In 1933, car-mad Adolf Hitler contracted the gifted designer Rudolf Porsche to develop a car that the ordinary working man could afford. Despite opposition from the German automobile industry, the Nazi state financed the building and testing of the first prototypes.

In 1938, Hitler personally laid the foundation stone of the first Volkswagen factory. A whole town was built upon reclaimed swampland – modern-day Wolfsburg. By the end of the war, the town's German population of 14,000 was outnumbered by more than 18,000 forced labourers from Russia and Poland. Today, 130,000 people live in Wolfsburg.

At the beginning of 1939, the regimented subjects of the totalitarian German state were encouraged to open special savings plans to enable them to buy a VW. But the 270,000 people who did so never saw the "car for the common man", whose arrival had been hailed for years by the Ministry of Propaganda. During the war civilian projects were sacrificed to the requirements of the *Wehrmacht* and the projected VW was transformed into an all-purpose military vehicle which could be adapted to all terrains and climates.

The Beetle's success after the war, its reputation as the world's best-built small car, is largely thanks to the punishing trials that Porsche's military vehicles had to undergo during the war: they had to be as reliable in the blazing sands of the North African desert as they were in sub-zero temperatures on the Russian steppe.

Immediately after the war in 1945, the British occupation authorities began the first limited production of the Beetle. Heinrich Nordhoff took over management in 1948. During his time at the company a car that had initially been criticised as having as many design faults as a dog has fleas, became a hallmark of the German "economic miracle", the symbol of quality German workmanship. During those 20 years, VW engineers developed 36 new prototypes, but Nordhoff clung to the myth of the Beetle and would not let any of them go into production. Seen from the outside, there is hardly any difference between the 1948 and 1958 models, but in fact practically every single part was redesigned. VW went on improving the Beetle right into the 1970s and it was only in the 80s that production finally ceased.

Thanks to its solid construction, the Beetle also became the most versatile of vehicles. Do-it-yourself freaks welded bodies of nobler cars onto its chassis, or souped up the engine so that it could be entered for rallies and autocross events. With modifications the Beetle served as a delivery van, a snowplough, a sand buggy and even as a locomotive on rails! Its popularity and shape inspired sculptors and graphic artists and it has played many a prominent role on the Big Screen.

While other models have now all but driven the Beetle off the road, the car lives on in the minds of men. Beetle fan clubs still survive and Beetle races are still held. It is one of the few cars that everybody knows, even non-drivers who normally shake their heads at the motorisation mania in Germany.

Wednesday, Saturday and Sunday.

From Bad Oeynhausen it is only a few minutes drive to **Porta Westfalica**, where the river has carved an 800-metre (2,620-ft) wide gorge on its way from the Weserbergland region into the northern German plains. These plains stretch to Denmark in the north, to Holland in the west and to Poland in the east.

North of Porta Westfalica is the old city of Minden whose 13th-century Town Hall is one of Germany's oldest. The nearby **Wasserstrassenkreuz** is where the **Mittelland Canal** crosses the Weser in a cement trough 375 metres long and 13 metres wide (1,230 ft by 43 ft). This technological work of art, a water-conducting canal-bridge with three sluices, serves as a link between the well-travelled waterways.

The monastery of **Loccum** (12th–13th century) lies to the north. The seat of a Lutheran Academy, it is renowned for its conferences on topics relating to religion and society. A smaller road leads from here to **Steinhuder Meer**, the largest German lake between Lake Constance and the North Sea. With a surface of 32 sq. km (12 sq. miles), it has a maximum depth of only 3 metres (10 ft). The junction of the Aller and the Weser rivers is in **Verden**. The **Cathedral** in the centre of the city, built in the year 786, is the oldest brick church in northern Germany.

Bremen: This old Hanseatic town (population 555,000) together with the port of **Bremerhaven**, 57 km (35 miles) further to the north, comprises Germany's smallest state. Bremen lies near the mouth of the "fairy tale" river. It is said that the Saxons departed from here on their way to conquer England in the year 449. The city itself was founded in the 8th century and was raised to the status of a bishop's city in 789 by Charlemagne. Bremen was known for a long time as the "Rome of the north" due to the fact that it was the departure point for the Christianisation of Scandinavia. In the year 1358 Bremen joined the Hanseatic League and in 1646 became a free city of the German Empire.

During these 300 years Bremen was

The Roland column still guards the marketplace in Bremen.

involved in a constant battle for power with Hamburg. Today, although the citizens of Bremen concede the fact that Hamburg may be Germany's gateway to the world, they contend that the key to the gate is in Bremen. This explains the key in the city's coat of arms.

Bremen itself is now Germany's second largest harbour after Hamburg. It is the traditional port of trade principally for grains, cotton and coffee. The **Overseas Museum** has an enlightening ethnographic collection as well as replicas of Japanese and Chinese gardens and buildings. Literally all of the attractions of the old part of the city can be reached within a few minutes from the market square. The first building of interest is the 15th-century Gothic **Old Town Hall** with its ornate Renaissance facade. Its **Great Hall** is the venue for the annual **Schaffermahlzeit**, the world's oldest fraternal dinner. The **Ratskeller** in the cellar is famous for its Gothic arches as well as for the more than 600 varieties of wine which are served here.

Close to the northwest tower is the city's second symbol, the *Bremen Town Musicians*. These four figures, a dog, a donkey, a cat and a rooster are from a Grimm Brothers' fairy tale. The third symbol, the 10-metre (33-ft) high statue of **Roland**, is located beside the Town Hall. It was erected in 1404 and serves as a symbol of Bremen's freedom and independence. Roland casts a challenging gaze at the **Cathedral** with its 98-metre (321-ft) high steeples embodying 1,200 years of history.

The **Bleikeller**, where Eygptian mummies are housed, is guaranteed to send shivers through the spines of visitors. Near the **Schütting**, the old merchants' house, is the entrance to **Böttcherstrasse** whose restored medieval buildings present a kind of open-air museum. From here it is only a few steps to **Schnoor**, which the oldest part of Bremen and the site of many homes, pubs and shops dating from the 15th century. Those who wish to have a complete change and enjoy a breath of North Sea air need only travel another 57 km (35 miles) to the north in order to find both.

Left and right, the Schnoor Quarter in Bremen.

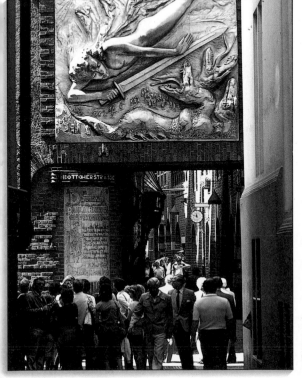

THE NORTH SEA COAST

Nordsee ist Mordsee (*The Treacherous North Sea*) is the title of a film made by Hamburg director Hark Bohm. It is a title which aptly describes the close relationship between the inhabitants of the northern German coastal regions and the sea on which these fishermen, ship-builders, merchants, pirates and wreckers depend for their livelihood. There was many a time when one of them set out to sea never to return and there was many a time when the ocean waves crashed through the doors of their homes and cottages. And there were even times when the "shining Hans", as they call the water, rolled into the interior of the countryside and simply swallowed an entire piece of land and everything on it.

Myths and legends about the North Sea abound. They tell of pirates like Klaus Störtebecker and Earls of dikes such as Hauke Haien. But the fateful force of the elements has affected everyone, the good and the evil, throughout the region's history. And thus the North Sea, this branch of the Atlantic with an average depth of only 100 metres (328 ft), has left its mark on an entire population. The East Frisians are sometimes depicted as reserved, perhaps even to the point of being stand-offish, and often as a bit stupid, making them the subject of a whole series of East Frisian jokes. These people have inhabited the area between the Dutch Ijssel Sea and the German Ems since the year 12 BC.

Forceably Christianised by Charlemagne in the 8th century, the Frisians were feared as potential rebels. These independently-minded peasants, with farmsteads surrounded by fertile farm land, formed their own republics which remained in existence until the Middle Ages when they were destroyed by the Crusaders. Ever since this defeat, the Frisians have concentrated on commerce and maritime-related activities in which they have been just as successful as they were in farming and animal husbandry.

Preceding pages: solitude in the North Sea – a holm. Left, home with the catch.

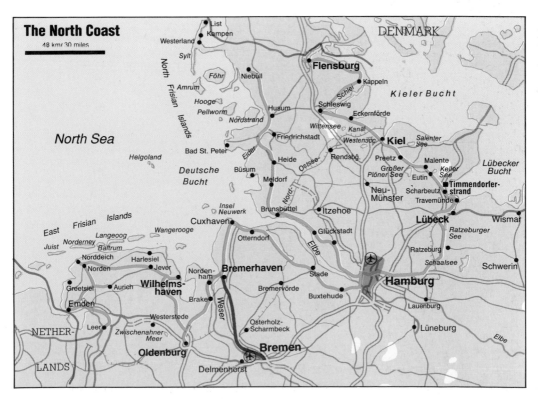

The North Coast

48 km/ 30 miles

They have learned to be reserved and not to brag about their wealth to outsiders. This clever diplomacy, fashioned to ensure that neighbouring folk would take little notice of them and leave them in peace, has been criticised by some of the more vocal ethnic groups as obstinacy.

Three types of landscape characterise this coastal region: The *Wattenmeer* (mud flats) with its unique life forms, an area flooded by the tide; the *Marschen*, the fertile flat meadowlands further inland which enabled the Frisians to become proud and independent farmers; and the *Geest*, the high and dry region of fields, moors and woods, located between the Elbe and the Ems, worn smooth by the retreating glacier at the end of the Ice Age 180,000 years ago.

The "German Riviera": The old harbour of **Leer** with its noteworthy **turning-bridge** spanning the Ems 3 km (2 miles) to the west was the gateway for travel from Holland and Emsland to the East Frisian Coast. The westernmost city on this coastline is **Emden** (population 55,000), an old pirate hideaway. During the Middle Ages many refugees from the Dutch liberation wars settled here, and the city grew into a centre for ship-building and maritime trade. In the 17th century, the German merchant marine used it as a base from which to sail to Africa and India. Today Emden is an industrial centre and Europe's largest loading port for the export of automobiles, especially Volkswagens. The **Town Hall** (1576) is a copy of the one in Antwerp and today houses the **East Frisian Regional Museum**. The publisher of the magazine *Stern* constructed the **Kunsthalle** art museum here and the **OTTO House** is a popular tourist attraction for fans of this contemporary German comedian. Here begins the stretch of coast known as the "German Riviera", with its 160 bathing areas. **Norden**, which occupies Germany's outermost northwesterly corner, is a name familiar to almost all German sailors. **Norddeich Radio** broadcasts from the nearby coast, sending greetings from those at home to loved ones at sea

The far north.

all over the world. Directly in Norden is the **Ludgeri Church** from the late 12th century. It is the largest medieval church in East Frisian. High dikes shield the entire coastline from the ravaging storm tides, a form of protection employed by the Frisians ever since they first settled here.

Out past the dikes is the **Wattenmeer** with an area of 565,000 hectares (1 million acres). It is one of Europe's last remaining nature preserves. More than 250 different species of animals live in this unique natural environment, each part of the food chain which is dependent on the North Sea's average 3.5-metre (11-ft) tidal fluctuation. At the northern edge of this region are the East Frisian Islands, a chain of islands between the mouths of the Ems and Weser rivers. They can be reached by ferry from various harbours.

From Emden it is possible to journey to **Borkum** with its 16th-century lighthouse. The neighbouring island of **Juist**, 17 km (10 miles) in length, is the longest of the seven islands, while **Norderney**, serviced by ferry from Norddeich, is the site of Germany's oldest sea-bathing area, founded in 1797. **Baltrum**, with its sandy beach, can be reached from Nessmersiel; **Langeoog** (ferry from Besmersiel) is particularly interesting for bird-lovers. From Neuharlingersiel one can travel to **Spiekeroog**, a former pirate hideaway, and the launches for **Wangerooge**, where the canopied beach chair was invented, leave from Harlesiel. Automobile traffic is allowed only on the islands of Borkum and Norderney.

The pier of tears: The bathing resorts along the coast have preserved their charm as fishing villages and their value as health resorts (owing to the stimulating climate) despite the annual summer influx of tourists. However, for those seeking quiet and long solitary walks along the beach, the main season is not the time to spend a holiday here. Set somewhat back from the coast, the meadowlands offer a taste of the original East Frisian atmosphere with thatched-roof farmhouses nestled in lush meadows filled with grazing Holstein

East Friesian traditional headgear.

THE HANSEATIC LEAGUE

What do the towns of Bruges and Novgorod, Lübeck and Bergen, Braunschweig and Reval have in common? Between the 12th and 17th centuries they and a further 200 cities joined together to form the Hanseatic League. This association enjoyed greater economic and political influence than any German state before 1871. In addition, its military might exceeded that of many a kingdom of its time.

This exercise of power was not one of the League's original aims. It was created as an association of German traders abroad, as a means of providing mutual protection from attack. It also offered a more effective means of representation, and the advantages of shared office and warehouse accommodation. The loosely-knit organisation expanded over the years to include more towns, especially in North Germany. From the middle of the 14th century, under the leadership of Lübeck, it controlled all trading on the North Sea and Baltic coasts. The economic, military and political power of the Hanseatic League lay in the strict code of regulations with which all members had to comply. The penalties for not doing so were severe. Council meetings were held at which decisions were taken on matters of common interest; these were then binding upon all members. Any trader who failed to abide by them was threatened with a total boycott by all members. A town sentenced to such sanctions could no longer sell its goods in any of the member towns nor was it permitted to use the League's offices and warehouses abroad. Thus the Hanseatic League governed not only the economic development of a town, but also its politico-social climate. When, for example, following lengthy arguments with the local patrician merchants the craftsmen of Braunschweig finally asserted their right to participate in the running of the city, the Hanseatic League boycotted the municipality, thus forcing a return to the old order. This subjection to external

influences stood in contrast to the considerable economic advantages of membership. No duties were levied on goods imported from member towns, they used a common system of weights and measures and all paid in the same currency. The combined representation lowered costs overseas, made transport cheaper and provided additional protection from unwelcome competition.

Over the years the Hanseatic League became so powerful that in 1370 it even dared to declare war on the King of Denmark in order to claim its rights in that country as well as access to the Baltic. The League was victorious, forcing the Kingdom to accept another king and insisting on the execution of all their requests. Thus the association protected its market, which extended from Bruges and London in the West to Novgorod in the East. Its role was to act as a turntable between East and West. In its cavernous *Koggen*, high-sided freight ships with a capacity of 120–160 tons, the Hanseatic League brought raw materials such as furs, wax, salt, honey and amber from the Orient and transported metal goods, textiles, wine and beer from the West. It maintained transport routes to almost every sizeable town in northern and central Europe.

The heavily laden *Koggen* were also a popular prey for pirates determined to make a quick fortune. For a long time the Hanseatic League undertook a campaign against such incursions. Pirate raids were particularly bad between 1370 and 1402. One of the boldest pirates, Klaus Störtebeker, plundered every ship unable to escape his clutches, yelling as he did so, "God's friend - man's enemy!" No prisoners were ever taken; any survivors were unceremoniously flung overboard. The other side was equally barbarous; vanquished pirates were summarily executed on shore.

The Hanseatic League had passed its zenith by the end of the 15th century. Increasing numbers of princes gained control over the cities within their jurisdiction, and the rise of nation states such as Sweden, Russia and England placed further restrictions on the League's expansion, thereby breaking its united front. In 1598 it abandoned its last overseas branch office, in London.

cows, fields surrounded by centuries-old hedges guarding against wind erosion and a landscape of quaint villages, windmills and woods.

Aurich was originally the dwelling place of Frisian chiefs and later of the East Frisian princes. A short distance to the east is **Jever**, famous not only for its brewery but also for the portrait hanging in the **Castle** (built in 1505) of the Russian czarina Catherine the Great who ruled Jeverland from Russia from 1793 to 1818.

Wilhelmshaven (with a population of 100,000), located on **Jadebusen**, was Germany's largest war harbour until the end of World War II. Supertankers now arrive here to deliver their oil into the pipeline flowing to the Ruhr industrial region.

Oldenburg (population 140,000) is an important industrial centre as well as being a university town. It has had a turbulent history. After belonging to Denmark for over 100 years, it developed into a cultural centre of northern Germany at the end of the 18th century. The

At the end of the day.

Regional Museum with its collection of Italian masters is housed in the 17th-century **Palace**.

Bremerhaven (population 150,000) is located where the Weser empties into the North Sea. It forms a part of Germany's smallest state. The "pier of tears", as the **Columbus Pier** is also known, was the point of departure for more than 10 million Europeans who travelled to an uncertain future when they journeyed to the New World. Today Bremerhaven is Europe's largest container and fishing port. A *Hansekogge*, a boat typical of the region, is on display at the **German Maritime Museum**.

Near the well-restored city of **Stade** is the **Alten Land**, Germany's largest fruit-producing region. The mouth of the Elbe at **Cuxhaven** (population 62,000) is 15 km (9 miles) wide. The **Alte Liebe**, an old pier whose name literally means "old love" and the nearby lighthouse are ideal places from which to watch the huge ocean liners travelling up the river toward Hamburg.

At ebb-tide, it is possible to stroll 13

km (8 miles) out into the *Wattenmeer* to the island of **Neuwerk**. However, don't forget to ask one of the natives exactly when the tide is due in before embarking on such a walk.

The sea cliffs: Boats for **Helgoland** depart from the *Alten Liebe* pier. This island lies 70 km (43 miles) off the coast. It has red sandstone cliffs which, according to legend, were brought here from Norway by the devil. The exposed position of the island accounts for its frequent changes in ownership. It was first used as a base by pirates in the 13th century. Later it was ruled by the Danes and then by the British until it was traded to the German Empire in 1890 for the island of Zanzibar. It served as a naval base during both world wars. The bombing of the island during World War II made it uninhabitable and the British Air Force used it subsequently for target practice. An extremely daring non-violent occupation by a group of German youths led to the return of the island in 1952 to its original inhabitants. These residents have now managed to turn it into a unique tourist attraction.

In **Otterndorf**, to the southeast of Cuxhaven, one can tour the world's largest waterworks. Somewhat further, in Wischhafen, ferries depart for Glückstadt (founded in 1617 by the Danish king).

Through Dithmarschen: In **Glückstadt**, on the other side of the Elbe, the turbulent history of today's Schleswig-Holstein becomes apparent. The reason for establishing the city was to outflank Hamburg, a goal never attained by the Danish king Christian IV. And the region from Glückstadt to Flensburg remained an area of contention between Germany and Denmark for centuries until the German-Danish war of 1863–66 brought an end to the dispute by making Schleswig-Holstein a Prussian province.

This made possible the construction of the **Baltic-North Sea Canal** which is still of great strategic and economic importance. On the way to **Brunsbüttel**, where the canal flows into the Elbe, one passes the **Brokdorf** atomic power plant. This was the site of many militant dem-

A lonely lighthouse.

onstrations during its construction, and it is still a subject of much dispute.

The fertile and flat lands around **Dithmarschen** were independent republics until 1559 when they were forced to surrender to the Danish king. The **"Cathedral of the Dithmarschers"** (1250) in **Meldorf** is evidence of the early Christianisation of the peasants. **Heide**, the economic centre of the former Ditmarschen, has one of Germany's largest market squares.

North of Heide, along the Eider, is **Friedrichstadt**, established in 1621 by religious refugees from Holland. They built their new homes in the same style as the ones that they had left behind, buildings which still stand today.

On the northern edge of the Eiderstedt peninsula is the old city of **Husum**, an inland city until the tidal wave of 1362. The catastrophe turned it into the "grey city on the sea" and marked the beginning of the city's economic ascent. **Theodor Storm**, who first gave the city the above-mentioned title, is buried in the St Jürgen Cemetery. Shrimp trawlers fill the harbour from where boats and ferries depart for the Halligen and **North Frisian Islands**.

St Tropez of the north: Just off the coast of Husum are the islands of **Nordstrand** (joined to the mainland by a dike), **Pellworm** and the **Halligen**. In former times this was all mainland, but the tidal waves of 1362 and 1364 washed over the meadowland and left only a few hectares (several acres) above water in the Wattenmeer. The few farms located on Halligen are built on *Warften*, mounds of earth designed to protect them from flooding when the next cries of "tidal wave" come.

Ferries depart from Halligen and from the small harbour of **Dagebüll**, north of Husum, for the three large North Frisian islands.

Amrun has a 15-km (9-mile) long sandbar, called the *Kniepsand*. It moves about 50 metres (165 ft) to the north each year due to the effects of wind and waves. The island **Föhr** has an area of 80 sq. km (30 sq. miles) and relatively abundant vegetation. The **Frisian Museum** in the island capital of **Wyk** is a reminder of the tribes who immigrated to these islands and coastal region in the 8th century.

Germany's northernmost point is located on the island of **Sylt**. Often called "the St Tropez of the north", it is a rendezvous point for members and would-be members of the jet-set. Car-laden trains leave from Niebüll, travelling across the **Hindenburgdamm** to this playground for high society, almost 100 sq. km (40 sq. miles) in area. The capital, **Westerland**, is the final stop on the train line and an El Dorado for gamblers.

The village of **Keitum** is somewhat removed from the hustle and bustle and has thus been able to preserve its lovely old buildings, including a 12th-century church. **Kampen**, the beach resort for the "upper 10,000", is located 4 km (2 miles) north of Wenningstedt with its stone-covered *Denghoog* grave site dating back to the neolithic age. Kampen is concerned that its 30-metre (98-ft) high **Red Cliffs** may be the victim of the next tidal wave.

Maintaining sea defences.

HAMBURG

Ludwig the Pious, son of Charlemagne, was perhaps the first to realise how profitable the location of the **Hammaburg** settlement, at the junction of the Alster, Bille and Elbe rivers, could be. His construction of a fortress here in the 9th century served the dual purpose of intimidating the inhabitants of the surrounding Saxonian villages as well as providing a secure harbour from which to carry out commercial trade with the neighbours to the north and to the west. The village, however, did not remain merely a depot for merchants: deep-sea fishermen journeyed from Hamburg far out into the North Sea as early as the 11th century.

The evolution of Hamburg into a prosperous commercial city began with the granting of free trade licenses in the year 1189 by Friedrich Barbarossa. Near the site of today's *Nikolaifleet*, a new city centre grew up with settlements housing sailors and merchants. Hamburg was, for a long time, the North Sea port for the wealthier city of Lübeck. The Hanseatic League developed out of this common trade bond. The eventual decline of this union brought no disadvantages for Hamburg. Through clever actions, mixed with a bit of luck, the one-time "junior partner" became an autonomous free German city in 1415 and was, in effect, an independent city-state. Owing to its well-constructed fortifications, Hamburg was able to withstand the Thirty Years' War unscathed.

The transport of raw materials and passengers from Europe to the new colonies, starting in the 17th century, proved to be very profitable for Hamburg's merchants. It was during this time that the city made its major contributions to the development of German intellectual life. Gotthold Ephraim Lessing became dramaturge at the German National Theatre in 1776. Matthias Claudius published the *Wandsbecker Bothen* in 1771–76. Hebbel, Heine, Brahms, Handel and Telemann all lived and worked in Hamburg.

The decision to join the German Customs League, vehemently opposed by many of the city's residents, actually brought immense trade advantages as well as the development of new industry. By 1913 Hamburg was the world's third largest seaport after New York and London. When Germany was forced to surrender almost its entire merchant fleet to the victors in 1918, Hamburg was hard hit. It did not take too many years, however, for the losses to be recouped. The towns of Harburg and Wandsbeck were incorporated into Hamburg in 1937 bringing the city to its present size of 750 sq. km (290 sq. miles).

Due to its strategic economic importance, Hamburg was the target for many bombing raids during World War II resulting not only in severe damage to the city but also in great losses to the civilian population which suffered a total of 60,000 casualties. Even this blow was met with typical Hanseatic composure as the rubble was cleared and a new start made.

Since the war Hamburg has been re-

Left, Hamburg – gateway to the Seven Seas. **Right**, Reeperbahn erotica.

markably successful in persuading new industry to settle within the city. This has made the competition from the port of Rotterdam, on the rise for the past 15 years, less threatening since Hamburg no longer relies solely on its revenues as a commercial seaport. Today Hamburg, with its population of 1.6 million, is Germany's second largest city.

The Hanseatic virtues of diligence, good business sense and a balanced view of the world displayed by the people of Hamburg are very similar to those of other great seafaring folk, earning them the nickname of "German Englishmen". And, in fact, English merchants and sailors were role models for Hamburg's citizens.

Gateway to the world: For many visitors to Hamburg the first point of attraction is the **St Pauli Landungsbrücken** near the **Old Elbe Tunnel**. In former times, before the centre of commercial shipping activities was moved to the outskirts, steamers and sailing ships berthed at these piers. Today they serve as the departure point for boat tours of the harbour. The smaller tour boats can pass under them and into the old harbour whereas the larger ones must remain in the more modern part.

The world's largest warehouse complex is found in the old **Speicherstadt** with its myriad canals. Coffee, tea, tobacco, spices and other goods are stored here in huge Gothic buildings of brick. Products stored in this **free port**, a fenced-in area measuring 10 sq. km (4 sq. miles), are not subject to customs formalities.

Almost all of the 15,000 ships which arrive annually in Germany's largest port are loaded and unloaded in **Steinwerder**. This is reached via the old Elbe tunnel with its vehicle elevators and tiled walls. The **Köhlbrand Bridge** stretches above this swarm of ships and cranes, large and small barges, tugboats and motor launches. The vast majority of north-south *autobahn* (motorway) traffic passes over this bridge and through the **New Elbe Tunnel**.

The **Hafenstrasse**, with its "autonomously" occupied houses, has been the

Warehouses in Hamburg's centre betray a maritime tradition.

scene of violent confrontations between the government and the lost children of a prosperous nation. The area has become a first-rate tourist attraction. The nearby **Reeperbahn** derives its name from the rope-makers (*reeper*) who formerly worked in this area producing the riggings for the sailing ships. Today this street and those which are immediately adjacent, the **Grosse Freiheit** and **Herbertstrasse**, form what is known as the port's "mile of sin". Appropriately, "Grosse Freiheit" translates as tremendous freedom.

Visitors from the countryside have been known to amuse themselves in this sector until the early hours of Sunday morning. They then head for the **Fish Market** to purchase a pot of flowers as a souvenir from the "Dutchman" who actually comes from Lübeck. Fishmongers are actually becoming a rarity at this market, though some of the more persistent natives do manage to make their way through the early-morning crowds to the fishing boats and carry home a fresh catch of the day before the

clock on the nearby **Church of St Michael** strikes 10. This baroque symbol of Hamburg with its outstanding view over the harbour is affectionately called "Michel".

Here one finds the **Shopkeepers' Flats**. These buildings were established by the shopkeepers' guild in 1676 and administered as a form of widows' pension. This function was finally abandoned in 1969, and the flats now house a museum, gallery and pub. Not far away, at the address Am Holstenwall 24, is the **Museum of Hamburg History**, which has a large selection of model ships. Here, too, is the Office of Emigration.

The more well-to-do, though perhaps not very authentic, part of Hamburg can be seen by strolling from the **Main Railway Station** into the city centre. Most of the "historic" buildings here are actually reproductions of those destroyed in earlier catastrophes, but the general impressions gained from such a walk make it well worth the effort. For those who would rather be driven, a

Backstreet restaurants.

small tractor-train takes visitors on tours of the downtown area, leaving from in front of the **Bieberhaus** (tourist information office). Next door is the **German Play House** (1900), whose productions have gained world-wide fame.

Around the corner are the tempting shops of the **Mönckebergstrasse**, but be sure not to miss the **Church of St Peter**, Hamburg's oldest church (1050). After being destroyed by the great fire, it was not rebuilt until 1842. East of this church, in Steinstrasse, is the **Church of St Jacob** (1340) with its precious 17th-century Schnitger organ and Lucas altar (1499).

At the end of Mönckebergstrasse is the **Town Hall**, built in 1886–87 and today the seat of Hamburg's government. Many of the building's 647 rooms can be seen on a guided tour. The facade is decorated in Renaissance style with figures depicting the German emperors.

The neighbouring **Stock Market** (founded in 1558) was rebuilt after the great fire which broke out in the nearby **Deichstrasse**.

Around the Alster: A few minutes away from the Town Hall is the **Inland Alster**. The **Jungfernstieg** with its department stores and shops facing the city and the **Alster Pavilion** facing the water, is the point of departure for guided boat tours of the city.

Near the inland Alster is the **Hamburg State Opera** (Grosse Theatre Strasse 35). Elegant shops, expensive department stores, glass arcades and first-class restaurants and cafés are located all around the inland Alster.

To the west is the neighbourhood of **Altona**, incorporated into Hamburg in 1937. Founded in 1520, the village came under the rule of the Danes 100 years later. The **Altona Museum** provides a good insight into the fascinating history of this area. The museum also has an interesting collection of model ships, figureheads and sea charts.

The **Elbchaussee**, lined with luxurious villas, follows alongside the river to the former fishing village of **Blankenese**. Only the very wealthy can today afford the romantic houses here

Shopping arcade in Hamburg's Hansa Quarter.

which look out over the Elbe. The common folk must content themselves with the view from the paths along the riverbanks. Somewhat further along the Elbchaussee is the **Willkomm-Höft** from where all ships entering or leaving Hamburg are greeted or bade farewell. The national flag of the ship's home port is hoisted and its national anthem is played over a loudspeaker.

Recreation in Hamburg: There are various opportunities to escape the routine of daily life in Hamburg. For friends of nature, the **Plant and Flower Park** offers greenhouses, playgrounds and fountains. The grounds of the **Wallanlagen** and the **Old Botanic Gardens** are wonderful places for a stroll as is **Hagenbecks Tierpark**, the world's first private zoo, in existence since 1907. Hamburg's **Kunsthalle** is worth a visit not only for its permanent collection including works by Picasso, Kokoschka and Warhol, but also for its fascinating special exhibits.

Excursion to the Lüneburg Heath: South of Hamburg lies an area of 720 square km (279 sq miles) of relatively infertile heath. The grazing heath-sheep prevent the spread of new growth, ensuring that the landscape retains its ecological balance. The barrows provide evidence of there having been early settlements here. The large **Lüneburg Heath National Park** is located near **Undeloh** and can be reached via the *autobahn* A7 from Hamburg.

The old commercial city of **Lüneburg** gave its name to the surrounding landscape. The monopoly on the salt trade which Lüneburg gained when the neighbouring city of Bardowick was destroyed brought immense wealth. The large number of Gothic brick homes ("Am Sande") is evidence of this affluence. The old warehouses, mills and harbour facilities, including a 640-year-old crane, which can still be found along the Ilmenau River, bear a lasting testimony to the splendid era during which Lüneburg and Lübeck controlled the salt trade. The magnificent **Town Hall** is itself a notable product of this period (1300–1706).

Left, "Banana Harry", one of the city's institutions. **Right**, the "Michel" is Hamburg's main landmark.

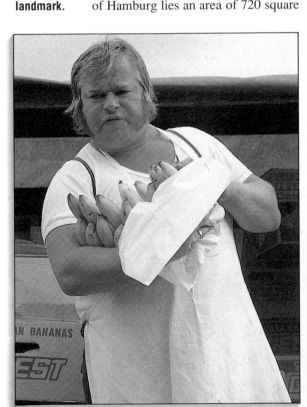

CONCORDIA DOMI FORIS PAX

FROM LÜBECK TO FLENSBURG

More than any other German state, "Schleswig-Holstein, surrounded by the sea" is the crossroads between Scandinavia and the Continent as well as between the Baltic Sea and the North Sea. This region was first formed into the *Cimbrian* Peninsula 8,000 years ago, at the end of the last Ice Age. It has been inhabited at various times throughout its history by the Angles, Danes, Stormarns, Holstens, Abotrites and Frisians. Some of these tribes lived here concurrently and some subsequently to one another. Accordingly, the history of the area, at least since recorded time, has been a turbulent one. This has resulted in a wide variety of literary and artistic characters being produced by the region: Matthias Claudius and Friedrich Hebbel, Theodor Storm and Emil Nolde, Ernst Barlach and Theodor Mommsen are all closely connected with Schleswig-Holstein. The fertile

meadowlands in the west and the rolling hills in the east with their deeply-carved fjords (Baltic Sea bays) make this an important agricultural district. And the residents have learned to protect the land by planting hedges to guard against wind erosion.

Lack of minerals has prevented the development of industry thus earning the region, in the post-war era, a reputation as a "structurally weak area", a polite term for a poorhouse. This was not always the case. During medieval times, Schleswig-Holstein's wealth came not only from agriculture but also from its strategic location. It controlled the land and sea routes across which people and goods from the surrounding areas, each an independent centre of power and influence, required to pass in order to trade with each other.

Queen of the Hanseatic towns: For 250 years **Lübeck** (population 220,000) was the undisputed commercial metropolis of Germany. By entering into a union with Hamburg, Bremen and many other cities of northern and central Germany, the merchants ensured the freedom, power and influence of their city until the Thirty Years' War (1614–48).

Founded by Henry the Lion as a fortified trading post on an island in the Trave River near Travemünde, the city defeated the Danes in the Battle of Bornhöved in the year 1227. As the city grew, due mainly to immigration from the Rhine region and Westphalia, it eventually developed into a point of departure for joint merchant trading ventures across the Baltic Sea with neighbours to the north and northeast. Fish and wood from the north was exchanged for Flemish cloth and iron from the lower Rhine. Furs, tar, honey and amber from the Baltic were used as barter for wool, copper and tin from England. The merchants alone, through the town council, controlled the destiny of the aspiring city.

The exact number of Hanseatic towns that joined in this commercial and political union was never known, but from 1356 onward Lübeck was considered the most powerful. At times, Lübeck and Cologne were in close competition

Left, the landmark of Lübeck is the Holsten Gate. **Below**, the Voss-Eck in Eutin.

for the title of Germany's largest city. During this long heyday, the style of brick Gothic, originally quite primitive, was developed to perfection. Buildings remaining from this era make a visit to Lübeck a visual delight.

Those arriving from the direction of Hamburg can spot Lübeck's seven towers from a great distance. **The Church of St Mary** was built in the 13th century and served as a model for many of the brick churches along the Baltic Sea. Henry the Lion laid the cornerstone for the **Cathedral** in 1173. This building, originally planned as a Romanesque pillared basilica, was constructed in its present Gothic form in the 13th and 14th centuries. Both the Cathedral and St Mary's Church were damaged in World War II and restored in 1959.

The 14th-century churches of **St Ägidien**, **St Catherine** and **St Peter**, as well as the 13th-century **Church of St Jacob** which houses one of Europe's oldest organs (15th century), are all grouped closely together in the old part of the city. This area is reached by crossing one of the many bridges or dykes. In former times, the rivers and canals provided protection for the city's inhabitants when the renowned diplomatic skills of the merchants failed. The **Holsten Gate** (1466), the most impressive of the few remaining parts of the city wall, formerly guarded the western entrance to the city and the nearby 16th-century **salt warehouse**, where Lüneburg salt was stored. Today it houses a museum with a large model of the city from the year 1650.

In the centre of the city, just a few minutes walk from the Holsten Gate, is the Gothic **Town Hall** built in 1484, one of the oldest in Germany. A monument to the Swedish king Gustav Wasa can be found in the lobby. The unique openings in the facade and arcades served as a protection against the weather for the numerous market booths well into the 19th century. A few steps further on is the 18th-century **Buddenbrook House**, former home of Thomas and Heinrich Mann. Thomas Mann's novel of the same name turned the house in

Shipbuilding in miniature in the Kiel museum.

Mengstrasse into a popular destination for literary pilgrimages. The nearby **Schnabbel House** is a good place to dine. The **Shippers Society House** (Breite Strasse), though less fancy, offers an interesting maritime atmosphere. The polished wooden furnishings, copper lamps and model ships hanging from the ceiling serve as reminders of the many Hanseatic ship captains who spent their last years here.

The **Holy Ghost Hospital** with 13th-century frescoes in the cross vaults was one of Germany's first public welfare establishments. Nearby are the *Wohngänge* settlements that were built in the 16th century in gardens behind large middle-class homes to house the ever-increasing population of the inner city. Cafés on the market square sell the world-famous Lübeck marzipan.

Beaches and bathing areas: Located to the northeast of Lübeck, in Lübeck Bay, is **Travemünde**, which has belonged to Lübeck since the 14th century. The rich and the powerful including many Scandinavians – Travemunde is a ter-minal for many sea services linking Germany and Scandinavia – have been enjoying this resort, whose main attraction is the **Casino**, since 1802. Stretching further to the north are the famous beaches and bathing areas of **Lübeck Bay**. Row after row of canopied beach chairs as well as diverse models of original German sandcastles are the trademarks of **Timmendorf Beach**, **Scharbeutz** and **Haffkrug**, to name the most famous. At **Hemmelsdorfsee**, located between Travemünde and Timmendorf, is Germany's lowest point – 44 metres (144 ft) below sea level.

A mere 10 km (6 miles) further to the north one encounters the "mighty" heights of Schleswig-Holstein's "little Switzerland" with its beech and oak forests surrounding approximately 200 lakes. The health resort of **Eutin** (population 18,000) is known as the "Weimar of the north". Here Johann Heinrich Voss translated Homer's epics. Historic pictures painted by the 18th-century artist Tischbein during his stay in Eutin are exhibited in the moated

The *Passat* recalls the days of sail.

castle. Summer concerts in honour of Eutin's most famous native son, Carl Maria von Weber, take place annually in the castle's park. North of Eutin, between **Kellersee** and **Dieksee**, is the resort of **Malente-Gremsmühlen**. Somewhat to the east is solitary **Ukleisee**.

At the centre of Schleswig-Holstein's Swiss landscape is **Plön**. A moated castle, built in Renaissance style and located on the shores of the **Plöner See**, is one of the region's main attractions. The history of Schleswig-Holstein is mirrored in the turbulent history of this castle ranging from its function as a ducal residence to its use as a training institution for cadets under the Nazis. Today it houses a public school. The tower of the Church of St Peter in **Bosau** provides a wonderful view across the entire region. Ten km (6 miles) to the west is **Bornhöved**, the site of two decisive battles against the Danes in 789 and 1227. North of Plön, in **Preetz**, is a 13th-century Benedictine monastery with its triple-nave brick church that was built in 1325. The **Seelenter See** north of Preetz provides a sanctuary for rare birds. Several manor houses and small castles are situated nearby as is the **Bungsberg**. This mountain, with its "impressive" altitude of 164 metres (538 ft) is the highest point in the "Switzerland" of Schleswig-Holstein.

The capital of the north: Schleswig-Holstein's capital, **Kiel**, has a population of 249,000. This important port has access to both the Baltic Sea and the North Sea. A centre for modern industry, Kiel is the largest and economically the most important city within this German state. Although it was founded in 1233 at the westernmost point of the **Kiel Fjord**, it did not gain significance until Prussia annexed Schleswig-Holstein in 1865. The construction of a canal linking the North Sea with the Baltic Sea (the Kiel Canal) and the establishment of Kiel as the main port for the German war fleet made the city strategically important. This, in turn, made the city the target of numerous bombing raids during World War II.

Schleswig-Holstein is a fertile land.

Kiel's attractions, in the light of severe damage suffered during the war, are mainly modern structures. An exception is the area around the **Market Place** with its 16th-century Town Hall and a few remaining half-timbered houses. The **Marine Memorial** in Laboe, the **Open-Air Museum** in the suburb of Molfsee and the bridge spanning the Kiel Canal are the most interesting sights around the city. The **Hindenburgufer** offers a wonderful view of the harbour facilities, docks and the bustle that occurs throughout the year in this increasingly busy harbour.

In the former duchy of Schleswig, 50 km (31 miles) north of Kiel, one passes through the Danish *Wohld* (woods) and arrives at **Eckern Fjord** where the famous freshly-caught Kiel sprats are smoked. To the west, shortly beyond the holiday resort of **Haddeby**, are the ring-shaped remains of **Haithabu**, the most important trading post of the Viking era. Located at the junction of the old north-south road and the east-west route across the Schlei, Eider and Treene rivers, this fortification was, until well into the 11th century, the most important centre for trade across the North and Baltic seas and between Scandinavia and central Europe.

On the other side of the Schlei is the successor to Haithabus, **Schleswig** (population 29,800). This is the oldest city in Schleswig-Holstein, having been granted its charter in 1200. Here one finds a remarkable old town sector as well as the Renaissance castle **Gottorf**, the largest royal castle within the state. It houses two important museums: the **State Museum** and the **Prehistoric and Early History Museum**, the largest of its kind in Germany. The **Nydam Boat,** a 4th-century Viking boat which was rowed by 36 men, is on display here. The **Bordesholmer Altar** (completed in 1521) by Hans Brüggemann with its 392 carved figures crowned by the Holy Virgin can be seen in the **Cathedral of St Peter**, a Gothic church built in the 12th century.

The peninsula of **Angeln**, northeast of Schleswig, also dates back far into the past. From here the Germanic tribe of the same name conquered England in the 5th and 6th centuries. Flensburg can be reached from Schleswig either via the old Oxen route between Hamburg and Denmark (today's B B76) or by travelling along the coastal road through **Kappeln**. The moated castle of **Glücksburg**, built in 1587 and formerly the residence of the Danish king, is located near **Ringsby**.

Flensburg (population 90,000) is Germany's northernmost city. It grew out of a fishing village in the 12th century and later served as a Danish trading settlement. The homes and public buildings are testimony to Flensburg's status as a wealthy commercial trading centre since the 13th century and its rank as Denmark's largest seaport in the late 16th century. The 16th-century **Norder Gate**, a brick structure, is the symbol of this capital of the rum industry. The city has been importing and blending this beverage from the Danish West Indies since the 18th century. Flensburg is situated on the border with Denmark, and Danish signs abound.

Nothing beats a salted young herring.

The two new federal states of Thuringia and Saxony stand for esprit and *joie de vivre*. In contrast to Berlin, bastion of Prussian militarism, or a hectic world city like Frankfurt, people in these two states have learned to take life casually. Goethe, the great German classical writer strolled through the Thuringian Forest and Augustus the Strong indulged in his sumptuous parties in Dresden.

As is the case everywhere else, the people of Thuringia and Saxony are influenced by the environment in which they live: gentle hills, endless forests, medieval villages. Few cases of big city neurosis are found in Thuringia or Saxony.

While in terms of area, Thuringia is the smallest of the new federal states, with a population of 2½ million it is also the most densely populated. One-fifth of industrial production in the former GDR came from Thuringia. The town of Eisenach was, until March 1991, the centre of production of Wartburg cars. Carl Zeiss in Jena produced world-famous optical instruments.

Five million people live in Saxony, a region that delivered about one-third of the former GDR's gross national product. From Chemnitz, called Karl Marx City during the SED era, come textiles while Dresden produces computers and other office machinery manufactured by "Robotron". It was in Saxony that the accidental discovery of European porcelain was made at the beginning of the 18th century – the person responsible was actually trying to alchemise gold.

The environmental pollution of the region is largely due to the mining of brown coal and uranium, but agriculture and the chemical industries around Leipzig and Halle have also played their part.

"Create ruins without weapons". This *leitmotiv* accompanies the traveller as he makes his way along the "culture trail" through the south of Eastern Germany between Eisenach, Weimar, Jena and Dresden. Tremendous cultural achievements and splendid restoration work in some cities stand out against the decay resulting from 40 years of GDR rule.

At one time both Thuringia and Saxony belonged to the realm of the Saxon Wettin family. About a hundred years before the Reformation they were separated and for centuries the destiny of Thuringia became linked with North Hesse, especially Kassel and Schmalkelden. The new Thuringian coat of arms with its red and silver lion on a blue background is very similar to the royal insignia of Hesse. Because of these present and historical associations a tour through the south of Eastern Germany begins in Kassel and, apart from a detour to the Thuringian Forest, remains oriented around the old trunk road (F 7) towards Dresden.

Preceding pages: two aspects of the Thuringian Forest. **Left**, the monument to Goethe and Schiller in Weimar.

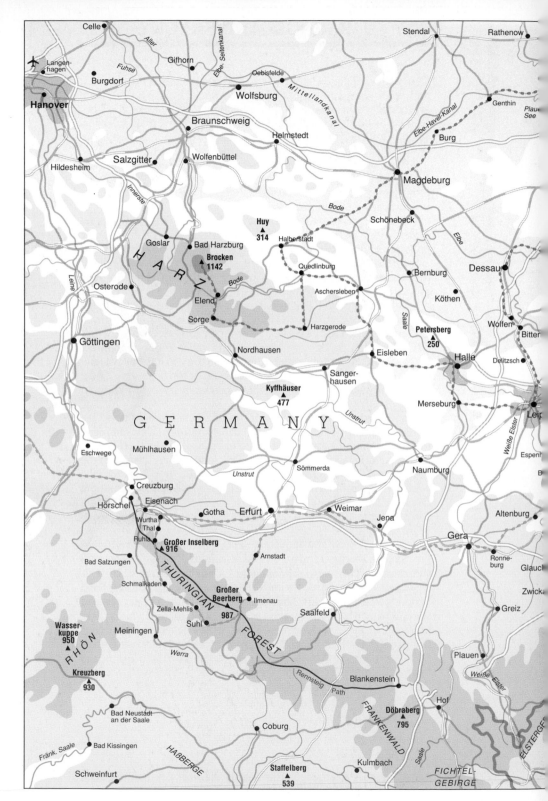

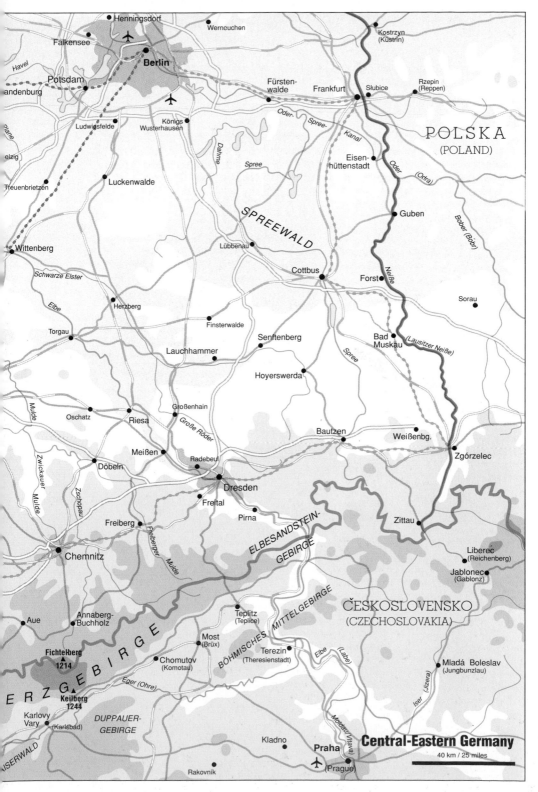

Central-Eastern Germany

40 km / 25 miles

EISENACH AND GOTHA

After the opening of the border in 1989, and the subsequent invasion of columns of "Trabis" towards the West, the National Highway 7 was soon dubbed "The Trans Banana". After 40 years of having to do without it, the simple banana had become the symbol of a western quality of life that could so easily have been achieved in the former GDR.

The attractions of Kassel, with its parks and museums, have already been described elsewhere in this book. In the direction of Eisenach, the B 7 (F 7) is now overloaded with traffic which thunders through the middle of helpless villages, suddenly awakened after decades of slumber on the other side of the border. There is no need to look for any signs in order to confirm that you are now in the former GDR: whereas in the West practically all the ancient avenues of trees had to make way for sanitised grass verges (supposedly in the interests of road safety), beyond the "border" they are all still there.

This is the centre of the new Germany. If one were to cut Germany out of the map and mount it onto cardboard, the pivotal axis would run through the magic triangle between Eisenach, Mühlhasen and Eschwege.

Creuzburg: What remains of the "death zone" – the bare deforested strip of land which once separated the two republics – is becoming less and less recognisable. Vegetation is beginning to fight back and is slowly eradicating this carbuncle of German history. Creuzburg lies some 70 km (45 miles) beyond Kassel and it is the first town reached after crossing the erstwhile border zone. The town once lay in a prohibited area so that even citizens of the GDR had to have a special permit to come here.

Archaeological finds attest to a long period of settlement by the Celts until they were displaced by the Germans around AD 200. In 724, St Boniface consecrated a chapel on the estate of the Frankish kings above the town. Leaving the town on the left, beyond the stone bridge over the Werra, is the **Liborius Chapel** a jewel of Gothic architecture which was built at the end of the 15th century. A few kilometres away on the F 7, situated in a valley basin often shrouded in the smoke of industry, lies **Eisenach**.

The most German Castle: Most people come to Eisenach to visit the **Wartburg** which stands on a rocky plateau high above the town. The castle was besieged only once in its 900-year history. It was never taken and never destroyed. It compares favourably with Neuschwanstein Castle in the popularity stakes, although from a historical point of view it is much more interesting. To the Wartburg came Luther, disguised as the young squire Jörg, to translate the Bible. Here, too, lived St Elizabeth. And within the Wartburg's walls there once resounded the song of medieval minstrels. While the Wartburg is not the largest and not even the most beautiful, it is undoubtedly the most "German" of all German castles.

The building is said to have been

Left, the Wartburg is neither the largest nor the most beautiful, but certainly the most historically interesting of all German castles. Right, the restored centre of Eisenach.

founded in 1067 by Ludwig dem Springer. "Hill wait, for thou shalt become my castle", he exclaimed, and had soil brought from Schauenburg so that the edifice stood on its own ground. The Landgrave Room, where a ceiling fresco describing the legend was painted by Moritz von Schmid in 1854, was dedicated to the founder.

It was during the time of Duke Hermann I (1190–1217) that the legendary "War of the Songsters" (1206–07) took place, at which the best known of all medieval *minnesingers* (minstrels) are said to have appeared, including Walther von der Vogelweide, Wolfram von Eschenbach and Heinrich von Ofterdingen. The theme of the performances was "Why is Duke Hermann so glorious?" Centuries later the history of the event provided material for E.T.A. Hoffmann's narrative *Serapionsbruder* (1812), for Ludwig Tieck's *Phantasus* (1816) and for Richard Wagner's opera *Tannhäuser*. The music festival is recalled by a massive fresco dating from 1855 in the Singers' Hall.

The fame of St Elizabeth (1207–31), who was canonised in 1235, also spread from the Wartburg. Daughter of a Hungarian king, Elizabeth married the 20-year-old Ludwig IV at the tender age of 14 and so became his countess. She bore her husband their first child, Hermann, only one year later. Elizabeth was greatly influenced by Franciscan monks who taught her that it was poverty that hid the eternal soul. With the necessary personal sacrifice she proceeded to found churches, old people's homes and hospitals. Her father confessor, a friend of the Pope, lord of all German monasteries and judge at the Court of the Inquisition, a much feared man indeed, commanded Elizabeth to a life of asceticism.

The well-known legend of the "Miracle of Roses" tells of Elizabeth bringing meat and bread hidden under her cloak for the poor in the hospital. When searched on the orders of the count, her offering had miraculously turned into a bunch of roses. In the Elizabeth bower, there is a mosaic depicting scenes from Elizabeth's life and legend.

Brown coal is the most common heating fuel in the former GDR.

The next prominent guest of the Wartburg was Martin Luther, who arrived here from Worms where he had been summoned to renounce his criticism of the Catholic church before Emperor Karl. He refused, saying: "here I stand, I can do nothing else". Luther's concept of the world liberated people from the power structures of the Middle Ages and created the basis of the Protestant ethic. The Pope and the emperor, realising the dangers, lost no time in declaring him an outlaw.

As the young squire Jörg, Luther lived in the Wartburg for 10 months. He became fat and depressed until his disciples gave him the necessary encouragement to render a correct translation of the Bible.

Luther made an epochal contribution to translating: "There is no need to ask the Latin letters how to speak German. All you have to do is look the common man in the eye." A critic caustically remarked that "all the tailors and cobblers, women and other simple fools" could now read the Bible. Martin Luther worked in a wood-panelled room and the desk at which he once wrote was so thoroughly destroyed by traditional believers that his followers supplied him with a much more solid late-Gothic monastery table.

The entire second floor is taken up by the splendid 12th-century banqueting hall whose wooden ceiling was added in the last century. Above the central chimney hangs the banner of the students' societies. In 1817, the societies marched to the Wartburg waving their banners of black, red and gold (the colours of the German national flag). Their aim was German unity and so they declared their fight against the divisive conservatism of the established barons and monarchs. The attraction of the Wartburg lies in the fact that it represents a microcosm of German history. In the 19th century, the edifice was in imminent danger of collapse, but was saved by Goethe who launched a programme of restoration, which was completed in 1890.

The town of Eisenach has a population of some 50,000. The **Castle**, the

Rural tranquillity.

Town Hall, the **Church of St George** and the **Residence** are all clustered around the Middle Age **Market Place**. One of the oldest and most beautiful houses in Eisenach provided accommodation for Luther when he was a Latin student of Ursula Cotta from 1498 to 1501. After being destroyed in 1944, the building was restored to its former splendour and named the **Lutherhaus**. Johann Sebastian Bach was born here in the Frauenplan on 21 March 1685.

The days of the "Wartburg" car, a kind of rich man's Trabi, are over. The factory was closed in March 1991 and the workforce of 8,000 is anxiously waiting to see whether they will be retained by General Motors. A new factory costing well over a billion DM is to be built for the production of Opel cars. Environmentalists now fear far-reaching climatic consequences. The Hörsel Valley, in which the new plant is to be situated, acted as a wind corridor and provided the town with much-needed fresh air.

Hörsel Mountains: Following the Hörsel on the F 7 in the direction of Gotha, turn left at the church in Sättelstädt. The road winds steeply into the **Hörsel Mountains**, a range of limestone hills only 7 km (4 miles) long, which is clearly visible from the nearby motorway. The Hörsel Mountains are steeped in legend. Especially when it is misty one might easily be confronted by Wotan, the old-German King of all gods. His companions the "wild hunt" carry on their backs their own heads, arms and legs that they lost in battle. They howl like a storm and their approach is heralded by the sound of horns and indescribable yelling. You are advised to steer clear of the "wild hunt", or at least to close your eyes.

From the restaurant on the 480-metre (1,575-ft) high ridge it isn't far to **Venus's Cave**. It is said that, clad only in typically sparse heathen dress, she snared the knight Tannhäuser for seven long years. Wagner created his opera of the same name from the different yarns handed down through the ages. He linked the lord Tannhäuser with the minstrel

The town hall in Gotha, city of cartography.

Heinrich von Ofterdingen, so joining the myths of the Hörsel Mountains with those of the Wartburg.

Grimm's Frau Holle is the most famous resident of the Hörsel Mountains. She rewards the busy and punishes the lazy. But there is another way of looking at it: Frau Holle's busy daughter Goldmarie picks the ripe apple at just the right time and never allows the bread to burn. Always working in harmony with the natural world, she is the model on which the ecology-minded feminists of today are based – and they are still waiting for their reward!

The Thuringian Forest, the green lung of Thuringia, stretches away to the south. It is a paradise for walkers and cross-country skiers with quaint old villages like **Oberhof**, **Friedrichroda** and **Bad Liebenstein** all easily reachable by road. Those in a hurry can continue along the F 7 directly to **Gotha**.

Gotha: Perched on a hill high above the town of Gotha, **Friedenstein Palace** comes into view long before the town is reached. The first baroque palace in Germany, it was built soon after the Thirty Years' War. The palace was always very productive: the royal houses of Sweden, England, Belgium and Bulgaria can all claim to have ancestors who were conceived here. The building houses several interesting museums. The **Museum of Cartography** recalls Julius Perthes, whose drawing office, founded in 1785, provided the basis for the Gotha publishing tradition.

The ducal apartments and reception rooms have been preserved in the **Palace Museum**. It houses paintings by a number of artists who include Lucas Cranach the Elder, Rubens and Franz Hals. The Ekhof Theatre in the West Tower is where, in 1774, for the first time in Germany, actors received fixed seasonal engagements. The stage of the theatre has been largely preserved in its original state.

In Gotha's **Old Town**, all preserved and restored buildings are tightly clustered around the square **Market Place**. The focal point of the ensemble is the red Renaissance Town Hall.

Standing before an uncertain future.

THE THURINGIAN FOREST

To the south of the towns of Eisenach, Gotha, Erfurt, Weimar and Jena lies the gently rolling walking country of the Thuringian Forest. The famous *Rennsteig*, a long-distance footpath of 168 km (104 miles) which runs over the hills, can now be rediscovered by walkers seeking clean air and relaxation. Goethe was probably the most famous person to complete the route, which winds its way over undulating fields and along green terraces, among trees often shrouded in mist or haze.

It is generally frosty for some 150 days a year on the high ground of the Thuringian Forest, so walkers should make sure that they have a warm jacket and, when the snow falls, skiers should ensure that their skis are freshly waxed. From its source near the Rennsteig, the River Werra forces its way down into the valley, forming the southern boundary of the Forest. Unfortunately, there isn't much life left in the river because of pollution from the local potash mines. The fish could never get accustomed to being fed salt solutions during the week and sweet water only at weekends.

Remote from the bustle of the city, far from the madding crowd, Thuringia is an easy-going place. Between the castles and the fortresses, on the fringes of the medieval villages at the foot of the valley, arose a culture of garden allotments where man built his *dacha* in order to escape from a constrained bureaucratic world, and to establish his own private niche. Here the people are tolerant and there is *Gemütlichkeit* in abundance.

Up to the Rennsteig: Coming from the Hörsel Mountains, leave the F 7 in Wutha and take the road to **Thal**. German history is reflected even in this small village. When in 1920 in Berlin, the East Prussian civil servant Kapp led the coup of right-wing nationalists, the workers staged a nationwide general strike in protest. In Thal they had confiscated all privately-owned weapons, whereupon 15 of them were captured and shot by the reactionary "students' Corps of Marburg". The culprits were acquitted, and a memorial was built in the graveyard in honour of those murdered.

On the road to **Ruhla**, deciduous woodland gives way to an increasing density of pine forest, as the climb up to the Rennsteig begins. With a population of 7,000, Ruhla is situated in the deep Erbstrom Valley and its houses cling to the steep slopes rising above the river. Ruhla is renowned for its manufacture of smokers' pipes, the history of which is described in the local museum. Its traditional watch-making industry developed into the production of automobile electrics on a massive scale, with 12,000 locals involved in the manufacture and export of everything from starter motors to ignition contacts. By and large, factories and workshops in the Thuringian Forest blend with the landscape. Unfortunately, Ruhla is an exception.

Along the Rennsteig: There is no doubt that Germany's most famous forest walk, which stretches all the way from Hörshel

Schmalkalden was at the centre of the Reformation.

near Eisenach to 15 km (9 miles) on the other side of the Bavarian border, is much older than its first documented mention in 1330 would suggest. The Rennsteig runs along the watershed dividing the catchment areas of the Weser and the Rhine from those of the Elbe and has always formed the natural boundary between Thuringia on the one side and Hesse and Franconia on the other. One can only guess as to who might have used this route in primeval times, though it could well have been a highway frequented by the hunters and gatherers of the Stone Age. It is also possible that the Celts used it as a means of retreat from their strongholds in the face of the advancing Germans. Perhaps it was a route for messengers, part of a quick route through to the Danube.

Whatever doubts there may be about its history, the fact remains that the hardened walker needs five days to complete the distance, following the "R" signs all the way. Some nature lovers assert that the reopening of the Rennsteig carries just as much symbolic significance as the reopening of the Brandenburg Gate in Berlin.

Bad Liebenstein: As in Ruhla, the cottage industries of **Liebenstein** are linked to life in the forest, in this case the curative properties of its water. The place has specialised in the treatment of heart disease ever since 1610. However, it cannot live from its hospitals alone. Biscuits are manufactured for domestic consumption and bicycle bells are produced for Benelux. Everything here happens behind the facades of the renovated half-timbered houses – the post office resembles a small medieval castle – and the new health resorts. Continuing along the hairpin bends up the narrow **Trusel Valley**, with its picturesque waterfall, the visitor duly arrives at the small town of **Schmalkalden**.

Fountain of the Reformation: Luther's democratisation of divine worship shattered the basis of traditional religious belief, and it was in Schmalkalden that the ideas of the Reformation were given their momentum. Here in 1530 the "Protestants" joined together as the

Time seems to have stood still in Arnstadt.

"Schmalkalden Association" to defy Catholic imperial power and to demand the Reformation.

At the peak of its power, the association held its decisive meeting on 10 February 1537. It comprised 18 Protestant dukes, 28 representatives of the imperial and Hansa cities, as well as envoys from Denmark, France and the German emperor. They were joined by the papal legate and 42 leading theologians, including Melanchton and Luther himself.

The composition of this meeting clearly indicated that what was at stake was the very power structure of the German states. The emperor's envoy met with unanimous rejection right from the start and the papal legate did not fare much better. Luther published his "Schmalkalden Article", the document which sealed the division of the Catholic and Protestant churches. As a counter blow, Emperor Charles V defeated the Protestant dukes in battle near Mühlberg on the River Elbe. They finally capitulated in Wittenberg on 19 May 1537. However, the victory did not succeed in halting the march of Protestantism; within 20 years no less than 90 percent of all German citizens had gone over to the Protestant church. Luther died in Eisleben in 1546 and so did not live to witness peace between the two sides, which was finally settled in Augsburg in 1555.

Schmalkalden was first mentioned in 874 when it belonged to the landowning families of Thuringia. They ruled it together with the dukes of Henneberg for 200 years before the property fell into the hands of the aristocrats of Hesse. **Wilhelmsburg Castle** was built by Wilhelm IV as a hunting lodge and summer residence. Most of the master builders and artists who worked on the castle came from the royal workshops in Kassel. The building is richly decorated with fine stuccos and paintings and has been splendidly restored. The exterior is rendered in red and white - the colours of the house of Hesse.

The museum within the building details the fortunes of the local iron industry which began here in the 15th century. Alongside the manufacture of common everyday articles, weapons were produced from 1745 onwards. In World War II hand-grenades were manufactured here.

Winter sports: Although when looking at the map one might easily get the impression that forest settlements such as Steinberg-Hallenberg, Zella-Mehlis and Oberhof are nothing but sleepy backwaters, this is not in fact the case. **Oberhof**, for example, boasts a splendid baroque church which is evidence of past prosperity as well as a number of cottage industries which indicate that the place continues to thrive.

At 830 metres (2,723 ft), the town of 3,000 has also developed into a prominent winter sports centre. Among the attractions for the 100,000 annual visitors are the ski-jump complex at the Rennsteig, the biathlon stadium and the bob-run. Locals can be recognised by the delightful smell of brown coal fumes in their hair; in the winter time the palls hang over the town, seeming to penetrate every last nook. Brown coal re-

A welcoming smile.

264

mains the most widely used heating fuel in the former GDR.

Talking of pollution: From Oberhof a steep, winding road descends to the town of **Ilmenau**, which is dominated by its glass factory. Goethe often visited Ilmenau, either on holiday or in an official capacity, inspecting the silver and copper mines on behalf of the Duke of Weimar. The 18-km (11-miles) long Goethe track leads from the town hall via Manebach to the Goethehause in Stutzerbach. Goethe's impressions of Ilmenau were entirely favourable. Here, in 1780, in the hunting lodge on the Kickelhahn Hill directly opposite the glass factory, he penned his most famous poem:

"Silence reigns on the hilltops,/in the treetops not a breath of wind;/not a sound from the birds of the forest./Wait awhile, for you too shall find your peace."

Goethe often visited Ilmenau, either on holiday or in an official capacity, inspecting the silver and copper mines on behalf of the Duke of Weimar. The 18-km (11-mile) Goethe track leads from the town hall in Ilmenau via Manebach to the Goethehaus in Stützerbach.

A town of arts and crafts: On the F 4 leading towards Erfurt, the town of **Arnstadt** was first mentioned in 704 and can thus claim to be the "oldest town in the GDR". The town has a long musical history, the fortunes of which came to be guided by no less a genius than Johann Sebastian Bach. He was the organist in today's **Bach Church** from 1703 to 1707. In the castle museum there is a unique collection of over 400 wax figures called Puppenstadt Monplaisir, which the duchess Auguste Dorothea collected from 1690 to 1750.

The town's most important export item remains its lead crystal. The art of its production was developed here during the 17th century and today the craft has been refined by glass cutters all over Thuringia and Bohemia. Eleven km (7 miles) to the northwest of the town, the cuisine of the **"Wachsenburg"** is known far and wide as being one of the top gastronomic delights in all Thuringia.

Thuringian sausages are legendary.

ERFURT AND WEIMAR

To rise again from the ruins – that might well be the dream of the new capital of Thuringia with its 220,000 inhabitants. **Erfurt**, the largest town in the state, could be made into a real jewel, perhaps even in time for its 1,250th anniversary in 1992. However, this would be a monumental task. Although the town was spared the bombing of the last war, it has since been allowed to crumble. The only buildings that were ever renovated are those lining the "official routes" along which party functionaries would lead their guests.

Buildings of architectural and historical importance, such as **Das goldene Rad**, the **Krone** the **Fruit Bazaar** are desperately waiting for the restorers to get going. Particularly depressing is the **Andreasviviertel**, the district in which the artisans once lived and worked – a scene of smashed window panes, broken gutters and plaster dropping off the walls. Only half of the 1,100 flats are habitable, and most of those are in a "medieval" state.

When it was planned to put a ring road straight through the heart of the district, the Evangelical Youth Club started their protest. In December 1989, thousands of townsfolk formed a human chain to protect their old city. It threaded its way past sites that had already been restored, like the medieval **Krämerbrücke**, the only medieval covered bridge north of the Alps. It used to be part of the old east-west trade route, and today houses artists' studios and antique shops. Or the **Cathedral**, which was founded in 742 and contains the "Gloriosa", one of the largest church bells in the world and the "Wolfram", a candelabra dating from the 12th century. Another attraction of Erfurt is the **Church of St Severin** whch stands next to the cathedral. The tomb of St Severin, who died in 1365, is contained within.

The city's skyline is characterised by the towers of further churches and monastery buildings of the numerous orders who settled in the town: Dominicans,

Augustinians, Benedictines and many more. It was from Erfurt that the monk St Boniface set out to convert the heathen Germans. He founded an independent bishopric in 742, although this was soon integrated with Mainz. In the Middle Ages, Erfurt derived a great deal of wealth from the export of blue dyes. Market gardening developed into an important source of revenue from the 17th century onwards, an industry from which the permanent garden exhibition, for which the town is famous, developed. The visitor can get an idea of the former wealth of the city by taking a stroll along the pedestrian precinct which fans out from the **Fish Market**, with its **Statue of Roland** (1591) and the splendid neo-Gothic **Town Hall**.

Erfurt actually only ceased to be the capital of Thuringia in 1952, when the old states were done away with and the country was divided up into new administrative districts. On 19 March 1970, the **Erfurter Hotel** was the site of the historic meeting between Willy Brandt and Willi Stoph that heralded the new

Erfurt has retained its historic character.

Ostpolitik of the Federal Republic, a policy of mutual cooperation rather than mutual antagonism.

Weimar: This world-famous city, only 20 km (12 miles) away from Erfurt, would have liked to become the new capital of the new state and thereby reclaim the position it held until 1920. However, with a population of only 60,000, the city lacked the necessary infrastructure – bad luck for Weimar and good luck for Erfurt. Nevertheless, the city remains a place of pilgrimage for culture vultures and lovers of tradition from all over the world. With the new accessibility that Weimar has now acquired, the locals are anxious to prevent it from becoming one great Goethe-Schiller Disneyland. An action group has been formed.

Duchess Anna Amalia: When Goethe and Schiller came here, the population was a mere 6,000. In those days, major contributors to the stench prevailing in the narrow streets were the cows which were led through the city and out to pasture in the mornings, and then back through again when day was done.

Duchess Anna Amalia was responsible for elevating Weimar into the position of a world-famous cultural centre. The daughter of Duke Karl I and niece of Frederick the Great, she was a lover of poetry, music and painting. The government of the Duchy of Saxony-Weimar-Eisenach was left in her hands after her husband Ernst August Constantin (1668–1758) died when she was only 19 years old. No tutor was good enough for her sons Carl August and Konstantin. In 1772 she summoned the poet and professor of philosophy Christoph Martin Wieland from Erfurt to educate Konstantin and in 1774 Karl Ludwig von Knebel, a Prussian officer, came to teach Karl August. He introduced his young protege to Goethe, who had already become famous through his work *The Sorrows of the Young Werther*. A year later, the Duchess withdrew from running the affairs of state in order to have time to follow her pursuits of literature and art at her baroque summer residence **Tiefurt Palace** on the river

The magnificent library in Weimar.

Ilm. Karl August took over and it was he who then summoned Goethe to Weimar. Goethe was to remain here for almost 60 years.

Goethe's rapid career: In 1777, Goethe took over as head of the Ilmenau commission of mines and succeeded in keeping them going and in keeping the state budget in the black. Two years later, as the first German to talk about disarmament, he reduced the troop force to a bare 200 infantrymen. Taxes could be lowered as a result. As an early champion of the trades union cause, he supported the pay demands of workers involved in the building of Weimar Castle. But these early efforts at reform did not get very far and in 1786 he left for a temporary sojourn in Italy.

Schiller: The relationship between the great minds of Weimar, Christoph Martin Wieland, the theologian and philosopher Johann Gottfried Herder and Goethe was characterised more by mutual respect than by any great degree of friendship. But when Friedrich Schiller came to Weimar in 1787, Goethe immediately had a close ally. Indeed, nowhere else in the history of German literature do we find such cooperation as that which existed between Goethe and Schiller. When, for example, Schiller's drama *Wallensteins Lager* was first performed, Goethe actively involved himself in the rehearsals. Goethe was the Weimar theatre's director for 26 years.

In 1792, the French National Assembly elected Schiller as an honorary citizen of La République – the premier of his play *Räuber* in Paris had created a sensation. But within a time-span of only a few years, the legend of Weimar collapsed. Herder died in 1803, Schiller in 1805, Anna Amalia in 1807 and Wieland in 1813. Goethe outlived them all. He died on 22 March 1832.

Apart from the historical sites, the traditional culinary venues of the city have also been preserved. There are the "White Swan", the "Black Bear" and the "Elephant Hotel" on the market place, which served as the location for Thomas Mann's novel *Lotte in Weimar*. Other popular inns in the city include the "Esplanade" and "Goethe's Café".

The **State Art Collection** is contained in the **Castle**. It contains masterpieces by Lucas Cranach the Elder, Tintoretto, Rubens and Caspar David Friedrich. Nearby, the Green Castle is the repository of the "Central library of German classical literature", containing 840,000 volumes. When it comes to books, Weimar seems particularly well-endowed: a further 600,000 volumes are contained in the **Goethe and Schiller Archives** on the opposite bank of the river Ilm.

On the same side of the river stands Goethe's old **Summer House**. Today, it still looks as if the great poet has just popped out and will be back any minute. It was here, while he was minister of state, that he and his lover Christiane Vulpitus spent their happiest days. They finally married in 1806 after living together for 18 years. Their life together was the subject of continuous society gossip.

It is possible to view 17 rooms in Goethe's classical residence, his **Haus am Frauenplan**. Everything is still there, just as he left it, a real treasure trove of his personal memorabilia. His living and working quarters at the back of the house, to which only very close friends had an entrée during his lifetime, are preserved from close public scrutiny. The library is protected by a screen. The 8,000 volumes contained within are still still ordered on their plain grey shelves according to Goethe's system. Of special note is his writing stand, which can be seen between the windows overlooking the garden. The **Goethe Museum** is beside the house.

A short distance away in the pedestrian precinct is the **Schillerhaus**, which the poet and playwright had built in 1802 with his entire fortune of 4,200 Taler. The new **Schiller Museum** next door, with its light and airy rooms, is considered to be the only really spectacular modern museum building in the former GDR. Anna Amalie spent a good 30 years of her life in the **Wittumspalais**, which contains a museum dedicated to the work of Christoph Martin Wieland. Immediately opposite, as the high point

THE GENIUS OF GOETHE

Born in Frankfurt, Johann Wolfgang von Goethe (1749-1832) first arrived in the little royal town of Weimar on 7 November 1775, when he was 26 years old. The young author had already won fame at home and abroad with his novel *The sorrows of the young Werther*.

But Goethe was much more than just a talented writer and it was Weimar which was to provide him with the stage on which to demonstrate what a universally gifted man he really was. It wasn't long before he had risen from being the friend and tutor of the 20-year-old Duke Karl August to become a top civil servant with a seat on the privy council. He was further promoted to the ranks of the nobility in 1782.

However, 10 years of carrying out onerous official governmental duties had not left him much time to follow his literary passions. He was also frustrated by his continuously thwarted attempts to introduce social and economic reform.

So Goethe resigned and went to spend a year in Italy. Returning to Weimar in 1778, he took up the posts of Education Minister and Director of Theatre. From now on Goethe was to devote much of his energy to literature and also to a wide spectrum of scientific subjects, writing numerous valuable theses on botany, zoology, and on climatology, as well as his famous treatise on colours.

Although Goethe's output was huge, his incomparable place in the history of German culture is not only the result of his writings. Of the works which truly stood out above the rest, he once said: "they are but fragments of a greater confession". This was something more than a *Weltanschauung* or perception of the world. Goethe was an extremely perceptive and practical person, no great friend of philosophy and mere theoretical sciences. He became a universal thinker because he wanted to live universally, exploring every avenue which was presented to him. He always felt compelled to achieve.

Goethe's greatest achievement, therefore, was life itself. Whether he viewed the world through the eyes of a lover, a natural scientist, a politician or a traveller, the profound effect that he was to have on later generations could only be compared to that of a classical work of art. All who followed in Goethe's footsteps could shape the model of their own existences by drawing on the multitude of life's designs that Goethe bequeathed.

His compulsive hunger for knowledge and the pursuit of his own personal development is also the theme of his famous drama about Faust, his "main work" which took him no less than 60 years to complete. The scholar Faust, weary of all the stagnant knowledge contained in books, submitted himself to the Devil, for it was only Mephistopheles who had the key to open the door to every possible experience that the world could offer. Despite all his experiences and successes, in the end Faust is a broken man; cleverer but not wise, rich but not happy. The angels save his soul from the claws of the devil, because: "we will deliver anybody who strives hard".

Viewing his own life in the same tragic light, Goethe sought similar salvation for himself. "My conviction as to our continued being is based on the notion of constant application to the task; for when I work tirelessly right to the end, nature is duty-bound to assign me another form of existence, should my present one no longer be able to endure my spirit."

Nature was Goethe's god, his guiding light, and the study of nature was his form of worship. The young Goethe became renowned as the greatest "original genius" of his time, as the prototype of that creative individuality, which, as far as it was manifested in his own emotions, gave birth to a new language.

When Goethe was old, he looked upon himself as a "collective being", for whom the wisdom of old age and all life's works were a loose synthesis of thousands of influences. He refused to be representative of a Germany heading towards a nation state; as a translator and critic and the writer of *East-west Divan*, he strove for the creation of a "world literature" in the hope that the embattled peoples of Europe "should become aware of one another, should understand one another, and if they cannot love one another, then they should at least learn to be mutually tolerant".

of our tour through Weimar, Goethe and Schiller stand side by side on a pedestal in front of the main entrance to the **German National Theatre**. During the time of the revolution in the east, when mass demonstrations were also held in Weimar, notices stating "We are staying here" were hung around their necks.

The **Museum** was the site of the meeting of the national assembly held in 1919, when the "Weimar Constitution" was passed, so giving its name to the first German republic. Other notable landmarks, many restored since World War II, include Weimar Castle, the Belvedere Castle, Tiefurt Castle and St Peter and Paul Church with an altarpiece by Lucas Cranach and his son.

Countless other famous people spent some time in Weimar. Before the time of "German Classicism", Johann Sebastian Bach worked here from 1708 to 1717 as the court organist. Later came Franz Liszt, director of music here for 17 years, and also Richard Strauss and Friedrich Nietzsche. It was here, too, that Walter Gropius founded his *Bau-* *haus* School, which soon moved to Dessau because, by the 1920s Weimar had begun to lose much of the old humanistic spirit of tolerance it once had.

The dark side of Weimar: However splendid a past Weimar might have had, the image of the city remains tarnished by the fact that it was the site of the infamous **Buchenwald** concentration camp. More than 60,000 people from some 35 countries were murdered in the camp, which was especially notorious for medical experimentation on living human beings. The camp's clock has stood still at 3.15, when on 11 April 1945 the prisoners succeeded in making a mass escape.

But the tragedy and the cruelty did not end there. The camp was taken over by the Russian secret police, and according to local estimates a further 13,000 people lost their lives between 1945 and 1950. They were supposedly political, national socialist prisoners, though many of them had been wrongfully denounced. One wonders why the world remained silent for 40 years.

The classicists Goethe and Schiller observe arts and the changing times.

JENA, GERA AND ALTENBURG

After Gotha, Erfurt and Weimar comes Jena, the last of those cities stretched out like pearls on a string along the F 7.

A town of glass: Jena first springs to mind as a major centre for the manufacture of glass and fine optics, whose production is closely associated with the name of Carl Zeiss, so famous for the production of camera lenses. At the age of 30, Zeiss realised that the emerging industrial development required a close cooperation between scientists and traditional craftsmen. He opened his workshop which produced optics in 1846, but it was only when he joined forces with the physicist Ernst Abbe in 1866 that his operation began to show any success from a business point of view. Abbe devised the first microscope constructed according to purely scientific principles. Precision optical instruments can only be made with the very best glass, and this was produced in Jena

by the chemist Otto Schott who invented the heat-resistant "Jena Glass" and founded the Schott glass factory.

Even today, the life of this town of 100,000 revolves around glass-making. The **Optical Museum** on Carl Zeiss Platz describes the road to success of the town's two great glass pioneers and no less than 13,000 optical instruments are on display, as well as 1,000 exhibits describing the history of optics. Founded in 1926, the **Zeiss Planetarium** is located at the botanical gardens. In 1985 it was equipped with a new giant projector which shows 9,000 planets in cosmic perspective.

The university: The renown of the university (founded 1558) was not created by scientists alone. Here in 1789, Friedrich Schiller presented his inaugural lecture on "freedom, equality and brotherhood" and other ideals behind the French Revolution. By the time he was 30, Schiller was already a well-known personality and the auditorium was full to the brim. He must have made quite an impression, for the university

The main market in Weimar.

still bears his name today. Schiller's memorial is situated in his former summer house, in which he wrote *The Maid of Orleans*.

In contrast to Schiller, the professor of philosophy Johann Gottlieb Fichte had real problems with the university. In 1799 he suffered the damning accusation of being an atheist. He defended himself by submitting a paper "which has to be read first before being confiscated". The poor man became the victim of his own wit and was immediately suspended.

The oldest university building, the "Collegium Jenense", dating from the 13th century, is situated at the edge of the **Market Square**. The monument in the middle of the square is that of its founder the elector Johann Friedrich, called Hanfried for short, brandishing a sword in his right hand. Perhaps this is the detail that gave the architects the necessary inspiration to design their mighty 120-metre (394-ft) high university office building right next door, an edifice which bears the epithet "Penis Jenensis". However contentious the aesthetics of the building may be, it nevertheless does not look totally out of place in a town that was virtually levelled during the war and which was rebuilt with concrete slabs. The visitor can take the lift to the restaurant on the 25th floor from which he is afforded an impressive panorama of Jena.

One of the town's few ancient buildings to have been preserved in its original state is the late-Gothic **Town Hall** with its two curved and overhanging roofs. It contains the moving figures "Schnapphans". After each strike of the hour, Schnapphans dressed in his fool's cap opens wide his toothless mouth and snaps it shut again on the offering being presented to him by the pilgrim. The cycle is completed by a croaking noise.

Gera: The town of Gera, also situated on the F 7, played a particularly notorious role in the dying hours of the GDR. In the district of Gera alone, no fewer than 2,500 snoopers and informers were employed by the Stasi, the State Security Service. And from these very of-

Evening shopping in Gera.

fices in Gera in December 1989 came the last counter-revolutionary appeal to halt the process of democratic reform. "Comrades, citizens, if we do not immediately succeed in exposing and paralysing the instigators of these venomous machinations, they shall incite the majority of the population to turn against their state and their government".

That is exactly what happened and a short time later the citizens' committee took over the building and ensured that not a single file was destroyed. The Department of Public Prosecution put all documents under its seal and they still await analysis. Only very few of the GDR's 86,000 persecutees were allowed to look inside their files, which had been assiduously compiled by full-time employees of the state security service.

Such blocks of flats surround many old town centres. This one is in Gera.

Right up until reunification, the dissolution of the Stasi became one of the most awkward questions with which the GDR was confronted. The issue resulted in Ministers resigning and many delegates to the People's Chamber had to abandon their brief.

Attractive town centre: The former Stasi complex is not far from the town centre which is well worth visiting because Gera's **Market Square** is one of the most attractive in all Thuringia. The focal point is the **Town Hall** dating from the 15th century with its richly decorated six-storey tower (57 metres/ 187 ft). The building is surrounded by the old Apothecary (1606), the three-storey baroque government building (1772) and a collection of houses dating from the Middle Ages. All these buildings were restored in the 1960s.

The Museum in the Strasse der Republik provides information about the history of the town. It is housed in the former **Penitentiary and Orphanage** built in 1738. The town's art gallery is to be found in the **Orangery** and contains impressive collections from Lucas Cranach the Elder, Rembrandt, Jan von Goyen and Max Liebermann. Well-known artists from the GDR such as Bernhard Heisig, Willi Sitte and Werner Tübke are also represented. The **Otto Dix Collection** is particularly im-

portant. The painter and graphic artist whose paintings deal largely with the miseries of war and with social injustices was born in Gera in 1891. He was forbidden to continue painting by the Nazis in 1934.

A number of interesting churches can be seen in Gera. The **Parish Church of St Mary** is a single nave late-Gothic edifice built in the 15th century. The **Church of Our Saviour** is a triple nave baroque building dating from 1720, although it was refurbished in Art Nouveau style at the turn of the century. The **Church of the Holy Trinity** dates back to the 14th century.

Deadly doses: Driving along the F 7 about 14 km (9 miles) the other side of Gera, the traveller can hardly miss the stark outlines of two enormous pyramids, both over 100 metres (330 ft) high. They are mounds of ore which was once known as black gold or pitchblende, but which is now called uraninite. More than 50,000 people used to work here in the uranium mines, obtaining the basic raw material for the manufacture of the Soviet Union's atomic bombs.

One guidebook to the GDR reads "It was in 1766 that the amazing healing potential of the radioactive springs at Ronneburg was discovered". For several decades Ronneburg established a reputation as being one of Europe's top spa resorts, but then, as luck would have it, its name was forgotten. Fortunate indeed, since it has been established that such radioactive healing properties bring anything but good health. A study carried out in 1926 showed that 71 percent of Gera miners died of cancer.

Today, the radioactive contamination levels around Ronneburg remain 300 times those of Berlin. Blown from the mounds of ore, radioactive dust settles over the surrounding area. And unfiltered water collecting at the base of the mounds also finds its way along ditches into the surrounding corn and potato fields. "No drinking water" is the only warning sign, although the words themselves are hardly readable through the rust. Billions of DM are necessary to cleanse the area, and by rights the

Uranium for the Soviet bombs, cancer for workers and residents in Ronneburg.

Soviet Union, which still has majority ownership of the uranium mine, should be the one to pay.

If, despite this carbuncle on the landscape, one still decides to head for Ronneburg, then there is always the late-Gothic **Castle** to visit, as well as the old spa facilities.

Altenburg: The last stop on the F 7 is a paradise for gamblers. Whoever knows the card game skat might have heard of **Altenburg**, where between 1810 and 1817 the game was devised from a number of older card games. Altenburg is the seat of the High Court of skat, and its decisions are recognised internationally. While on the oldest market square in the town, the **Buhl**, it might be possible to overlook the baroque **Seckendorfsche Palais** (1725), the **Town Hall** (1604), and the handsome **Merchants' Houses**, but it is impossible to miss the **Skat Fountain** standing in the middle. It must be the only monument in the world dedicated to a card game. A **Playing Cards Museum** is housed in the castle. The wide collection of all differ-

ent kinds of playing cards and tarots, including hand-coloured cards printed from woodcuts in the 15th century, as well as the card maker's workshop dating from the turn of the 17th century, all testify to the importance that cards have had for Altenburg, the most easterly town in the state of Thuringia.

Home of the "Trabi": Thirty-five km (22 miles) to the south, over the border in Saxony, lies the industrial town of **Zwickau**. This is where the legendary Trabants are produced, cars which achieved overnight world fame when they came streaming over to the West after the collapse of the Wall. "Trabis" were born here back in the 1950s. Powered by a single two-stroke engine, they are made of plastic and possess no crush section, which means that when they crash, even at the modest speed of 30 kph (19 mph), they disintegrate. The greatest danger to life and limb is the steering column which, even through the slightest impact, is catapulted into the interior of the car. The positioning of the petrol tank also leaves much to be

desired – it is located under the bonnet, directly at the zone of collision. Although they really belong on the scrap heap, 3.4 million of these moving environmental disasters are still on the road. At least the vehicle is no longer produced and Volkswagen is now investing billions in replacing it with the Polo.

First mentioned in 1118, Zwickau seems to have made every effort to ensure that it appeared at the very end of any alphabetical listing. Its name was originally written Zzwickau! The town became important as a customs post along the trade route between Halle and Prague. In the 15th century it blossomed as a centre of cloth manufacture and silver mining in the Erz Mountains. Until 1977 it was the GDR's chief centre of coal production.

The town's main attractions are located around the main **Market Place**. There is the **Town Hall**, rebuilt in neo-Gothic style in 1862, the **Cloth Merchants' Warehouse** dating from 1525 (a theatre since 1825) and a number of fine **Patrician Houses**, including the

birthplace of the composer Robert Schumann (1810–56), whose legacy is maintained in the Museum, the Schumann Society and the Conservatory.

One of the noblest houses on the market place belonged to the silver mine owner Martin Römer. On his way to Italy he visited the master carver Michael Wohlgemut, teacher of the famous Albrecht Dürer. To honour the Creator, "who alone guides the miners to treasure beyond their wildest dreams", Römer ordered a magnificent winged altar-piece (1479) for the Cathedral, "for whose gold and figures no costs should be spared". The altar is a true masterpiece, bathed in Gothic light.

It is well worth taking a stroll along the pedestrian precinct, with its restored period architecture. There are a number of inviting street cafés.

Concrete city: Our journey continues from one industrial centre to another. But in contrast to Zwickau, the city centre of **Chemnitz** was almost entirely destroyed during the war. It is now a **Patches of urban decay.**

place of broad boulevards lined with ugly concrete blocks. One edifice that stands out amidst all the monotony is the gigantic head of Karl Marx. Created in the 1960s, it is a mighty monument indeed; all of 7 metres (23 ft) high, its 42 tons are supported by a plinth of granite from the Ukraine.

But Karl Marx is now something of an anachronism in Chemnitz, particularly as he never actually set foot in the place. This, coupled with the fact that many East Germans now tend to lay the GDR's failures squarely at his door, would indicate that he is hardly the most revered of historical personages. Understandably enough, the citizens voted to have the name Karl Marx Stadt, as the city was known from 1953, revert to Chemnitz.

Since the 15th century it was ore mining in the local Erz (ore) Mountains that provided the basis of the city's prosperity. Chemnitz served as a centre of supply and transshipment to and from the mines. As in Zwickau, cloth also played an important role in the city's

development. It was initially produced by weaving families in their cottage industries, and later (from 1800) in large spinning mills which were powered first by water and then by steam. Chemnitz soon acquired the reputation of being a "German Manchester"; while a few clever entrepreneurs became extraordinarily wealthy, many of those whose cottage industries had been dismantled became the victims of unimaginable poverty. The fact that, even before the changes in the East, Volkswagen produced engines here (for Wartburg cars) is indicative of a certain slowness in economic development.

The city centre: The only unsullied part of the old city centre is around the **Theaterplatz**, with the **Opera House** and the **Museum**, whose splendid Art Nouveau interior has been preserved. The amazing Petrified Forest is probably unique among museum exhibits. The old **Town Hall** dating from 1498 was yet another victim of bombardment, but it has now been rebuilt to look like the original.

DRESDEN

Dresden is the most beautiful city in Germany – or at least that's what the locals say. But millions of annual visitors also marvel at the Zwinger, the Semper Opera House, the River Elbe and Pillnitz Palace. Magnificent gardens and the resplendent creations of voluptuous baroque provide a sumptuous stage for this stronghold of Augustus the Strong (1670–1733). The sights to be seen in Dresden today are mostly down to that one man, the Hun with the boyish soul, who not only enjoyed life to the full but as a man of great vision also set about the planning of this *his* city.

More culture, more art, less military strength and less power were his priorities. "Princes become immortal through their creations", was his motto. That is why he summoned the most capable architects and artists to his court. The monument to Augustus the Strong was created during his own lifetime, and with masterful success. The only exception is his actual memorial, the golden equestrian statue, which looks rather out of place on the market place in Neustadt.

Augustus made sure that life would continue after death by fathering a total of 352 children. The best-known of his mistresses was the Duchess Cosel whom he incarcerated for 47 years in Stolpen Castle, a sentence which continued even after his death. Society intrigue and the accusation that she had involved herself in politics caused her downfall.

Augustus was no angel. This is clearly demonstrated by his oppression of the peasants, the ever-more ruthless tax squeeze that he imposed on them, and the abysmal wages he paid the workers building the Zwinger. There was severe punishment for the slightest murmur of discontent. Although Augustus maintained a standing army, he did not need to use it to become king of Poland. That he achieved by corruption.

The Venice on the Elbe: As if blown there by the wind, Dresden came to settle on a broad bend in the River Elbe. This was Augustus' "Grand Canal" and he had Venetian gondolas escort him to and from Pillnitz, the palace he had built in Chinese style. The nobility that flocked here from all over Europe needed to be entertained, so he employed a chief treasurer specifically to control the unbelievable sums of money required. The Prussians denounced this lifestyle. "When the pomposity of the Saxon Albertine so graciously mingled with the prostitution of the Polish nobility, then did German absolutism lose all its virtue".

Numerous artists added to the city's fame: the composers Heinrich Schütz, Carl Maria von Weber, Richard Wagner and Robert Schumann; the writers E.T.A. Hoffmann, Erich Kästner and Karl May; the painters Canaletto, Philipp Otto Runge and Caspar David Friedrich. And then there are the equally impressive and venerable names of the city's musical tradition: the Kreuzchor, the State Orchestra, the Semper Opera and the Dresden Philharmonic.

Preceding pages: Augustus the Strong had the Zwinger built as the setting for a wedding. Left, Augustus's monument in Dresden. Right, renovation awaits the palace in Dresden.

Past and present: Today Dresden lives somewhere between the restored splendours of its past and the ostentatious, but architecturally hidebound, pedestrian precinct Prager Strasse. It lives between untreated sewage, polluted air and the attempt to develop itself once more into a metropolis of classical tourism.

It promises to be a hard struggle. In the "valley of the ignorant", as the region was known because it was unable to receive Western television, the number of people seeking to leave the country in 1989 was well above the national average. In that summer alone, no fewer than 22,000 people fled to the West. Since the collapse of the Wall, numerous local firms have had to close down, such as the camera manufacturer Pentacon with the loss of 6,000 jobs.

Historic Dresden has had its fair share of hardship in recent years. During the night of 13/14 February 1945, in the dying days of World War II, the city was annihilated by a massive allied bomb attack. Sanctioned by Churchill, the bombing was calculated to inflict as much damage on the city as possible. At least 35,000 people lost their lives in the inferno. Coventry was more than avenged.

First orientations: A good view of the city can be had from the top of the town hall tower, which can be reached by lift. Directly beneath is the **Kreuzkirche** which was rebuilt in baroque style and is said to contain a fragment of the Holy Cross. Every Saturday vespers are sung here by the Kreuzchor. Across on the Neumarkt (new market) stand the imposing ruins of the Church of Our Lady as a lasting reminder to the ravages of war. It was on this site that the foundations of Dresden were laid in the middle of the 11th century, when a Christian missionary centre was established by monks out to convert the heathen Slavic Sorbs.

Merchants settled here on the crossing point over the Elbe. In the Middle Ages there was already a stone bridge in place, at the point where the **Augustusbrücke** now joins the two halves of the city. In 1485 the Albertine,

The Semper Opera House by night.

the Saxon line of the ruling Wettin family, elevated Dresden to a royal city. But when the Europe of the Middle Ages began to open up to the ideas of Luther and the Reformation, Georg the Bearded sided firmly with the Pope. It was only after the Thirty Years' War that the city really blossomed with the arrival of the baroque and Augustus the Strong. A new world emerged, a world that cast aside all links with the past.

Zwinger: After establishing our bearings from the town hall, the **Zwinger**, the crowning achievement of the baroque on the Elbe, now stands as the focal point of our tour of the city. Augustus' original intention was an orangery, because every ruler had to have an orangery. Located as it was between the inner and the outer defensive walls, the complex came to be called "Zwinger" – the outer bailey. With its mighty gateways, its pavilions, galleries and gardens, the building expanded to take up an enormous area. It was provisionally completed in 1719, just in time for the marriage of Prince Friedrich August II

Sunset behind the Hofkirche.

(1696–1763) to the Archduchess Maria Josepha (1699–1757), a daughter of Austria's Habsburg empress Maria Theresia.

The grounds were embellished with fountains and statues and the occasion was celebrated in grand style on this "outdoor festival ground". The court architect Matthäus Daniel Pöppelmann and the sculptor Balthasar Permoser had taken as their model just about every conceivable representative building that had ever been created: not only from Rome, Vienna and Prague but also from the orangery at Versailles. Augustus had admired this building while visiting Louis XIV.

The Zwinger houses a number of art galleries and collections, of which the **Gemäldegalerie Alter Meister** (the Old Masters' Art Gallery) is the most important. Completed in 1854 it was the creation of Gottfried Semper. The collection itself, founded by Augustus, consists of 2,000 works of painters from Germany, Flanders, Holland, France and Italy. The most famous paintings are Raphael's *Sistine Madonna*, Rembrandt's *Self-portrait with Saskia* and Dürer's *Sieben schmerzen der Maria*. The **Historical Museum**, located in the east wing of the same building, contains a superb collection of ceremonial weapons. The **Porcelain Collection**, after Topkapi Serayi in Istanbul the largest such collection in the world, can be viewed in the Long Gallery.

The Semper Opera House: World famous for both its architecture and its music, the **Semper Opera House** stands next to the Zwinger on the expansive **Theaterplatz**. Named after its architect Gottfried Semper (1803–79), it was built in the style of the High Italian Renaissance. The equestrian statue of King Johann and the memorial to the composer Carl Maria von Weber stand in front of the main entrance. The reopening of the opera house after restoration work was completed in 1985 and was marked by a performance of Weber's *Freischütz*, the first German opera. Weber was the court conductor from 1817 to 1826.

At the beginning of the 20th century

the first nights of Richard Strauss's *Salome* and *Elektra* received rapturous applause here. Even before the opera house was built, another theatre had stood on the same site from 1719 until 1869, when it was destroyed by fire. It was here that the first performances of Wagner's operas *Rienzi* (1842), *The Flying Dutchman* (1843) and *Tannhäuser* (1845) were staged. Wagner became an idol, at least until he was forced to take refuge abroad. In 1849 he had sided with the underdogs, the bourgeois rebels taking part in the German Revolution. He had sent signals from the tower of the town hall to warn the provisional government (which included the Russian anarchist Michael Bakunin) of the imminent approach of the Saxon-Prussian loyalist forces.

The **Old City Guard House** is situated on the eastern side of Theaterplatz. The building was designed by the classicist architect Karl Friedrich Schinkel, who is most famous for his classical buildings in Berlin. With its six sandstone Ionic columns this particular edifice is reminiscent of a Greek temple.

Theaterplatz is dominated by the Catholic **Hofkirche** (1739–55). Planned by Augustus III it is Saxony's largest church. As well as the 78 statues to be found in the external niches of the building, the intricately carved wooden pulpit (by Balthasar Permoser) and the magnificent organ (built by Silbermann 1753) are worthy of attention.

In 1985 work began on rebuilding the completely destroyed **Castle** (1547), although the **Georgentor** had been completed in 1967. This is where the State Art Collection will be housed in the future. From here the **Lange Gang** (long passage) leads to the **Johanneum**, the erstwhile royal stables on the Neumarkt, which now houses the **Transport Museum**. Along the external wall of the passage 35 Wettin rulers are depicted in a royal parade. In 1876, the mural was rendered in scratchwork, but then in 1906 this was overlaid by 24,000 ceramic tiles from Meissen.

War memorial: There is some debate as to whether the ruins of the **Church of**

Resting the legs.

Our Lady (1726–43) should be left as they are or should rise again. The dome of the church, which was once 95 metres (312 ft) high, came crashing down amidst the rain of bombs in 1945. The Frauenkirche was the most important Protestant church in Germany. Martin Luther continues his vigil in front of the ruins, sternly pointing at his Bible.

Passing the **Hotel Dresdner Hof** (opened 1989) the visitor will arrive at the **Sekundogenitur**, the library which automatically came into the possession of every second-born prince. Today it is a café and wine bar and leads to the **Brühlsche Terrasse** (1738) on the Elbe. Known as the "window to Europe", this is now the quay at which the White Fleet steamers pull in. It was here in the **Jungfernbastei** with its pleasure pavilions that Johann Friedrich Böttger, while attempting to alchemize gold, succeeded in discovering porcelain.

The **Albertinum** was originally built as an arsenal. In addition to its sculptures and collection of coins, the Grüne Gewölbe, or **Green Vaults**, contain a unique collection of treasures from the Saxon electors: jewellery, precious stones and priceless paintings from the 14th–16th centuries. In the **Galerie Neuer Meister**, the paintings are not contemporary as the name might imply, but from the 19th century. Works on display include such masterpieces as Caspar David Friedrich's *Cross in the Mountains* and Paul Gauguin's *Two Ladies from Tahiti*.

Around Dresden: The most popular weekend excursion for the people of Dresden, **Loschwitz**, was once a haven of peace for the nobility and educated elite of the city. The painter and writer Wilhelm von Kügelen (1802–67) describes in his "childhood memories" how he spent his holidays with his parents in Loschwitz: "From the upper floor it was possible to step out onto a balcony which was shaded from the sun by old walnut trees."

The composer Heinrich Schütz and Augustus the Strong's goldsmith also spent their holidays here. And Christian Gottfried Körner, the art patron, invited

Pillnitz Palace on the Elbe viewed from the rear. Augustus the Strong liked to come here by gondola.

his literary friends, including Friedrich Schiller who spent most of his sojourn writing *Don Carlos*. Since 1896, Loschwitz, lying to the east of Dresden, has been accessible by tram. A **funicular railway** leads up the hillside to the Luisenhof café whose terrace affords fine views of the Elbe and the city.

The most important recreation area close to Dresden is the **Dresden Heath**. In devising an organised system of paths through the woods Heinrich Cotta (1763–1844) was an early pioneer of nature walks. In **Klein-Hosterwitz** there is a museum dedicated to Carl Maria von Weber. The composer would come here to recover from the toils of court life. He wished to alter the seating arrangement of the orchestra and to introduce the baton. Until then cues had always been given by the pianist. Although King Friedrich August I forbade this innovation, the orchestra stood by Weber and he eventually had his way.

The visitor can find out all he ever wanted to know about Richard Wagner at the museum in **Graupa**, where the composer lived on a farm estate. As director of the opera, Wagner was beset by constant problems. He neither managed to increase the size of his orchestra nor to achieve higher wages for his musicians. He spent a great deal of time in the *Sächsische Schweiz* – the Switzerland of Saxony – to the south of Dresden, and there, atop the crags of the **Bastei**, he gained much of the inspiration for his music.

By crossing the Loshwitzer Brücke and then taking the road to Pillnitz, the traveller will soon find himself on a narrow country road leading directly to **Pillnitz Palace**. This "Indian pleasure palace" complete with "Turkish and Persian furniture" became the summer residence of the kings and queens of Saxony. It was primarily the creation of the architect responsible for the Zwinger, namely Matthäus Daniel Pöppelmann. With its sweeping pagoda roofs, it conformed to the exotic tastes of the courtly late-baroque and today rates as an important example of the Chinese vogue so prevalent at that time. The main fa-

The Karl May Museum in Radebeul.

cade, with its broad two-tiered staircase, looks out across the river.

Excursions downstream: In the other direction, following the river downstream, are three further sights connected with Augustus the Strong: Radebeul, Moritzburg and Meissen. The tram ride to **Radebeul** provides an opportunity to sample the outlying districts of Dresden which, unlike the city centre, largely escaped the destruction of 1945. Radebeul emerged in 1924 from the fusion of 10 communities and this town of 35,000 therefore has no clearly defined centre. When you arrive at the stop "Landgasthof Weisses Ross" you can continue to explore on foot or change for the tram to Moritzburg.

Passing through old wine growing estates you arrive at the yellow **Spitzhaus**, today a popular restaurant. At the bottom of the flight of steps (designed by Pöppelmann) leading up to the building, stands **Haus Hoflösnitz**, which contains the **Viticulture Museum**. This was originally Augustus the Strong's "summer-house" and he would

European hard porcelain was invented in Meissen.

come here during the grape harvest to join in the vintage festivals and the vintner parades. The showpiece of the museum is a phylloxera which can be viewed through the microscope. It was these insects that were responsible for devastating the vineyards back in 1885. Phylloxera-resistant vines from America were introduced in 1920.

With his gripping tales of lands he had never even visited, Karl May was Germany's answer to Henry Rider-Haggard. The Karl May Museum is located in **Villa Shatterhand**, where the writer lived out his final years. Despite receiving 250,000 visitors every year, the building is in a poor state of repair. May was ostracised in the GDR until 1984 when the regime officially rehabilitated him as a "mediator of humanist values". More fascinating, particularly for children, is a visit to the **Puppet Theatre Collection** in the **Hohenhaus**, the interior of which is preserved in its original state. The richly furnished rooms have an overwhelming atmosphere, brought alive by the puppets themselves.

Moritzburg is accessible via a narrow gauge railway which spookily howls its way through the forest. Augustus the Strong used the Mansion, which could accommodate 100 guests, as his official hunting lodge. The splendid museum describes how they were entertained.

Meissen: The bridge over the Elbe rattles disconcertingly as you cross it on the way to Meissen, the city of porcelain. Over 1,000 years old, Meissen used to be the hub of Saxony. Most of the buildings surrounding the market place date from the Middle Ages and this atmosphere has been preserved.

The **Albrechtsburg**, completed in 1525, was the first of the Wettin family's residential palaces. In 1710 Augustus the Strong moved the production of porcelain here in order to keep the formula a secret. Augustus had apprehended the runaway apprentice chemist Friedrich Böttger so that he might employ his alchemy skills in the production of gold and thereby rescue the shattered finances of the state. However, Böttger's experiments only resulted in porcelain.

J.H. Böttger laboriret in der Burgk auf Gold, flcms.

THE ELBSANDSTEIN MOUNTAINS

Whatever excursions one decides to embark on from Dresden, the chances are that Augustus the Strong went the same way. He certainly spent some time in the *Sächsische Schweiz*, Saxony's "little Switzerland", the Saxonian part of the Elbsandstein Mountains, the sandstone uplands which lie to the southeast of Dresden and straddle the border with Czechoslovakia. In his day the area was much more isolated. It was only in 1850 that the railway was completed, opening up the region to tourism. In 1857 the area also became accessible by steamer from Dresden. In earlier times the wealthy were carried by litter through these rugged mountains.

The gateway to the hills: The last bridge over the Elb before the Czechoslovakian border was a decisive factor in the development of the town of **Pirna**. Until the late-Middle Ages the town was a trading post for the entire region. Today, the city centre is classified as a historical monument. Although Pirna was spared the aerial bombardments of World War II, many of the town's buildings have since been allowed to fall into a sad state of disrepair. Once splendid houses now lie empty and decaying; many have been demolished.

Gothic, Renaissance, baroque and neoclassical buildings lie side by side in a heap of despair. Yet, it is still possible to sense the prosperity the place once had, and like an impoverished nobleman trying to rescue his birthright, the people of this town are now set on recapturing the glories of days gone by.

The area around the market place has been partly restored. In the centre, the **Town Hall** stands alone. The building displays architectural influences spreading over five centuries, starting with the ground floor which dates back to 1485. The portals and gables are of Gothic origin and the tower was added in 1718.

The residences surrounding the market place excel with their fine arcades and oriel windows. Particularly worth inspection are No. 3 with its five cano-pied niches (1500) and No. 7, the **Canalettohaus**, with its steep and richly decorated gable. Not long ago it would have been possible to appreciate fully the "Canaletto view" which presented itself to the master as he painted scenes of this market place. A picturesque place it certainly must have been, otherwise Canaletto, famous for his precise depictions of Dresden, Warsaw and Vienna, would not have been attracted here.

The tower of the **Church of St Mary**, to the east of the town centre, is a good vantage point from which to view the town, the rolling foothills of the eastern Erz Mountains and the Switzerland of Saxony. The twin-naved church with impressive ribbed vaulting was built around 1300.

The **Sonnenstein Fortress** rises above the city. Although it has a history dating back to medieval times, the present buildings actually date from the 19th century when the complex was converted into a sanatorium. During the Third Reich, the fortress was used for the euthanasia programme. Some 10,000

Left, the Switzerland of Saxony is a paradise for climbers. Right, the Elbe winds its way through the Elbsandstein Mountains.

sick people were murdered. Even a GDR guidebook on the region suppresses this dreadful period in the fortress' history. After the war, aeroplane engines were developed at the Sonnenstein, and today it is a centre for treating psychologically disturbed children.

Five km (3 miles) outside Pirna are the romantic **Grossedlitz Baroque Gardens**. The property was acquired by Augustus the Strong in 1723. He completely redesigned the place to provide a suitable setting for his extravagant parties, commissioning the addition of statues, free flights of steps and an array of waterworks and fountains from his specialist Matthäus Daniel Pöppelmann. Nowadays the mirrored hall of **Friedrichs Castle** is used by newly-weds to celebrate their Big Day.

The Elbsandstein Mountains: The Switzerland of Saxony was only "discovered" as a walker's paradise around the turn of the 19th century. Two local men, Wilhelm Leberect Götzinger (1758–1818), a magistrate, and the priest Carl Heinrich Nicolai (1739–1823), through their many publications, were responsible for introducing hikers and climbers to the region. However, the name "Switzerland of Saxony" was actually coined by two Swiss artists who studied at the academy in Leipzig. The paintings of Adrian Zingg (1734–1816) and Anton Graff (1736–1813) can still be seen in the galleries of Dresden.

The most popular path in those days was known as the "Malerstrasse", the "painter's road". It was a three- or four-day walk from Dresden to Prebizschtor, which lies just over the border in today's Czechoslovakia. Caspar David Friedrich lost his heart to the region when he walked this route. He returned by taking the steamer down the Elb.

What is it that continues to draw people to this part of the world? With the Grosse Winterberg topping out at just 552 metres (1,713 ft), it can't be the height. The mountains here are molehills when compared to the mighty Alps. No, the biggest lure of the region is the fascinating topography with cliff faces carved in a multitude of forms, freestanding pillars of rock and deep ra-

vines running between them. The land was sculpted by the Elb and its tributaries which over millions of years eroded the single sandstone plateau of which the region was originally composed. Today the process continues. Roads and tracks are constantly threatened by falling rocks. Climbers often underestimate the difficulty of some routes and some crags have now been closed due to the instability of the rock. Acid rain is accelerating the process of erosion.

After the Baltic, the Switzerland of Saxony was the second most popular tourist destination in the GDR. Encompassing 368 square km (142 sq miles), it was visited by 3 million people annually.

River trip: One of the best ways to appreciate the countryside is by taking the steamer from Dresden to the border town of Schmilka. The Elb is more playful, friendly and lively than the broad, majestic Rhine. Against the current, the trip lasts six-and-a-half hours: the return journey to Dresden only four. A double-decker train also runs along

The library of the Sorbs, one of Germany's Slavic minorities.

the banks of the river. The first really stunning feature are the rugged cliffs of the **Bastei**, from the top of which there are superb views of the Elb plateau. At the "Rockfall", one of the most popular crags, a 76-metre (250-ft) long stone bridge crosses the impressive **Mardertelle Gorge**.

The ship soon draws in at the health spa of **Rathen**, a town closed to vehicles. In the summer time, the amphitheatre of cliffs provides a natural backdrop to the open air theatre which has a seating capacity of 2,000. The programme is extremely varied. Beyond Rathen, **Königstein Fortress** stands sentinel 360 metres (1,181 ft) above the river. Augustus the Strong was responsible for the construction of this pleasure palace. The largest wine vat in the world with a capacity of 250,000 litres is housed in the building's vaults. The prison dungeons were once occupied by Michael Bakunin, the Russian anarchist who was incarcerated here for his part in the Dresden Revolt of 1849.

Bad Schandau stretches along the river for some distance. Built in 1704, the local church is a great attraction. Both the pulpit and the altar are carved from local sandstone and the altar is also set with locally occurring precious stones. Hikers can take the **Kirnitztal Railway**, incorporating the very best technology that the 1920s could provide, to the **Lichtenheiner Waterfalls**. This is the starting point for the climb to the "Cow Shed", a deep cave 11 metres high by 17 metres wide (36 ft by 56 ft) in which the robber knights would hide the cattle they had stolen.

After 51.5 km (32 miles), the steamer reaches the border town of **Schmilka**, after which the Elb forms the international boundary for several kilometres. The fact that at this point the river falls no more than two centimetres along a length of one kilometre means that it is often frozen over in the winter time.

After this tour of the countryside, we come to a particularly neglected part of Germany, the far southeastern corner of the former GDR. Three minorities live here; the Slavic Sorbs in Bautzen, the

Religious motifs are the theme of this Sorbian woodcarver's creations.

Moravian brotherhood also near Bautzen and a community of Silesians in Görlitz.

Prison and mass graves: For many thousands of people who opposed the GDR regime, the town of **Bautzen** has bitter memories. Here was the prison in which they served out their long sentences, although some of them managed to make it over to the West, after the Federal Government had paid the necessary ransom.

It was only after the changes in 1989 that a grisly discovery of bones revealed the true extent of the terror inflicted by the Russian Secret Service between 1945 and the early 1950s. The largest mass grave of the German post war era is said to be the one lying next to the prison in Bautzen. It contains the remains of some 17,000 prisoners. Bautzen was one of 11 Soviet internment camps in which a total of 70,000 people lost their lives.

Standing on a granite outcrop, **Ortenburg Castle** was built as a border outpost during the eastwards expansion of the Germans. It first belonged to Bohemia and after 1635 to Saxony. In Bautzen's **Old Town**, the historic facades of many buildings have been renovated. The nondenominational **Church of St Peter**, with its 85-metre (283-ft) high tower, has been used by both confessions since the Reformation (1524), when it was agreed that the Protestants take the nave and the Catholics the choir. An iron grill continues to divide the church.

The Sorbs: Totalling about 60,000 in number the Sorbs, the smallest Slavic group, live scattered between Bautzen and Hoyerswerda and as far as Cottbus and the Spree Forest. Their parent organisation, the "Domowina" (homeland) is based in Bautzen. Under the Nazis the Sorbs were degraded as a "leaderless band of peasants" and their patriots ended up in the concentration camps. Later, in the GDR, they were regarded as nothing more than a token minority. Although they were allowed to wear their traditional costumes and to continue to paint their Easter eggs, their rights were not protected. The traditional village communities were ruth-

This castle at Muskau has seen better days.

lessly destroyed by the collectivisation and the loss of land brought about by the development of opencast coal mining.

The Stasi even maintained a separate department responsible for shadowing the Sorbs. Today they continue to have a hard time preserving their cultural traditions and their language, not least because the language itself is spoken in two quite different dialects – upper-Sorbian and lower-Sorbian. It is astounding that the Sorbs have managed to survive as an independent people.

Moravians: To the south of Löbau, between Bautzen and Görlitz, lies **Herrnhut**, the home of the religious minority of the Moravians (or Herrnhuter). The brotherhood was founded in 1722 by the pious Count Nikolaus von Zinzendorf and his Bohemian-Moravian fellow-believers.

The especially moving thing about the Moravians is their piety. For example, early on Easter Sunday morning, when it is still dark, the entire community joins in a procession to the graveyard accompanied by the resonant sounds of bassoons. Sunrise heralds the celebration of the Ascension of Christ. The simplicity of the graves is intended to express the equality of man after death. The Museum of Anthropology in Herrnhut shows the result of the sect's missionary work in places as far-flung as Southern and East Africa, Tibet and Kashmir, Alaska, Labrador and Greenland.

Border town: Situated on both sides of the **River Neisse**, **Görlitz**, Germany's most easterly town, is divided between Germany and Poland. The Görlitz Agreement of 1950 made the **Oder-Neisse Line** the "inviolable border of peace and friendship" between the GDR and Poland, although it was closed in 1980 in an attempt to stop the spread of the Solidarnosç virus. The final signing of a further border agreement prior to Germany's reunification in 1990 put the seal on any visions anybody might have had of the new Germany expanding once more towards the east. The Oder-Neisse border remains sacrosanct and has now been reopened.

With a present population of 76,000, compared to 100,000 in 1949, Görlitz is now in decline. The town experienced its most prosperous period in the 15th century. At that time the most important crossing over the Neisse blossomed into a centre for the trading of cloth and blue dyes. Here was the junction of two important land routes; that from Stettin via Frankfurt on the Oder to Prague and from Leipzig to Breslau.

Those flourishing times are recalled by a number of late-Gothic churches, merchant's houses and the town hall. The towers of the **Parish Church of St Peter and Paul** soar heavenwards. Particularly beautiful features within the building are the altar (1695) and the pulpit (1693). Still older is the double-winged altar in the upper church of the erstwhile **Franciscan Monastery** dating from 1510. The baroque altar in the same church was installed in 1713. The oldest church in Görlitz is the triple-naved **Church of St Nicholas** which was dedicated in 1492.

To Berlin: Following the F115 through a seemingly empty part of Germany

Bautzen has bad memories for political detainees.

near the Polish border, the traveller arrives in **Bad Muskau** with its 16th-century castle. It was here that in 1785 Duke Hermann von Pückler-Muskau came into the world. The **Castle Museum** describes how the duke laid out his large 200-hectare (450-acre) country park between 1815 and 1835. With its smooth transition into the adjacent countryside this is a jewel of landscape design.

To the west of Bad Muskau, **Kromlau Castle** (1845) is also surrounded by beautiful parkland, as is the nearby hunting lodge at **Weisswasser** whose grounds – another of the duke's creations – were planned along typically "English" lines. Duke Hermann lived in Muskau Castle with his wife Lucie. They were soon joined by his Abyssinian girlfriend Machbuba whom he had discovered at a slave auction when she was 12. Lucie was not impressed. The duke's name lives on in a famous brand of German ice-cream, although what is now available in the supermarkets bears little resemblance to his original recipe.

Passing abandoned farmyards and taking care to avoid occasional families of ducks and turkeys waddling down the road, the rural idyll is soon destroyed by the emergence of the brown coal mines around **Cottbus**. The town became important due to its advantageous position on the Salt Road. Scarcely a trace of this early prosperity remains. Urban blight is well-established here; rows and rows of decaying houses, many abandoned, windows boarded up. Practically the only surviving testimony to better days is the lovingly restored Art Nouveau **Theatre**. Inside and out the building is richly decorated with little obelisks and allegorical figures, marble and mirrors.

Frankfurt on the Oder: The bridge over the River Oder to Poland is situated in the centre of Frankfurt and is today the only outstanding sight. The prosperous days of the city are long-gone. As early as 1368, Frankfurt was a member of the Hanseatic League, the influential medieval alliance of trading cities. From 1506 to 1811 it was home to the first university in the Brandenburg Marches and then greatly expanded as a result of industrialisation in Upper Silesia.

But the university was moved to Breslau and the eastern part of the city now lies in Poland. Commerce and cultural life became oriented towards Berlin which is only 70 km (43 miles) away. Frankfurt's most famous son is the poet Heinrich von Kleist (1775–1811). His memory is kept alive in the Museum, housed in a miniature baroque palace.

The journey to Berlin continues along the F 5 and F1, the road tunnelling its way through dense avenues of trees. This is something of a novelty for West Germans, for in West Germany most of the trees which line the roads have been felled. Occasionally, the road passes idyllic villages with carefully-tended gardens nestling next to small ponds at clearings in the forest, although for much of the journey the scenery consists of huge fields of maize. Eventually the countryside gives way to the city as the first grey blocks of flats start to appear along the route and the gardens give way to balconies.

Left and **right**, the former GDR still retains a rich baroque legacy.

BERLIN: MYTH AND HISTORY

"Zurückbleiben!" If you've ever been on the underground in Berlin, then you will doubtless recall this particular command, the raw Prussian voice demanding, not even remotely politely, that you "stand back". And when the train pulls in you'd better have your wits about you, otherwise you might well find yourself having to wait for the next one, or maybe even the one after that.

The mad scrimmage to get through those doors is indicative of the character of Berlin: you have to be quick, no waiting around, always on the point of doing something – and whoever gets there too late might have to wait a while before he gets another chance.

Berlin, the racy city. It seems that history is continuously made here, and not only when walls start to collapse. History always was and continues to remain plainly evident, whether in matters cultural, political or simply in matters of daily life.

The Berliners themselves seem unperturbed by the fact that most visitors are here to see Berlin the myth rather than Berlin the reality. When the world was still moved to tears by the events of reunification, the West Berliners were already on the look-out for weekend retreats in all that newly acquired countryside, whilst the East Berliners were equally busy looking for lucrative jobs in West Berlin. And the main topic of conversation was already old hat as the heated debate about Berlin's future status got underway in Bonn. After all, whether as a capital city or not, Berlin was always a metropolis. In Berlin history and change are always more quickly digested than elsewhere.

But the stimuli which were born in Berlin were not always of a positive nature. In this century alone two world wars have been waged from this city, and in Berlin the destruction of the Jews was decided upon and organised. But despite the evil of Nazi rule and the almost total destruction of the city in the last war, the metropolitan identity remained intact in "that pile of rubble next to Potsdam". The people, or more precisely the women, rebuilt the city and the Berliners survived the Blockade, the Cold War and the building of the Wall. Instead of sinking into apathy and provincial oblivion, Berlin once more became the fountainhead of innovation. It was here that the student protests of the 1960s began and a short while afterwards the young people of this "capitalist island in a socialist sea" created for themselves an alternative lifestyle. And the Wall also provided an alternative: should the train have already pulled out, then one simply waited patiently for the next one.

Nowadays, people in the eastern half of the city do not see things very differently. Of course, the grey old men of the Politburo attempted, with the help of parades and red flags, repression and control, to create a socialist capital in which they and only they could dictate the terms. But even the socialist East Berliners remain first and foremost Berliners, and there were always niches in which they could find their own free space, could give vent to their own free opinions. Politically contentious art was simply displayed in private flats or garages; protest and subversive resistance were articulated in the form of a church service.

And today? Signs of the past are to be found all over the place. Fine works of art and architecture, the Prussian legacy, remain from the times of the Hohenzollern who ruled Berlin as electors, kings and emperors for over 500 years. The "open all night" entertainment from the "raving twenties" has also remained. The Nazis left deep scars on the souls of their victims. By contrast, the "alternative" scene from both East and West maintains a thriving subculture in which all resistance is granted a voice. And the Wall is now regarded as nothing more than a museum piece.

The trains of history don't halt for long in Berlin. They quickly get rid of their freight and take more on board, hardly waiting for the order "Zurückbleiben" before steaming off once more.

Preceding pages: symbol of German unity, the Brandenburg Gate. Left, the Memorial Church on the Kudamm with the TV Tower on Alexanderplatz.

THE WALL

Every city has its landmark. For some it is a cathedral, for others a telecommunications tower. Berlin had the Wall. Not a particularly inspiring feature for, after all, it shut the West Berliners in and the East Berliners out – or vice-versa. Yet, it was still one of the most unusual features ever to have dominated a city: 161 km (100 miles) long and 4 metres (13 ft) high and, on the East Berlin side, equipped with watch towers at regular intervals, which by night would light up the ugly grey concrete and present a deadly threat to every single citizen in the GDR.

On the West Berlin side it was painted in colourful graffiti, and at some points viewing platforms were constructed. Whether for individual gardens or for entire districts like Kreuzberg, the Berlin Wall acquired the significance one might attach to a garden fence. Private households had creepers growing up it and it provided shelter for patches of cucumbers and lettuces. But in the East it was nothing but a permanent prison wall. Visitors to Berlin would regard it with a mixture of fascination and revulsion. It was the cause of the death of some 70 people who had tried to escape, and this grim fact undoubtedly contributed to its touristic appeal.

The Wall as a piece of art, as a city landmark and as a zone of death has now practically been relegated to history. Anybody wishing to see the Wall today can only look at bits of it in a museum. Only at very few places such as the Gropius building in Kreuzberg, can vestiges of this monstrosity still be seen standing. It is questionable whether these sections will remain for very much longer. The "wallpeckers", with their hammers and chisels, have been laying into them for some time now.

Most of the old course of the Wall is just about unrecognisable apart from strips of wasteland which it left behind. The streets which for so long stopped at a dead end have once again been opened to through traffic and cars can once more ply freely from one district to another. City planners are busy debating how this wasteland should best be exploited. After all, the Wall ran through the very heart of the city and for many contractors the land now made available would seem to promise lucrative returns. There are those, of course, who advocate a "green" approach and suggest that the fallow land left by the Wall should now be parkland. No chance. The city budget is in a sorry state and having this potentially very profitable titbit planted with lupins and rhododendrons simply isn't on.

If such debates suggest that the 28 years of the partition of Berlin are now forgotten, the scars which the Wall left on the lives of the Berliners are nowhere near healed.

13 August 1961: The day on which Berlin was so abruptly and brutally divided into two parts started just like every other day in post-war Berlin. People from East and West were commuting back and forth as usual between the two parts of the city, between two social

Killed while trying to escape.

systems, without hindrance. From the eastern sector, officially under Soviet administration but long since declared the capital of the GDR, the public had poured over to West Berlin which, with the help of the allied powers, had been turned into one long window display of glittering capitalism.

However, for too many people the open border simply provided a one-way ticket to prosperity, a golden opportunity to turn their backs on the socialist GDR. The number of "refugees" had risen to thousands, thousands of valuable workers who simply contracted out of attempting to develop an economy that was already on its knees. On Saturday the 13th alone, 2,662 refugees from throughout the GDR had been received at the refugee camp at Marienfelde.

For the leaders of the SED in the middle of the Cold War this hole in the Iron Curtain had been a thorn in the flesh for long enough. At the beginning of August, a meeting of the party chairmen of the Warsaw Pact had already decided on the action to be taken. A wall designated as a national boundary should be built to halt this one-way traffic and to banish the influence of capitalism once and for all.

On the night of 12/13 August the tanks began to roll through the eastern sector of Berlin. The People's Army unravelled kilometres of barbed wire along the entire length of the sector boundary and then erected their "screen". By morning, the border through the city had been sealed.

The populace couldn't believe its eyes. The barbed wire and the hastily erected Wall cut into the living city like a surgeon's knife, sometimes running down the middle of a street. It not only divided east from west, capitalism from socialism, but it also separated families and friends, parents and children, worker and work-place. Some managed to escape in the nick of time, though they had to leave most of their belongings behind. Final goodbyes. A helpless, desperate rage. In Berlin an unprecedented political and human tragedy had begun.

Despite this almost impenetrable cor-

The death zone of the "anti-Fascist protection wall".

don, the months following its construction saw quite a number of East Berliners attempting to make it over to the West. People jumped from the windows of houses standing directly adjacent to the Wall; they crawled through sewage conduits linking one side of the city with the other or swam under water across the River Spree. Business was good for the escape agents who aided their clients through tunnels, hid them in their cars or provided them with false identity papers.

But no sooner had one means of escape been discovered than it was plugged by the East German authorities. Underground connections between the two halves of the city were barred and entrances to underground stations with lines leading to the West were walled up. With prefabricated concrete slabs the height of the Wall was increased to 4 metres (13 ft). Watch towers, dog runs and automatic shooting galleries were installed. The "anti-capitalist protective wall" reached ever-greater perfection evolving from a makeshift "first gen-eration" Wall to a hi-tech "fourth gen-eration" affair. As the years passed fewer and fewer made it over.

The fact that Berlin was now divided meant that the two halves developed separately. After years of chaos, the "capital of the GDR" remembered its Prussian legacy and set about creating a representative metropolis. The "inde-pendent political unit West Berlin" be-came something of a curiosity, though with all its subsidised wealth and its experiments in alternative living, it grew more provincial in character. Berliners on both sides of the Wall made the best of their situation. Old folk pondered wistfully on better days and the young took their chance to realise their own dreams. Those growing up could soon hardly remember an undivided Berlin. That one day the Wall might fall was a notion that lay only on the very distant horizon. In the spring of 1989, Erich Honecker claimed that the Wall would still be standing in 100 years.

9 November 1989: Despite the fact that signs of change in the GDR had been

The Wall was also a canvas for artists.

302

evident for months, nobody really imagined that the collapse of the Wall would come so soon and so suddenly. In the summer of 1989 the detente policy of Michail Gorbachov had led to the opening of the Hungarian border. The resulting mass escape of GDR holiday makers towards the West was the signal for those who stayed behind to start demanding reforms from their SED government, along the lines of "the last one in bed turns the light out".

On 4 November almost 1 million people gathered on Alexanderplatz in East Berlin to demonstrate against the despised SED regime. And finally, at one of those endless and utterly boring press conferences, government spokesman Günter Schabowski, apparently unaware of the implications of his utterance, nonchalantly announced the lifting of travel restrictions for GDR citizens, including those who lived in Berlin. It took a couple of hours before the journalists and then the Berliners themselves had cottoned on to what had been said, and that night there was nothing to stop

Dismantled at last.

the avalanche. By car, by bike and on foot, the people of East Berlin poured over the border into the western part of the city. They were given a rapturous reception by crowds of West Berliners, cheering and clapping. Champagne corks flew. Total strangers embraced one another, the tears flowed and the whole of Berlin celebrated. The euphoria lasted several weeks, during which time columns of Trabis were enthusiastically greeted at the border. But the routine of daily life and the expected reunification of the two parts of Germany soon caught up with the Berliners.

The dismantling of the Wall required first and foremost a lot of hard work. While visitors to the city came and chipped off their souvenirs, the disposal of this erstwhile landmark of Berlin was a considerable task. It wasn't only a matter of knocking down the Wall: roads had to be re-joined and underground connections, interrupted for so long, had to be restored. The immense social and economic problems of the reunited Berlin began to emerge.

And the Wall itself? Where it hasn't been stored to be broken up and used as material for road building, or where it hasn't been chiselled away by the wallpeckers, it has been sold off in complete, painted segments by a trading company of the former GDR. One year after the collapse of the Wall, its component parts had brought in a total of 2.1 million DM, a sum which is now being put to charitable use, including the protection of monuments in Berlin.

Twenty-eight years of mutual isolation have left behind another very different wall in the city, one that can neither be torn down nor sold off. It is a wall between people from two different social systems, who have gathered different experiences and different values. Gingerly one treads the streets on the other side, for this is still somehow foreign territory. Increasing conflict brings increasing abuse and new barriers are built. Yet, the daily grappling with the situation also brings people closer together. Berliners will certainly manage to dismantle that wall which is now inside their heads.

Berlin and Surroundings

4 km/ 2,5 miles

Hohen - Neuendorf

Mühlenbeck

Mathiasberg
▲ 56

Bötzow

Henningsdorf

Schild

Glienicke / Nordb.

Schönwalde

FROHNAU

BERLINER
FORST
TEGEL

HERMSDF.

LÜBARS

WAIDMANNS-
LUST

HEILIGENSEE

Humboldt-Palace

NORI

Falkensee

BERLINER FORST
SPANDAU

KONRADS-
HÖHE

TEGEL

BORSIG
WALDE

WITTENAU

WILHEL
RUF

F.-FALKENHÖH

TEGELORT

REINICKENDORF

HAKENFELDE

SPANDAU-
NEUSTADT

Airport
Berlin-Tegel

K.-Schumacher-
Damm

WEDDING

SPANDAU

Citadel

HASELHORST

SIEMENS
STADT

KLOSTER-
FELDE

STRESOW

Charlottenburg
Palace

TIERGARTEN

STAAKEN

WILHELM-
STADT

WESTEND

Brandenbur
Gate

Seeburg

PICHELSDORF

CHARLOTTENBG

Bellevue Palace

Victory Column

Radio Tower

AB.-Dr.
Funkturm

WILMERS-
DF.

Finkenberg
▲ 75

GATOW

BERLINER

Karlsbg.
▲ 78

GRUNEWALD

SCHÖNE

AB.- Kr.
Schöneb

Fahrland

Groß-
Glienicke

Gatow Airfield

FORST

Grunewald
Hunting Lodge

SCHMARGEN-
DF.

FRIEDENAU

P.-NEDLITZ

KLADOW

GRUNEWALD

DAHLEM

STEGLITZ

Havel

ZEHLENDF.

P.-BORNIM

P.-SACROW

NIKOLASSEE

LICHTER-
FELDE

LANKWTZ

Cecilienhof
Palace

WANNSEE

Berlin-
Zehlendorf

273

Kl. Glienicke
Palace

MARIENFEL

Sanssouci
Palace

Babelsberg
Palace

SCHÖNOW

Kleinmachnow

Teltow

Potsdam

P.-KLEIN-
GLIENICKE

STEIN-
STÜCKEN

P.-
BABELSBERG

Stahnsdorf

Kl.
Ravensberg
▲ 114

P.-DREWITZ

Bergholz

Güterfelde

Großbeeren

Mah

Rehbrücke

304

TWO CITY CENTRES

Now that the Wall has gone, perhaps the most striking thing about Berlin is that it possesses two city centres. On the one side, on Alexanderplatz, the TV tower, built as the unmistakeable emblem of the "capital of the GDR", marks the historical centre of Berlin, **Berlin-Mitte**. On the other, the shining blue Mercedes Star affixed to the Europa Center marks the location of the **Kurfürstendamm**, the bustling centre of the western part of the city. The *still* bustling centre. Yet, since the collapse of the Wall the elegant boulevard **Unter den Linden** has begun to usurp the position held by the "Kudamm" as *the* street for taking a stroll. And as far as the "No. 1 business address" is concerned, **Friedrichstrasse** is busily making up for lost years, at least in property prices.

The Kurfürstendamm: Nevertheless, the Kudamm has not yet lost its powers of attraction. "I so long for my Kurfürstendamm", once sang Berlin's very own inimitable singer and actress Hildegard Knef. However, these sentiments cannot have been inspired by the architecture or by any historical corrections. The Kurfürstendamm as we see it today only emerged 100 years ago. Ever since the 16th century it had just been a broad track leading out into the country, serving as a bridle path for the electors who would ride out from the royal palace in the direction of Grunewald to go hunting. Kurfürstendamm means "The Electors' Road".

Only with Germany's rapid industrial expansion from 1871 onwards did the street begin to take shape. Inspired by the Champs Elysées in Paris, Bismarck decided that he wanted just such a boulevard for the new capital of the *Reich*. Building work proceeded in "Wilhelmenian" style: generous, ornate and even florid; truly representative of the age. Proverbial Prussian frugality suffered its heaviest defeat at the hands of the Kurfürstendamm.

The Kurfürstendamm became the

Berlin remains two cities: the bustle and colour of the west...

place where Berlin was youthful, where the wildest entertainment could be had and where everything considered Bohemian was on offer. That was particularly the case during the "raving twenties". The most famous meeting-place in those days was the **Romanische Café**, situated where the austere Europa Center now stands. Its list of regular guests read like the *who's who* of Berlin's artistic elite.

In 1933 all the colourful goings on were abruptly halted. The decadence of the New West had for long been considerable cause for concern for the Nazis. The mostly Jewish people engaged in this cultural sector were ousted, and carried off to their grim fate. A traditional centre of entertainment had become the stage for a *danse macabre*.

But the memories of the once bustling boulevard remained. After the ravages of World War II and the division of the city into East and West, the Kurfürstendamm redeveloped as the cultural centre of West Berlin. The actual city centre was over in the East and, particularly after the building of the Wall, could not be reached. But despite all the effort, the old splendour of the Kudamm could never be recreated. Ugly new buildings with mirror facades and workaday single-storey structures which bear a close resemblance to barracks, came to dominate the character of the Kurfürstendamm. Nevertheless, because the city centre had been lost to the East, this famous street was assigned the function of carrying out the social duties of the business world.

The broad pavements are lined by expensive shops, cinemas and any number of cafés. Concerned about the good reputation of this address, the authorities turned away all the junk shops, porno shops and snack bars. That the Kurfürstendamm has been elevated to world-city level, is demonstrated by controversial works of art which were erected along the central reservation in time for the 750th anniversary celebrations in 1987.

During the post-war years the Kudamm developed into a symbol of

...and the relative drabness of the east.

western prosperity and acquired dazzling night life. It was not for nothing that on the night after the collapse of the Wall it was to the Kudamm that East Berliners flocked. And it is not just for the East Berliners that "To the Kudamm and back" is an absolute must. For many, it's like drinking Champagne for the first time.

The first place on the Kudamm most people head for is **Breitscheidplatz** with the ruins of the **Kaiser Wilhelm Memorial Church**, together with its blue-glazed rebuilt version. Since 1983, particularly in the summer, all sorts of people have tended to gather around the **Wasserklops**, a huge fountain created by the sculptor Schmettau which stands next to the **Europa Center**. The building is one of the tallest in Berlin, crowned by that highly symbolic Mercedes Star mentioned above. It is practically a city in itself, at least with respect to the shops and entertainment amenities offered. Everything can be had here, from the highly precious to the downright *kitsch*. Meals are overpriced and a casino tries to emulate Monte Carlo. In short, the Europa Center is a good place to head for when it's raining, but only when you're prepared to splash out.

More stylish is the **KaDeWe**, the "Store of the West" on the adjacent **Wittenbergerplatz**. Here, in Europe's largest department store, is everything that anyone could possibly wish to buy, though admittedly they don't have pink elephants – yet. Never mind, a visit to Berlin without popping in to the KaDeWe is like visiting London for the first time and not going to Harrods.

A stroll along the Kudamm from Wittenbergerplatz to Breitscheidplatz and all the way to **Lehiner Platz** might well last a whole day. All possible wants for day or night are provided for here. On could start by going shopping in the KaDeWe, then visiting the Memorial Church and stopping for a lunchtime snack at **Café Kranzler**. Admittedly it's no longer the Kranzler of the pre-war days – that was in Berlin-Mitte – but it nevertheless offers a taste of the elegant Berlin. When you've had enough of all those Kudamm shops and their

not-always-so-elegant wares, then you could try venturing down one of the side streets. Here begins the so-called **Off-Kudamm** containing rather more tasteful, but not necessarily more reasonable, shops. But the restaurants, cafés and pubs are definitely more original, better places for whiling away the afternoon.

Entertainment of a cultural nature can be enjoyed in the evening by booking seats for the **Schaubühne am Lehiner Platz**. Originally in Kreuzberg, this theatre made a name for itself through the brilliant productions of its director Peter Stein. It remains one of the city's best theatres, although, since moving into its technically perfectly-equipped new domicile, performances have tended to lack something of their experimental vivacity.

If you wish to sample nightlife, then the **Discothek Far Out** next to the theatre and the **Nachtclub Eden** on **Adenauerplatz** are both recommended. Which one you plump for depends on your age and taste. However, you might choose to do the same as most Berliners and sample the venues up and down the Kudamm all night long. Most places are open until the early morning.

Historical centre: Things are a lot more leisurely over in **Berlin-Mitte**. That isn't to say that it's boring – quite the contrary. Here one is endlessly confronted by Berlin and Prussian history. Here was also the very cradle of the city, the small merchants' settlement which established itself on the ford across the Spree where the Mühlendammbrücke now crosses the river.

Of course, most of the historical buildings to be seen here are not the originals and much such as the **City Palace** of the Hohenzollern Emperors, for example, has been lost forever. Although severely damaged during the war, it was the Stalinist authorities of the former GDR who actually finished the building off, back in the 1950s. The copper-coloured **Palace of the Republic**, seat of parliament and popular amusement during SED rule, now stands in its stead. But this building had to be closed in 1990 because of the health hazard from the

Right, Nefertiti, wife of the Egyptian Pharaoh Akhenaton, whose bust is in the Egyptian Museum.

MUSEUMS IN BERLIN

Like so many other things in Berlin, some museums are available in duplicate. During the period when the city was divided, East Berlin expanded the historic Museum Island, and West Berlin countered with the "Foundation for Prussian Cultural Possessions". It is now planned to unite all the capital's museums under the simple title "The State Museums of Berlin".

Below is a selection of the most important museums to be found in the city.

The Museum Island lies between the two arms of the Spree. The Pergamon Museum houses the most valuable art treasure in the city: the Altar of Zeus from Pergamon in west Turkey. Also on view in the Collection of Antiquities is the Market Gate from Miletus. The Near Eastern section boasts the throne room facade from Nebuchadnezzar II's Babylon.

The Bode Museum contains Egyptian antiquities from prehistoric until Graeco-Roman times. The papyrus collection, which includes 25,000 papyri, parchments and wax and wooden tablets, is one of the most important in the world. The Department of Prehistory and Early History contains some of Heinrich Schliemann's collection of Trojan antiquities as well as finds from virtually every period of prehistory and early history in Europe.

The Museum of Natural History houses the zoological, mineralogical and palaeontological collections of Humboldt University. The focal point is a a brachiosaurus skeleton – the largest dinosaur skeleton on show anywhere in the world.

The Arts and Crafts Museum is housed in the baroque Palace of Köpenick. It contains antique furniture, porcelain and leather items from various periods.

The principal museums in former West Berlin are located in Dahlem, in the Charlottenburg Palace and in the new Art Forum in the Tiergarten.

The Painting Gallery in Dehlem contains fine examples of virtually every movement in Western art before 1800. It was discovered that one of its most valuable paintings, the *Man with the Golden Helmet*, was not painted by Rembrandt, but most probably by one of his pupils.

The Prints and Drawings Department houses one of the most extensive collections of its kind in the world: 25,000 drawings by world-famous artists, 50,000 sheets of prints and 1,500 illustrated books. There are examples of work by every painter of significance, from Dürer to Brueghel and from Botticelli to Picasso.

The Museum of Islamic Art, through paintings and arts and crafts, traces the development of the Islamic religion from its foundation in AD 600.

The largest museum in West Berlin is the Museum of Anthropology. The collections from four continents include paintings, sculpture, religious objects and utensils of every description. The newest of the specialist department, is the Museum of Indian Art, opened in 1963. Its 12,000 exhibits make it the most important collection of its kind in the German-speaking world.

The most famous exhibit in the Egyptian Museum in Charlottenburg is the bust of Nefertiti, a limestone sculpture of the wife of the Egyptian Pharaoh Akhenaton. Ancient papyri, the oldest bearing a text over 3,000 years old, recall the remarkable civilisations of the land of the Nile.

The Museum of Antiquity contains Greek and Roman works of art, including statues, portraits and antique miniature art.

The New National Gallery on the south side of Tiergarten, contains late 19th-century and 20th-century paintings up to the present day. It was completed in 1968 in accordance with a design provided by the Bauhaus architect Ludwig Mies van der Rohe. Many world-famous contemporary artists are represented in the collection, as are 19th-century Realists and Impressionists.

The Bauhaus Museum exhibits teaching material and works by artists who graduated from the Bauhaus or taught there: Gropius, Mies van der Rohe *et al.*

Every city needs to document its own history. With its models and maps, furniture and fashions, signs, prints, pictures, portraits, busts, china and household utensils the Berlin Museum in Kreuzberg provides a cross-section of the cultural history of the city.

asbestos which had been used in its construction. This irony of history brought a wry smile to the faces of long-time and recent SED opponents.

It was only later, in the 1970s, that the DDR regime remembered its Prussian heritage and sought to make amends. While many of the projects had the best of intentions, they did tend to overshoot the mark. An example is the Nikolai District. It must be said that the **Church of St Nicholas**, Berlin's oldest edifice dating back to the 13th century, was rebuilt in exemplary fashion. But the buildings around the church square were at the same time converted into doll's houses, into a Berlin "Disney World". Nevertheless, they are certainly more appealing than the functional blocks strewn around Alexander Platz and Leipziger Stasse.

The gateway to Berlin-Mitte is unquestionably the **Brandenburg Gate**. Since its inauguration in 1791, this structure has always been a symbol of the fate of Germany, and as such has engendered a great deal of pathos. Napoleon marched through it on his triumphant way to Russia, and slunk round it on his humiliating retreat. The Quadriga, the goddess of victory on her chariot drawn by four horses, was stolen from the Brandenburg Gate, to be brought back in triumph by Marshal Blücher eight years later, in 1814.

Barricades were erected at the Gate during the German Revolution of 1848. Kings and Emperors paraded here. The revolutionaries of 1918 streamed through it on their way to the palace to proclaim the republic. The Nazis also staged their victory parades through the Brandenburg Gate, and after their downfall in 1945, Soviet soldiers hoisted the Red Flag on the Quadriga.

Following the construction of the Berlin Wall, the entire area around the monument was cordoned off, both from the East and the West. During and after the collapse of the Wall, the Gate became a central symbol of the hopes and expectations of a united Germany. It also became the meeting place for all those who counted themselves, in the words of the former West Berlin mayor

Walter Momper, among "the happiest people in the world". So much for the pathos. Plans without the least trace of pathos are being hatched to turn the Brandenburg Gate into a traffic island. Despite the protests from Berliners and outsiders alike, roads are due to "run closely past" the monument.

The most Prussian of Berlin's streets is undoubtedly the **Unter den Linden**. Here, too, much was annihilated during the war and ruined by socialist misplanning in the post-war years. However, strolling down this elegant boulevard today the ambience of the old metropolis can almost be touched. The classical structures conceived by the 19th-century architect Friedrich Schinkel, which transformed the city into "Athens on the Spree", testify to the fact that Berlin once ranked amongst the most beautiful European cities.

It is open to debate which of Schinkel's buildings is the most beautiful. Some maintain that it is the **Schauspielhaus** (theatre) on the **Platz der Akademie**. Framed by the German Cathedral and

An attraction on Breit-scheidplatz.

the French Cathedral the entire square is an aesthetically perfect ensemble. Others point to the **Neue Wache** on Unter den Linden as being Schinkel's most complete work. It was his first building in Berlin, and it certainly possesses the harmony of Classical simplicity. This is where in DDR days, People's Army soldiers goose-stepped in front of the Neue Wache which served as a memorial to the victims of Fascism and militarism. The future memorial role of the Neue Wache is uncertain. The decision about who and what should be commemorated has not yet been made.

A third favourite candidate for Schinkel's masterpiece is the **Old Museum** on the **Museum Island**. This is indeed his most impressive building. Inside and out it was entirely designed to serve its purpose, namely to display works of art. But then the whole museum island is, in both form and content, an extraordinary artistic ensemble. It requires more than just one afternoon to visit all the museums, the Old and **New Museum**, the **National Gallery**, the **Pergamon Museum** and the **Bode Museum**.

But Berlin-Mitte is more than just royal Berlin. It is also Fascist and Socialist Berlin. The old Opern Platz, now renamed Bebel Platz, is where the Nazis burnt more than 20,000 books in 1933. The **Forum Fridericianum**, round this square, is graced with structures from every epoch. There is the baroque **Zeugaus**, the old arsenal which is now a museum. The **German State Opera House** was conceived in Classical style, but has been renovated and rebuilt so many times that it now bears little resemblance to the original edifice. **Berlin Cathedral** is a monument to the Wilhelmenian expression of splendour. The equestrian statue of Frederick the Great looks beyond the TV Tower, which dominates everything on Alexanderplatz, to the Palace of the Republic and the Marx-Engels Forum. There, somewhat lost and out of place, the statues of the two fathers of historical materialism, Karl Marx and Friedrich Engels, await an uncertain fate.

Vigil at the Stasi headquarters in 1990.

BERLIN'S BOROUGHS

With a total area of 883 sq. km (341 sq. miles), Berlin is the largest city in Germany. Yet anyone who thinks that its present size is the result of gradual development over centuries is mistaken. Until shortly after World War I, Berlin consisted solely of its historical centre and a few isolated suburbs. It was a splendid place but could never have been described as a large city. It was only in 1920 following borough reforms that numerous villages, estates and small towns were integrated into the city area, so giving Berlin the boundaries that it has retained to this day.

The different boroughs of the city were also organised and named at this time. Smaller areas have often retained their original village names, as for example has Dahlem in the borough of Zehlendorf and Karlhorst in Lichtenburg. So some of the characteristics of a small town have been kepted over the years and the map of Berlin is dotted with several "town centres". In many cases on the edge of the city the village structure has remained largely intact.

Concrete blocks: Berlin has a total of 23 boroughs, three of which, in the eastern city, were only founded in the 1970s and 1980s. **Marzahn**, **Hellersdorf** and **Hohenschönhausen** are giant concrete estates were built to solve the acute shortage of housing which was prevalent in the GDR at that time. Without so much as a thought for aesthetics, they were simply dumped on the sands of the Brandenburg Marches. Although equipped with all mod cons, most of the flats are far too small. It is purely the result of the residents' own initiative that the oldest development at Marzahn has now been transformed into something approaching an urban character. They planted bushes and trees, installed playgrounds for the children and filled those bare walls with life. Geraniums now blossom on the balconies.

This same kind of self-help was instigated by the residents of the **Märkische Viertel** (Brandenburg Marches District)

in the borough of Reinickendorf in the north of Berlin, and the residents here are truly proud of their achievements. However, that is in no way typical of the majority of such developments. In **Gropiusstadt** in the southern borough of Neukölln acute social problems are endemic. Such places provide ideal breeding grounds for crime and right-wing radicalism.

Workers' settlements: But most of Berlin is occupied by traditional working-class suburbs such as: **Friedrichshain**, **Kreuzberg**, **Wedding** and **Prenzlauer Berg**. It was in the middle of the last century when industrialisation and land speculation were just beginning that wretched accommodation for the workers shot up like mushrooms before the gates of the city. Many of the houses at the rear have now been demolished to leave airy yards where children can play and the parents can enjoy barbecues.

Prenzlauer Berg, which the Berliners also lovingly call "Prenzelberg" is without doubt the liveliest residential district in the city. It is primarily young

Pop art in Kreuzberg.

312

people from the alternative scene who have made their home in these dilapidated barracks. Squats, pubs, galleries and workshops were all part of the Prenzelberg scene even in the days of the GDR when conditions weren't exactly conducive to individual initiative.

However, the SED government's preference for "Disneyland" also managed to plant itself here. One street, **Husemannstrasse**, was styled to look like the old Berlin and the visitor might easily be fooled into thinking that it was one big open-air museum. Particularly when one looks at the rest of the Prenzlauer Berg, where plaster falls from the walls of houses whose condition has continuously deteriorated since the preWorld War I days in which they were built.

"Prenzelberg" is often compared to **Kreuzberg** over in the western half of the city, at least with regard to the kinds of people that live there. However, despite its wild reputation, Kreuzberg has long become a showpiece of the so-called "multi-cultural" way of life. In

Kreuzberg's terms this only really means that the large proportion of foreign residents are tolerated, nothing more. Sadly, the degree of tolerance is on the decline.

The "scene" has nevertheless managed to establish itself here, and since the house battles of the early 1980s an alternative culture has been maintained. The borough of Kreuzberg is in fact a product of the borough reforms of 1920. It consists of the old Berlin suburbs of Friedrichstadt and Luisenstadt. It got its name from the hill (Berg = Hill) where the **Victoriapark** is now located.

The Kreuzberg street battles of the 1980s, whether they were waged for squats or just for the pure hell of it, have long since moved to another part of town. In November 1990 in **Friedrichshain**, **Mainzer Strasse** became the theatre for the toughest battle between police and squatters ever waged in Berlin. The whole street was laid waste.

But Friedrichshain has always been a problem area. As a worker's settlement which was created last century with no particular provision for hygiene, its in-

Out for a walk in Prenzlauer Berg.

WOMEN'S LIB

Berlin is a feminine city. "Berlin", enthuses Johanna, a younger woman from the Stutgart region, "Berlin is like a love affair. First comes the tingling sensation of attraction, then the confrontation with the unexpected harshness of reality, and finally the realisation that you must be prepared to take your life into your own hands, and that then everything is possible." Her eyes sparkling, she laughs as only true Berliners can, even if they were born in Munich, Dresden or Istanbul. It is a full-throated laugh with the charm of those who do not take themselves unduly seriously.

A women's city. No other metropolis has been so indelibly imprinted by the character of its women. The famous 19th-century salons of Rahel Varnhagen, Henriette Hertz and Bettina von Arnhim are just a handful of obvious examples. Everybody who could lay claim to be somebody gathered here, provided they were also quick-witted. Those who wished to match up to these well-educated women needed to be in possession of more than an academic title and a literary reputation. And it was Queen Sophie-Charlotte who, during the 18th century, supervised the founding of the Academy of Science and summoned scientists such as Leibniz to Berlin.

Over the years, the women of Berlin have added a fighting spirit and social commitment to this propensity for wit. The artist Käthe Kollwitz took up the cause of the poorest of the poor, the children who lived in abject poverty. At the end of the last century Lina Morgenstern founded the first educational association for women factory workers, and Else Lasker-Schüler chose Berlin as the city in which to find inspiration for her literary works.

But the women of Berlin have sometimes won back their city in a highly subversive – even a radical – way. The first women's centre in Germany was opened in the Stresemannstrasse and during the student revolts the "Women's Council" threw tomatoes at the SDS, the male-dominated socialist student union.

Playgroups were formed as a way of escaping domestic isolation and refuges were set up for maltreated women and girls. Prostitutes joined together to form the association known as *Hydra*, which fought for their rights and their recognition. In 1990 the first old people's home run exclusively by women was also established.

Women have also achieved a great deal in less spectacular ways. Their early efforts were often greeted with derision, which rapidly changed to admiration in the light of their success. The first house to be occupied exclusively by women, a former sweet factory, is now a feminist centre for the entire district. Today there are galleries, cafés, bars, information offices, health centres, even a hotel for women (*Artemisia*, tel: 878905). The list is endless. It sometimes seems as if masculine establishments have become totally superfluous.

Even the Senate of West Berlin was dominated by women from 1989. There were, admittedly, reasons for this: it was a clever move to gain popularity by the newly elected Socialist mayor, Walter Momper. He chose five women to fill senatorial posts, and a further three were proposed by the Alternative List, the SPD's smaller coalition partner. Eight women against five men – a situation greeted with scepticism and celebrated with euphoria. In any case they were observed far more critically than their masculine colleagues.

One of the woman senators instilled fear not only into her opponents in Berlin; she pitted herself against the entire atomic power industry of the land. Michaela Schreyer, the Senator for Development and Environmental Protection, was an independent appointed by the Alternative List. Despite opposition from the highest quarters she refused to licence the controversial atomic research reactor of the Hahn-Meitner Institute because of insufficient provision for waste disposal. During her period in office she asserted herself in an expert manner and won lasting respect.

The women of Berlin are simply tougher when it is a question of claiming their rights. They are also fairer when it comes to sharing – a fact documented by past history as well as the present. Come what may, Berlin's future is bound to be feminine or nothing.

habitants succumbed to illness and infirmity more rapidly than elsewhere. More than 100 years ago, therefore, the progressive city fathers decided to compensate for this state of affairs by putting some open space at the residents' disposal. Together with its **Märchenbrunnen** (fairytale fountain), the **Volkspark Friedrichshain** was dedicated to the sick, rickets-stricken children of the borough.

Today's **Karl Marx Allee**, once known as the Frankfurter Allee, a street on which no house remained standing after the war, was rebuilt in true Stalinistic block-style in the 1950s. While the sheer immensity of the construction may not be to everybody's taste, the flats inside at least fulfilled the requirements of the age, not only in terms of comfort but also in terms of natural lighting and ventilation.

In contrast to the other three boroughs, the "scene" never settled in **Wedding**. The borough remains a bastion of the Berlin working class. From the beginning of the century to the arrival of the Nazis, Wedding was a communist stronghold. The squalor of domestic life and the indescribable working conditions in the factories were part of the reason why the borough was denounced as "red Wedding". Wedding is now a town in itself. Computer technology has now settled here and "red Wedding" has meanwhile changed its name to "silicon Wedding".

The small town feel: Many boroughs have managed to maintain their small town character. **Weissensee**, for example, is both an industrial and residential district with the typical atmosphere of a suburb. One of Berlin's countless lakes, the **Weisse See** which gave the borough its name, is one of the main attractions of the area. It is surrounded by parkland and there is an open-air stage. But what makes the borough famous is the **Jewish Cemetery** where a substantial proportion of the Jewish cultural and business elite lies buried: at least, those who were not exterminated by the Nazis.

With its wonderful tombs and gravestones, the cemetery has existed here for over 100 years. But many of the graves

have fallen into decay, and not only the sands of time are to blame. Even today, they are repeatedly vandalised by extreme right-wing mobs.

The "sights" in the borough of **Lichtenburg** are of a totally different nature. Right in the middle of this workers' settlement the SED built the monumental headquarters of its spying apparatus. It was in **Normannenstrasse** that the Ministry of State Security, better known in its abbreviated form *Stasi*, carried out decades of surveillance on every single citizen of the GDR.

It was in **Karlhorst**, a part of Lichtenberg, that Germany's capitulation to the Allies was signed in May 1945. Even today a part of the Soviet Army command is stationed here. The friendly relations enjoyed during the time of the GDR are no more. Many Berliners now seem to regard the Russians as an unwelcome occupying force.

If Lichtenberg has maintained its small-town character, the borough of **Treptow** has succumbed more or less totally to industrialisation. But not quite. The real attraction of this part of town is its parks, and in the **Treptow Park** you can gaze at the remnants of Hitler's Chancellery of the Reich: the stones were brought here and used in the construction of the **Soviet Memorial**.

Naturally enough, however, most visitors tend to head straight for the **Plänterwald**. The amusement park is packed just about every day of the year. But the biggest attraction, now for the whole of Berlin, is the famous **Restaurant Zenner** whose traditions stretch back over 400 years.

There is not much in the way of amusements in the neighbouring borough of **Neukölln**. Most Berliners are of the opinion that if you live here then you're right at the bottom of the pile. This is something which the people of Neukölln do not like to hear: they proudly maintain that anybody living here does so because he wants to. Be that as it may, with the highest density of dog excrement per metre in all of Berlin plastering its pavements, Neukölln does look rather *triste*. Squalor, a lack of open spaces and a great deal of boredom

Left, women have played a key role in the rebuilding of Berlin.

among the local population are some of the characteristics of this borough, which was known as Rixdorf until 1912 when, in memory of Berlin's erstwhile sister town of Cölln, it was renamed – the new Cölln. Noteworthy are the pubs on the corner whose no-nonsense sparse interiors smack of the old Berlin.

Neukölln practically fuses with the next-door borough of **Tempelhof**. Tempelhof's main claim to fame is as the location of Berlin's first airport, though its importance has declined since the construction of the airport at Tegel. There are plans to reactivate Tempelhof in the future. As far as the past is concerned, it was here during the 1946 blockade that the Allies' "raisin bombers" daily landed with their care parcels to relieve the marooned population. The **Airlift Monument** at the airport is the borough's main landmark.

Schöneberg is where the prostitutes hang out. All the weird cafés and bars are on **Nollendorfplatz** and **Winterfeldplatz**, interspersed by a number of junk and antique shops. **Potsdammer Strasse**, which was for years denounced as the "brothel mile", has now been developed by the alternative scene. One of the most recent places to have opened up (1990) is the **Quartier**, a variety theatre which lives up to the vital metropolitan consciousness. But the name Schöneberg is first and foremost linked with its **Town Hall**, which is where the West Berlin chamber of deputies was housed. Behind the royal colonnade, in the **Kleistpark**, there is a building with a particularly shameful history. Here stands the **Superior Court of Berlin** where the judges of the People's Court sentenced the 20th July resistance fighters to death. After the war, the building was used by the Allied Control Council.

Posh suburbs: Berlin doesn't only consist of history, the alternative culture and the working class. The city simply wouldn't be complete without all its wealthy suburbs and smart villas. **Steglitz** is just such a borough, in which businessmen and the educated elite lead their leisurely lives. However, they haven't been able to escape the real

The Oberbaumbrücke.

world completely. During the past few years and especially since the collapse of the Wall, Schloss Strasse, the main thoroughfare running through Steglitz, has lost something of its tranquillity. Particularly on Saturdays the shops are so busy that you'd think they were giving it all away. And it isn't only the locals of Steglitz who throng here. Half of Potsdam, only 30 minutes away by car, does all its weekend shopping here.

Things are rather more peaceful out in **Zehlendorf**. This borough basks in its pleasant surroundings and cultural amenities. **Dahlem**, part of Zehlendorf, is not only the location of the second largest museum complex in Berlin but it is also home to the **Free University** which back in the 1960s was the starting point of the students' revolt. However, the days of unrest and mass demonstrations are over: students now have other things to worry about than world politics. Finding a place to live, for example: the shortage of flats in Berlin is acute and digs that students can afford are extremely hard to come by.

The real charm of Zehlendorf is to be found in the **Grunewald** with all its lakes, particularly the **Wannsee** which has a beach for bathing. And who would guess that a metropolis like Berlin would possess a jewel like the **Pfaueninsel**, a beautiful little island, worth heading for if you're in need of rest and relaxation?

At the opposite side of the city, namely in the north, is another oasis. **Reinickendorf** is full of contrasts. On the one hand there is the **Berlin Tegel Airport**, a source of considerable annoyance to residents who live near the main flightpath, and on the other there is the **Tegeler Fliess**, a melt-water channel left over from the Ice Age which is one of the most beautiful of Berlin's nature reserves. With its high-rise flats, the **Märkische Viertel** is an ugly monstrosity, but right next door is **Lübar**, a place which has retained much of its original village structure.

East Berliners, too, possessed and continue to possess their very own high-class residential district. By GDR standards **Pankow**, in the north of the city, is unusually well maintained. This can be easily explained: in all those villas in the neighbourhood of the **Majakowski-Ring** the most important members of the old SED regime once lived, at least until the 1970s when most of them moved out to Wandlitz. The government of the GDR was therefore disparagingly referred to as the "Pankow Regime". The borough has now largely been taken over by successful artists and diplomats.

The New West: The dividing up of Berlin after the war was partly also along traditional lines. The "Red East" was therefore taken over by the Russians and the "New West", consisting of the most elegant boroughs, fell into the hands of the Allies.

In the borough of **Tiergarten**, there is not much left to see of the menacing scale and chilling grandeur of the erstwhile government sector. Hitler's Chancellery of the Reich was reduced to a pile of rubble. The imposing villas of the old diplomatic enclave are still there, though, as is the mighty **Reichstag**, which after decades of po-

Fine houses in Badstrasse.

litical redundancy became the centre of attention once more with the reunification celebrations on 3 October 1990. Nevertheless, the name Tiergarten is primarily associated with the largest and most famous of Berlin's parks, on the edge of which lies the third cultural centre of the city. The **Kulturforum** was planned in the post-war years to complement the Museumsinsel. The most impressive building is the **Philharmonie** designed by the architect Scharoun. Here under Herbert von Karajan, the Berlin Philharmonic Orchestra triumphed.

But Tiergarten is not just culture and history. Its district of **Moabit** out towards Wedding, for example, is industrial and working-class. Its somewhat doubtful reputation is based on its prison. Inmates were not only the big and small fish of Berlin's criminal world, but after the account was settled with the SED many a prominent person did time here.

Before its compulsory incorporation into Berlin, the neighbouring borough of **Charlottenburg** was the richest town of the Brandenburg Marches. Although the place is now hardly recognisable, north of the Kurfürstendamm there are still a number of exceptionally noble residences. They have steps in front of their doorways and contain generously proportioned flats. But the best preserved building in Charlottenburg is undoubtedly the **Palace**. With its beautiful grounds it compares very favourably with Sanssouci.

Less elegant by comparison is the **ICC**, the International Congress Centre, an aluminium-faced colossus that looks rather like a spaceship. The **Radio Tower** and the **Trade Fair Centre** look decidedly old-fashioned against this futuristic-looking edifice.

The most elegant and in some areas the most expensive part of Berlin is the borough of **Wilmersdorf**, which contains the highest proportion of green open spaces in the city. Around the administrative district on **Fehrbelliner Platz** live the educated middle class and the academics, together with the upper echelons of civil service employees. The "Wilmersdorf widows" are prover-

bial in this part of town. And it isn't only the multitude of expensive old people's homes that have created this image, rather the ladies of advanced years who, as wealthy widows, have chosen to remain in their enormous flats. Considering the housing shortage among more lowly folk, some believe that such behaviour is highly antisocial. The most expensive address, not only in Wilmersdorf but also in the entire city, is the **Grunewald District**. Elegant modern houses and noble villas exude a dignified wealth, which for many is the object of envy.

Older than Berlin: When, along with its sister city of Cölln, Berlin was founded on the Spree at the beginning of the 13th century, it lay right between two fortified towns, **Spandau** and **Köpenick**. Both are much older than Berlin and have retained their essential character. In 1920 they successfully fought off all attempts to make them part of their much younger neighbour, and even today a man from Spandau will be offended if someone calls him a Berliner.

Squatters' houses in the eastern part of the city.

Before they moved into the little double city of Cölln-Berlin, the Askanians ruled from the **Citadel** in Spandau, a fortress complex dating back to the Middle Ages. However, their departure by no means marked an end to Spandau's strategic importance. During the time of the Soldier King Friedrich Wilhelm I the town, together with Potsdam, became the centre of the Prussian armaments industry. And its favourable position at the confluence of the Spree and the Havel enabled it to develop into a prosperous trading centre.

Recent history, however, has brought Spandau a rather more gloomy reputation. It was here that Hitler's vice chancellor **Rudolf Hess** spent all those decades behind bars in the war crimes prison. After he committed suicide in 1987, the building was demolished. The site is now occupied by a shopping centre.

Köpenick also acquired wide fame through a criminal deed, though by no means as dreadful. At the beginning of the century, the cobbler **Wilhelm Voigt** decided to dress up in the guise of a captain of the city treasury. Even the Emperor, who had heard about the case, is said to have laughed out loud at the audacious manner in which he carried out the offence.

Berlin's most beautiful lake area, together with its largest lake **Müggelsee**, is in Köpenick. In the days when Berlin was still divided, this was where the whole of East Berlin flocked in the summer months. Now that the area is accessible to people from West Berlin, the final destruction of this idyll seems ensured. But the West Berliners will probably wait and see how the place is developed. They will first take a good, hard look at their newly-acquired countryside, so perhaps green Berlin will not become quite so swamped as some have feared.

Perhaps, conservationists hope, a growing awareness of "green" issues will save this lovely area from development along ultra-commerical Western lines, with all the discarded polystyrene packaging and garish plastic waste that such development entails.

The School of Art at Weissensee.

POTSDAM

Why the Prussian rulers took a fancy to Potsdam, of all places, remains a mystery to this very day. Some say that the Great Elector of the 17th century liked the hunting here, for hunting indeed was one of his passions. Others maintain that the kings, especially Frederick the Great, came here to flee the bustle and the stress of Berlin society. The town was hardly suitable as a health resort. Because of its lakes and swamps, colds and rheumatism are still the most common complaints among those who live here.

Potsdam is a good deal older than Berlin. It received its first official mention in AD 993 as Potztupimi ("under the oak trees"). For centuries the Wendish fishing village on the River Havel was of no significance, economically or strategically, and most certainly not in any cultural terms. Nevertheless, in 1660 the Great Elector somehow fell in love with this sleepy backwater and by building his residence here elevated Potsdam to a royal city. The **Game Park**, as it is known today, was his favourite hunting ground.

Potsdam first appeared in Prussian history because of the famous Tolerance Edict of 1685. It was from Potsdam that the Great Elector guaranteed asylum to his fellow Huguenots who had just been expelled from France by the Edict of Nantes.

However, it was his son Frederick I, the first and self-proclaimed king of Prussia, who really transformed Potsdam into a pleasure garden. Quite literally so, because, as his Grandson Frederick the Great was later to confirm, there was unrestrained merriment in the Potsdam residence. With constant binges and amazing orgies, it was a rave-up from start to finish. The king himself was never inclined to involve himself in battle. "Make love not war" appears to have been his motto.

Later, under the soldier-king Friedrich Wilhelm I, Potsdam became a perma-

Preceding pages: the splendour of bygone days in Sanssouci. **Below**, a limit to the number of visitors will help to preserve the palace.

nent residence city. But Friedrich had no time for the frivolities of his father. He introduced cutbacks in expenditure almost to the point of being miserly. His vassals now had to honour that, meanwhile legendary, Prussian virtue. To accommodate his beloved household guard, his "big boys", he now made Potsdam a garrison town – Prussian militarism, another myth, was born.

This favoured Prussian seat before the gates of Berlin gained its present day appearance, and indeed its fame, when Frederick II, later to be called Frederick the Great, took over the reins of government. He had his architect Knobelsdorff build the famous **Sanssouci Palace** to his own design. And here he retreated from the bustle of Berlin, fled from the rather too inquisitive and demanding burghers, whose cockiness had become a source of considerable annoyance. He expanded the town itself into a real jewel and the "pearl on the Havel" emerged.

The Orangery in Potsdam. His successors continued to develop the town. At the beginning of the 19th century the Prussian chief builder and star architect Karl Friedrich Schinkel added his own classical creations to the existing baroque elements. The landscape architect Peter Joseph Lenné transformed the park at Sanssouci to what it is today: a unique symbiosis of art and nature.

The Hohenzollern emperors also admired Potsdam. The opening of the city railway between Potsdam and Berlin in 1886 facilitated communications between the two royal cities. Even during World War I, when a sizeable proportion of the population was either dying in battle or almost starving to death, the heir, who never actually ascended the throne, saw fit to have another palace built in Potsdam. **Cecilienhof Palace** was completed in 1917 and after the 1918 revolution this was the only building that the Hohenzollern were allowed to continue to use. The erstwhile Prussian ruling family remained here until 1945. When fleeing before the advance of the Red Army at the end of the war, they were careful to pack as many valu-

ables as possible. A lot of the furniture disappeared.

In the summer of 1945 Cecilienhof was the location of the conference of the representatives of the three victorious Allies who were to decide Germany's fate. The building was fitted out to enable the delegations to carry out their task and the famous "round table" and the offices of Churchill, Truman and Stalin can still be seen in their original state. It was the "Potsdam Agreement" that gave this town its place in world history. Since the days of the GDR the Cecilienhof has also housed a hotel. The restaurant is a fine place to go and have dinner.

For the victorious powers the terms of the Potsdam Agreement were intended to enforce the democratic development of a united Germany. However, until the winter of 1989, any visitor who while touring the building glanced from the window of the Blue Room, was confronted with the reality of a Germany divided – the Wall. For almost 30 years the border zone blocked the approach to the lake and to much of the park.

Sanssouci: Anyone who talks about a visit to Potsdam will almost certainly be referring to Sanssouci. And Sanssouci doesn't only mean the relatively small palace created by Frederick the Great, but also an extensive area of parkland covering some 290 hectares (700 acres) which contains a number of other architectural and historical jewels.

The palace itself actually looks quite modest from the outside. Almost as if wanting to hide, it hardly rises above the level of the palace terraces. Frederick designed it for his own needs and despite a whole series of objections from his architect Knobelsdorff, carried his concept through in 1745. The interior, even if only consisting of 12 rooms, is splendidly decorated. However, not everyone has the good fortune to be able to view it.

Since the collapse of the Wall and the resultant flood of visitors to both park and palace, the continued upkeep of these precious creations can no longer

The future of Germany was decided by the victorious Allies at the Potsdam Conference.

be reliably guaranteed. A limit has therefore been set on the number of visitors allowed in.

Frederick found his peace in Sanssouci. Here he involved himself in the *beaux arts* and performed his famous flute concerts. But he wasn't alone. Frederick was a Francophile and one of his most illustrious guests was Voltaire, who came here for several years. The debates between these two sharp-witted and headstrong personalities are legendary. But Voltaire finally left Potsdam a frustrated man. It seems that, as he got older, the king became ever more cranky and stubborn, qualities that the Frenchman with the sharp tongue could no longer abide.

While the palace is the central attraction of Sanssouci, in its very variety the park holds a number of wonderful surprises in store. At the other end of the mile and a half long main drive there is the **Neue Palais**, a representative building which fell out of Frederick's favour as soon as it was completed. This is where he accommodated his retinue and his guests. Opposite stand the **Communs**, the domestic offices in which the servants were housed. The maintenance of these and other buildings has clearly been sorely neglected. Bushes are sprouting from the ridges of the roofs and the figures on the gable ends are blackened by the dirt of centuries, and the corrosive smog of the present epoch. Draughty windows and an abundance of damp allow mildew to thrive in the interiors, causing serious damage to irreplaceable paintings.

Hidden behind ingeniously positioned copses of trees and bushes along the main drive, are a number of buildings representing the most varied collection of styles. The **Chinese Teahouse**, for example, shines golden out of its green surroundings. Surrounded by gold Chinese statues, the little building is a good indication of the 18th-century Prussian fad for things Chinese. The mansion of **Charlottenhof**, on the other hand, is a pure classical building designed by Schinkel, as indeed are the **Roman Baths** which clearly display a predilec-

Russian soldiers hunting for bargains.

tion towards recreating the works of classical antiquity. The largest building is the **Orangery** which was built in Italian Renaissance style. In addition to providing a home to all manner of exotic plants, it was also used as a guest house.

The park is criss-crossed by numerous paths which provide for constantly changing vistas: a planned garden here, a group of marble figures there. Whoever strolls in the grounds of Sanssouci will soon understand why the Hohenzollern rulers came to be so attached to the place.

But the lover of seclusion Frederick the Great would most certainly have blanched at the thought of so many visitors. And he would turn in his grave if he knew that even just a small proportion of these use it as a depository for their litter and even break off little bits of building here and there to take home as souvenirs.

The city centre: But the tourists are not responsible for the state that Potsdam finds itself in today; that can be blamed on the petit-bourgeois ignorance of the founding fathers of the GDR. This pearl of the Prussian baroque, the jewel of the Brandenburg Marches is in a tragic, pitiful state. Alongside Dresden and Würzburg, Potsdam used to be one of the most historically beautiful cities in all of Germany. It could become so again, but only with a great deal of money and effort.

If you wander through the streets of the capital city of the federal state of Brandenburg, you will only find scattered remains of the glorious past. Sometimes it is possible to detect a trace of baroque and Classical Potsdam, but usually only under the crumbling plaster of the facades, although occasionally you might find a house, or even a whole street, that has been restored. For appearance's sake the SED potentates would sometimes preserve a facade, but permit what stood behind to decay.

The **Dutch Quarter** is a good example of this willful neglect. The Soldier King Friedrich Wilhelm I had this residential district built in Dutch style at the

Polish restorers, here working at Sanssouci, are in demand Europe-wide.

beginning of the 18th century. These fine red-brick houses survived intact for 250 years. Only in the last few decades were they demolished, one after the other. Socialist Germany maintained different standards and demanded, as did East Berlin, the eradication of the feudal Prussian past. A few houses still stand and are now being renovated, but only **Brandenburgerstrasse**, now a pedestrian shopping precinct, has been fully restored. The worst example of misplaced socialist architecture is the **Interhotel Potsdam**, a massive concrete block which completely destroys the city's skyline.

Another particularly tasteless piece of city planning came with the construction of the **New Theatre**, a concrete edifice which was dumped in front of the **Church of St Nicholas**, one of Schinkel's buildings. The **Potsdam Residence** stood here on the **Old Market Place** until 1961. Admittedly, like so many other buildings, it had suffered a fair amount of damage during the war. But it wasn't completely destroyed. And what did the socialist planners do? They demolished the 17th-century creation of the Great Elector. The politicians, of course, wanted to make room for an impressively broad boulevard, broad enough for them to have their march-pasts.

So that something cultural came out of their scheme, they decided to erect on this central square a theatre which they called the "Multi-purpose Culture Hall". Despite all the protests, the architect responsible for the airport buildings at Schönefeld was called in to do his worst – and succeeded. You can imagine what charm this new theatre building exudes! Some people have recently been toying with the idea of rebuilding the old residence facade on the site and installing a modern hotel behind it.

Alongside the restoration of the old city, there is much support for the idea of encouraging the development of a new, young Potsdam. At least some stimulus for this could come from the DEFA (German Film Atelier) Film Studios in Babelsberg. The film company Bioscop established its first studios when the German film industry was in its infancy, way back in 1912.

A short time later the High Command attributed the disastrous course of World War I partly to the failure of the propaganda films produced on these very premises. In the days of the GDR the exceedingly tedious nature of many of the productions – they banned all good films – led critics to dub the studios "Honecker's Hollywood". Be that as it may, the studios survived and their future now seems assured by the creation of a special-effects studio based on the American model.

Film Museum located in the former stable buildings offers a fascinating insight into the history of film-making.

So Potsdam is indeed a city of contrasts: of the sublime and the ridiculous. And it is a city where it is easy to dwell on what might have been if the idiocies of its former socialist rulers had not been allowed full play. One shudders to think what the Great Elector would have done with those who so nearly managed to wreck his city.

Frederick the Great.

SACHSEN-ANHALT

A journey through Sachsen-Anhalt is a varied one because the different regions of the state are worlds apart. In the Harz Mountains the traveller is transported into the picture-postcard landscape of German Romanticism. Quaint half-timbered buildings in cities and villages that lie nestled amidst the pine forests and which are only accessible by cobbled roads, alternate with fields of the best quality dark loam where sugar beet, wheat and barley are cultivated.

Further back in time is the fantastic mythological world of the Brocken, the highest mountain in the Harz. The magic that this place exudes on a misty autumn evening continues on the journey to Meresburg. "*Eiris sazun idisi, sazun hera duodor…*" so begins the Old High German spell with which a lame horse could be healed by supplication to the Germanic gods. In the vicinity, over the border in Saxony, another phantom came and vanished: 40 years of GDR. It was in Leipzig, the second largest city in the former republic, that the impressive "Monday demonstrations" took place. A journey, then, into the most recent German past. A good 60 or 70 years further back, the traveller finds himself in another area which could have provided the setting for a film about the Russian revolution, in which "Manchester capitalism" stands accused: the industrial region of Bitterfeld and Wolfen. Foul-smelling chimneys, pale and prematurely-aged workers, smashed and boarded-up windows, illness and depression. Finally, already en route to Berlin, lies the town of Wittenberg on the Elb, the city in which the great reformer Martin Luther lived and worked from 1508 until just before his death in 1546.

Sachsen-Anhalt, the main destination of this trip, cannot exactly look back on a long history. The state was in existence for only seven years. It was created after the war from the free state of Anhalt and the Prussian province of Sachsen (Saxony), which, however, has nothing to do with the kingdom of Saxony. In 1952, Sachsen-Anhalt disappeared, as did every other state, in the administrative reforms. Nevertheless, this new federal state with an area of 20,400 square km (7,900 sq miles) did have a kind of forerunner in the archdiocese of Magdeburg that existed from AD 968 to 1680.

Preceding pages: washing day. Left, fruits of the forest.

BERLIN TO THE HARZ MOUNTAINS

After you've successfully procured your genuine piece of the Wall, got a cold chill down your spine on the Glienicker Bridge, where the spies used to be swapped, and experienced something of the more peaceful side of Prussianism at Sanssouci, then you can continue on your journey along the F 1. In days gone by this was the "Pan German" connection from Königsberg (today in Russia!) via Berlin all the way to Aachen.

Werder: Before the last war, the 40-km (25-mile) stretch between Berlin and Brandenburg was very popular with Berliners for its views of the **River Havel**, the trees in blossom and the copious quantities of fruit wine. Traditionally, the island town of **Werder** was the place to head for in the spring when the trees blossomed. And it was here, in one of the many inns, that the apple flan, and later on in the year the plum flan, tasted best of all.

The most famous of these hostelleries is the "Friedrichshöhe", a somewhat decrepit brick building replete with towers and spires. After negotiating a total of 196 steps to reach it, visitors can still enjoy the view over the river. Sadly, little remains of the original orchards. Now, like nearly everywhere else, the trees are planted in long, uniform rows of "Golden Delicious". The visitor is better off stocking up at one of the wayside stalls selling "biological" strawberries, cherries, apples and plums.

Under its canopy of oak trees, linden trees, alders and maples, the road continues across the broad Havel plain, the flat landscape only interrupted by the rounded hillocks of a terminal moraine.

Brandenburg: If the Brandenburg Marches was the home of the Prussian monarchy, then one might have thought that the town that gave the state its name would possess at least something of the splendour of days gone by. With its skyline dominated by steel and rolling mills, however, this is plainly not the case! And the visitor will be even more disappointed when he discovers that not even Johann Sebastian Bach's Brandenburg Concertos were dedicated to the town. Bach actually composed them for the young Duke Leopold of Anhalt Köthen, a sleepy little town north of Halle and it was only some years later that he sold them to the Margrave of Brandenburg. The fact that these were then named the "Brandenburg Concertos" is the result of the marketing skills of Bach's first biographer Spitta.

The town was originally a Slavic fortified settlement called "Brennabor" containing a shrine to the Slavic god Triglav. The fortress, lying on a ford-point across the Havel, was taken by Heinrich I in AD 928. Brandenburg only really established itself when it was elevated to a diocese after the arrival of German craftsmen and tradesmen in the 12th century. In the 14th and 15th centuries it flourished as a centre of cloth manufacture and trade. The town's diocese status ceased, and its importance thus declined, after the elector of Brandenburg Marches established Berlin as the seat of the royal court in 1470.

Left, these half-timbered houses in the Harz are due for restoration. Right, sad ruins in front of the cathedral in Halberstadt.

Fortunes were revived once more, however, with the arrival of the Huguenots. Banished from France at the end of the 17th century, they brought with them new tanning skills and this trade soon became one of the mainstays of the local economy.

Brandenburg has also witnessed dark days. In 1933 Brandenburg-Görden was built as one of the first concentration camps. A total of 1,800 political prisoners were murdered here. Among those who survived was Erich Honecker, imprisoned here for 10 years for his role in the communist resistance against the Nazis. He was released only in 1945.

Magdeburg: For travellers heading to Berlin in the days of the GDR, whether from the *autobahn* or the railway station, Magdeburg had the appearance of being nothing more than an industrial city surrounded by tasteless concrete housing estates. These fleeting impressions were not entirely wrong. The pedestrian precinct, the **Breiter Weg**, was described in GDR brochures as being "a notable example of contemporary urban planning". Note that the authors did not speak of "design". It is a mercy that the worst architectural crimes are mellowed somewhat by the presence of parks and gardens.

The best way to discover Magdeburg is on foot. In the centre of the city is the university bookshop "Otto von Guericke". Guericke was not only the inventor of the air pump: by creating a vacuum in the "Magdeburg Hemispheres" that he devised in 1656, he was able to prove, through experiments conducted in public, that the two halves were held together by nothing more than external air pressure.

In front of the baroque town hall on the **Old Market Place** stands what is thought to be the oldest free-standing **Equestrian Statue** in Germany, dating from around 1240. Astride the horse is the emperor Otto the Great, who had founded Magdeburg back in the 10th century. Along the Elbe, opposite the pier of the White Fleet, stands one of the most important Romanesque monastery complexes in the land, the **Monastery**

Massive fields are a typical feature of agriculture in the former GDR.

of Our Dear Lady, whose concert hall is dedicated to the composer Georg Phillip Telemann who was born in Magdeburg in 1681.

The city is dominated by the **Cathedral** which was originally founded in AD 955. After being destroyed by fire in 1207, it took no less than 311 years to recreate it in French Gothic style. The 14th-century choir stalls have been preserved, as has the 16th-century pulpit. Any negative impressions which might have been gained of the city are ameliorated to some extent by the presence of these few remaining monuments to the distant past.

To the Harz Mountains: On its way to Halberstadt the F 81 passes fields farmed by agricultural cooperatives. Interrupted by neither hedges nor trees, they stretch away to the horizon, their massive scale recalling the prairies of North America. While providing a sharp contrast to the small fields west of the former border, which through the partition of estates are becoming increasingly uneconomical, the rich soils of the Magdeburg

Plain are now unprotected from wind erosion. Tractors spreading their liquid manure across fields of maize as far as the eye can see indicate the presence of huge pig-fattening farms. However, leave the main road at small villages such as **Egelen**, **Kropenstadt** or **Gröningen** and it is still possible to discover the rural GDR as it once was. On cobbled streets flanked by well-preserved half-timbered houses, you will see men in groups chatting, women in their frocks knitting and children playing with the cats in the poultry yards. Only the electricity pylons and the TV aerials awaken the visitor to the reality of the present day.

Halberstadt: The old capital of the diocese, Halberstadt was almost completely destroyed in World War II. Six hundred historical buildings survived, but 300 of them were later demolished, albeit long after the war. The Gothic **Cathedral**, dedicated in 1491 after taking 250 years to complete was, however, painstakingly restored, as was the **Church of Our Dear Lady** on the opposite side of

Rape and bees at the edge of the Harz.

the cathedral square. In the cathedral's cloister is an impressive collection of treasure including a beautiful Romanesque tapestry, crucifixes made of rock crystal and raiments once used for mass. The **Heineaneum** next door houses a collection of 16,000 stuffed birds and 10,000 bird's eggs. With a population of 47,000, Halberstadt is destined to become a model town. As is the case with Meissen, Weimar, Brandenburg and Stralsund, millions of Deutschmarks have been made available to help preserve and restore its Medieval heritage.

An open-air museum: Even visitors familiar with half-timbered houses will be amazed that in **Quedlinburg** there are no less than 2,000 such buildings constructed over a period of 600 years. The town centre has been declared a historical monument and UNESCO has proposed that it join the "World Heritage" list. Above the roof tops of this town of 30,000 rises the Romanesque **Collegiate Church of St Servatius** (1129) whose altar and pews were destroyed by the Nazis. Thus desecrated, the church, which contains the tomb of the founder of the first German empire Heinrich 1, became the "shrine" of the Third Reich, replete with a massive swastika.

Near Heinrich's palace, Queen Mathilde, to whom he had granted the town of Potsdam, founded an institution for the education of the daughters of nobility in 919. Another daughter of the town played a distinguished role during the Age of Enlightenment. **Dorothea Christiane Erxleben** not only accompanied her father, a doctor, as he made his rounds, but with the permission of Frederick the Great, became the first German woman to study medicine. While still awaiting royal leave, at the age of 23 she wrote that it was "necessary, possible and useful" to allow women to study. She qualified just after giving birth to her fourth child. The theme of her thesis was that it was the doctor's job to discover the causes of illness and not just to treat symptoms.

Into the mountains: The **Harz Mountains** can be reached via Luther's town of Eisleben on the road to Leipzig. From

Wernigerode is dominated by its castle.

the summit of the **Brocken Mountain** you can imagine the same splendid view that Hans Christian Andersen beheld when he visited the area from his native Copenhagen in 1831: "Soon it became clearer and clearer and the towns and the church spires appeared as the tiniest miniature paintings: Magdeburg, Halberstadt and Quedlinburg, the large cathedral in Erfurt and the Wilhelmshöhe near Kassel."

Another route to the Harz is past the station at Quedlinburg southwards to **Harzgerode**. The mountains rise steeply above the village and the numerous orchards make a valuable contribution to the rural economy and provide the basis of winter warmth. Fruit schnapps and liqueurs are produced legally in **Gernrode**, otherwise from a multitude of farmhouse stills. From Harzgerode the route continues along the F 242 towards **Hasselfeld**, right into the heart of the Harz Mountains. A wild, lonely landscape with nothing but miles of pine forests stretches towards the horizon. At **Sorge** there is a small station for

the railway that runs along the Harz. Since 1899 this narrow gauge track has followed the line of the only ancient path through the mountains, a stretch of 60 km (40 miles) linking **Wernigerode** and **Nordhausen**.

A German mountain: For the great German poet Heinrich Heine (*Travels to the Harz* 1824), the climb to the top of the Brocken was a hazardous undertaking: "The higher one climbs, the shorter, the more dwarf-like become the fir trees, until only clusters of bilberries and mountain flora remain. And then it gets noticeably colder." At a height of 1,142 metres (3,747 ft) the summit of the Brocken rises above the tree line.

Few other German mountains can be surrounded by so much myth and legend Heine wrote: "Only now do the strange formations of granite become clearly visible. They must be the balls that the evil spirits threw to each other during Walpurgis Night" (that spring festival of the witches who arrived here on their broomsticks and pitchforks to pay homage to their satanic master). As

he was making his ascent, Heine pondered "On the great mystical German national tragedy of Doctor Faust. It always seemed to me as though his cloven foot trod next to mine. And I believe that even Mephistopheles has to fight for breath as he climbs his favourite mountain."

For the 28-year-old Göethe, the experience seems to have been similar: "I stood on the summit of the Brocken and between those ominous granite crags I cast my gaze over endless snow. Beneath me I saw a motionless sea of cloud, the position of the surrounding mountains only indicated by the varying levels at which it had settled."

Safely at the Brockenhaus you soon realise that the solitude of earlier times has been transformed. Nowadays, scores of tourists climb the Brocken. However, the variety of flora and fauna has remained intact in this unique nature reserve, which for decades was protected from man. From 1971 the Brocken was a strictly prohibited area in the hands of the military and, as such, was not even marked on the weather map.

Aschersleben: After this sojourn in legend we can return to Quedlinburg and continue on the journey to Leipzig. Aschersleben is a typical industrial town. It lives from its woollen blanket factory, machine tool plants and the manufacture of packaging material. After thriving for hundreds of years, the mining of potash and brown coal has now declined, and the mines are being dismantled. Of the Middle-Age watch towers which once dominated the town, 15 remain. Careful restoration work has now begun on the town centre.

A short distance off the F 180 towards Eisleben, the old mining town of **Mansfeld** presents a pitiful scene of poverty and decay. The heavy-industrial with its ore mine, rolling mill and production plant has reached the end of the road. The place typifies the legacy that the dawdling socialists have left behind. Nationwide, tens of thousands of workers are now having to be laid off because their industries have no chance of competing on world markets. Not far from

These decorations are almost 500 years old.

Mansfeld, in the shadow of the gigantic copper slag heap at **Sangershausen**, the fate of the 800 miners at the "Thomas Müntzer" copper mine has already been sealed.

Here, at the start of the 16th century the reformer **Thomas Müntzer** amassed his rebels and set the Peasants' Revolt into motion. He rid the divine service of its "Papist buffoonery", including the Latin language and the "hypocritical" confession and abolished the privileges of the clerics. In contrast to Martin Luther, Müntzer's tone was militant: he preached "that the people should resist with their pitchforks". He denounced the traditional scribes as "foolish philosophisers" and regarded Luther as a "brother fattened pig". By 1525, a third of Germany had risen up against the feudal lords and the Church. However, the counts banded together and in **Frankenhausen**, at the foot of the **Kyffhäuser**, only a few kilometres from Sangershausen, 5,000 peasants were slaughtered. Münzer was beheaded.

To provide a fitting memorial to the Peasants' Revolt, the GDR leadership donated 53 million DM for the construction of a monumental tower on the top of the Kyffhäuser hill. Here between 1983 and 1987 Werner Tübke created his massive mural depicting the peasant's struggle.

Luther's birthplace: The **Statue of Martin Luther**, who was born in **Eisleben** in 1483 and died here on 18 February 1546, stands larger than life in front of the **Town Hall** on the market place. Following a fire in 1532, the building was reconstructed in late-Gothic style. The life's work of the great reformer is recreated in the **Luther Museum**, the house where he died. As was the case with Mansfeld, Eisleben was always dependant on mining for its livelihood. Even Luther's father managed a small mine. Huge heaps of copper slag still visible in the suburbs testify to the fact that bronze has been produced in this region for over 4,000 years. The collections of weapons and tools in the **Local Museum** provide further evidence of this tradition.

Left, stocking up with beer. **Right**, beware of witches!

HALLE, MERSEBURG AND LEIPZIG

Before we reach Leipzig, there are two other traditional cities on the River Saale: Halle and Merseburg. Situated as they are between the romantic heart and the industrial core of Eastern Germany, both can look back on a distinguished history. Prosperity not only came from the rich, fertile land in which they lie but also from industry. And industry has left its mark on both the health of the inhabitants and on the environment.

Halle: Those who do not know **Halle** imagine it as being an ugly industrial city. However, its age alone would indicate that this simply can't be the case, and the prejudice is immediately dispelled by a stroll through the city centre, which was spared the Allied bombs. A number of residential areas near the city centre were once very noble indeed. Here are street after street of solid brick houses from the turn of the century, some of them Art Deco.

With a present population of 230,000, Halle came into the possession of the Bishops of Magdeburg in AD 968. *Halhus* is the Old High German word for salt which was already being produced here at that time. The salt trade flourished and the 15th century saw bitter struggles between the rich and powerful citizens and their episcopal overlords. The bourgeoisie lost and the **Moritzburg** was built as a means of controlling the activities of the salt merchants. The Bishops, however, could not maintain their position for long: the Reformation put paid to their secular power. The fortress was destroyed but was later rebuilt and since the beginning of this century it has housed a **Museum** in which primarily the works of German artists are exhibited: Caspar David Friedrich, Franz von Stuck, Wilhelm Lehmbruck and Ernst Barlach.

The university was founded in 1694. In the 18th century it became a bastion of enlightened ideologies. After the abolition of Bismarck's law against the socialists, the first party conference of the SPD (Socialist Party of Germany)

was held in Halle in 1890. Halle has always had a strong labour movement and this stood up particularly against the right-wing nationalist tendencies of the 1920s. After the war Halle became a centre of the chemicals industry and in 1964 **Halle-Neustadt** was built as a massive dormitory town accommodating well over 100,000 workers and their families.

The large **Market Square** in the centre of Halle, with its fascinating ensemble of churches and other historical buildings, reflects the former prosperity of the city. Especially impressive are the town hall and the **Church of St Mary** with its four spires which was dedicated in 1537. Martin Luther preached here and George Friedrich Handel, Halle's most famous son, played the organ. His monument stands opposite the church. The centre of the market place is dominated by the **Red Tower**, an 84-metre (275-ft) high free-standing clock-tower erected in the 15th century. The tower is now completely black.

Merseburg: The road to Leipzig con-

The Monday demonstrations in Leipzig first demanded reform of socialism, later the reunification of Germany. Right, "Chiquita" arrives in Leipzig.

tinues through the industrial complexes of Schopkau and arrives once more at the dawn of German history. The Merseburg Hill, where Heinrich I constructed his fortified palace at the beginning of the 10th century, became the focal point of the town, where today the two main attractions, the cathedral and the castle, stand harmoniously side by side. The emperors of the old German Empire favoured Merseburg: between 933 and 1212 more than 20 Imperial Diets were held here.

The buildings are situated within the relaxing, well-kept palace gardens, together with the assembly house of the estates, a palais, the orangery and a café. The whole ensemble is a charming, if somewhat dilapidated, jewel of German history. The **Castle** stands on the walls of the old palace and was built between the 15th and 17th centuries.

More important from a cultural point of view is the **Cathedral**, which was originally founded in AD 931 as the palace chapel of Heinrich I and which became a cathedral after the establishment of the diocese in 968. The building as we see it today was begun in 1015 and underwent a succession of alterations until the 16th century when the addition of the four spires completed its present countenance. Showpieces of the unusually opulent interior are the bronze-cast epitaph (1080), the font (1150) and the beautifully carved choir stalls.

World famous is the **Cathedral Chapter Archive** founded by Bishop Wigbert in 1004 and containing a collection of manuscripts from the Middle Ages, including the **Merseburg Spells** which are among the oldest works of German literature. Dating from the 9th or 10th century and thought to have come from Fulda, they were only discovered in 1841 in the library. Both verses contain magic formulas, one for freeing prisoners and the other for healing lame horses. In 1842 the philologist Jakob Grimm acknowledged the importance of this discovery for the history of literature: a treasure with which even the most famous libraries in the land have nothing to compare.

Leipzig: The city has grown so much that Merseburg is now almost one of its suburbs. Today, Leipzig calls itself the "city of heroes". They were peaceful heroes who brought about the revolution in the GDR. The demands of the marchers involved in the demonstrations of autumn 1989 were short and to the point: "We are the people", "We are one people" and "If the Deutschmark comes we stay, if it doesn't we leave".

Autumn 1989 saw the vigils in the Church of St Nicholas spill out into open protests on the streets. On 2 October 15,000 demonstrators marched through the centre of the city. One week later, on 9 October, the security forces from the entire country had closed in on Leipzig and a major confrontation seemed unavoidable. However, a message sent out over the local radio station from the director of the Leipzig Philharmonic, Kurt Masur, appealed for a peaceful settlement. Indeed, one of the main slogans on that fateful Monday was "No Violence". There was the dread of the "Chinese solution", that had been witnessed a few months earlier in Peking.

The cathedral in Halle.

Despite the fact that the entire city centre was closed to camera teams, the GDR opposition secretly filmed the event and smuggled the video cassette to West Berlin. And on that same evening the whole world, including many people in East Germany, could witness on their TV screens the unabashed will of the people for peaceful change. By reacting with violence, the regime would only have discredited itself further. The free city of Leipzig, which had never been a royal city, had successfully stood up against the leadership in East Berlin. Exactly one month later, the Wall came tumbling down.

With a population of 556,000, Leipzig is the second largest city in the former GDR. In the task of regenerating the run-down infrastructure, the city faces seemingly insurmountable problems. Thirty thousand flats are no longer habitable, the public transport system requires a complete overhaul and the streets are pitted with pot-holes. One-third of all the water mains pipes are leaking and need replacing. The neces-

Currency union came into force on 1 July 1990 (here pictured in Eisleben).

sary repairs to the sewage system alone will cost billions. Nevertheless, there are already some glimmers of a brighter future. One year after the collapse of the Wall, the emissions of sulphur dioxide into the air have already been reduced by 25 percent. This is the result of the closure of the carbonising plants in Espenhain and Böhlen.

However, the city's population continues to decline. At the time of writing there are 22,000 fewer people here than there were in 1970, 150,000 fewer than in 1930, and that during a period when most other large cities witnessed unrestrained growth.

History: The history and prosperity of the city is inseparably linked to the **Leipzig Trade Fair.** This is said to have had its premier in 1268 when the Margrave of Meissen declared the city a centre of free trade. By that time Leipzig, founded at the junction of the König-strasse and the Reichsstrasse, had long played a leading role in East-West trade.

A Slavic Sorb settlement called *Lipzi* (under the linden tree) was established

here in the 7th century. Trader's and craftsmen's settlements developed on the same site. With the bestowal of trade fair privileges by the Emperor Maximilian I in 1497, Leipzig's role as a trading centre was secured. From the east came spices, oriental goods and meat, while from the west came cloth and jewellery

In 1507 the area in which Leipzig was permitted to store goods was increased and no other fair was allowed to take place within a circumference of 115 km (70 miles). By this time the population had reached 45,000 and Leipzig had surpassed Frankfurt as Germany's number one trade fair city. The privileges granted the city included allowing publicans and retailers to increase their prices during the fair, though of course any abuses were strictly controlled. Tax debtors who normally had to live on the periphery of the city were allowed to go freely about their business in the city centre.

In 1839 the first German rail connection, that between Leipzig and Dresden, was opened. In contrast to what happened in Dresden, World War II "only" destroyed about one-quarter of Leipzig.

The university: Two other factors contributed to the development of Leipzig: the university and the production of books. In 1409 nationalistic tendencies at the university in Prague had led to a walk-out by German professors and students and Leipzig University was founded as an alternative place of study. It is an institution which continues to dominate the city, particularly with the 142-metre (466-ft) high tower, known locally as the "sharp tooth". The university has since been joined by a multitude of other colleges and polytechnics, including the Centre for the Science of Sport, which became the sweatshop responsible for turning out all those top East German athletes.

Goethe had the highest praise for the university: "That's just what I like; a city that educates its people." Later he was to bestow upon the city the title of "little Paris". The university turned out a host of important people: the historian Leopold von Ranke, the philosopher

Baron Gottfried Wilhelm von Leibnitz, the poets Friedrich Gottlieb Klopstock and Gotthold Ephraim Lessing, as well Jean Paul and the philosopher Friedrich Nietzsche.

City of publishers: Science always needs books and these have been printed in Leipzig since 1481. In this regard too, the city soon outshone Frankfurt, where publications were subjected to the strict censorship of the Archbishop of Mainz. The Reformation provided the book trade with a great deal of stimulus. In the 16th century every new title that Luther produced became an immediate bestseller. The first edition (5,000 copies) of his "New Testament" sold out within a few weeks. Over the next 15 years, no less than 200,000 copies were sold. Sixty-six out of a total of 74 editions were pirated.

Leipzig achieved its monopoly position in the book trade through a unique system which still functions to this day. Publishers distributed their books in Leipzig through a central company founded in 1842. Booksellers submit-

Bin women in Leipzig.

ted their orders to this organisation first hand and (until 1945) so received books from 80 percent of all publishers. By cutting out the middle men, considerable savings could be made in both cost and time. Even people not familiar with the history of publishing may recognise some of the great names of Leipzig: Karl Baedeker, Breitkopf & Härtel, Goldmann, Grieben, Reclam, and Georg Thieme.

The Battle of Nations: Publishing companies even made a killing from the Battle of Leipzig. After a few months they were presented with the battle plans and the portraits of the most important politicians and military. One author, Ludwig Husserl, created two volumes from the material, together with two collections of anecdotes. The Battle of Nations (1813) marked the end of Napoleon's rule in Europe. 190,000 troops on Napoleon's side, French, Belgians, Dutch, Poles as well as forces from the German states of Baden, Hesse, Württemberg and Saxony, were blockaded in Leipzig by the allied army con-

Many old buildings are simply being demolished.

sisting of 205,000 men. There were Russians, Prussians, Austrians (including Hungarians, Czechs and Croatians), Swedes and English. Hardly had the battlefield been cleared of the 22,000 dead Russians, 16,000 Prussians, 15,000 Austrians and 35,000 French before plans to erect a monument were discussed. But it was only on the occasion of the 100th anniversary that Kaiser Wilhelm II inaugurated the 91-metre (298-ft) high edifice which stands atop a 30-metre (100-ft) high earth mound. The creation of this monument just before the outbreak of World War I, was intended as an expression of German nationalism. The view from the observation platform is today one of the main attractions of the city.

Labour movement: Less nationalistically minded, the German labour movement had its roots in Leipzig. It was here in 1863 that Ferdinand Lassalle founded the German Worker's Association, the forerunner of social democracy in Germany. Well-known socialists like Clara Zetkin, Rosa Luxemburg

and Franz Mehring worked on the *Leipziger Volkszeitung* (a left-wing newspaper) which was founded in 1894.

The station: That building which many travellers to Leipzig first confront is the **Main Station**, completed in 1915. This enormous building is the largest station in Europe: it is 240 metres (787 ft) long and spans 24 platforms. The apparent symmetry of the building is not the result of aesthetic considerations. Originally it was shared by two independent railway authorities, the eastern part belonging to Saxony and the western part to Prussia. Behind is the main booking hall which is almost 300 metres (1,000 ft) long.

Most points in the city centre are within 15 minutes of the station. To reach the historic market square, cross the broad Sachsenplatz, whose design completely lacks fantasy as do most new city squares – in both east and west.

The Town Hall: In strange contrast to the station, the **Old Town Hall** is actually asymmetric in design. The tower rises above the main entrance, but this is flanked on the right by four gable roofs and on the left by only two. The people of Leipzig were cost-conscious tradesmen and built their Town Hall in only nine months – between two trade fairs – in 1556. It was built on the foundations of an even earlier Gothic Town Hall and the erstwhile spinners' guild. The colonnade was only added in 1907. Today the old Town Hall houses the **City History Museum**. The historic character of the **Market Square** would be preserved if it wasn't for the presence of the office building of the trade fair authority. Built in 1965, it completely destroyed the harmonious ensemble.

Opposite the town hall, the **Craftsmen's Arcade**, which replicates street life in medieval Leipzig, was reopened in 1989. Above the entrance of the **Kaffeebaum**, the oldest coffee house in the city at Fleischergasse 4, the life-sized model of a Turk hands a bowl of coffee to a cherub. According to the proprietor, Augustus the Strong was so excited about the wonderful coffee that he donated the statue.

A refuge for cats.

Thomasgasse leads to the **Church of St Thomas** which was built in 1212 as an Augustinian collegiate church by Margrave Dietrich the Afflicted from Meissen. The church went through a number of major conversions before Claus Roder gave it its late-Gothic appearance in the 15th century. At the inaugural celebrations for the university in 1409, the **Thomas Boys' Choir**, the *Thomaner*, had already been singing in this church for 200 years. The choir started off with 12 boys who went around singing the mass in schools for the children of poor families. And they sang whenever there was anything to celebrate in the church or in the city: local elections, coronations, conclusions of peace. They eventually became the one and only important boys' choir of German Protestantism.

When Johann Sebastian Bach took over as the choirmaster-organist on 13 March 1723, he complained about the poor quality of some of the singing and sacked 17 of the 54 choristers. Nevertheless, he wrote most of his motets for "his" choir. Today the choristers perform in the same "sailor suits" in which they became world-famous.

Back behind the Town Hall is the **Old Trading Hall** (Alte Handelsbörse) which was built in 1687 according to the style of Italian and Dutch models. It served as a meeting place of bankers and merchants visiting the trade fair. Festive events take place here today. A statue of the young Goethe stands before the building, and if you follow the direction in which he is walking, you will arrive at the **Auerbachs Keller** in the Mädlerpassage. It is a famous students' pub with a long history and provides the setting for one of the scenes in Goethe's "Faust". A glockenspiel made of Meissen porcelain chimes in this elegant arcade.

At the exit to the arcade on the right is the **"Städtische Kaufhaus"**, part of the trade fair complex which has been here since 1901. This is where the old cloth hall used to be, in which, apart from the cloth trade, the orchestra was also housed. Hence the name of the Leipzig Orchestra – the **Gewandhaus** (cloth hall). The "Gewandhaus" now plays in a new building on Karl Marx Platz. The orchestra was founded in 1781 and Felix Mendelssohn Bartholdy was probably its greatest conductor.

Back on our tour of the city, we come to the **Church of St Nicholas**, Leipzig's main church. The building was started in Romanesque style in the 12th century. The choir is 200 years younger and the late-Gothic nave was dedicated in 1523. Stucco work on the columns and vaulting as well as the classic interior design testify to the former wealth of the city, whose people in 1989 still held this sacred building to be a suitable place for secular meetings.

Outside the city centre, the southerly district of **Connewitz** provides an insight into domestic architecture as built during the period of rapid industrial growth in Germany towards the end of the last century. A local action group made up of residents, young people, city planners and architects is fighting to save these fine buildings from further decay and ultimate demolition.

Western culture on sale in Leipzig station.

THE BITTER TASTE
OF BITTERFIELD

As far as carrying out the slogan "Hit capitalism where you can" was concerned, the industrial districts of Halle and Leipzig certainly achieved more than was required of them in one respect: the region was beyond any doubt the most polluted area of Europe.

The general state of health of people in the eastern part of Germany is decidedly worse than that of West Germans. One does not need to look far to see why: take the constantly high levels of sulphur dioxide in the Erz Mountains and the region north of Leipzig around Bitterfeld that lead to retarded growth in children and a weakening of the immune system. The children in Bitterfeld are frail and have low blood counts. Around the brown coal processing plant in Espenhain south of Leipzig every second child suffers from respiratory ailments.

Forty percent of the population of the former GDR lives in areas where the amount of sulphur dioxide in the air far exceeds legal limits. Leipzig, Halle and Chemnitz are the most heavily polluted areas. In 1982, the old regime responded to the environmental disaster by simply declaring all environmental data classified information.

Now that the statistics are there for all to see, a few comparisons indicate the scale of the catastrophe. The power station in Cottbus pumps more sulphur dioxide into the air than all the power stations of Norway and Sweden put together. The total emissions of this poison, whose effects can also be seen in the dying forests, exceed those of any other region in Europe by 5.6 million tons a year. Each day the chemical plants at Buna near Halle release more mercury into the River Saale than the West German giant chemical concern BASF in Ludwigshafen jettisons into the Rhine in one year.

The inhabitants of Mölbis want to leave their village. They have witnessed how the fumes from the gigantic plants at Espenhain (closed down in 1991) have eroded the bricks of their houses, and naturally they are concerned about the effect those same fumes have been having on their lungs. The skies over eastern Germany are five times as polluted as those over the old Federal Republic. The Trabis have also played a major role in contributing to these statistics: one Trabi releases as much carbon monoxide as 100 cars equipped with catalytic converters.

The old GDR also came top of the world league of energy wasters. The energy squandered by its archaic and highly inefficient power plants would comfortably provide a country such as Denmark with its entire energy needs.

Bitterfeld: the name of this town has become synonymous with environmental catastrophe. Camera teams from the world over have reported on Bitterfeld. Even Jane Fonda came here. She visited a person whom one cannot escape in matters environmental: Hans Zimmermann. Long before the changes in the East, the trained plumber had formed an environmentalist action group whose activities were continuously monitored by the Stasi, the secret power. He was responsible for a video film *The Bitter taste of Bitterfeld*, which created uproar in the West. It dealt with the appalling living and environmental conditions that the locals had to put up with, in a place where each and every day one pound of brown coal dust came to settle on one square yard of earth.

Some miles further on in Wolfen, the phototechnical company ORWO has been pumping its waste products into the Silber See for 16 years producing a silvery-brown foaming chemical cocktail which then flows into the River Elbe. Greenpeace discovered that the level of chlorides in this river is 600 times higher than that found in the Rhine. The quality of the drinking water in eastern Germany can only be maintained at acceptable levels through the addition of huge quantities of chlorine.

Not all the filth in the old GDR is home-produced. Near Berlin are the refuse sites of Vorketzin and Schöneiche to which millions of tons of West Berlin's domestic waste continue to be brought. Add to this poisonous wastes from Austria, Switzerland and Holland, and you have the beginnings of an ecological problem that will not be easily or rapidly solved.

DESSAU AND WITTENBERG

Returning from Leipzig to Berlin, there are two towns beyond the industrial region and Bitterfeld that are well worth visiting, especially because of the enormous importance they have had for the development of mankind, in two entirely different spheres. **Dessau** is the original home of the Bauhaus, regarded as the most important school of art in this century, and **Wittenberg** is the town from where Martin Luther set out to preach the Reformation. Apart from revolutionising the times in which they were born, the movements had something else in common: both were castigated by the ruling powers of the day.

The Bauhaus: Lying to the east of the main station, the old Bauhaus school building is the principal attraction of Dessau, a town of 104,000 on the River Mulde. Founded in Weimar in 1919, the Bauhaus moved here in 1925. But in Dessau the group of artists, architects, planners, designers and photographers who had gathered around Walter Gropius could only remain intact until 1932. Ultra-conservative politicians in Weimar and then National Socialists in Dessau used every means to obstruct the new Bauhaus ideas. A final attempt to move the Bauhaus to a factory building in Berlin failed. The building was searched by the Nazis and closed in 1933 on the pretext of it being a hotbed of corruptive Bolshevist ideologies.

What did they want to achieve, these aesthetic revolutionaries, with their simple forms that did away with all frills and decoration, whose ideas spread to dictate the design of whole new cities in America; schools, factories and office blocks in Western Europe? In the words of Walter Gropius: "The Bauhaus seeks to unify all the individual components of artistic creation, to reunite the disciplines of sculpture, painting, applied art and handicraft as indivisible elements of a new style."

In order to emphasise the close relationship between craft skills and artistic

Children hoping for a healthier future.

creativity, Gropius called his teachers "masters" and his students "apprentices". The Bauhaus not only aimed to bridge the gap between handicraft and art: in the opinion of the masters Ludwig Mies van der Rohe, Lyonel Feininger, Moholy-Nagy, Paul Klee, Wassily Kandinski, and Gerhard Marcks, there were no irreconcilable contradictions between handicraft and technology. As far as they were concerned, it was a matter of working in the real interests of the people by creating the most practical solution in terms of function and material.

That is what dictated the beauty of the product or the style of the building. Teaching and learning, theory and practice were inextricably linked. Today, the ideas of the Bauhaus remain stylistically instructive for modern architectural and industrial design.

From 1937, the Bauhaus found its successor in Chicago. In the GDR, however, it died at the hands of "socialist realism". Only in 1977 was the Bauhaus building converted into a museum. In addition to the Bauhaus, other buildings have been preserved, including the former labour exchange designed by Gropius on August Bebel Platz, the Bauhaus settlement with the Co-op building in the district of Törten and the Masters' houses in Ebert Allee.

War damage: Junkers aeroplanes and the products of other armaments firms in Dessau also enjoyed world-wide success. The result: On 7 March 1945, over 80 percent of the town was destroyed by a massive British bombing raid. Practically the only historical building that remained standing was one decaying wing of the **Royal Palace** (1530), which has subsequently been restored. The **Church of St George** (1712–17) was also rebuilt after a fire in World War II.

Dessau, first mentioned in 1213, was the residence of the dukes of Anhalt-Dessau (1471–1918). The town's undoubted heyday was during the reign of Duke Leopold Friedrich Franz of Anhalt-Dessau (1740–1817), who gathered around him artists, poets and architects. He was responsible for Castle

Luther's town Wittenburg.

Mosigau, a short distance to the southwest of the town, and also for the Wörlitz Country Park.

In 1742 Duke Leopold granted his daughter Anna Wilhelmine the estate of **Mosigau**. She moved her official residence here some 10 years later and commissioned the architect Knobelsdorf to build the rococo palace (1752–57). The building, now a state museum and picture gallery, contains collections of arts and crafts, porcelain and faience, and paintings by Rubens, van Dyck and Jordaens. The park has a maze and a Japanese teahouse, features which were trendy among the nobility of the day.

One of the finest "English style" country parks in Germany is at **Wörlitz**. Lying not far from Mosigau on the road to Wittenburg, this jewel of landscape architecture nowadays compensates for the otherwise bleak industrial landscape. Duke Leopold Friedrich Franz had the park laid out around his hunting lodge on what were formerly swampy pastures beside the River Elbe. Built between 1769 and 1773, Wörlitz Castle was the first neoclassical building in Germany. The walls and ceilings of the banqueting and dining halls were embellished with opulent frescoes. Today it contains a valuable art collection with works by Averkamp, Canaletto and Rubens.

It is possible to take a boat trip along the canals linking the artificial lakes. However, this is no substitute for a stroll through the 112 hectares (276 acres) of this wonderful park which contains over 800 species of deciduous trees and a multitude of exotic plants growing between the hills, along the winding paths, on the bridges, into the caves and around the statues and antique sculptures. The park is also dotted with buildings and follies representative of many architectural styles: an Italian farmhouse, Doric columns, a Greek temple, a Gothic castle and a palm house. Millions of visitors used to visit annually to experience the "old Dassauer's" dream come true.

Wittenberg: Continuing along the road from Wörlitz, the first landmark to catch the eye is the mighty dome of the **The Bauhaus Museum.**

Schlosskirche, whose form recalls a stranded emperor's crown. Until the Easter week of 1990, a tank stood in the square in front of this church, its gun directed towards the West.

Wittenberg is Luther's town although he was born in Eisleben. On 31 October 1517, after the peasant uprising in Hungary, Czechoslovakia, Switzerland and southern Germany, he nailed his 95 theses to the door of this church and thereby launched the Reformation. The bronze *Thesentür* – "Thesis Door" actually dates from 1858. Luther and Melanchton lie buried in the church.

At that time Luther was alarmed by the special offers made by the seller of indulgences Johann Tetzel, who only charged a paltry eight Ducats for the pardon of manslaughter. Purely by accident, Luther foiled a dubious triangular transaction of European high finance. Luther's archbishop Albrecht, Cardinal of Mainz, had purchased his title in Rome and wanted to continue his illegal activities by acquiring a number of bishoprics. To this end the 25-year-old Albrecht needed a special arrangement with Rome. No problem: the necessary 23,379 Ducats were financed by the Augsburg banker Jakob Fugger. Pope Leo duly made out a letter of indulgence the profits of which were intended not only to reimburse Fugger, but to go towards the building of St Peter's. The general agent in these transactions was the Dominican Tetzel.

Luther's "working paper" was a bestseller in Europe within only a few weeks. Politically more significant was the break with the Pope on 10 December 1520. At the **Luther Oak** in the east of the city, now a dying tree, Luther burnt the Pope's bull of excommunication together with all the volumes of canonical law, the very legal basis of the Middle Ages. The **Lutherhaus** is located close to the old oak tree, as is the **Lutherhalle**, which houses the world's largest museum devoted entirely to the Reformation. On display are paintings by Luther's artist friend Lucas Cranach the Elder which depict the great reformer, his wife and the "Ten Commandments".

Objets d'art on display within the building.

FROM BRANDENBURG TO THE BALTIC

Visitors wishing to see the northeast of Germany can approach the area from Berlin by travelling on the *autobahn* to Rostock which lies on the North Sea coast. It may be more interesting, however, to leave the capital at Staaken and follow the old Berlin-Hamburg trunk road, the F 5. Until the *autobahn* was built in 1982, this was the only route available to those wishing to drive from Hamburg to West Berlin. Day and night the traffic would thunder along the road, through the avenue of trees accompanying it for mile after mile.

For the children who grew up along this road the colourful cars were the only link with the other world, a world for which they secretly longed. The children liked to stand on the verge and wave to the cars as they flashed by, although their teachers did not approve. The transit travellers themselves were forbidden to stop or to leave the designated route.

The Prussian province: The road runs directly across the Brandenburg Marches, with its typical landscape of fields, forests, meadows and avenues of trees stretching away across the flat countryside whose sandy soil is proverbially famous – the *Märkische Sandboden.* The route passes through one village after another. Their farmhouses have generous steps leading up to their front doors, as if they were pretending to be the manor house of some wealthy estate. Indeed, it was the old noble families like the Bredows and Ribbeck von Ribbecks that gave the villages their names.

The writer Theodor Fontane (1819–89) hailed from these parts. The trained chemist from Neuruppin turned his hand to journalism and writing after the failure of the German Revolution in 1848, and spent much of his time travelling – also in the service of the Prussian government. An anglophile, he translated Shakespeare into German and in his years spent in the United Kingdom (1855–59), he wrote about Scotland

(Beyond the Tweed). It was this journey that inspired him once more to return and write about his homeland in *Walks through the Brandenburg Marches*, in which he describes the history, legends and anecdotes of the region. He regarded the relationship between England and Scotland as being very similar to Prussia and its border regions.

Today 28,000 people live in **Neuruppin**. The uniform, classical character of the city emerged after the great fire of 1787 and its oversized squares were useful for holding military drills. Neuruppin was always an important garrison town, first for the Prussians and in more recent times for the Red Army. Now the withdrawal of the Russian troops has begun and the Federal Army is showing interest in the facilities left behind, particularly the airport. Some of the locals most affected by the noise have formed an action group and are demanding the permanent closure of all military facilities.

The local museum in Neuruppin not only recalls the life and works of Theodor

Preceding pages: the day awakes in the Brandenburg Marches. **Left**, Rheinsberg Palace. **Right**, at the bus stop.

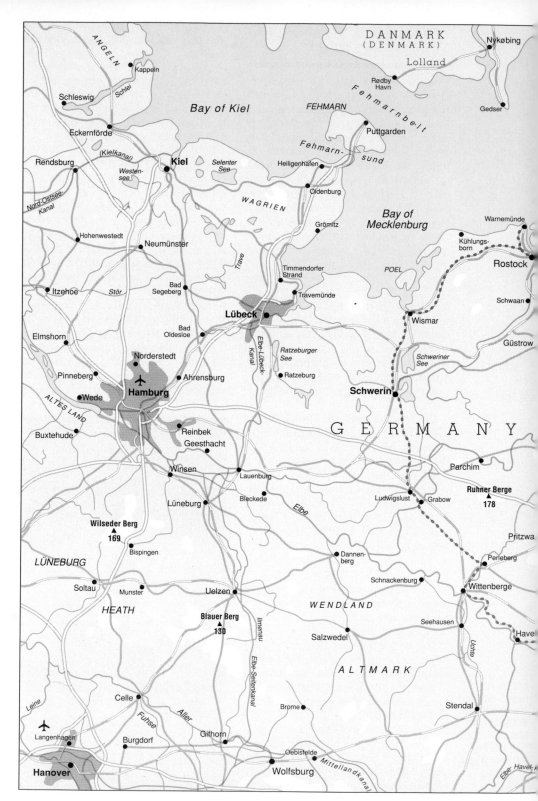

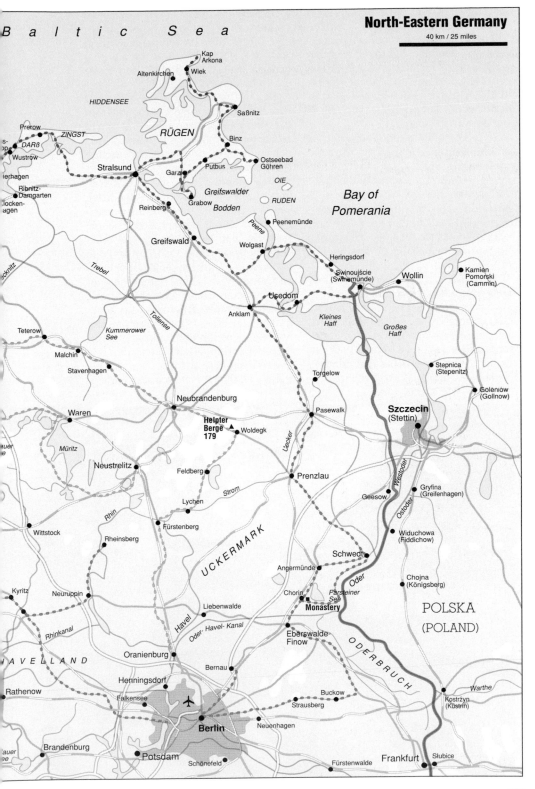

North-Eastern Germany

40 km / 25 miles

Baltic Sea

Kap Arkona

Altenkirchen

Wiek

HIDDENSEE

Saßnitz

ZINGST

Prerow

DARß

Wustrow

RÜGEN

Binz

Ostseebad Göhren

ierhagen

Stralsund

Garz

Putbus

OIE

Ribnitz-Damgarten

Grabow

Greifswalder

RUDEN

locken-agen

Reinberg

Bodden

Peene

Peenemünde

Greifswald

Wolgast

Bay of Pomerania

Trebel

Heringsdorf

Świnoujście (Swinemünde)

Wollin

Kamien Pomorski (Cammin)

Tollense

Usedom

Kleines Haff

Großes Haff

Teterow

Anklam

Stepnica (Stepenitz)

Kummerower See

Goleniów (Gollnow)

Malchin

Stavenhagen

Torgelow

Neubrandenburg

Waren

Helpter Berge 179

Woldegk

Pasewalk

Szczecin (Stettin)

Müritz

Uecker

Neustrelitz

Feldberg

Strom

Prenzlau

Geesow

Gryfina (Greifenhagen)

Wittstock

Lychen

Rhin

Fürstenberg

Rheinsberg

UCKERMARK

Widuchowa (Fiddichow)

Kyritz

Neuruppin

Schwedt

Chojna (Königsberg)

Angermünde

Oder

Rhinkanal

Chorin

Parsteiner See

Monastery

POLSKA (POLAND)

Liebenwalde

Havel

Oder-Havel-Kanal

Eberswalde-Finow

ODERBRUCH

HAVELLAND

Oranienburg

Bernau

Rathenow

Henningsdorf

Falkensee

Buckow

Warthe

Kostrzyn (Küstrin)

Strausberg

Berlin

Neuenhagen

Brandenburg

Potsdam

Schönefeld

Fürstenwalde

Frankfurt

Słubice

Fontane, but also its other famous son, the architect Karl Friedrich Schinkel (1781–1841). As well as being a painter and stage designer, Schinkel was the most important architect of the Prussian world. He designed the Neue Wache and the Theatre in Berlin as well as Charlottenhof Palace in the gardens of Sanssouci in Potsdam.

The oldest building in Neuruppin is the 13th-century Dominican **Monastery Church** which was renovated according to Schinkel's plans in the middle of the last century. Also worth close inspection is the baroque **Temple Garden** created by Schinkel's predecessor Georg Wenzeslaus von Knobelsdorff, who was Frederick the Great's architect.

The town became famous through the *Neuruppiner Bilderbogen*, a pictorial broadsheet published by Gustav Kühn, a folksy fore-runner of the illustrated magazine. It regularly reported on world events and between 1810 and 1935 no less than 100 million sheets were printed. For decades the aims and principal of the Neuruppin office was to provide the public with a continuous flow of up-to-date information on topical matters. It was one of the few thin threads that connected the broad tracts of this country to the outside world.

On the first night of the August full moon, the locals organise a regatta from the Neuruppiner Lake along the Rhin to Altruppin. It passes illuminated gardens with fancy dress parties depicting the theme of the night.

Near Neuruppin is the "Luch", an area of low-lying ground that the Prussian king Frederick the Great had drained 200 years ago. It was settled by people from Swabia, Württemberg and other German states who turned it over to cultivation. With its canals and locks and water-wheels this flat expanse of countryside is reminiscent of Holland.

Local romances: Rheinsberg is about a 25-minute drive from Neuruppin. Before his accession to the throne, Crown Prince Friedrich, later Frederick the Great, lived here for four years in the **Palace** on the lake, which was built by

On Lake Kyritz, one of 650 lakes north of Berlin.

the court architect Knobelsdorff. It was here that Frederick discovered the qualities of his otherwise plain wife Elizabeth Christina.

This was also the setting for Kurt Tucholsky's most beautiful romance *Rheinsberg* (1912). Since its publication, many have come here in search of the flame of passion, particularly those who, like Tucholsky's characters Claire and Wölfchen, want to escape the monotony and stress of life in Berlin. The memorial to Tucholsky is located within the castle. Outside in the park are allegorical depictions of the four elements fire, earth, wind and water.

For years the palace served as a sanatorium for diabetes sufferers, but now the local art association is trying to find other uses for the building in the hope of attracting tourists to Rheinberg. It is planned to continue the old summer music traditions by introducing a festival of chamber music.

Of knights and reforms: We return to join the trunk road at **Kampehl**. In the annex of the village church it is possible to view the mummified corpse of a knight. The story goes that he murdered a shepherd, but to protest his innocence he exclaimed before the court: "If I really am the murderer then God will not let my body decompose!" When he was exhumed 90 years later, his corpse was found to be intact.

In **Kyritz** (population 10,000) a monument in front of the local culture centre recalls the land reform introduced by the first GDR president Wilhelm Pieck on 2 September 1945, whereby the landowners were all expropriated. The town itself lies on a series of lakes which can be explored either by steamer or rented craft.

Kyritz, Pritzwalk, Wittstock and Perleberg belong to the district of **Prignitz**. The flat countryside with its small lanes and scattered villages lends itself to cycling excursions in the summer. GRAF (*Galerie Rosenwinkel Ausbau Fünf*) is an independent culture project in **Rosenwinkel** which organises theatre performances, concerts and sports competitions such as the

Frederick the Great lived in Rheinsberg Palace before he became emperor.

"Rosenwinkler Bauernolympiade" – the "Farmers' Olympics of Rosenwinkel".

Havelberg, not far from the confluence of the Havel and Elbe rivers, is dominated by its Gothic **Cathedral**. On the first weekend in September, many visitors are attracted to the large **Horse Market** on the Havel meadows. The event developed over the years into the largest flea market in the GDR. In former times the horse market was also a marriage market and today much flirting still goes on along the main bazaar during this annual event.

A little farther down the River Elbe we come to **Wittenberge**. The main problem facing this industrial and port town is the restructuring of the economy. Paper-making used to be an important local industry. Despite the resultant pollution to both air and river, around 100 pairs of storks still continue to nest in the vicinity of the town.

On the market square in **Perleberg** stands a **Roland's Column**. Such sculptures depicting the bareheaded man with his sword were erected in the Middle Ages in many northern German towns in order to commemorate their fight for political and judicial independence.

Mecklenburg residences: Leaving the Brandenburg Marches, our journey continues through Mecklenburg. From 1757 the Mecklenburg dukes resided in **Ludwigslust**, during which time it went through baroque and then Classical building phases. Particularly worth seeing is the **Palace** and its park covering 135 hectares (335 acres). In 1837 the seat of the Grand Duchy was moved back to the beautiful cathedral city of **Schwerin** (population 130,000), 40 km (25 miles) to the north, and a magnificent residence was built (1846–57) in neo-Gothic style. It lies on an island between the Burgsee and the 66-sq. km (25-sq. mile) **Schweriner Lake**. It is a fairytale castle, the Neuschwanstein of the north, and it is still said to be haunted by its ghost, the "Petermännchen".

Pleasure steamers, which pull in close to the castle, ply back and forth to **Kaninchenwerder Island**. The visitor can observe the sailing boats on the lake

Left, this statue of Roland once symbolised the independence of Brandenburg. Right, a memorial to fallen Russian soldiers.

from a restaurant or the observation tower. It is possible to travel by boat from Schwerin all the way to Berlin – only by rowing or sailing boat, however! Only by taking to the water can the visitor really enjoy the attractions of the surrounding countryside. Since 27 October 1990, Schwerin has been the capital city of the new federal state of Mecklenburg-Vorpommern.

To the sea: The **Baltic Sea** coast is only a half hour's drive from Schwerin. This border region used to be the favourite destination for GDR holidaymakers. Places in the state-owned holiday homes were much sought after. There is now a lot of empty space on the beach and in the large guest houses and bed and breakfast homes. Because many businesses have been forced to close down, the only chance of survival for many local people is the opening up of the region. "Now we can take visitors for cruises on the open sea" explains a fisherman from Ahlbeck. This, like sailing and surfing, used to be forbidden. And if anyone decided to travel out too

far on their inflatable lilos they could be arrested for violating the frontier. Many a romantic beach hut flirt would be interrupted by the regular patrols of the border officials.

The landscape here is extremely varied. Rugged cliffs alternate with long beaches of fine white sand. Behind lies the forest and the typical Baltic salt water lagoons and *haffs*. Promontories, sounds, outlying islands and peninsulas make it difficult to see where the land ends and the sea begins. Our journey takes us along the coast from west to east, from Wismar via Rostock to Greifswald and Usedom.

The small port town of **Wismar** (population 57,000) was seriously damaged during World War II and decayed even further during subsequent decades. It now lives primarily from the ship-building yard.

In the 13th century Wismar signed a pact with Rostock and Lübeck to combat piracy and this alliance soon developed into a branch of the Hanseatic League. From 1648 to 1903 the town

The rural heart of Mecklenburg.

belonged to Sweden and in 1803 it was mortgaged to Mecklenburg for 100 years. The Swedes developed Wismar into the largest coastal fortress in Europe and during the many Swedish wars the town was often prone to attack. Only the 37-metre (121 ft) high nave of the **Church of St Nicholas** survived the successive bombardments.

On the large market place stands the "Old Swede", the oldest house in the town built at the end of the 14th century, with its triple-gabled roof. Within there is a cosy little sailors' pub. The waterworks on the market place, built in the style of the Dutch Renaissance, provided Wismar with water until 1897. Down by the harbour the old piers and warehouses still stand. From here the visitor can take the boat to **Poel Island**, a popular excursion. Nobody knows quite what the two Swedes' heads are doing on the quayside: some say that they were put there to deter any would-be pirates.

To the north-east of Wismar lies the spa town of **Külungsborn**, one of the largest tourist resorts on the Mecklenburg coast, and the attractive **Bad Heiligendamm** with its whitewashed spa hotels. Founded in 1793, this is the oldest coastal spa in Germany. On the rocky coast the visitor can observe students of the local college of applied arts as they go about their nature studies. A romantic narrow-gauge railway nicknamed "Molli" links both places with **Bad Doberan**, formerly the summer seat of the Mecklenburg court, today a small town of 12,400 souls.

The tombs of several Mecklenburg dukes are found in **Doberan Minster**, which developed from a monastery church founded in the 13th century. Established in 1807, the Doberan racecourse is the oldest in Europe.

The "gateway to the world": By developing **Rostock** (population 250,000) into an international port in the 1950s, the GDR ended its dependence on the port of Hamburg. Here in 1419 the first university in northern Europe was established. The mighty **Church of St Mary**, which dominates the city, was

Stralsund, the old Hanseatic town on the Baltic.

begun in 1230. On the wall of the cathedral is an astronomical clock which merchants donated to the city in 1472. Opposite the town hall, the old patrician houses are still in a good state of repair.

On Universitätsplatz the so-called "Porno Fountain" bubbles forth, with its highly risqué sculptures true to the style of Socialist Realism. The visitor can recover from the shock of this confrontation by popping in at the "Kogge", an olde-worlde pub in Wokrenter Strasse. Also worth seeing are the remains of the old fortifications. The old city centre is now surrounded by new housing estates in which two-thirds of the total population lives. The concrete blocks extend along the Unterwarnow all the way to **Warnemünde**, Rostock's huge resort and site of its ferry terminal.

Nineteenth-century novelist Theodor Fontane, who wrote particularly about middle-class life in Northern Germany enthused about the style of architecture in Warnemünde, which distinguished itself by the "glass boxes attached to the house fronts, which whether they be called balconies, verandas, or pavilions ultimately remain the same old glass boxes which make this place so special, for guests and locals alike. It is these glass extensions and porches that give the place its character and the bather his enjoyment"

In the days of the GDR the mole at Warnemünde was where the locals silently longed for far-off places, as they watched the ferries and merchant ships head out into the open sea towards Denmark.

The "amber island": The long sandy beach at Warnemünde is a bastion of naturism. While in the 1960s the naturist area was still signposted, in the course of time the nudists succeeded in taking over the entire Baltic coast. Nowhere else in Europe will you find such a long naturist beach. The freedom of nudity was one of the few real freedoms tolerated in the GDR.

Beyond this the large peninsula which was formed only a few hundred years ago when the islands of **Fischland**, **Darss** and **Zingst** coalesced. It is now a

Rostock, historic bridgehead of the north.

conservation area. On the way to Darss is the **Klockenhagen Open-air Museum**, with its carefully preserved Mecklenburg half-timbered houses. **Ahrenshoop** is the diva of the Baltic resorts. It has been an artists' colony for centuries and even during the socialist era was a meeting place for intellectuals who would stay in the holiday homes provided by the GDR culture association. The **Darss Forest** starts behind Ahrenshoop, and can be explored either on foot or by bicycle – the area is closed to motor traffic. On the western side of the peninsula the trees have been bent into obscure forms by the storms. The typical colourful house doors can be found in Perow and Zingst, and the villages of Born and Wiek with their wild dunes are also well-worth a visit.

Another name for Darss is the "amber island", for this is where the most copious quantities of Baltic amber are to be found. Find out more about the "gold from the north" by visiting the **Amber Museum** in Ribnitz-Dammagrten. The nearby Recknitz stream forms the natural border between Mecklenburg and Vorpommern.

Stralsund: Situated opposite the island of Rügen, the Hanse city of Stralsund has been called the most beautiful city in northern Germany. The trading port was granted its city charter as long ago as 1234 by the Slavic Count Wizlav I. In 1648, along with the rest of Vorpommern, it fell to the Swedes, and then after the Vienna Congress of 1815 to the Prussians. In the old city entire streets, such as Fährstrasse, have been preserved and still look as they did when first built in the 13th and 14th centuries. The centre, with the Gothic town hall, the churches of St Nicholas and St Mary, the monastery buildings, and the fortifications, is surrounded by parks and lakes.

Until the 18th century the merchants' houses were designed according to the same architectural principals. The ground and first floors of one half of the house were given over to the living quarters while the other half consisted solely of an atrium, two storeys high, from which the merchants would hoist

Bound for the rubbish tip of history.

their goods into the store under the roof.

In the Monastery of St Catherine, the **Maritime Museum** includes the 16-metre (52 ft) long skeleton of a fin-backed whale as well as 120 different species of marine life swimming in a sea water pool. Since 1936, Stralsund has been linked to the island of Rügen by a dyke. From time to time a lift-bridge allows ships to pass through.

Rügen: The chalk cliffs of Rügen, which sometimes rise 100 metres (330 ft) or more vertically above the sea, were made world-famous through the paintings of Caspar David Friedrich. A Romantic contemporary of his Philipp Otto Ruge praised the place "where the peaceful solemnity of sea is interrupted in manifold fashion by the peninsulas and valleys, the hills and cliffs." And Karl Friedrich Schinkel regarded the island with such varied landscape as "a wonderful piece of art".

...but the future is anything but certain.

A special feature of the island are the seams of flint running through the chalk cliffs, which in some areas have been eroded by the waves. Sometimes the cliffs slant inland in a series of great ramparts. The steep coastlines of Wittow, Jasmund, Grabnitz and Mön-chut are gradually being eroded by the sea and retaining walls have had to be built in some places.

To the west of these rocky peninsulas lies the main core of the island with the settlements of Bergen, Putbus, Ganz and Gingst. Further to the west the long narrow island of **Hiddensee** acts as an effective breakwater protecting Rügen's western shore. The highest points on Rügen are Piekberg near Hagen, the Trenzer Berg north of Sassnitz, the Rugard and the Königstuhl which is right on the coast. All provide wonderful views of land and sea.

The interior of this 926-sq. km (358-sq. miles) island is every bit as beautiful as the coast. Quaint villages are joined by long avenues of linden and chestnut trees and by the sides of the roads are fields of rape, corn and sunflowers. The island also boasts a great deal of lovely woodland, with picturesque castles nestling among the trees. **Spyker Castle**

looks out over the bay of Jasmund Bodden and the **Granitz Hunting Lodge**, now a hunting museum, near Binz, has a commanding view over the Greifswald Bodden. The large meadow in front of **Ralswiek Castle** is transformed into an open-air stage during the annual Rügen Festival.

There are numerous pre- and early-history monuments on the island and megalithic burial places and barrows testify to the early presence of man. Indeed, historians maintain that during the neolithic period the Lietzow culture provided large parts of central Europe with weapons made of Rügen flint.

Just like England: In **Garz**, the oldest town on the island, a museum recalls Rügen's most famous son, the poet and scholar Ernst Moritz Arndt (1769–1860). The writer was a German nationalist through and through, who enjoined his countrymen to fight Napoleon and to banish the French to the west of the Rhine. With its classical mansions, **Putbus** has the appearance of an English south-coast resort. Above the town is the "circus" surrounded by white-washed houses, in the middle of which is an obelisk erected to the memory of Duke Malte of Putbus. His palace was badly damaged during the war and finally demolished in 1962.

An especially pleasant area for walking is the peninsula of **Mönchgut**. Here there are still a large number of the original Rügen farmhouses which convey a feeling of the past. The old resorts of **Sellin** and **Binz** have become one of the main attractions for visitors to the island. In the north of the island are the famous chalk cliffs depicted by Caspar David Friedrich, including the 117-metre (384-ft) high **Königstuhl**.

From the nearby ferry port of **Sassnitz** there have been regular services to Trelleborg in Sweden since 1897. On the very northern tip of Rügen, at **Cape Arcona**, there used to stand a temple to the Slavic deity Svantevit. In 1168 this sacred place was captured and destroyed by the Danes and all that remains today are 13-metre (43-ft) high embankments.

A small track from the cape leads down to **Vitt**, which is located in a depression protected from the winds. The tiny village is also protected by the seamen's chapel perched high on the cliff top.

University and atomic power: Back on the mainland, the journey continues along the Baltic coast towards the Polish border. The next town of any size is the **Greifswald**, where Caspar David Friedrich was born. The town developed from the Eldena Monastery which was built here in 1248 on the banks of the Ryck stream. The ruins of the monastery, which were the inspiration for one of Caspar David's most famous paintings, can still be seen today.

From 1278 Greifswald was a member of the Hanseatic League. The university was founded in 1456 by the legendary mayor of the town Heinrich Rubenow. Some of the great minds of German history studied and lectured here, including the reformer Ulrich von Hutten, the writer Ernst Moritz Arndt and the doctor Ferdinand Sauerbruch.

As a result of the repeated fires that ravaged the town in the 18th century, many of the original medieval buildings were destroyed and only the occasional Gothic brick building dates from this period. Nevertheless, the old part of town is still very attractive, saved as it was from the ravages of World War II by the decision of the local commandant to surrender to the Russians before even a shot was fired. Today Greifswald has a population of 64,000.

In recent times the name of Greifswald has been associated with the nearby atomic power station, which used to deliver one-tenth of all the GDR's energy needs. In 1976 a fire in the plant nearly ended with a melt-down. This was only the worst of a long chain of mishaps and in 1990 the power station was decommissioned because it no longer satisfied the much more rigourous safety standards applied in the West. It still hasn't been decided whether to close it permanently or carry out the necessary renovations and continue production. Either way, it will remain a monument to a utopian socialist energy policy that seriously misfired. Meanwhile, a hurriedly-built conventional power sta-

Gerhart Hauptmann was among the guests at Hiddensee.

VISITORS TO HIDDENSEE

The first visitors to arrive on this 17-kilometre (11 mile) long thin strip of land, a gigantic breakwater in front of Rügen's western shore, were Cistercian monks. They founded a monastery on the island, which at that time belonged to Denmark, in 1297. The monks continued to live here even after the secularisation of their property in 1536. They didn't want "to leave such a beautiful place". All that now remains of the ecclesiastical building is one entrance arch.

For centuries, fishing and a limited amount of farming provided the basis of the local population's livelihood. In the island museum displays of household effects and sailors' souvenirs testify to the simple life that the people once led here. At the end of the last century the island, Rügen's little sister, was discovered by artists and intellectuals and was developed, as Gerhart Hauptmann wrote in 1899 "into the most intellectual of all coastal resorts." The dramatist Hauptmann when he first visited the island some 14 years previously at the age of 23, immediately fell in love with the place and wrote a whole series of poems about it.

From that time on summer visits to the island became part and parcel of his life. Here he could find his inspiration and

was able to concentrate, and here he would take his morning "productive strolls", when he would think about everything that he was going to pen in the afternoon. It was 50 years after his first visit that he acquired the house Seedorn at the ruined monastery.

Today it is the Gerhart Hauptmann Memorial and the visitor can take a peek inside his tiny, dark bedroom. Above his bed he inscribed the words "the greatest art of all is silence". Hauptmann's grave, in which the urn containing the mortal remains of his wife are also interred, can be seen in the island graveyard near his house.

After World War I the island was well and truly transformed into an artists' colony. Thomas Mann visited Hauptmann, who subsequently appeared in his novel the *Magic Mountain* as "Mynheer Peeperkorn". Albert Einstein took strolls here in his worn-out coat, through the wind and the rain. For the actress Asta Nielsen, who said "Nowhere does one feel so young and so free as on this island" Max Taut built a house with flowing contours, the "carousel". Many visitors appear to have felt the same way as Asta Nielsen. They came in droves: Sigmund Freud, Käthe Kollwitz, Max Reinhardt, Joachim Ringelnatz, Ernst Barlach, Stefan Zweig, Gottfried Benn, Heinrich George, Carl Zuckmayer and even the burgher's wit George Grosz, who came to poke fun at Hiddensee society.

After World War II the Central Committee of the SED built holiday homes on Hiddensee. The Central Committee always chose the very best places. Here the GDR spy Günter Guillaume, who was responsible for the downfall of the Federal Chancellor Willy Brandt, came to relax under the roof of the "house on the hill". Artists continued to arrive, including the director Walter Felsenstein, who drew attention to himself by the fact that he gave his donkey a gold tooth. It is said that his wife used to go horse-riding along the beach – in the nude. Nobody ever spoke well of the SED holiday homes.

During the GDR revolution the church was packed with up to 500 worshippers, half of them locals. Earlier, the enlightened Protestant vicars of Hiddensee had always put the interests of the locals before those of the "political barons". The holiday homes, inclusive of restaurant and rooms to let, now belong to the community.

Further faithful visitors to Hiddensee are all the birds that flock back here year after year, either to rest during their migration or to stay the whole winter. They include Canada geese, knob-bill geese and swan geese which arrive at the still-water reserves by the thousand. The island has been declared a wildlife sanctuary and cars are forbidden. Hiddensee, otherwise known variously as the "Sylt of the north", the "Capri of Pomerania", and the "pearl of the Baltic" is loved by rich and poor alike. The wealthy of Berlin keep a holiday home on the heath and, in the low season, art students, traditionally impoverished, sit with their easels on the hilltops, painting and sketching.

tion has taken over the supply of local energy needs.

Usedom: The island of Usedom is the last port of call on our journey along the coast. The eastern end of the island is Polish territory. The island is connected by a bridge to the mainland near **Wolgast**, the birthplace of the Romantic painter Philipp Otto Runge.

The oldest resort town on the island is **Heringsdorf** which was opened in 1822. Together with its neighbours **Ahlbeck** and **Bansin**, it has developed into a veritable tourist conurbation. On the leeward side of the island a number of picturesque fishing villages located on the *haffs*. Nowadays, the fisherman can hardly even scrape a living together. The murky waters of the River Oder have poisoned most fish stocks and what remains to be caught is scarcely edible.

Art lovers should head for **Lüttenort**, on the narrowest point on the island, where it is possible to view the studio of the painter Otto Niemeyer-Holstein. Hardly any other artist this century has painted as many seascapes as Holstein,

who died in 1984 at the age of 88. Today, however, it is not possible to explore the whole of the island because of its unfortunate military past. In the Luftwaffe testing site of Peenemünde West the German physicist Wernher von Braun developed the first liquid-fuel rocket, the forerunner of the dreaded V2 which Hitler used to bombard the south of England. Nowadays an airforce base occupies the site.

The route back to Berlin runs parallel to the Polish border. First though, comes the town of **Anklam**, another Hanse city of whose glorious past little remains apart from the Church of St Mary, the old powder magazine and the stone gateway. There is a memorial to the great aviation pioneer Otto Lilienthal, who was born in Anklam in 1848 and died after losing control on one of his test flights in 1896.

The border country to Poland, the **Ucker Marches**, is a rolling landscape speckled with a multitude of lakes. A peaceful land, criss-crossed by canals on which barges slowly chug.

Left, tranquillity on Rügen. Right, visitors to Warnemünde.

Two places to the northeast of Berlin, are well worth visiting: **Chorin Monastery** and **Buckow**. The monastery was founded in 1273, and although it was destroyed during the Thirty Years' War, it was partly restored in the middle of the 19th century. Theodor Fontane's description of the old building is still valid today: "Whoever comes here at dusk and beholds the splendour of this peaceful, lonely building as it emerges through the poplars, half magic, half ghostly; on him is bestowed the very best of what this ruin, which is hardly a ruin, has to offer. The atmosphere of this place is like a vision, like some romantic picture passing before the eyes, where not even the silent desolation of the inner self can destroy the magic of the moment." Today, classical concerts are performed here during the Chorin "music summer".

Coming into Buckow there is a sign describing the place as "The Pearl of the *Märkische Schweiz*" – the Brandenburg "little Switerland". Fontane penned the following words about the region:

"Mountain and lake, slopes of pine and wooded gorges, springs bubbling over gravel and birches half uprooted by the force of the wind, their long branches stooping to the forest stream".

This paradise lies within easy reach of Berlin. Berthold Brecht and Helene Weigel had their summer house in Buckow. Today it is a memorial. Here Brecht wrote his last poetry cycle, the *Elegies of Buckow*. He not only describes the tranquillity of the Schmermützel Lake, but also the threat to this summer idyll:

The silver poplar, a well-known
local beauty,
today an old hag. The lake
a pool of dish water, don't touch it!
The fuchsias cowering under the
snapdragon,
all shoddy and worthless. Why?
Last night while dreaming
I saw fingers pointing at me,
like at an outcast. They were
withered and/they were broken.
Ignorant people! I cry,
full of my own guilt.

A breather for cyclists.

THE MECKLENBURG LAKE DISTRICT

One of the least populated regions of Europe stretches directly to the north of Berlin and to the east of Hamburg. Even today, this wonderfully tranquil region, which has largely escaped the ecological disasters visited on other areas, has hardly been discovered by tourists. This is not too surprising, since the Mecklenburg lake district does not offer very much in the way of facilities for visitors. A round trip though this moraine landscape should give some idea of just how much there is to discover in this region of rivers and lakes.

Oranienburg (population 25,000) lies 25 km (15 miles) north of Berlin on the F 96. The town, originally named Bötzow, was founded around AD 1200. When the ruling Great Elector of Prussia built a new Dutch-style residence here in 1651, he named it for his wife Louise Henriette from the House of Orange. In time the name came to be applied to the town. In 1814, a sulphuric acid factory moved into the palace, and it was here that the chemist Friedrich Ferdinand Runge succeeded in separating aniline and carbolic acid, two of the most important raw materials for the chemical industry, from coal tar. The palace and its pleasure garden have now been restored to their former glory.

The town was the site of the first Nazi concentration camp, which was established in an old brewery in 1933. In 1936 an extermination camp was constructed a short distance to the north, at Sachsenhausen. 100,000 people perished here, about half the total number of prisoners. Only in the winter of 1990 was it discovered that after the war Stalin's secret police had murdered political opponents at the very same site, and had buried them in mass graves in the nearby forest.

The journey continues along the F 96 to the small town of **Fürstenberg**, which is picturesquely situated on three islands where the River Havel broadens out into the lakes, Röblin, Baalen and

374

Schwedt. The **Palace** (1752) is a splended baroque building whose heavy oak door is embellished with rococo ornamentation. In the district of Ravensbrück stood the largest of the Nazis' concentration camps for women, today yet another memorial to those appalling atrocities.

Strelitz lake district: Fürstenberg marks the beginning of the Strelitz lake district, and the route continues in an easterly direction towards **Lychen**, where the prosperity of days gone by is recalled by the remains of the town walls and the old Stragard Gate. Further to the north lies **Feldberg** from where a romantic ridge path leads to the small fishing village of **Carwitz**. The German writer and social critic Hans Fallada (1893–1947), whose novels dealt with the plight of the common man, fled here at the beginning of the 1930s. He had to escape a Berlin that was becoming increasingly nervous and find his peace in the tranquillity of Mecklenburg. Fallada was plagued by financial misery, alcoholism and blighted love affairs as well as

the unexpected success of his novel *Kleiner Mann – was nun?* (*What now, little man?*) It had only taken him 16 weeks to write the book, which describes the fight for survival of ordinary folk caught up in the crisis of high unemployment. Fallada did not flee from Berlin as a romantic refugee from the Big City, but as somebody who had already lived and worked on the land. Many writers left the city in those months of 1933: some even left the country altogether. "I prefer Carwitz to Hollywood", wrote Fallada. However, bouts of illness continued to prolong him and he had to spend much time in a psychiatric clinic. Neverthless, after the war he became mayor of the town. In 1947 at his grave side, his friend and colleague Johannes R. Becher said that Fallada, "was endowed with a command of the broadest range of human emotion and could express the most unusual and complex of matters in a language that everybody understood. But although he could see into the hearts of others, he remained a stranger unto himself."

A Mecklenburg farmer.

Return to Feldburg and then travel north on the F 198 to arrive back on the old transit route at **Woldegk**. It is well worth stopping here to inspect the wonderful old windmills. One of them contains a pottery and a museum of mills and another a quaint little café. From here the F 104 continues west towards Neubrandenburg.

The **River Havel** has its source in this lake district. The Havel, with its many tributaries and canals, casts a dense network of waterways over the landscape. The small **Neustrelitz Lakes** are linked via the Müritz-Havel canal to the **Mecklenburg Lake District** which consists of over 1,000 open stretches of water. Both areas were created during the Ice Age when massive lowland glaciers stopped here and deposited all their debris in a series of moraines. The ice also gouged out large depressions that remained after the ice had melted. Only during our geological age, the Holocene, did these depressions fill up with water, so creating the lakes that now shimmer between the hills. While much of the area remains forested, parts have been turned over to cultivation. In the more remote and sparsely populated areas between the lakes there are countless secluded country houses and cottages, some built in half-timber technique and others which are truly representative manor houses. Forsaken and decaying brick-built cottages are patiently waiting for the day when people might live in them once more.

Before turning eastwards to the centre of the Mecklenburg Lake District, it is well worth taking a side-trip to the northerly town of **Neubrandenburg** (population 80,000). In World War II the town was so badly damaged that it is possible to speak of a "second founding" in the post-war era. The 2,300-metre (1.5-mile) long Middle Age fortifications have been restored. The wall itself is 8 metres (27 ft) high and is flanked by a series of three moats. There are several watch towers strung out along its length as well as four city gates, the most famous of which, the **Treptow Gate**, houses a museum of early his-

A blustery day at Muritz Lake…

tory. Mecklenburg's famous poet Fritz Reuter (1810–74) lived in "Nigenbramborg", as the place is known in local parlance, from 1856 to 1863. He was actually born in the town of **Stavenhagen**, also referred to on some maps as "Reuterstadt".

The house on the market place where he was born is now a museum dedicated to this popular poet who, through his works, transformed the local Mecklenburg Low German dialect into a language of literature. Reuter's *oeuvre* exposed the slightly sentimental, humorous, if somewhat coarse nature of the Mecklenburg mentality. His favourite characters are depicted at the base of his statue: farm girls and stable lads, squires and merchants, lawyers and clergymen, all from the Mecklenburg of the 19th century.

To the north-west of Stavenhagen begins the Mecklenburg's "**little Switzerland**", a hilly moraine landscape, which, by north German standards, contains some unusually high ground (Hartberg, Röthelberg). With its ancient forests and lakes, rare wildlife and numerous country houses once occupied by the local nobility, the region has remained untouched by modern industry. Far from the madding crowd, this is an ideal place to get away from it all. The local tourist authority in Teterow does not wish to see the place become over-developed and over-run and promotes "holidays on the farm" and the like. The only events that disturb the peace in this part of the world are the annual Whitsuntide motorcycle races which take place on a grass circuit near Teterow.

The route continues along the F 4 into the valley of the **River Nebel**. The town of **Güstrow** (population 37,000) possesses the most important extant Renaissance building in all Germany. The **palace of the Dukes of Mecklenburg-Güstrow** was built in 1588 and became the royal residence of all Mecklenburg when Marshal Albrecht von Wallenstein became Duke in 1628. After the ducal family had died out in the 19th century the palace was converted into a hospital

...but some manage to brave the waters.

and was only restored to its former splendour between 1964–72.

A walk through the Lavender Garden transports the visitor into a landscape more typical of southern climes. Indeed, according to the sculptor, graphic artist and poet Ernst Barlach, Güstrow could easily be placed along side a Tuscan town. He lived here from 1910 to 1938 and created the bronze sculpture *Der Schwebende* ("the floating one") for the northern transept of the Gothic **Cathedral**. Barlach was ostracised by the Nazis and his masterpiece was melted down for use in the armaments industry in 1944. A copy of the sculpture was found buried in the Lüneburg Heath and after the war found a home in the church of St Anthony in Cologne. That parish then created a new mould and donated the casting to Güstrow in 1952, since when it has occupied its original position.

Further Barlach creations include the **Chapel of St Gertrude** (1430) which is located in the park adjacent to the cathedral. In 1978 a memorial to Barlach was installed in his studio (Heidberg 15): the museum contains drawings, sculptures, printed graphics and books from the artist's estate.

Passing a seemingly endless chain of lakes, we now alter course towards the south via Krakow (F 103) and Malchow (F 192) and arrive at **Müritz**. With a surface area of 116 sq. km (48 sq. miles) this is the largest of the Mecklenburg lakes. When it gets stormy the lake almost has the appearance of a sea, with high waves breaking on the shore. Come rain or shine, Lake Müritz is well worth visiting.

The best-known of the lakeside towns is **Waren** (population 23,000), which has been a bathing and health resort for over 100 years. The houses are built on terraces rising up from the lake shore and are representative of a variety of 19th-century building styles. Balconies draped with vines recalling Italy lie side by side with rabbit hutches, clothes drying areas and new one-family houses. The church spire is not crowned by a saint, but by a swan. As is the case with many other towns in the former GDR, a local action group is campaigning for the preservation of the rapidly decaying old town.

The large nature reserve on the eastern shores of the lake include the hunting ground of the former GDR president Willi Stoph. Environmentalists are now campaigning to have this converted into a wildlife sanctuary. The western flanks of the reserve are occupied by the 15-km (9-mile) long **Plauer Lake**, whose towns of Plau, Malchow and Bad Stuer were already well-established health resorts in the middle of the 19th century.

The town of **Neustrelitz** (population 27,000) lies at the northern end of the Neustrelitz Lakes. Planned in the shape of a star radiating out from the central market place, it became the capital of the Dukes of Mecklenburg-Strelitz in 1733. From 1918 to 1933 it was the capital of the Mecklenburg-Strelitz Free State. Although the palace was destroyed in 1945 a number of buildings of architectural significance still stand in the park, including the orangery, the Luisentempel and the royal stables.

Below, running repairs. Right, the challenge that lies ahead.

TRAVEL TIPS

GETTING THERE

BY AIR

Most air-routes into the Federal Republic of Germany lead to Frankfurt; Rhine Main Airport, with 50,000 passengers a day, is the second busiest airport in Europe after London's Heathrow Airport, with up to 600 international departures and arrivals daily. Germany's other international airports are: Berlin, Bremen, Düsseldorf, Hamburg, Hanover, Cologne, Munich, Nuremberg, Saabrücken, Münster/Osnabrück, Dresden and Stuttgart.

Lufthansa, the German national airline, serves most of the world as well as operating a domestic service. If you book in advance, you may take advantage of special APEX fares and thereby save up to 40 percent on domestic and international flights. The main domestic airports are interconnected by regular Interflug, Aero Lloyd and Lufthansa services. From within Germany, Berlin can now be reached by a number of airlines including Euro Berlin, Interflug and Dan Air.

From Rhine Main Airport there is a 15-minute shuttle service (S15) to the main transport junction, the Hauptwache, where the suburban railway (S-Bahn) and the subway (U-Bahn) meet. From this point you can travel to anywhere in town by public transport. Alternatively, bus number 61 shuttles between the airport and the town centre (Sachsenhausen). Official taxis are ivory-coloured Mercedes or BMW models with a black "TAXI" sign on the roof.

BY SEA

There are ferry connections from northern Germany (Hamburg and Rotterdam) with Scandinavia and the UK (Scandinavian Seaways sailings on the Harwich – Hamburg route). The East German port of Warnemünde has sailings to Trelleborg in Sweden.

BY TRAIN

From northern Europe, the best train connections to the north of Germany are from the Hook of Holland in the Netherlands. Trains leave in the direction of Venlo and Emmerich. The south of Germany is better reached via Ostend, from where trains go to Aachen and Cologne, connecting with Euro-City and Inter-City trains to the southern federal states. From the UK, ferry links with the Hook of Holland are via Harwich and with Ostend via Dover.

TRAVEL ESSENTIALS

VISAS & PASSPORTS

A valid passport is the only requirement to enter the Federal Republic (including all parts of new Germany). Members of the European Community (EC) only need identity cards. Holders of Australian, Canadian, Japanese, New Zealand, South African and United States passports automatically get three-month permits on crossing the border, but visas are required for longer stays. Visitors from outside the EC are not allowed to enter any form of employment.

MONEY MATTERS

The German Mark (D-Mark) is a decimal currency made up of 100 pfennigs. The coins come in denominations of 1, 2, 5, 10 and 50 pfennigs, and 1, 2, and 5 DM. The notes are in denominations of 5, 10, 20, 50, 100, 200, 500 and 1,000 DM. Money may be changed at any bank and local money changers (*Wechselstuben*) usually found in train stations, airports and in tourist areas. (*For banking hours, see below*). It is advisable to carry traveller's cheques instead of cash, as the former can be replaced if lost or stolen; remember to keep the cheque numbers separately noted. Although the Germans are not

The central part of Europe offers an abundance of classic travel destinations. **Insight Guides** *and* **Cityguides** *are indispensable companions here: in Paris, the most romantic capital; in Florence, the city of art; in picturesque Alsace or on a boating trip on the river Rhine, with legendary landscapes and castles along the way.* **Insight Guides** *show you the famous sights and intimate hide-aways.*

Alsace
Amsterdam
Austria
Barcelona
Belgium
Berlin
Brittany
Brussels
Düsseldorf
Florence
France
Germany
Hamburg
Loire Valley
Munich
Netherlands
Paris
Rhine
Switzerland
Vienna
Waterways of Europe

A P A
INSIGHT
GUIDES

very fond of credit cards you can pay your bills in hotels, restaurants or big department stores with American Express, Diner's Club, Visa or Master Charge cards. You may have problems, however, in smaller towns or villages. Eurocheques can be cashed practically everywhere.

WHAT TO WEAR

Whatever the season, pack both a raincoat and your sunglasses because the weather can be very unpredictable indeed. Even if you come in the hottest summer months (July and August) you are advised to bring one warm sweater or cardigan. And for your trip to the North Sea and the Baltic Sea you should bring a jacket or a raincoat.

In case you forget to bring one, you can "go native" and buy a *Friesennerz* (a yellow rubber raincoat) and a pair of rubber boots quite cheaply. Good walking shoes are necessary for anyone wanting to walk in the Black Forest, the Harz, the Lüneburger Heide, the March of Brandenburg or to go hiking in the Alps. Otherwise, casual clothing is acceptable. Most Germans are very fashion-conscious, especially in big urban areas like Berlin, Hamburg or Munich. Long evening dresses and tuxedos are still worn when attending the opera, although this is beginning to change.

CUSTOMS

There are no restrictions on the amounts of local or foreign currency you can bring into the Federal Republic. You are also allowed to bring any personal belongings and equipment as well as reasonable quantities of food for your own consumption. In addition, visitors may bring in limited quantities of tobacco, alcohol, etc., duty free. European (EC) citizens can import 300 cigarettes or 150 cigars or 75 large cigars or 400 gm tobacco; 1½ litres of ordinary wine; 750 gm of coffee (beans) or 300 gm instant coffee; 150 gm of tea or 60 gm of instant tea; 75 gm of perfume; and 3/8 litres of toilet water.

These limits apply to goods bought in ordinary shops. If bought in duty-free shops, there are slightly lower limits. European nationals other than those from the EC have a slightly smaller allowance.

VAT

VAT (*Mehrwertsteuer*) in Germany comes in two rates: 14 percent and 7 percent. Fourteen percent VAT (MWST) is added to all goods except food, books and newspapers which are taxed at 7 percent. All services such as the hairdressers add 14 percent VAT. Restaurant menu prices include 14 percent VAT. The tax can be deducted if you buy expensive articles, provided you fill in a sales form when buying the article. Present both the form and article at customs when you return home, have it stamped and send it back to the shop where you bought the article, which will then reimburse you.

GETTING ACQUAINTED

GEOGRAPHY & POPULATION

The two former Germanys have now become one country: the five Länder (administrative regions) of Mecklenburg-Western Pomerania, Brandenburg, Saxony-Anhalt, Thuringia and Saxony have joined the Federal Republic of Germany, so that there are now 16 federal states in all, with Hamburg, Bremen and the united Berlin as separate city states. The decision to move the capital from Bonn to Berlin was taken in summer 1991 and will be put into practice in due course. Nevertheless, in some cases different conditions are still applicable for each of the areas of the two former countries during a transitional period. In the following information we have indicated the different origins: W = West Germany and E = East Germany.

At its longest point, Germany is approximately 1,000 km (620 miles) from north to south, and at its widest (Aachen to Görlitz) it measures approximately 650 km (400 miles). The population of 79.2 million people is spread over a total of 350,000 sq. km (135,150 sq. miles), with the south being more densely

Germany (Federal States)

120 km/ 75 miles

SWEDEN

Copenhagen

Malmö

BORNHOLM

DENMARK

Odense

Baltic Sea

North

Sea

FEHMARN

RÜGEN

Kiel

SCHLESWIG-
HOLSTEIN

Rostock

MECKLENBURG

Neu-
brandenburg

HAMBURG

Schwerin

Szczecin

Hamburg

Groningen

BREMEN

NETHERLANDS

Oldenburg

Bremen

LOWER SAXONY

Elbe

BRANDENBURG

POLAND

Potsdam

Berlin

Frankfurt

Arnhem

Weser

Hanover

Braunschweig

Magdeburg

Münster

SACHSEN-
ANHALT

Cottbus

Rhine

NORTH RHINE-WESTPHALIA

Essen

Dortmund

Halle

Elbe

Düsseldorf

Kassel

Leipzig

Dresden

Bonn

HESSE

Erfurt

THURINGIA

SAXONY

Chemnitz

G E R M A N Y

Eger

RHINELAND -

Wiesbaden

Main

Cheb

Prague

Moselle

Mainz

Frankfurt

Bayreuth

Plzeň

PALATINATE

SAARLAND

Nuremberg

CZECHOSLOVAKIA

Saarbrücken

Ansbach

FRANCE

Karlsruhe

Regensburg

BAVARIA

Stuttgart

Strasbourg

Rhine

Landshut

Linz

Colmar

BADEN-
WÜRTTEMBERG

Danube

Augsburg

Munich

Inn

Freiburg

*Lake
Constance*

Belfort

Salzburg

Doubs

Basle

Zürich

AUSTRIA

SWITZERLAND

384

populated than the north. As a rule, the north is very flat and characterised by waterways and marshes, while the south embraces the mountainous part of the country. The most impressive mountains are the Harz, the Variscian mountains of the Schwarzwald (Black Forest), the Elbesandstein Mountains or "Little Switzerland" and the magnificent Bavarian Alps with the highest mountain, the Zugspitze (2,963 metres/9,721 ft).

TIME ZONES

Germany keeps Central European Time (MEZ) which means it is an hour ahead of Greenwich Mean Time and 6 hours ahead of New York time. In summer (from the last Sunday in March to the last Sunday in October) the clocks are put forward by one hour.

CLIMATE

Germany lies within the continental climate zone which means it can be really hot in the summer and bitterly cold in the winter. You will, however, experience a slight change in climate when travelling from the northwest to the southeast. In the north around Hamburg and in Schleswig-Holstein and along the Baltic Sea the weather is more oceanic with milder winters and moderately warm summers. Further south the weather becomes more continental with greater variations.

The average winter temperature varies from –1°C (30°F) in Berlin and surroundings to 2.5°C (37°F) in Cologne; in the mountains it varies between –10°C and –15°C (14°F and 5°F). The hottest month is July when it can be as hot as 35°C to 40°C (95°F to 104°F). If you come in summer you will hardly ever be disappointed by the weather since German summers are mostly hot and dry, even though July is the wettest month with an average rainfall of 750 mm (30 inches) in the north and 620 mm (26 inches) in the Rhine Valley. The average rainfall in Bavaria, for example, is 1,300 mm (52 inches) with Oberstdorf in the lead, with rainfall up to 1,750 mm (70 inches).

The Alps are by far the wettest region, which also has another climatic phenomenon – the Föhn, a warm dry wind which blows down the Alps into South Bavaria and Swabia. The Föhn has two effects: it clears the sky so that one can see the Alps even in

Munich, and it also tends to give many people headaches!

The best time to travel to Germany is in the summer from late May to early October. Skiers will find the best conditions between mid-December and March.

WEIGHTS & MEASURES

Germany uses the metric system. Some useful metric equivalents:

1 gram = 0.03563 oz
1 kilogram = 2.2046 lbs
1 metric tonne (1,000 kilos) = 0.9842 ton
1 litre = 1.7598 pints
1 centimetre = 0.3937 inch
1 metre = 3.281 ft
1 kilometre = 0.62137 mile
1 sq. cm = 0.155 sq. inch
1 sq. metre = 10.764 sq. ft
1 hectare (10,000 sq. metres) = 2.4711 acres
1 cu. cm = 0.061 cu. inch
1 cu. metre = 35.315 cu. ft

TEMPERATURES

In Germany, temperature is measured on the Centigrade (C) scale.

Celsius	Fahrenheit
100	212
90	194
80	176
70	158
60	140
50	122
40	104
30	86
20	68
15	59
10	50
+5	41
0	32
–5	23
–10	14
–15	+5

ELECTRICITY

Germany's electrical supply works on the 220-volt system. Two-pin plugs are in use throughout new Germany.

BUSINESS HOURS

Most shops are open from 9.30 a.m. to 6–6.30 p.m. Small shops such as bakeries, fruit and vegetable shops and butcher's shops open as early as 7 a.m., close for 2½ hours about noon, re-open at around 3 p.m. and remain open until 6.30 p.m. in the evening. Shops located in the railway stations and airports usually have late shopping hours (some are open till midnight). Business hours are usually 8 a.m. to 5.30 p.m. Government offices are open to the public in the mornings from 8 a.m. to noon.

Banking hours are Monday to Friday from 9 a.m. to 12 noon and 1.30 p.m. to 3.30 p.m. In most towns, banks are open until 5.30 p.m. on Thursdays. There are slight variations in the different federal states.

PUBLIC HOLIDAYS

Public holidays draw a line right through the Federal Republic. On the one side are the Catholic states and on the other the Protestant. The dates in parentheses are national public holidays:
New Year's Day: 1 January.
The Magi: 6 January.
Good Friday: changes from year to year; refer to German calendar.
Easter Monday: changes from year to year; refer to German calendar.
May Day: 1 May.
Christi Himmelfahrt (Ascension Day): changes from year to year; refer to German calendar.
Whit Monday: changes from year to year; refer to German calendar.
Fronleichnam (Corpus Christi Day): in Catholic states. Changes from year to year; refer to German calendar.
Mariä Himmelfahrt: in some Catholic states. Changes from year to year; refer to German calendar.
Day of German Unity: 3 October.
All Saints' Day: 1 November in Catholic states.
The Day of Prayer and Repentance: changes from year to year; refer to German calendar.
Christmas Day: 25 December.
Boxing Day: 26 December.

FESTIVALS

Germany is a country where festivals are given pride of place. In the calendar below you will find listed the most important local festivals throughout the year. For more detailed information ask at the local tourist information office (variously known as Fremdenverkehrsamt, Verkehrsverein, Verkehrsamt, Verkehrsbüro or Fremdenverkehrsverein).

(**W** = former West Germany, **E** = former East Germany)

JANUARY

W–Villingen-Schwennigen
Villinger Fasnet. Parade and traditions, famous for their frightening and colourful traditional costumes.

W–Munich
Schäfflertanz Shrovetime. Parade. (Usually February/March).

FEBRUARY

E–Berlin
Musiktage. Festival of political songs. Alternates bi-annually with the *Musikbiennale*.

E–Wasung
Wasunger Karneval.

W–Cologne
Karnevalszug (parade).

W–Mainz
Rosenmontagszug (Rose Monday parade).

MARCH

W–Verden
Lätare-Spende. On the first Monday after Laetare Sunday (third Sunday before Easter), the people of Verden are given bread and herring following an old tradition.

W–Rothenburg ob der Tauber
Schäfertanz. Shepherds' Dance in the marketplace at the end of March, and several dates in the summer.

E–Arnstadt, Eisenach, Erfurt, Gotha, Weimar
Thüringer Bachtage. Johann Sebastian Bach festival.

E–Frankfurt an der Oder
Musikfesttage.

E–Leipzig
International Book Fair.

APRIL

E–Weimar
Shakespeare Tage. Shakespeare festival.

E–Werder (near Potsdam)
Baumblüte. Folk festival and various events.

MAY

W–Rothenburg ob der Tauber
Meistertrunk. The Master Draught is a historical play commemorating the rescue of the town in the 17th century. Performed at Whitsun and on certain Sundays in summer.

E–Dornburg
Rosenfest. Festival of the roses.

E–Dresden
Internationales Dixieland-Festival und Dresdner Musikfestspiele. Dixieland and other music performances, various venues.

W–Höxter
Conveyer Musikwochen. Classical concerts which take place in May and June.

E–Finsterbergen
Holzhauer- und Fuhrmannsfest. Woodcutter's and ferryman's festival.

W–Überlingen
Schwedenprozession. The procession takes place on a Sunday in May and another Sunday in July.

E–Vogtland
Vogtländische Musiktage and Internationale Festtage der Harmonika. Traditional music festival and international harmonica celebration.

W–Nördlingen
Stabenfest. Historical festival usually on the second Monday in May.

W–Island of Reichenau (Lake Constance)
Blutfest. Festival in traditional costume on the last Sunday.

W–Brühl
Schlosskonzerte. In the castle of Brühl the works of the classical masters are performed from May to September.

W–Hameln
Rattenfänger-Spiele. Pied Piper Play is an open air performance from May to September, Sundays from 12 p.m.–12.30 p.m.

W–Oberammergau
Passionsspiele. The Passion Play takes place every 10 years. (Next performance in the year 2000).

W–Schwalmstadt-Ziegenhain.
Salatkirmes. Every year on the second weekend after Whitsun.

W–Regensburg
Orgelwochen. The organ concerts are held in the church of the friary (Minorettenkirche) of the Municipal Museum every Sunday from May to October.

W–Donauwörth
Kammerkonzerte. Candlelight concerts are held in the Castle of Leitheim from May to October.

WHITSUN
W–Rothenburg ob der Tauber
Reichsstadtfesttage. Traditional festival held at Whitsun and on the second weekend in September.

W–Schwäbisch Hall
Kuchen- und Brunnenfest. This cake and fountain festival of salt makers is held at the market square of this town near Stuttgart.

JUNE

E–Arnstadt
Wollmarkt. Wool market.

E–Berlin
Köpenicker Sommer and *Pankower Sommer*. Summer festival in the Köpenick and Pankow area.

E–Chorin
Choriner Musiksommer. Festival of music.

E–Greifswald
Greifswalder Bachwoche. Music by J.S. Bach.

E–Halle
Händelfestspiele. Händel festival.

E–Leipzig
Internationaler Bach-Wettbewerb. International Bach competition.

E–Potsdam
Parkfestspiele Sanssouci. Festival in the gardens of castle Sanssouci.

E–Nordhausen
Rolandsfest. Summer festival.

E–Weimar
Internationaler Musiksommer. International music festival.

W–Lüneburg
Bach-Woche. Mainly the works of Johann Sebastian Bach are performed in daily concerts in the second week of June (8 p.m.).

W–Göttingen
Händel-Festspiele. Händel's concerts and operas are staged daily for a week.

W–Oldenburg
Kultursommer. A festival of indoor and outdoor concerts, folk dances and theatre performances.

W–Bad Segeberg
Karl-May-Spiele. Wild West in Germany. Open air performances June-August.

W–Bad Hersfeld
Festspiele in der Stiftsruine. Romeo and Juliet is one of the plays performed in the ruins of the Stiftskirche each summer.

W–Passau
Die Europäischen Wochen. During the European Week operas, concerts and dramatic performances are held at the Nibelungen Halle, mainly in the evenings.

W–Meersburg
Internationale Schlosskonzerte. Classical concerts in the castle every Saturday.

Ongoing events from previous months:
See May: W–Höxter, W–Brühl, W–Hameln, W–Oberammergau, W–Regensburg, W–Donauwörth.

JULY

W–Cuxhaven
Wochenende an der Jade. Festival in the harbour with windsurfing and music.

W–Ansbach
Rokokospiele im Schloss. Plays, concerts and dances from the 18th century. Several performances daily.

W–Kaufbeuren
Tänzelfest. Children's festival with crossbow-shooting, puppet theatre and parades.

W–Mindelheim
Frunsberg Festspiele. Festival pageants all over town.

W–Straubing
Agnes-Bernauer-Festspiele. Tragic plays by Agnes Bernauer every four years. (Next performance in 1992).

W–Überlingen
Schwerttanz. Sword dance at town hall.

W–Neunburg
Burgfestspiele. Pageant plays at the edge of the Bavarian forest.

W–Kiefersfelden
Ritterspiele. Pageant of medieval times.

W–Altdorf (near Nuremberg)
Wallenstein-Festspiele. Theatre performances and processions.

W–Heidelberg
Schlosspiele. Classical concerts in the castle of Heidelberg.

W–Constance
Internationale Musiktage. An international musical festival.

W–Bayreuth
Wagner-Festspiele. At this festival, the famous works of Wagner are performed daily for one month.

Ongoing events from previous months:
See May: W–Überlingen, W–Brühl, W–Hameln, W–Oberammergau, W–Regensburg, W–Donauwörth.
See June: E–Arnstadt, E–Berlin, E–Chorin, E–Halle, E–Potsdam, E–Nordhausen, E–Weimar, W–Oldenburg, W–Bad Segeberg, W–Bad Hersfeld, W–Passau, W–Meersburg.

AUGUST

W–Schwalmstadt-Treysa
Hutzelkirmes. Every year on the second weekend in August.

W–Frankfurt/Main
Mainfest. This festival in August takes place on the Römer and by the banks of the river Main.

W–Kassel
Zissel. Folk festival.

W–Straubing
Gäubodenfest. Folk festival.

W–Grafenau
Säumerfest. Festival in commemoration of the salt industry.

E–Frauenwald
Rennsteigfestspiele. Festival around the famous walking trail, the "Rennsteig".

E–Weimar
Festabende zu Goethes Geburtstag (around 28 August). Performances around Goethe's birthday.

Ongoing events from previous months:
See May: W–Brühl, W–Hameln, W–Oberammergau, W–Regensburg, W–Donauwörth.
See June: W–Bad Segeberg, W–Bad Hersfeld, W–Passau, W–Meersburg.
See July: W–Neunburg, W–Kiefersfelden,

W–Altdorf (near Nuremberg), W–Heidelberg, W–Constance, W–Bayreuth.

SEPTEMBER

E–Berlin
Festtage des Theaters und der Musik. Theatre and music festival.
Weissenseer Blumenfest. Flower festival.

E–Cottbus
Cottbuser Musikherbst. Music festival.

E–Dresden
Internationales Schlagerfestival. International festival of pop music.

E–Freyburg
Winzerfest. Vintners' festival.

W–Stuttgart
Cannstatter Wasen. Folk festival in the suburb of Cannstatt.

W–Koblenz
Rhein in Flammen. Fireworks along the Rhine.

E–Leipzig
Musiktage. Music festival.

W–Nuremberg
Nürnberger Kulturzirkus. Festival with music and theatre performances.

E–Baltic Sea
Zeesbootregatta in Bodstedt. Boat regatta.

W–Munich
Oktoberfest. Also known as *Wies'n* among the local people. Traditional beer-drinking festival with a ceremonial participation of innkeepers, the mayor and other VIPs. Usually begins in the last week of September and continues through the first week of October.

Ongoing events from previous months:
See May: W–Brühl, W–Hameln, W–Oberammergau, W–Regensburg, W–Donauwörth.
See Whitsun: W–Rothenburg ob der Tauber.
See June: W–Meersburg.

OCTOBER

W–Bremen
Bremer Freimarkt. This folk festival is held in the second half of October.

E–Halle
Hallische Musiktage. Music festival, various venues.

E–Leipzig
Internationale Dokumentar- und Kurzfilmwoche. International documentary and short film week.

E–Weimar
Zwiebelfest. "Onion festival".

Ongoing events from previous months:
See May: W–Regensburg, W–Donauwörth.
See September: W–Munich.

NOVEMBER

W–Hamburg
Hamburger Dom. Big fair on the Heiligengeistfeld.

W–Nuremberg
Christkindlmarkt. The most famous Christmas market in Germany. It begins in the last week of November and lasts until Christmas Eve, December 24.

E–Schneeberg (Ore Mountains)
Fest der Freude und des Lichts. Festival of Joy and Light. Christmas festival with many wooden carvings and candle lights in the windows.

Ongoing events from previous months:
See October: E–Halle, E–Leipzig, E–Weimar.

DECEMBER

Ongoing events from previous months:
See November: W–Nuremberg, E–Schneeberg.

COMMUNICATIONS

MEDIA

The press in the Federal Republic is diverse. The range extends from conservative newspapers like the *Frankfurter Allgemeine Zeitung*, socialist newspapers like the TAZ (*Tageszeitung*) highbrow papers like the *Süddeutsche Zeitung*, to the popular press, the most infamous being the *Bildzeitung*. The former GDR newspaper *Neues Deutschland* is now published with a new, rather serious image, whereas the *Junge Welt* has a more critical and defiant approach. For information on cinema, theatre, exhibitions and concerts, consult any local paper. Foreign newspapers and magazines are available in every town. There are also international bookshops especially at railway stations, airports and city centres.

Radio and television broadcasting in Germany is under public control. There are two national TV stations, the ARD and ZDF, with the ARD having local stations in each state. The DFF (formerly the East German channel) now broadcasts ARD programmes. The ARD also maintains nine radio stations: NDR, RB, SFB, WDR, HR, SWF, SDR, SR and BR. On the third channel of all these stations you can hear the current traffic reports (on VHS). Currently negotiations are under way to merge the four East German stations with the Sender Freies Berlin (SFB).

Younger listeners may appreciate the more relaxed radio stations Radio 110 in Berlin or (probably) the former Eastern station DT-64. For those who speak or understand German the main news programmes on TV are *Heute* at 7 p.m. (ZDF), and *Tagesschau* at 8 p.m. (ARD).

POSTAL SERVICES

The post offices (*Postamt*) are usually open from 8 a.m. to 6 p.m., with smaller ones closing at noon for lunch. You can have your mail sent care of an individual main post office provided it is marked "poste restante". Your mail will be left at the counter identified by the words *Postlagernde Sendungen.* The postal rates for letters and postcards within the old German states of what used to be West Germany are DM1.00 for letters up to 20 gm and 60 pfennigs for postcards. The same rates apply for mail to Andorra, Austria, Belgium, Denmark, France, Great Britain, Italy, Liechtenstein, Luxembourg, Monaco, the Netherlands, San Marino, Switzerland and Vatican City. Standard letters (up to 20 gm) to all other countries cost DM1.30 plus 20 pfennigs for air mail; postcards must have an 80-pfennig stamp.

For the five new German states the following rates continue to be applicable:
Abroad:

letters up to 20 gm	70 pfg
postcards	50 pfg

Inland:

letters up to 20 gm	50 pfg
postcards	30 pfg

The inland rates quoted above are also applicable for letters and postcards to Albania, Bulgaria, China, Yugoslavia, North Korea, Cuba, Laos, Mongolia, Austria, Poland, Rumania, Soviet Union, Czechoslovakia, Hungary and Vietnam.

Local post boxes (*Briefkasten*) are emptied at least twice a day (morning and evening); those designated with a red point are emptied more frequently. On Saturdays, however, there is only one service. For sending telegrams you have either to dial 1131 on a private telephone or go to the post office. The charges are 80 pfennigs per word within Germany and Europe; for overseas telegrams inquire at the post office.

TELEPHONE

In public pay phones insert 30 pfennigs for local calls. For long-distance calls you can also dial direct from most of the yellow public phone boxes but remember to have enough coins with you (10-pfennig pieces and 1- and 5-mark pieces), or you may go to a post office where an operator makes the connection. Every place of any size in Germany has its own dialling code, which is listed under the local network heading. Should you have a language problem, dial 00118 (international directory enquiries). The East German directory enquiry service is not yet standardised and differs from town to town. Phone calls from foreign countries to Germany must still be preceded by (49) for the West and (37) for the East.

EMERGENCIES

MEDICAL SERVICES

The Federal Republic has a national health system whereby doctors and hospital fees are covered by insurance and only a token fee has to be paid for medication. Treatment and medication is also free of charge for EC members and certain other nationalities (Austrians, Turks and Yugoslavians). All other nationals should ensure that they have adequate health insurance before they leave their home country as medical fees are expensive in Germany.

People under special medication should either bring a sufficient supply or a prescription from their own doctor. If you have to consult a doctor, contact your consulate for a list of either English-speaking doctors, or doctors who speak your native language.

In the event of an accident, dial 110 for the police, 112 for the fire brigade or 115 for an ambulance or call the Rotes Kreuz (Red Cross). All accidents resulting in personal injury must be reported to the police.

Useful address for **diabetics**: Diabetiker-Verband e.V., 6750 Kaiserslautern, Hahnbrunnerstrasse 46, tel: (0631) 76488.

Pharmacies (Apotheken) have normal opening hours (8 a.m.–6.30 p.m.) Every pharmacy carries a list of neighbouring pharmacies which are open during the night and on weekends.

GETTING AROUND

ORIENTATION

When driving in Germany observe the following rules: traffic travels on the right with oncoming traffic on your left. Main road traffic has the right of way. At the junctions of two main roads or two minor roads, traffic coming from the right has priority unless otherwise indicated. Traffic signs follow international standards. The general speed limit (*Geschwindig-keitsbeschränkung*) in towns and villages is 50 kph (31 mph) and on open roads it is 100 kph (62 mph). The recommended speed limit on motorways (*autobahnen*) is 130 kph (80 mph). This is changing, however. Recently the government has been promoting a general speed limit of 100 kph (62 mph) on motorways and 80 kph (50 mph) on open roads due to the rapid increase in the number of dying trees and forests. Vehicles towing trailers are limited to 80 kph (50 mph) on all roads outside towns and villages. Vehicles with trailers and vehicles where rear visibility is impaired due to bulky loads etc must fit additional outside mirrors to both sides of the car.

Rear and front seat safety belts must be worn while travelling. Violation of this results in a hefty fine. Children under 12 years of age are not allowed to sit in the front if the car is fitted with rear seats, unless special safety devices for children are fitted.

Spiked tyres are prohibited. Driving with dipped headlights is obligatory in darkness, fog, heavy rain and falling snow. Driving on parking lights alone is prohibited. Dipped headlights are obligatory for motor-cycles at all times. Crash helmets are compulsory for the drivers and pillion-riders of motor-cycles capable of a maximum speed of more than 25 kph (15 mph).

Before setting out make sure you have a first-aid kit and a warning triangle in your car. Should you have an accident, switch on your hazard lights and put up the warning triangle at a safe distance from the scene of the accident. Depending on the severity of the damage, you should summon the police. Always ring the police when an accident results in personal injury. Ask the other party for the name of their insurance company and insurance policy number, and take note of possible witnesses. Do not forget to contact your own insurance company immediately.

The maximum permitted blood alcohol level is 80 mg/100 ml. However, this does not apply for the new federal states of Saxony, Thuringia, Saxony-Anhalt, Brandenburg and Mecklenburg-Western Pomerania. In these states it is absolutely prohibited to drink alcohol when driving. Speed limits for cars in what used to be East Germany are restricted to 100 kph (62 mph) on motorways and to 80 kph (50 mph) outside built-up areas. Vehicles can only be towed on the motorway at a speed of 70 kph (43 mph). Stopping is prohibited within 100 metres before or after stop lines (other than at the lines themselves), pedestrian crossings, crossroads and junctions. Parking is prohibited on trunk roads.

DOMESTIC TRAVEL

BY CAR

Germany is renowned for its motorways, the *autobahnen*. Altogether there are about 13,600 km (8,500 miles) of motorways throughout the Republic, making it one of the densest in the world. The *autobahnen* are marked with an "A" on blue signs while the regional roads are marked with a "B" on yellow signs.

There are rest stops (*Raststätten*) every 30 to 50 km (20 to 30 miles) along the *autobahnen*. Here you may drink, eat and use the toilet facilities. Often you will also find hotels at these rest stops. In addition, there are small rest stops every 4 to 5 km offering the opportunity to stretch your legs.

Despite many excellent roads, traffic congestion is the order of the day during the holiday season (from the end of June to the middle of September). It is therefore advisable to check traffic conditions on the local radio stations (*Traffic Broadcast/ Verkehrsfunk*). The respective wavelengths (VHR) are indicated on the blue square road signs along the motorways and roads. Should you get held up by traffic or some other obstacle, use the diversions indicated by blue signs with the letter "U" (*Umleitung*) and a number referring to the diverting road.

If your car breaks down on the motorway you can call the breakdown services. Use the orange telephones at the roadside. Black triangles on the posts along the side of the motorway indicate the direction of the next telephone. Listed below are 24-hour breakdown services.

Club	Town	Telephone
ACE	Stuttgart	(0711) 50671
ADAC	Berlin	(030) 868686
	Bremen	(0421) 446262
	Dortmund	(0231) 171981
	Düsseldorf	(0211) 19111
	Frankfurt/Main	(069) 74306
	Hamburg	(040) 23999
	Hanover	(0511) 8500222
	Munich	(089) 767676
	Nuremberg	(0911) 5390222
	Stuttgart	(0711) 2800111
AvD	Frankfurt	(0611) 6661666
DTC	Munich	(089) 8111212

Former East Germany:

Club	Town	Telephone
ACE	Berlin	(02) 2793742 (24 hours)
	Cottbus	(059) 30481
	Dresden	(051) 48530
	Erfurt	(061) 5380
	Frankfurt/Oder	(030) 311112
	Gera	(070) 6900
	Halle	(046) 8720
	Chemnitz	(071) 6590
	Leipzig	(041) 39440
	Magdeburg	(091) 33681
	Neubrandenburg	(090) 6950
	Potsdam	(033) 4761/4311
	Rostock	(081) 3839
	Schwerin	(084) 5371
	Suhl	(066) 5120
ADAC	Berlin	(02) 5588888
	Dresden	(051) 434050
	Erfurt	(061) 554202
	Frankfurt/Oder	(030) 311111
	Gera	(070) 26330
	Halle	(046) 29575
	Chemnitz	(071) 3682222
	Leipzig	(041) 80555

Lübbenau	(05887) 2501
Magdeburg	(091) 30071
Michendorf	(0853) 2611
Neubrandenburg	(090) 681323
Parchim	(03355) 2733
Rostock	(081) 37271
Suhl	(066) 40139

Regional repair and recovery services in former East Germany can be contacted on the following telephone numbers:

Berlin	(02) 5243565
Chemnitz	(071) 3682222
Cottbus	(059) 735490
Dresden	(051) 23230
Erfurt	(061) 5540
Frankfurt/Oder	(030) 24101
Gera	(070) 26330
Halle	(046) 29575
Leipzig	(041) 80555
Magdeburg	(091) 30071
Neubrandenburg	(090) 681323
Potsdam	(033) 21351
Rostock	(081) 37271
Schwerin	(084) 49225
Suhl	(066) 40300

The ADAC (Allgemeiner Deutscher Automobil Club) provides road assistance free of charge provided the damage can be repaired within half an hour. Should it take longer, you will have to pay for the repair as well as the cost of all spare parts needed. Road assistance is also free of charge and all recovery costs will be refunded if you have an *Auslandsschutzbrief* (insurance certificate). In fact, you should take out the insurance with your national automobile association before you leave home. The other automobile clubs (ACE, AVD, DTC) charge for spare parts, fuel and towing.

Cars can be rented (*Autovermietung*) practically everywhere. International companies are Hertz, InterRent, Avis, Europcar, etc. For local car rentals inquire at your hotel's tourist information desk. If you use the services of an international company such as InterRent and you come from an English speaking country, probably all that is needed is your national driver's licence and cash, credit card or cheque deposit. Smaller companies may insist on an international driver's licence.

BY TRAIN

Two railway systems – the Deutsche Bundesbahn (DB) with a network of some 28,000 km (17,400 miles) and the Deutsche Reichsbahn (DR) with a network of approximately 15,000 km (9,320 miles) – together comprise the most important transport undertaking in Germany. On the whole, both networks are efficient and will get you to all major places. An hourly service runs to and from more than 50 major towns and cities in the Republic by the intercity trains (IC). The new states are now included in the IC-network. As an example, Hanover-Berlin and Fulda-Dresden offer a two-hourly service; moreover you can travel from Munich to Hamburg in less than 6 hours. There are lunch-cars, first- and second-class cars and even telephone services on the intercity trains, for which an additional one-way fare of DM6 (*IC-Zuschlag*) is required.

Since 1988 Interregio (IR) trains in postmodern blue-white design transport travellers at two-hourly intervals from city to city. However, as the carriage production is rather slow, pseudo-IRs (same intervals, no "bistro cars") may be found on some of the routes until 1992. Euro-City (EC) trains connect major European towns and cities but are rather expensive. IC trains do not run at night. If you wish to travel at night board a D-Zug, which travels more slowly because it makes more stops on the way.

Another type of train, the E-Zug, stops even more often, but has the advantage of reaching the smaller towns.

Many overnight trains have couchette cars. The supplement is normally DM24 (6 persons per compartment). A couchette supplement on the DR currently costs DM6.50 per person. Seat reservations are possible for DM3.50 on DB and DM1.00 on DR trains.

The railways are not only very efficient, they also have some attractive fare structures. Cheap tickets (*Super-Sparpreise*) are valid for return journeys where the outward journey is made before and the return journey made after a weekend. Even cheaper are the "pink" town connections (*rosaroten Städteverbindungen*) to some cities at off-peak times. Families with three or more children can use the family pass (*Familien-Pass*) which allows a 50 percent reduction on the DB network. Pensioners may obtain the *Senioren-Pass* for DM75 (excluding weekend travel) or DM110 (including weekend travel). The tourist tickets are especially designed for long distance rail travellers. If you travel a minimum of 250 km (155 miles) by rail to your holiday destination, using, for example, a "saver" ticket or an international return ticket, you can obtain a tourist ticket at the resort. This ticket is valid for 21 days and entitles you to travel second class on a network of some 1,000 km (620 miles) as often as you like within 10 days. Tickets cost DM50 for one person, DM70 for 2 persons and DM85 for a family. Sunday return tickets are another easy way of saving money.

The German Rail Pass and German Rail Youth Pass (for young people aged 12–26) are personal network tickets for travel for 5, 10 or 15 days in one month. They are not only valid on DB and DR networks but can also be used for a variety of regional DB- and Deutsche Touring GmbH-buses and on some Rhine and Moselle ships as well as entitling the holder to free admission to the Museum of Transport in Nuremberg. Other reductions for young travellers can be achieved with the annual Junior-Pass which costs DM110 and entitles the owner (aged 17–22, students up to 26) to a 50 percent reduction on the whole DB network. Transalpino and "Twen" tickets are for young people up to the age of 26.

DR offers reduced return tickets, return tickets valid for a longer period, minigroup tickets and pensioners' tickets. Since fare structures change from year to year it is advisable to check at any railway station.

BY BUS

Buses are a primary means of transport in cities and connect the smaller villages in the countryside. But there is no national coach network such as the Greyhound system in the United States. The overland buses are a substitute for the railway system and wherever the railways do not go to, there will be a bus even to the remotest corners of Germany. Information on the regional bus service is available at either the railway stations or the tourist information centres.

CITY TRANSPORT

A widespread network of public transport systems is available in every large city. Those cities with a population of 100,000 and more offer an efficient bus system that runs frequently and usually very punctually. You can buy the bus tickets from the driver or at automats available in the bus or at the bus stop. In large cities like Berlin, Hamburg, Cologne, Munich, Frankfurt and Stuttgart, the bus lines are integrated with the underground (U-Bahn) the tram, and the overground (S-Bahn) into one large public transport system. The same ticket may be used for all four means of transport.

Trams (*Strassenbahn*) run on rails throughout the cities. The speed at which they travel allows for sightseeing, although there is the danger of getting into a traffic jam. Look out for yellow signs with a green "H" at bus and tram stops; they list the time schedules. Underground (U-Bahn) stations are usually identified by a sign showing a white "U" on a blue background. Every station has detailed route maps displayed on the wall. The S-Bahn will transport you at about the same speed as the U-Bahn. The S-Bahns are short trains that travel to the suburbs of the larger cities, and within the city they travel mostly underground. For people living in the suburbs it is a fast way of getting into the city. S-Bahn stations are identified by a white "S" on a green background. The price of tickets varies from town to town. For more detailed information contact the respective information office in each town or city.

Taxis are more comfortable than public transport although they are the most expensive form of transport available. There are special taxi stands in every large town, but you can also call for them. (Usually the telephone numbers are listed on the first page of the telephone directory.) You should memorise the taxi identification number in case you leave something behind in the cab or wish to complain about the driver. In some towns there are also minicabs and call cars which are cheaper and which also have ample space for luggage.

CYCLING

Many book and bicycle shops including the German bicycle club, Allgemeiner Deutscher Fahrrad-Club, Postfach 10 77 44, 2800 Bremen offer a variety of books and maps for cycling holidays. The Bund Deutscher Radfahrer (Association of German Cyclists), Otto-Fleck-Schneise 4, 6000 Frankfurt 71 has cycling guides for special regions on offer, whereas RV Verlag publishes cycling and walking maps entitled *Regio Concept*.

The alternative to taking your own bicycle is the railway service *Fahrrad am Bahnhof* (bicycle at the station) which offers bicycle hire at railway stations from 1 April to 31 October (in some areas also all the year round). Current hire prices are DM8 per day for train users and DM12 for non-train users. The brochure *Fahrrad am Bahnhof* also contains touring suggestions from and to the stations which offer this service.

ON FOOT

A sophisticated system of well-kept and signposted regional and long distance walking routes such as the Rennsteig in the forest of Thuringia make walking one of the main pastimes in Germany. Many round trips (*Rundwanderwege*) lead through nature resorts.

Some long distance walks are organised by clubs and associations (Youth Hostel Association), tourist offices or tour operators (Ameropa). Further information can be obtained from:

Deutsches Jugendherbergswerk
Bismarckstr.8
4930 Detmold 1
Tel: (05231) 740117

Touristenverein
"Die Naturfreunde"
Bundesgruppe Deutschland e.V.
Grossglocknerstr. 28
7000 Stuttgart 60
Tel: (0711) 337687/88

Deutscher Alpenverein
Praterinsel 5
8000 München
Tel: (089) 235090

Deutsche Wanderjugend
Wilhelmsstr.39
7263 Bad Liebenzell
Tel: (07052) 3131

WHERE TO STAY

Travellers should have no trouble finding suitable accommodation anywhere. It may not be as luxurious or inexpensive as you would wish, but even in the smallest village there is always some room available. In the peak season (June–August) it is advisable to book in advance if you are visiting a popular place. You may do so through the Allgemeine Deutsche Zimmerreservierung, Beethovenstrasse 69, W-6000 Frankfurt/Main, tel: (069) 75721.

YOUTH HOSTELS

German youth hostels are no longer as old and stuffy as they used to be. Many have been turned into new leisure centres which offer windsurfing as well as computer courses. Contact the Deutsche Jugendherbergswerk, Bismarckstrasse 8, W-4930 Detmold 1, tel: (05231) 740117, for a map of all German youth hostels. Information about youth hostels in the former East Germany can be obtained from Jugendherbergsverband, Friedrichstrasse 79a, O-1080 Berlin.

A new development in the youth hostels area are the so-called "Umweltjugendherbergen" (environmental youth hostels) which offer an insight into ecological issues. Here, you can book excursions, do open-air studies and other "nature awareness" courses. The hostel managers themselves are also known for their ecological management:

Umweltstudienplatz Prien/Chiemsee
Carl-Braun-Strasse 46
W-8210 Prien
Tel: (08051) 2972

Umweltstudienplatz Benediktbeuern
Don Bosco-Strasse 3
W-8179 Benediktbeuern
Tel: (08857) 88350

Naturschutzjugendherberge Altenahr
5486 Altenahr/Ahr
Tel: (02643) 1880

Jugendumweltherberge Hoherodskopf
W-6479 Schotten 12
Tel: (06044) 2760

Umweltstudienplatz Mönchengladbach-Hardter Wald
Brahmstrasse 156
W-4050 Mönchengladbach
Tel: (02161) 559512

Umweltstudienplatz Tönning
Badallee 28
W-2253 Tönning
Tel: (04861) 1280

Euro-Umweltstudienplatz Brilon
Auf dem Holsterloh
W-5790 Brilon
Tel: (02961) 2281

Euro-Umeltstudienplatz Forbach-Herrenwies
Franz-Köbele-JH Haus Nr. 33
W-7564 Forbach-Herrenwies
Tel: (07226) 257

CAMPING

Camping sites are widespread in Germany. The *Campingführer* (camping guide) published by the automobile clubs provides information on relatively comfortable places. Local tourist authorities and information offices (*see Tourist Information*) will also have lists of local sites. For more global information, also on places in the East, write to: Deutscher Camping-Club, Mandelstrasse 28, W-8000 München 40.

B&B, PRIVATE ACCOMMODATION

Please enquire in the local tourist offices for *Pensionen* and *Privatquartiere*. Prices may vary and are not always a clear indication for the facilities offered. Many travel organisers of package holidays have already included locations in the East in their new holiday offers.

Families with children or large groups may find *Ferienappartements* (holiday apartments) or *Ferienhäuser* (holiday homes) more attractive. You should book your individual apartment or house in your travel office where you can choose from the brochures of the main holiday home companies.

Those who would like to spend their holidays on a farm are advised to write to Landschriften-Verlag, Heerstrasse 72, W-5300 Bonn 1, where the *Handbücher für naturnahe Freizeitgestaltung* (Manuals for Outdoor Holidays) with more than 3,000 holiday farms in the West and inns in the eastern country side, as well as the brochure *Zu Gast beim Winzer* (Holidays at the Vintner's) are available.

HOTELS

In the list below you will find the type of accommodation arranged according to prices: LL stands for Deluxe (over DM250), L stands for Luxury, where the starting price is DM180. M stands for Moderate and costs between DM100 and DM179. E stands for economy with a price range of under DM100. If not otherwise stated, all prices are for one double room for one night, including breakfast.

The list below is arranged so that it follows the chapters in the rest of the book.

JOURNEY ALONG THE RHINE

Mainz
Hilton, Rheinstrasse 68, tel: (06131) 2450. Super-luxurious hotel near the Rhine. Breakfast buffet or continental breakfast not included. (LL)

Central-Hotel Eden, Bahnhofsplatz 8, tel: (06131) 674001. Near the station. (M)

Am Römerwall, Römerwall 51–55, tel: (06131) 232135. Near the station. (M)

Wiesbaden
Aukamm-Hotel, Aukamm Allee 31, tel: (0611) 5760. Luxurious hotel in Wiesbaden-Bierstadt. (LL)

Luisenhof, Bahnhofstrasse 7, tel: (0611) 39431. Only 500 metres from the city centre and the station. (M)

Hotel de France, Taunusstrasse 49, tel: (0611) 520061. (M)

Eltville am Rhein
Sonnenberg, Friedrichstrasse 65, tel: (06123) 3081. Outside town. (E)

Rüdesheim
Central-Hotel, Kirchstrasse 6, tel: (06722) 2391. (M–L)

Lorch
Arnsteiner Hof, Schwalbacher Strasse 8, tel: (06726) 9371. In the city centre, 15 minutes from the station. (E–M)

Lahnstein
Kaiserhof, Hochstrasse 9, tel: (02621) 2413. Cosy hotel near the Stadthalle. (E)

Boppard
Bellevue-Rheinhotel, Rheinallee 41, tel: (06742) 1020. Luxurious hotel near the ferry across the Rhine. (L–LL)

Rheinlust, Rheinallee 27, tel: (06742) 3001. With view over the Rhine. (M)

Bingen
Köppel, Kapuzinerstrasse 12, tel: (06721) 14770. In a quiet side street in the pedestrian zone. (E)

Rheingau, Rheinkai 8, tel: (06721) 17496. Close to the river. (E)

ALONG THE MOSELLE

Winningen
Moselblick, tel: (02606) 2275. Directly on the Moselle. (M)

Beilstein
Langhans, Auensteinerstrasse 1, tel: (07062) 5436. (E)

Traben-Trarbach
Bernkastel Kaiser, Markt 29, tel: (06531) 3038. (E–M)

Neumagen-Dhron
Zur Post, Römerstrasse 79, tel: (06507) 2114. Small hotel in the city centre. (E)

Trier
Europa Parkhotel Mövenpick, Kaiserstrasse 29, tel: (0651) 46021. Luxurious hotel with play facilities for children. (L)

Deutscher Hof, Südallee 25, tel: (0651) 46021. Situated in the city centre, opposite the station. (M)

THE ROAD TO COLOGNE

Koblenz
Brenner, Rizzastrasse 20, tel: (0261) 32060. Situated in the city centre, with sauna and solarium, new building. (M–L)

Kleiner Risen, Kaiserin-Augusta-Anlage 18, tel: (0261) 32077. New building near the Rhine, no children's facilities. (L)

Düsseldorf
Minerva, Cantadorstrasse 13a, tel: (0211) 350961. New building, only 700 metres from the station. (M)

Günnewig Hotel Uebachs, Leopoldstrasse 3–5, tel: (0211) 360566. Near station and shopping centre, very good hotel restaurant. (M)

Köln
Haus Lyskirchen, Filzengraben 26–32, tel: (0221) 20970. Right in the city centre, with indoor swimming pool, sauna, solarium. Dogs allowed. (L–LL)

THE RUHRGEBIET

Duisburg
Duisburger Hof, König Heinrich-Platz, tel: (0203) 331021. Situated in the city centre, next to the state theatre. Offers cheaper weekend prices, children and dogs (extra charge) welcome. (LL)

Novotel, Landfermannstrasse 20, tel: (0203) 22375. In the city centre, close to the station. Sauna, solarium and swimming pool, own underground car park. Children under 16 stay for free in their parents' room. Dogs allowed. (L)

Essen
Sheraton, Huyssenallee 55, tel: (0201) 20951. Only 2 minutes from the station. Cheaper weekend prices. Sauna. Dogs allowed. New building. (LL)

Arcade, Hollestrasse 50, tel: (0201) 24280. New building in city centre near station. (M)

Parkhaus Hügel, Freiherr-vom-Stein-Strasse 209, tel: (0201) 471091. Out of town, near Lake Baldeney. (M)

Münster
Haus Eggert, Handorf a.d. Werse, Zur Haskenau 81, (0251) 32083. Outside Münster, in beautiful surroundings with view over the Werse valley. Half-timbered house with sauna, playground for children and bicycle hire. (M)

HEIDELBERG

Speyer
Löwengarten, Schwerdstrasse 14, tel: (06232) 1051. Near the pedestrian zone. (M–L)

Am Wartturm, Landwehrstrasse 28, tel: (06232) 36066. Outside town. (M)

Worms
Domhotel, Obermarkt 10, tel: (06241) 6913. Right in the middle of town, near the station. New building. (M)

Mannheim
Steigenberger Hotel Mannheimer Hof, Augusta-Anlage 4, tel. (0621) 40050. Situated in the city centre, near the water tower. (LL)

Holländer Hof, U1, 11-12, tel: (0621) 16095. Six-floor building in the pedestrian zone of Mannheim. (M)

Heidelberg
Prinzhotel, Neuenheimer Landstrasse 5, tel: (06221) 40320. Breakfast not included. Opposite the historical city centre. Newly renovated building with view over the Neckar, steam sauna, solarium, jacuzzi. Dogs not allowed. (L–LL)

Schönberger Hof, Untere Neckarstrasse 54, tel: (06221) 22615. Established in historical building (since 1772), in the city centre near the Neckar. Children's playground nearby. (L–LL)

Romantik Hotel Zum Ritter St. Georg, Huaptstrasse 178, tel: (06221) 20203. Adjacent to the marketplace, in the pedestrian zone. Over 400 years old. (L)

A JOURNEY TO FRANCONIA

Erbach
Odenwälder Bauern- und Wappenstuben, Schlossgraben 30, tel: (06062) 2236. Small and cosy little half-timbered house near the castle. 12 rooms. (L)

Miltenberg
Hopfengarten, Amberggasse 16, tel: (09371) 2031. Small hotel in the city centre, close to the station. 3 single/ 11 double rooms. (E)

Wertheim
Schwan, Mainplatz 8, tel: (09342) 1278. Situated in a beautiful park in the inner city. (M)

Würzburg
Maritim, Peichertorstrasse 5, tel: (0931) 50831. 292 rooms in a new building, only 10 minutes from the station. Swimming pool, sauna and solarium. (LL)

Grüner Baum, Zeller Strasse 35, tel: (0931) 47081. Near the bridge across the Main. Two minutes to the river. 38 rooms. (M–L.) Interesting restaurant "Melchior-Keller" in the vaults (16th-century).

Bamberg
Bamberger Hof Bellevue, Schönleinsplatz 4, tel: (0951) 22216. 100-year-old building opposite the park. (M–L)

National, Luitpoldstrasse 37, tel: (0951) 24112. Near the station, built beginning of 19th century. (M)

Barock Hotel am Dom, Vorderer Bach 4, tel: (0951) 54031. Situated in the old city centre. (M)

Coburg
Blankenburg, Rosenauer Strasse 30, tel: (09561) 75005. Towards Neustadt, outside the city centre. Next to the municipal swimming pool (entrance free for hotel guests). Newly renovated, 45 rooms. (M)

Lichtenfels
Preussischer Hof, Hambergerstrasse 30, tel: (09571) 5015. In the city centre, near the post office. Sauna inclusive. 40 rooms. (E)

Gasthof Müller, Kloster-Banz-Strasse, tel: (09571) 6021. Outside Lichtenfels with its own huge garden. 68 beds. (E)

Kulmbach
Hansa-Hotel Hönsch, Weltrichstrasse 2a, tel: (09221) 7995. Ten minutes from the station. 56 beds. Book early for July (10-day beer festival). (M)

Christl, Bayreuther Strasse 7, tel: (09221) 7955. New building at the town entrance, 40 beds. (E–M)

Bayreuth
Bayerischer Hof, Bahnhofstrasse 14, tel: (0921) 22081. Cosy family hotel with sauna and swimming pool, built in the 1950s. 50 rooms. (M–L)

Königshof, Bahnhofstrasse 23, tel: (0921) 24094. In the city centre. (M–L)

Gasthof Goldener Löwe, Kulmbacher Strasse 30, tel: (0921) 41046. Very small and established hotel near the city centre, historical gabled house. (E)

Nürnberg
Carlton-Hotel, Eilgutstrasse 13, tel: (0911) 20030. Close to the station, sauna and solarium included. (L–LL)

Deutscher Hof, Frauentorgraben 29, tel: (0911) 203821. 50 rooms. (L)

Burghotel, Schildgasse 16, tel: (0911) 203040. Situated below the castle. New building with 35 beds. Swimming pool. (M)

ALONG THE ROMANTIC ROAD

Tauberbischofsheim
Henschker, Bahnhofstrasse 18, tel: (09341) 203040. Near the station. Sandstone turn-of-the-century building. 24 beds. (E–M)

Bad Mergentheim
Bundschu, Cronbergstrasse 15, tel: (07931) 3043. Situated in a residential area near the city centre, close to a large park. (M)

Rothenburg o.d. Tauber
Eisenhut, Herrengasse 3, tel: (09861) 7050. Close to the marketplace, 80 rooms. (L–LL)

Merian, Ansbacher Strasse 42, tel: (09861) 3096. Modern building shortly before the city walls, 60 beds. (M–L)

Gasthof Glocke, Am Plönlein 1, tel: (09861) 3025. Children very welcome. Family rooms and play room available. (E–M)

Ansbach
Am Drechselgarten, Am Drechselgarten 1, tel: (0981) 89020. Five-minutes walk to the castle, on a hill. (M–L)

Christl, Richard-Wagner-Strasse 41, tel: (0981) 8121. 20 rooms, hotel on the north side of Ansbach. Large rooms available for a small extra fee. (M)

Feuchtwangen
Gasthof Wilder Mann, Ansbacher Berg 2, tel: (09852) 719. (E)

Romantik Hotel, Greifen-Post, Marktplatz 8, tel: (09852) 2002. Traditional hotel on the marketplace, city centre. Swimming pool and sauna. Separate house with large group apartments for up to 8 people. (M–LL)

Dinkelsbühl
Blauer Hecht, Schweinemarkt 1, tel: (09851) 811. 300-year-old building in town centre, with swimming pool, sauna. Restaurant traditional German style serving regional and international dishes. 44 rooms. (M)

Nördlingen
Mondschein, Bauhofgasse 5, tel: (09081) 86074. Hotel in the centre of town with "pick-up" service from the station. Park and playground nearby. Restaurant "Zum Mondschein" with traditional food. (E)

Donauwörth
Traube, Kapellstrasse 14, tel: (0906) 6096. New building with restaurant. (M)

Park-Café, Sternschanzenstrasse 1, tel: (0906) 6037. Hotel with restaurant. Municipal swimming pool next door. 50 beds. (M)

Augsburg
Steigenberger Drei-Mohren-Hotel, Maximilianstrasse 40, tel: (0821) 50360. (LL)
Álpenhof, Donauwörther Strasse 233, tel: (0821) 42040. Grand hotel with 200 beds in the direction of Norden-Oberhausen. Small garden. (M–L)

Langer, Gögginger Strasse 39, tel: (0821) 578077. Small hotel opposite park and playground. Larger rooms for groups available for a small extra fee. (M)

Füssen
Fürstenhof, Komotener Strasse 23, tel: (08362) 7006. Small hotel close to the station, 30 beds. Larger rooms available. (M)

THE GERMAN ALPINE ROAD

Oberammergau
Alte Post, Dorfstrasse 19, tel: (08822) 1091. First registered 550 years ago as an inn on the Roman road. Situated in the town centre, surrounded by green areas. Family rooms available, 60 beds. (E–M)

Garmisch-Partenkirchen
Grand-Hotel Sonnenbichl, Burgstrasse 97, tel: (08821) 7020. Large hotel on the outskirts of Garmisch. Swimming pool and sauna. Dogs welcome for a small extra fee. 93 rooms. (LL)

Rheinischer Hof, Zugspitzstrasse 76, tel: (08821) 72024. Family-run hotel on the outskirts of Garmisch. Outside swimming pool and garden. Family apartments available. Restaurant with traditional food and salad bar. (M)

Rottach Egern
Gästehaus Haltmair am See, Seestrasse 47, tel: (08022) 2750. Cosy hotel, situated directly at the Tegernsee. (M)

Tegernsee
Seehotel zur Post, Neureuthstrasse 23, tel: (08022) 3951. Medium-sized hotel with direct access to the Tegernsee (sailing, etc), tennis courts and gardens close by. (E–M)

Schliersee
Schliersee-Hotel, Kirchbichlweg 19, tel: (08026) 6080. Large hotel in the vicinity of the Schliersee. Swimming pool and sauna. Dogs welcome for a small extra fee. (M–L)

Gästehaus Effland, Bayerischzell, Tannermühlstrasse 14, tel: (08023) 263. Small hotel, approximately 12 kms from Schliersee. Swimming pool and garden. (E)

Reith im Winkl
Zum Löwen, Tirolerstrasse 1, tel: (08640) 8901. Small hotel in the town centre. (E)

Altenburger Hof, Frühlingstrasse 3, tel: (08640) 8994. Small, family-run hotel at the town entrance, opposite municipal swimming pool and lido. Park nearby. (E)

Bad Reichenhall
Kurhotel Alpina, Adolf-Schmid-Strasse 5, tel: (08651) 2038. Cosy hotel in country-style. Half and full board available. (E–M)

Kurfürst, Kurfürstenstrasse 11, tel: (08651) 2710. Small hotel with separate family house (incl. terrace). Bicycle hire. (M)

Berchtesgaden
Alpenhotel Kronprinz, Am Brandholz, tel: (08652) 6070. Medium-sized hotel higher up the mountain with 130 beds, prices vary depending on view. Sauna and solarium. (M)

MUNICH

Munich
Hilton, Am Tucherpark 7, tel: (089) 38350. Super luxurious hotel by the "Englischer Garten" in the city centre. Swimming pool, sauna, hairdresser, fashion shop, jeweller, car hire. (LL)

InterCity Hotel, Im Hauptbahnhof, tel: (089) 558571. Situated in the main station, close to city centre and "Englischer Garten" (approximately 10 minutes). Noise protection windows. (L)

City Hotel, Schillerstrasse 3a, tel: (089) 558091. Newly renovated, medium-sized hotel near the old botanical gardens and "Sendlinger Tor-Park". 65 rooms. (M)

Europäischer Hof, Bayerstrasse 31, tel: (089) 551510. New hotel close to the station. Prices vary with the seasons. (M)

Blauer Bock, Blumenstrasse 16, tel: (089) 231780. Former monastery (16th-century) directly next to the "Viktualienmarkt". 75 rooms. Vegetarian restaurant. (E–M)

Starnberg
Seehof, Bahnhofsplatz 4, tel: (08151) 6001. Small hotel at the Starnberger See. Directly opposite the lake promenade. (M)

Wolfratshausen
Gasthof Humplbräu, Obermarkt 2, tel: (08171) 7115. Typically Bavarian inn in the centre of town, 30 rooms. The restaurant serves traditional dishes. (E–M)

Rosenheim
Parkhotel Crombach, Kufsteiner Strasse 2, tel: (08031) 12086. New hotel and restaurant with local and international cuisine. Dogs welcome. (M)

RELAXATION IN EASTERN BAVARIA

Freising
Isar-Hotel, Isarstrasse 4, tel: (08161) 81004. Medium-sized hotel with 70 beds, built in 1984. (M)

Landshut
Kaiserhof, Papiererstrasse 2, tel: (0871) 6870. New hotel at the river Isar, about 3 minutes from old city centre. Close to the castle. (L)

Romantik-Hotel Fürstenhof, Stethaimer Strasse 3, tel: (0871) 82025. Art Deco building with 4 floors in a quiet side street. (M) New: "Non Smoking" floor (L) with individual apartments. Sauna and solarium.

Kelheim
Ehrntaler, Donaustrasse 22, tel: (09441) 3333. Medium-sized modernised hotel with good restaurant serving national and international dishes, fish and game. (E–M)

Regensburg
Parkhotel Maximilian, Maximilianstrasse 28, tel: (0941) 51042. Listed rococo building, 52 rooms, opposite station. Park close by. (L)

Bischofshof, Krauterer Markt 3, tel: (0941) 59086. The foundation stone of this former bishop's residence was laid in 1648. Beer garden. Danube and huge park only a few minutes away. (M–LL)

Weiden
Stadtkrug, Wolframstrasse 5, tel: (0961) 32025. New hotel close to the town centre,

with country-style decorations. Children welcome (suitable beds for a small extra fee). Traditional restaurant. (M)

Straubing
Wenisch, Innere Passauer Strasse 59, tel: (09421) 22066. Small, quiet hotel close to the historical town centre and church. (E–M)

Bodenmais
Andrea, Am Hölzlweg 10, tel: (09924) 7710. Small hotel close to river Riesbach. Half and full board available. Swimming pool. (M)

Zwiesel
Kurhotel Sonnenburg, Augustinerstrasse 9, tel: (09922) 2031. New hotel with 40 beds and own swimming pool. (E)

Passau
Wilder Mann, Rathausplatz, tel: (0851) 35071. Four 14th-century patrician houses were inter-connected to form this comfortable hotel. Close to the historical town centre and town hall. Swimming pool. Gourmet restaurant. Also houses the glass museum. (M–L)

Weisser Hase, Ludwigstrasse 23, tel: (0851) 34066. City house, 230 beds at the entrance of the pedestrian zone, 10 minutes from the river Inn. Small children free. (E–M)

Dreiflüsse-Hof, Danziger Strasse 42, tel: (0851) 51018. New hotel, 130 beds, on the outskirts of Passau. Forest behind the building. Restaurant with traditional dishes. (M)

LAKE CONSTANCE

Lindau
Bayerischer Hof, Seepromenade, tel: (08382) 75055. Traditional hotel close to the station and harbour. Swimming pool. Small children stay for free. (L–LL)

Insel-Hotel, Maximilianstrasse 42, tel: (08382) 5017. Small hotel in pedestrian zone. (M)

Toscana, Aeschacher Ufer 12, tel: (08382) 3131. Built in the 1960s. The nearby park leads directly to the lake. (E–M)

Konstanz
Steigenberger Inselhotel, Auf der Insel, tel:

(07531) 25011. Old monastery (AD 300) on Lake Constance with own lakeside lawn and access to the water. With wine cellar and restaurant. (LL)

Seeblick, Neuhauser Strasse 14, tel: (07521) 54018. New, large building with swimming pool. Municipal park close by. (M)

Radolfzell
Am Stadtgarten, Höllturmpassage Haus 2, tel: (07732) 4011. New building with view over the town gardens. Approximately five minutes from Lake Constance. (M)

Kreuz, Obertorstrasse, tel: (07732) 4066. Traditional hotel with restaurant on ground floor (local cuisine). Close to the lake. (M)

Reichenau
Strandhotel Löchnerhaus, Schiffslände 12, tel: (07534) 411. Turn-of-the-century building, restaurant, lakeside lawn and garden. (M)

Überlingen
Romantik Hotel Hecht, Münsterstrasse 8, tel: (07551) 63333. Tiny hotel, 14 beds. (M)

Parkhotel St Leonhard, Obere St-Leonhard-Strasse 83, Tel: (07551) 8080. Traditional house dating from 1896, own swimming pool, playground and game park. Outside of town on a hill. (M–L)

Friedrichshafen
Zeppelin, Eugenstrasse 41, tel: (07541) 25071. Comfortable hotel with 20 rooms. Double rooms and apartments available. (M)

Zur Gerbe, Hirschlatter Strasse 14, tel: (07541) 51084. Situated in Eilingen, 3 km from Friedrichshafen. Own swimming pool and garden. Restaurant. (E)

THE BLACK FOREST

Freiburg
Colombia-Hotel, Rotteckring 16, tel: (0761) 31415. Hotel in city centre, close to the university. Own car park. (LL)

Zum Roten Bären, Oberlinden 12, tel: (0761) 36969. Oldest restaurant in Germany (first mentioned 1120 AD). Small patio. Restaurant with regional dishes. (L)

Hinterzarten

Park-Hotel Adler, Adlerplatz, tel: (07652) 711. City hotel close to the station. Swimming pool and playground. Restaurant dates back from 1446, regional cuisine. (LL)

Schwarzwaldhof, Freiburger Strasse 2, tel: (07652) 310. Old shingle-covered house with 40 beds in the city centre. (M)

Titisee

Seehotel Wiesler, Strandbadstrasse 5, tel: (07651) 8330. Small hotel with access to the Titisee, 60 beds. Lido next door. (M)

Bären, Neustädter Strasse 35, tel: (07651) 8223. Old hotel close to a forest, with own swimming pool and fitness centre. Restaurant: local and international cuisine. Close to town centre. (M)

Badenweiler

Blauenwald, Blauenstrasse 11, tel: (07632) 5008. New hotel with 46 rooms close to a sport centre. (M)

Römerbad, Schlossplatz 1, tel: (07632) 700. (LL)

Breisach

Am Münster, Münsterbergstrasse 23, tel: (07667) 8380. Medium-sized hotel on a hill. Swimming pool. Hotel extension opened in July 1991. (M–L)

Furtwangen

Kussenhof, Kussenhofstrasse 43, tel: (07723) 7760. Small hotel opened in 1970s. (E)

Nagold

Romantik Hotel Post, Bahnhofstrasse 2, tel: (07452) 4048. New hotel with (real) antique furniture, approximately 1 km from the station. Car park. Children stay free of charge (housekeeper is a children's nurse). Restaurant "Alte Post" serves international and national dishes. (M)

Calw

Ratsstube, Marktplatz 12, tel: (07051) 1864. 16th-century building in the marketplace full of half-timbered houses. Restaurant with Swabian cuisine and salads. Park close by. (M)

Tübingen

Krone, Uhlandstrasse 1, tel: (07071) 31036. Built during the Romantic period, close to river Neckar (boat hire) and park. Approximately 5 minutes from the station. (M–LL)

Barbarina, Wilhelmstrasse 94, tel: (07071) 26048. Small hotel near the botanical gardens and university quarters. Cellar-restaurant serving local dishes. (M)

Am Bad, Europastrasse, tel: (07071) 73071. New building close to lido, park and university stadion. (M)

Stuttgart

Steigenberger Hotel Graf Zeppelin, Arnulf-Klett-Platz 7, tel: (0711) 299881. Large city hotel (280 rooms) opposite the station. Summer rates until the end of August. Swimming pool and sauna. (LL)

Ricker, Friedrichstrasse 3, tel: (0711) 221311. Purpose-built city hotel opposite the station. Close to the Rosensteinpark. (L)

Seyboldt, Fenchelstrasse 11, tel: (0711) 445354. Newly decorated family hotel. Closed in August. (M)

Pforzheim

Goldene Pforte, Hohenstaufenstrasse 6, tel: (07231) 37920. 115-room hotel with swimming pool and sauna. Summer terrace. Close to jewellery exhibitions and museums. (LL)

Ruf, Bahnhofsplatz 5, tel: (07231) 106011. Turn-of-the-century building with all amenities. Close to town centre and station. Opposite old castle church. (M)

Karlsruhe

Ramada Renaissance, Mendelssohnplatz, tel: (0721) 37170. Large city hotel with own underground car park. (LL) Prices excluding breakfast, except at cheaper weekends (M). Two restaurants: "Zum Markgrafen" – Gourmet-cuisine; traditional restaurant (closed during the summer).

Kaiserhof, Karl-Friedrich-Strasse 11, tel: (0721) 26615. 200-year-old, newly renovated hotel with 40 beds in the town centre (marketplace). Three-person bedrooms available. (M–L)

Hasen, Gerwigstrasse 47, tel: (0721) 615076. Small hotel, built in 1912. Gourmet restaurant. (M)

Baden Baden
Brenners Parkhotel, Schillerstrasse, tel: (07221) 9000. Very expensive, traditional house with two restaurants, swimming pool, sauna, hairdresser, park, etc. Extra beds for a substantial extra fee. 1992: 120th anniversary. (LL)

Allee-Hotel Bären, Lichtentaler Allee, tel: (07221) 7020. Relaxed hotel surrounded by park, 80 rooms. 7 kms from station. Restaurant serving French and traditional cuisine. (L)

Greiner, Lichtentaler Allee 88, tel: (07221) 71135. Turn-of-the-century building with new annexe (1974), 52 beds. 3-person bedrooms available. (E–M)

ON THE TRAIL OF THE THE BROTHERS GRIMM

Frankfurt/Main
Hessischer Hof, Friedrich-Ebert-Anlage 40, tel: (069) 75400. Special offers during the summer. Close to natural history museum Senkenberg. (LL)

Jaguar, Theobald-Christ-Strasse 17, tel: (069) 439301. New hotel close to the zoo. (M)

Motel Frankfurt, Eschersheimer Landstrasse 204, tel: (069) 568011. 65 double rooms outside the city centre, approximately 4 kms from the station. Own car park and playground. (M)

Am Zoo, Alfred-Brehm-Platz 6, tel: (069) 490771. New building with 86 rooms, close to the zoo and city centre. (M)

Pension Uebe, Grüneburgweg 3, tel: (069) 592109. Medium-sized hotel, 3-person bedrooms available. Close to Grüneburgpark. (E–M)

Waldhotel Hensels Felsenkeller, Buchrainstrasse 95, tel: (069) 652086. Double and 3-person bedrooms in medium-sized hotel close to the Schärwaldpark. (M)

Airport Frankfurt/Main
Sheraton Hotel, Hugo-Eckener-Ring 15, tel: (069) 69770. Large hotel close to the airport. Cheaper weekend prices, more expensive during the fair. Swimming pool. Close to aeroplane-exhibition at the airport. S-Bahn to the city centre. (LL)

Bad Homburg
Maritim Kurhaus-Hotel, Ludwigstrasse, tel: (06172) 28051. Recently built hotel with own swimming pool, sauna and solarium. Cheaper summer rates. Very close to the Taunustherme (water fitness-centre). Bicycle hire. (L–LL)

Hardtwald-Hotel, Philosophenweg 31, tel: (06172) 81026. Old and new buildings connected, 70 beds. Apartments for families and larger groups available. Forest and playground nearby, riding hall next door. (M–L)

Kronberg
Viktoria, Viktoriastrasse 7, tel: (06173) 4074. Purpose-built hotel with 42 rooms. Close to forest lido. (L)

Königstein im Taunus
Zum Hirsch, Burgweg 2, tel: (06174) 5034. 30 rooms in new and old building with summer terrace. Close to park, castle ruins and countryside (walking). (M)

Oberursel
Parkhotel Waldlist, Hohenarkstrasse 168, tel: (06171) 2869. Medium-sized hotel on the outskirts of town, surrounded by a park. S-Bahn station in front of hotel. (M–L)

Hanau
Brüder-Grimm-Hotel, Kurt-Baum-Platz 6, tel: (06181) 3060. Purpose-built hotel close to pedestrian zone. Sauna, jacuzzi. Roof terrace restaurant, international cuisine. (L)

Gelnhausen
Grimmelshausen-Hotel, Schmidtgasse 12, tel: (06051) 17031. Traditional hotel, modern rooms and garden, relatively close to the town centre. 12th-century facade. (E–M)

Bad Orb
Stadt Hamburg, Sälzerstrasse 3, tel: (06052) 2063. Small hotel in the town centre, 1 km from the station. Own garden. (E)

Bad Soden

Park-Hotel, Am Kurpark, tel: (06196) 26050. Newly built hotel with 130 rooms, adjacent to a large park. Family apartments available. Close to thermal baths. (L)

Rheinischer Hof, Königsteiner Strasse 76, tel: (06196) 26050. Listed building connected with new area, with own underground car park. Close to large park and S-Bahn station. Three-person bedrooms available. (M–L)

Fulda

Maritim Am Schlossgarten, Pauluspromenade 2, tel: (0661) 72820. Former orangery and newly built area with 113 rooms. Swimming pool, skittles, mini golf. Close to castle gardens and cathedral. (LL)

Zum Kurfürsten, Schloss-Strasse 2, tel: (0661) 70001. 18th-century building with 113 beds in the baroque quarter of town. Close to cathedral and castle. Restaurant also serves children's menus. (M–L)

Marburg

Waldecker Hof, Bahnhofstrasse 23, tel: (06421) 63011. Old hotel (1864) with 70 beds. Swimming pool and sauna. Close to station and old town centre. (M–L)

Bad Hersfeld

Parkhotel Rose, Am Kurpark 19, tel: (06621) 14454. Cosy family-run hotel with 20 rooms, built at the turn of the century. Restaurant with national and international menu. Opposite spa gardens. (L)

Romantik Hotel Zum Stern, Lingplatz 11, tel: (06621) 1890. The oldest part of this hotel, a supporting column, was built in AD 1000. Swimming pool, car park. Babysittingservice. Close to the old town centre at the market place. (L)

Kassel

Waldhotel Schäferberg, An der B7, tel: (05673) 7951. Traditional hotel in beautiful forest surroundings, 10 kms outside Kassel. 95 rooms and "Bauernstube" restaurant with traditional cuisine. Sauna/solarium, fitness centre and skittles. Own car park. Dogs welcome. (M)

Westend, Friedrich-Ebert-Strasse 135, tel: (0561) 103821. Newly renovated hotel in the residential area of "Vorderer Westen". (L)

Royal, Giesbergstrasse 53, tel: (0561) 85018. 80-bed hotel near the "Holländisches Zentrum". (M)

Göttingen

Eden, Reinhäuser Landstrasse 22a, tel: (0551) 76007. Newly decorated hotel with 100 rooms, swimming pool and sauna. Restaurant serving traditional German food. New annexe with a further 100 beds finished in September 1991. (M–L)

Central, Jüdenstrasse 12, tel: (0551) 57157. Medium-sized hotel in the town centre close to the pedestrian zone. (E–M)

ALONG THE WESER

Münden

Schmucker Jäger, Wilhelmshäuser Strasse 45, tel: (05541) 5049. 58 beds in renovated half-timbered house and new annexe (family rooms). Own car park. Restaurant serving German dishes. Close to forest. (E–M)

Beverungen

Pension Bevertal, Jahnweg 1a, tel: (05273) 5485. Small, new hotel in quiet area, close to town centre. Own garden. (E)

Höxter

Niedersachsen, Möllinger Strasse 4, tel: (05271) 35333. (M)

Holzminden

Parkhotel Interopa, Altendorfer Strasse, tel: (0551) 2001. Small half-timbered house with own restaurant (gourmet) and car park. Close to park. (M)

Hameln

Dorint Hotel, Weserbergland, Am 164er Ring 3, tel: (05151) 7920. Medium-sized purpose-built house close to the "Bürgergarten" with own swimming pool, restaurant, disco, beer bar. Bicycle hire can be arranged. (M)

Bellevue, Klüstrasse 34, tel: (05151) 61018. Small, family-run hotel in art nouveau villa in art nouveau street. Approximately 10 minutes to town centre. (E)

Hanover

Maritim, Hildesheimer Strasse 34, tel: (0511) 16531. Newly built hotel with 293 rooms, own swimming pool and sauna. International restaurant. Close to "Herrenhäuser Garten", town hall and city centre. (LL)

City-Hotel, Limburgstrasse, tel: (0511) 326681. Established hotel, newly decorated, 70 beds. Opposite town hall in city centre. (M)

Hospiz am Bahnhof, Joachimstrasse 2, tel: (0511) 324297. Interesting hotel directly in the city centre, run by the church. (E–M)

Braunschweig

Deutsches Haus, Ruhfäutchenplatz, tel: (0531) 444422. The former guesthouse to the castle with a view over the cathedral offers 123 beds and an in-house beauty farm. (M)

Mövenpick Hotel, Welfenhof, tel: (0531) 48170. Newly built hotel in the pedestrian zone, adjacent to shopping arcade. Breakfast not included. "Saunaland" with "snow shower", fitness-centre, swimming pool. (LL)

Ritter St Georg, Alte Knochenhauerstrasse 11-13, tel: (0531) 13039. 14th-century half-timbered house with single and double rooms as well as family apartments. Cheaper weekend prices. Two restaurants. (M)

Wolfsburg

Holiday Inn, Rathausstrasse 1, tel: (05361) 2070. Large hotel on 9 floors, approximately 2 kms from the town centre. Swimming pool and sauna. Opposite planetarium. Lunch and dinner restaurant with special menus (Thursdays: "noodle buffet"). (M–LL)

City Hotel, Kaufhofpassage 2, tel: (05361) 23333. Tiny hotel built after World War II, 10 beds, in town centre. Restaurant. (M)

Hildesheim

Schweizerhof, Hindenburgplatz 6, tel: (05121) 29081. 55 rooms in hotel right in the town centre. Old marketplace close by. (L)

Bad Oeynhausen

Hotel Bosse, Herforder Strasse 40, tel: (05731) 28061. Hotel with 33 rooms. About 10 minutes to the town centre. (M)

Minden

Kruses Parkhotel, Marienstrasse 108, tel: (0571) 46033. Small hotel on northern outskirts of Minden, situated in beautiful surroundings at a canal lock, 1.5 km from station. Restaurant and skittles. Dogs welcome. (M)

Verden

Haags Hotel Niedersachsenhof, Lindhooper Strasse 97, tel: (04231) 6660. Newly built hotel in German country-house style outside Verden on the A27. Restaurant and summer terrace. Sauna, jacuzzi, solarium, skittles. (M)

Bremen

Marriott-Hotel (former Plaza), Hillmannplatz 20, tel: (0421) 17670. Now American-owned, 228 rooms, close to "Bürgerpark". Mini golf, horse riding. Cheap weekend offers (E) if booked 14 days in advance (deposit). Fitness centre and shopping area under glass dome. Three restaurants: gourmet; bistro; piano bar. (E–LL)

Park-Hotel, Im Bürgerpark, tel: (0421) 34080. 150 rooms in historical hotel surrounded by the "Bürgerpark" (mini golf, horse riding). Free bicycle hire. Hairdresser and chauffeur, babysitter service. (LL)

Heldt, Friedhofstrasse 41, tel: (0421) 213051. Family-run hotel with 60 rooms on the outskirts of Bremen. Restaurant open Monday–Thursday. (M)

Bremerhaven

Nordseehotel Naber, Theodor-Heuss-Platz, tel: (0471) 48770. Medium-sized hotel in the town centre with restaurant, banquet and club rooms, bar and summer garden. (L)

Parkhotel, Im Bürgerpark, tel: (0471) 27041. Medium-sized 19th-century hotel in a park, about 5 minutes from the station. Three-person bedrooms available. Conservatory, beer garden, playground, own car park. Restaurant serves traditional German food. (M)

THE NORTH SEA COAST

Emden

Schmidt, Friedrich-Ebert-Strasse 79, tel: (04921) 24057. This 100-year-old building is one of the oldest in Emden. 50 beds, 3-person bedrooms available. Garden. (M)

Aurich
Piqueur Hof, Bahnhofstrasse 1, tel: (04941) 4118. Medium-sized hotel in the pedestrian zone close to the old station and post office. Swimming pool and sauna, skittles, television room and cosy restaurant with genuine Frisian cuisine. (M)

Norden
Reichshof, Neuer Weg 53, tel: (04931) 2411. Small hotel with 40 beds at the town entrance. The restaurant menu features more than 300 regional, national and international dishes. (E–M)

Borkum
Nordsee-Hotel, Bubertstr. 9, tel: (04922) 3080. This hotel has been in the same family for generations. Some of the 78 rooms overlook the sea. "Badeland" facilities: sauna, jacuzzi, solarium, etc. and own spa facilities: seawater pool, massage. Special diets available. Dogs welcome. (M–L)

Juist
Hotel Pabst, Strandstr. 15-16, tel: (04935) 1014. Small family-run hotel with solarium, bicycle hire, library, restaurant and Frisian tea room. Mid-September to mid-June low season rates. Dogs welcome. (M–LL)

Norderney
Kurhotel Reinke, Bismarckstrasse, tel: (04932) 3051. 70-bed hotel in the centre (zone 1) of the island, close to the beach. (E)

Baltrum
Strandhotel H. Wietjes, Haus Nr. 58, tel: (04939) 237. Medium-sized hotel on the sea promenade. Restaurant. (L)

Langeoog
Haus Westfalen, Abke-Jansen-Weg 6, tel: (04972) 265. Small hotel on the outskirts of the village. Bicycle hire. The Westphalian owner serves East Frisian and Westphalian dishes in his restaurant. (M)

Spiekeroog
Upstalsboom, Pollerdiek, tel: (04976) 364. 10-year-old hotel with 60 beds close to the old island church. Lawn and children's playroom. Restaurant with East Frisian and German cuisine. (M)

Wangerooge
Strandhotel Upstalsboom, Strandpromenade, tel: (04469) 611. Medium-sized hotel close to the water. Indoor swimming pool and restaurant. (M–L)

Jever
Hotel-Pension Stöber, Hohnholzstrasse 10, tel: (04461) 5580. Tiny, family-run hotel with garden, only a short walk from the castle. (E)

Wilhelmshaven
Koppernhörner Mühle, Köppernhörner Strasse, tel: (04421) 202096. 23 rooms in a former 17th-century mill, close to the town centre. Small pub. (E–M)

Oldenburg
City-Club Hotel (CCH), Europaplatz 20, tel: (0441) 8080. Modern, purpose-built hotel outside the town centre, close to the "Weser-Ems-Halle" (festival hall). Sauna, solarium, jacuzzi. (L)

Hotel Wieting, Damm 29, tel: (0441) 27214. Old and new building combined to house 105 beds. Very close to the castle, "Lamberti"-church and English castle gardens.(M)

Cuxhaven
Donners Hotel, Am Seedeich 2, tel: (04721) 5090. New building with 86 rooms. Restaurant with sea view serves North German cuisine. Swimming pool and sauna. (M–L)

Island of Heligoland
Hotel Heligoland, Am Südstrand, tel: (04725) 220. Small hotel in new building, one-minute walk to the main road. (M)

Husum
Thomas Hotel, Zingel 9, tel: (04841) 6087. Two-star hotel with 40 double and single rooms. Four-person bedrooms available in guesthouse-annexe. Café, dance bar, international restaurant. Close to the harbour, old town centre and museums. (M)

Nordstrand
Landgasthof Kelting, tel: 04842 (335). Small hotel on the peninsula, approximately 20 minutes drive from the station of Husum. Restaurant. (E)

Föhr-Wyk
Duus, Hafenstrasse 40, tel: (04681) 708.
Small hotel in old building with new annexe
on the "outskirts" of Wyk. Very close to the
beach and jetty. Pedestrian zone nearby. (M)

Sylt-Westerland
Stadt Hamburg, Strandstrasse 2, tel: (04651)
8580. Medium-sized hotel with English-
Frisian decor in the town centre and close to
the beach. Bicycle hire can be arranged.
Restaurant serves German and French-style
cuisine. (L–LL)

HAMBURG

Hamburg
Vier Jahreszeiten, Neuer Jungfernstieg 9,
tel: (040) 34941. 100-room hotel in the city
centre. Hairdresser and massage facilities.
Two restaurants: the upmarket "Herlin" and
a barbecue-bar. Many other features planned
for the future. (LL)

Europäischer Hof, Kirchenallee 45, tel: (040)
248171. Large turn-of-the-century hotel
opposite the station with leisure centre, swimming pool and water slide, sauna. (L–LL)

Fürst Bismarck, Kirchenallee 49, tel: (040)
2801091. Medium-sized hotel close to the
main station. (M)

St Raphael, Adenauerallee 41, tel: (040)
248200. Recently redecorated, relaxing hotel with a beautiful view over the port. Fitness centre with sauna, jacuzzi, etc. (M–L)

Lüneburg
Hotel Residenz, Münstermannskamp 10, tel:
(04131) 45047. Cosy hotel with 35 rooms,
own garden and restaurant "Die Schnecke".
Close to spa gardens. Bicycle hire and underground car park. Dogs welcome. (M)

Bremer Hof, Lüner Strasse, tel: (04131)
36077. Family-run hotel close to the river
Ilmenau. Close to "Nikolai" church and
"Liebesgrund" (love ground!!) park. Restaurant. (E–L)

Lauenburg
Möller, Elbstrasse 46, tel: (04153) 2011.
Three houses were connected to form this
newly renovated small hotel with view over

the river Elbe right in the centre of the old
town. 3-person bedrooms available. Restaurant with German and seasonal dishes. (M)

FROM LÜBECK TO FLENSBURG

Lübeck
Hotel Jensen, An der Obertrave 4-5, tel:
(0451) 71646. Only 900 metres from the
station, this former Patrician residence is
situated in the historical city centre. The
family-run hotel consists of 46 rooms. Car
park, dogs welcome. (M)

Lysia-Mövenpick, Auf der Wallhalbinsel,
tel: (0451) 15040. Newly renovated, large
hotel in the historical quarter of the city.
Breakfast not included. Children under 16
stay free of charge. Playroom. Restaurant
and conference rooms. (L)

Eutin
Voss-Haus, Vossplatz 6, tel: (04521) 1797.
17th-century building with 16 rooms in the
town centre. Small garden and restaurant
with German and regional dishes. (M)

Malente
Intermar, Hindenburgallee 2, tel: (04523)
4040. With 10 floors the largest hotel in
town, special weekend rates (M-L). Apartments for larger groups. Sauna, solarium,
bar, restaurant "Friesenstube". Twenty km
from theme park "Hansaland". (LL)

Plön
Kurhotel, Ölmühlenallee, tel: (04522) 8090.
Relatively new hotel with 53 rooms, featuring its own therapy rooms with swimming
pool, sauna, massage, solarium, etc. The
restaurant serves regional and health food.
Only 200 metres from the large "Plöner See"
lake and a jetty. Forest nearby. (M)

Kiel
"Kieler Kaufmann", Niemannsweg 102, tel:
(0431) 85011. Small hotel in a quiet location, surrounded by gardens and featuring an
ancient open fire place in the hall. Swimming pool, sauna, bicycle hire. Exquisite
restaurant with beautiful decor. (M–LL)

Berliner Hof, Ringstrasse 6, tel: (0431)
62050. Medium-sized hotel opposite the station and close to the town centre. The

"Mozartwiesen" park and the sea are only 10 minutes away. (M)

Schleswig
Strandhalle, Strandweg 2, tel: (04621) 22021. This ideally situated hotel close to a marina and the station consists of 26 rooms with all mod cons. Cosy restaurant with seaside view, garden terrace. Swimming pool, solarium, table tennis, bicycle and boat hire. Tennis and horse riding facilities nearby. (M)

Flensburg
Historischer Krug, Oeversee, An der B 76, tel: (04630) 300. The oldest inn in the area (since 1519) has been in the same family for many generations. It has a gourmet restaurant with regional specialities, swimming pool, sauna, solarium, massage, fitness centre, beauty farm as well as canoe, kayak and bicycle hire. (M)

Flensburger Hof, Süderhofenden 38, tel: (0461) 17320. Beautifully renovated hotel close to the shopping centre, with international restaurant. 4-person bedrooms available. (M)

EISENACH & GOTHA

Eisenach
Stadt Eisenach, Luisenstrasse 11-13, tel: (0623) 3682. The modestly furnished hotel with 85 beds serves Thuringian dishes in its small restaurant. (E)

Parkhotel, Wartburgallee 2, tel: (0623) 5291. A small hotel, often full of tourist groups, with a gift shop and a restaurant. (E)

Gotha
Hotel Slovan, Hauptmarkt 20/21, tel: (0622) 52069. The 19th-century building on the outskirts of Gotha consists of 15 rooms with bathroom en suite. Restaurant and café. Park nearby. (M–L)

Harry Heinemann, Märzstrasse 73, tel: (0622) 53568. Smallest of small B&B places. (E)

Arnstadt
Bahnhofshotel, Am Bahnhof 8, tel: (0618) 2481. 70-bed hotel close to the station and the town centre. Breakfast not included. Zoo nearby. (E)

ERFURT & WEIMAR

Erfurt
Erfurter Hof, Am Bahnhofsvorplatz, tel: (061) 51151. This famous hotel with 182 rooms has hosted many VIPs. Four restaurants, a café, night club and flower shop add to the flair. Opposite the station. (M–LL)

Hotel Kosmos, Juri-Gagarin-Ring, tel: (061) 5510. Large tower block with 319 modern rooms. Restaurants and car rental. (M–L)

Bad Liebenstein
K.H. Karn, Rückertstrasse 3, tel: (0621) 61471. B&B in a separate villa for 4 people south of the Thuringian Forest. (E)

Weimar
Hotel Elephant, Am Markt, tel: (0621) 61471. 17th-century building with elegant facade and beautiful terracotta roof where Tolstoy and Bach used to stay. 106 rooms close to the historic marketplace. Excellent restaurants, Elephantkeller and Belvedere, famous for their salads. (M–L)

Hotel Russischer Hof, Goetheplatz 2, tel: (0621) 2331. 19th-century building, originally inhabited by a Russian aristocrat. The modern annexe in the centre of town houses comfortable bedrooms. (M)

JENA, GERA & ALTENBURG

Jena
Schwarzer Bär, Lutherplatz 2, tel: (078) 22543. 500-year-old building with 65 rooms in the centre of town. Restaurant. Close to lido. (E–M)

Gera
Hotel Gera, Strasse der Republik, tel: (070) 22991. Seven floors with 314 rooms are surrounded by a beautiful lawn with flowers blooming all the year round. Beer hall, café, terrace and three restaurants with Thuringian specialities. (M–L)

Altenburg
Zum Wenzel, Karl-Liebknecht-Strasse 21, tel: (0402) 311171. Newly renovated building, 65 beds, close to park. Three-bed rooms available. Restaurant with terrace serves local dishes. Ten minutes' walk to the castle. (E)

Chemnitz (Karl-Marx-Stadt)

Hotel Kongress, Karl-Marx-Allee, tel: (071) 6830. Modern concrete block near the Stadthalle, 369 rooms. Facilities include 4 restaurants, bars, a café, nightclub, fitness room, sauna, solarium and massage. (M–L)

Chemnitzer Hof, Theaterplatz, tel: (071) 6840. Huge, traditional hotel with 109 rooms. Three restaurants, bar, nightclub. (M–L)

DRESDEN

Bellevue, Köpckestrasse, tel: (051) 56620. The modern hotel with 328 rooms on the banks of the river Elbe was opened in 1985. The old part with its beautiful double court was integrated in the new structure. Five restaurants, bar, wine bar, beer cellar, night club, fitness room, sauna, bowling, massage and shopping arcade. (LL)

Dresdner Hof, An der Frauenkirche, tel: (051) 48410. Architecturally interesting five-star hotel in the baroque quarter of Dresden. 327 elegant rooms, 15 restaurants and cafés. The partial glass roof offers a view over the Elbe. Fitness centre, sauna, swimming pool, solarium, underground car park. (LL)

Interhotel Newa, Leningrader Strasse 34, tel: (051) 496 7112. Large hotel with 307 rooms in the middle of a green lawn opposite the station. Several popular restaurants serve national and international cuisine. Sauna and flower shop. From the upper floors you have a superb view over the city. (M–L)

Hotel Königstein, Prager Strasse, tel: (051) 48560. 303 rooms near the station. Restaurant with roof garden, sauna. (M–L)

Hotel Dresden, Münzmeisterstrasse, tel: (051) 475857. This medium-sized hotel 3 kms from the city centre is surrounded by a green landscape. Restaurant, sun terrace and souvenir shop. (M–L)

Meissen

Hamburger Hof, Dresdener Strasse, tel: (053) 2118. Small hotel in the centre of town. Hot and cold water in the rooms. Three-bed rooms available. Breakfast not included. (E)

THE ELBSANDSTEIN MOUNTAINS

Pirna

Schwarzer Adler, Platz der Solidarität, tel: (056) 3488. Small hotel with 40 rooms, showers on every floor. Close to park and old town centre. Steamship rides on the river. (E)

Bautzen

Lubin, Wendischer Graben, tel: (054) 511114. 22-year-old hotel with 130 beds. Apartments and 3-bed rooms available. Close to old town centre and shopping facilities. (E–M)

Weisses Ross, Äussere Lauenstrasse, tel: (054) 42263. 30 rooms with showers on every floor. The original turn-of-the-century decor is now being restored. (E)

Görlitz

Monopol, Platz der Befreiung 9, tel: (055) 5667. Small hotel near the town centre, rooms with hot and cold water. Apartment (with shower) available. Restaurant. Close to small theme park. (M–L)

Frankfurt/Oder

Frankfurter Hof, Wilhelm-Pieck-Strasse 1-2, tel: (030) 387421, fax: 387587. Ten floors with 150 rooms with a barbecue lawn and a peninsula park on the river Oder behind the hotel. Volleyball pitch. The restaurant "Oderblick" serves regional dishes, barbecue every Thursday. Fitness centre. (M)

Stadt Frankfurt/Oder, Karl-Marx-Strasse 193, tel: (030) 3890. This 20-year-old building with 186 rooms will be demolished in 1992 and rebuilt by 1993. The Helenensee is only 10 minutes away. (M–L)

Cottbus

Zum Schwan, Bahnhofstrasse 57, tel: (059) 22334. 45 beds in an old building which will be redecorated in 1991. Breakfast not included. The new Greek owner serves traditional Greek cuisine in the small restaurant. Close to the Branitzer Park (old and rare trees) and the planetarium. (E)

BERLIN

Berlin (West)

Alsterhof, Augsburger Strasse 5, tel: (030) 219960. The large and central hotel close to the "Ku-Damm" features a German restaurant, swimming pool, sauna, solarium, massage and an underground car park. (L–LL)

Hotel Hamburg, Landgrafenstrasse 4, (030) 269161. 240 rooms. The modern building is situated close to a shopping centre and only a few minutes' walk from the "Tiergarten" park and the "Gedächtniskirche". It offers a bar and an international restaurant. Dogs welcome. (L–LL)

Inter-Continental, Budapester Strasse 2, tel: (030) 21080. The old and new buildings house 680 rooms close to the zoo. The hotel features a swimming pool, sauna, solarium, massage, hairdresser, boutique, etc., as well as two restaurants: the Brasserie and an elegant establishment serving international specialities. (LL)

Meineke, Meinekstrasse 10, tel: (030) 882811. Small hotel with 60 rooms in a quiet side street near the "Ku-Damm". 3-bed rooms available. (M–L)

Berlin Plaza, Knesebeckstrasse 63, tel: (030) 884130. The newly redecorated turn-of-the-century building has 130 rooms on 7 floors. It is close to the "Ku-Damm" and a residential area full of distinguished, elegant villas. Restaurant with terrace. (L)

Berlin (East)

Grand Hotel, Friedrichstrasse 158, tel: (02) 20920. This establishment puts the "grand" back into grand hotels. 350 elegant and extremely comfortable rooms close to erstwhile Checkpoint Charlie. With fitness club, hairdressing services, swimming pool, sauna and solarium. Don't miss the monumental staircase, the "Peacock Bar", or any of the six exceptional restaurants in the hotel. Multi-storey car park. (LL)

Palasthotel, Karl-Liebknecht-Strasse 5, tel: (02) 2410. Large mod-cons hotel near the Palace of the Republic with 8 eating places from haute cuisine to quick snack. Apart from 3 bars it also offers all fitness facilities

and a bowling alley. In-house offices include car hire, flight and theatre bookings, a hairdresser and a souvenir shop. (LL)

Interhotel Unter den Linden, Unter den Linden 14, tel: (02) 2200311. Modern hotel with more than 300 bedrooms on this famous street close to many interesting museums. It features a bar, a café and a restaurant with international cuisine. (M–L).

Hotel Müggelsee, Am Müggelsee, tel: (02) 652100. The large hotel on the northeastern outskirts of Berlin lies close to the Müggelsee-complex, but within easy reach of the city centre (by bus, S-Bahn or taxi). 3- and 4-bed rooms as well as apartments for larger groups available. Several restaurants serving excellent food, particularly in the "Jagdkeller" with its large grill. Sauna, solarium, massage and beauty treatment. Sports facilities include tennis, horse-riding and surfing. Enjoy a walk in the nearby forest. (M)

POTSDAM

Hotel Potsdam, Lange Brücke, tel: (033) 4631. Large hotel with all modern amenities on the outskirts of the city close to the river Havel. Several restaurants such as the Sanssouci and a garden restaurant serve very good food. Nightclub, sauna, massage, souvenir shop. Various watersports facilities available. (L)

Hotel Cecilienhof, Neuer Garten, tel: (033) 23141. Charming hotel in the former residence of Crown Prince Wilhelm with 42 rooms. The dining room offers international and regional dishes of outstanding quality. (L–LL)

BERLIN TO THE HARZ MOUNTAINS

Brandenburg

Stadt Berlin, Thälmannstrasse 2, tel: (038) 522692. The newly decorated and refurbished hotel will re-open in September 1991. (M)

Jörg Stelter, Friedensstrasse 30, tel: (038) 25609. Small B&B place. Separate bungalow for 4 with open fireplace and garage. Close to municipal pool and gliders' aerodrome. (E)

Magdeburg

Note: Hotel rooms anywhere in Magdeburg need to be booked 6 weeks in advance.

Hotel International, Otto-von-Guericke-Strasse, tel: (091) 3840. Simple but comfortable, 344 rooms surrounded by a green landscape in the centre of town. Restaurants, café, salons de thé, night club, souvenir shop. (M–L)

Grüner Baum, Wilhelm-Pieck-Allee 40, tel: (091) 30862. Medium-sized hotel in a busy street. The half-timbered house has showers on every floor. Close to the "Elbe-Schwimmhalle" and the shopping centre. (E–M)

Halberstadt
Weisses Ross, Johann-Sebastian-Bach-Strasse, tel: (0926) 21176. Small sandstone building opposite a park. The restaurant serves German cuisine. (E–M)

Eisleben
Parkhotel, Bernhard-Koenen-Strasse 12, tel: (0443) 2335. The old building (1889) houses 13 rooms and a restaurant serving German dinners. 3-bed rooms available. Close to the centre and park. (E)

HALLE, MERSEBURG & LEIPZIG

Halle
Stadt Hale, Ernst-Thälmann-Platz 17, tel: (046) 38041. Massive building in the city with 338 units featuring restaurants, a wine bar, café, sun terrace and night club. (L)

Marthahaus, Adam-Kuckhoff-Strasse 5-8, tel: (046) 24411. 120-year-old residential home with small separate hotel unit near the theatre in a quiet side-street. (E–M)

Merseburg
Dessauer Hof, Dammstrasse 4, tel: (0442) 211145. 35 rooms in the vicinity of the castle and cathedral. The restaurant serves regional dishes. (E)

Leipzig
Merkur, Gerberstrasse, tel: (041) 7990. Large hotel (445 rooms) near the fairground in the city centre. The rates go up during the fair. You can choose from many restaurants, in-

cluding a Japanese and Italian establishment. View the city from "Club 27". Facilities include a flight and travel office, bowling alley, swimming pool, sauna, solarium and massage. (L–LL)

Leipzig, Richard-Wagner-Strasse, tel: (041) 288814. Large hotel opposite main station with two restaurants, café and night club. (L)

Am Ring, Karl-Marx-Platz, tel: (041) 79520. This large, modern building opposite the "Neues Gewandhaus" offers several restaurants, cafés and a night club. (M–L)

Zum Löwen, Rudolf-Breitscheid-Strasse, tel: (041) 7751. The 108 rooms with basic amenities are spread over 8 floors. The two restaurants have a regional and international menu. (M–L)

DESSAU & WITTENBERG

Dessau
Stadt Dessau, Kavalierstrasse, tel: (047) 7285. This old building with 50 rooms (including 3-bed and apartments) and a garden restaurant serving local food, is situated in the centre of town opposite the town park and close to the historical post office building. (M)

Wittenberg
Goldener Adler, Markt 7, tel: (0451) 2053. This small hotel has rooms with basic facilities. (E)

Wittenberger Hof, Collegienstrasse 56, tel: (0451) 2590. Very basic hotel in the centre of town. (E)

BRANDENBURG TO THE BALTIC

Neuruppin
Märkischer Hof, Karl-Marx-Strasse 51, tel: (0362) 2801. 20 rooms in a small hotel near the Tempelgarten. The restaurant with international dishes displays pictures by the famous architect Karl Schinkel. Close to the museum of folklore. (E-M)

Kyritz
S. & F. Grigull, Thälmannstrasse 39, tel: (0365) 366. Small B&B close to lakes. Horseriding and aerodrome nearby. (E)

Wittenberge

Germania, Bahnstrasse, tel: (08546) 3311. Medium-sized hotel with basic facilities and shared bathroom in the centre of town, only 10 minutes from a large park. (E)

Schwerin

Stadt Schwerin, Grunthalplatz 5, tel: (084) 5261. Interesting and pleasant establishment with a very good restaurant. Popular with Danish tourists. (E–M)

Wismar

Hotel Wismar, Breite Strasse 10, tel: (0824) 2498. Old hotel close to shops with hot and cold water in every room. (E)

Rostock

Warnow, Hermann-Duncker-Platz, tel: (081) 37381. Tower block with 338 rooms and balconies, surrounded by lawn. The six restaurants offer a regional menu. Other facilities include the Café Riga, a sun terrace, bar, night club and souvenir shop. (L)

Congress-Hotel, Leningraderstrasse 45, tel: (081) 7030. Small concrete hotel with 23 rooms outside Rostock. (M)

Warnemünde

Strandhotel, Seestrasse 12, tel: (081) 5335. 45 small and large rooms in an older hotel with basic amenities and shared bathroom, opposite the beach and the promenade. The restaurant serves excellent fish dishes. Close to the shopping centre and station. (E)

Ahrenshoop

Ostseehotel, Dünenstrasse 41, tel: (08268) 8132. 100-bed hotel with turn-of-the-century facade, opposite the beach. Two restaurants serving regional and national dishes. (E)

Stralsund

Hotel Baltic, Leninplatz 2-3, tel: (0821) 5381. 70-year-old hotel with 40 rooms, next to the station. 3-bed rooms available. Restaurant with good fish menu. Sea museum close by. (M)

Island of Rügen

Wilhelm Krause, Streuer Weg 62, 2331 Schaprode, tel: (082799) 1360. Small B&B with kitchen for self-catering, directly on the island. (E)

Greifswald

Boddenhus, Karl-Liebknecht-Ring 1, tel: (0822) 5241. New building with 80 rooms and bathrooms en suite on the outskirts of town. The "Stadtrestaurant" serves German cuisine. (M)

Island of Usedom

Gerda Gliesner, Dorfstrasse 8, Usedom-Gneventhin, tel: (082692) 843. Small B&B on a farm, meals on request. Guided tours and motor yacht excursions available. (E)

MECKLENBURG LAKE DISTRICT

Neubrandenburg

Vier Tore, Treptower Strasse 1, tel: (090) 5141. Huge, newly built establishment with 249 rooms with German restaurant. Approximately 5 minutes from the station and 15 minutes from the sea. Museums nearby. (M–L)

Dieter Müller, Ikarusstrasse 2, tel: (090) 73765. Bungalow in Penzlin/Werder on a peninsula with its own fishing jetty. Rowing boat with engine available. (E)

Güstrow

Stadt Güstrow, Markt 2/3, tel: (0851) 4841. Medium-sized hotel in the centre of town, close to the historic town hall and church. Restaurant with traditional food. (E–M)

Waren

Am Bahnhof, Strasse der Freundschaft 19, tel: (0993) 3619. Small hotel close to the station. (E)

R. Porsche, Rosa-Luxemburg-Strasse 17. Small B&B with separate apartment, balcony and view over the river Müritz. (E)

Neustrelitz

Rolf Seidler, Willi-Bredel-Strasse 62, tel: (0991) 40150. Holiday bungalow with direct access to the Canower See lake, with terrace and open fireplace. (E)

FOOD DIGEST

German cooking differs from region to region. For example, the Northern Germany *Labskaus* will not be found in Southern Germany. Listed by region below are the most typical meals encountered while travelling from south to north.

WHAT TO EAT

Bavaria
Krautwickerl: Minced meat rolled into white cabbage, usually eaten with potatoes.
Weisswürste: Spiced veal and pork sausages which are mainly eaten with sweet mustard (*Weisswurstsenf*). They usually accompany a late-morning beer.
Leberkäs: Meat paste, taken hot or cold.
Semmelknödel: Bread dumplings often served with *Schweinebraten* (roast pork).
Reiberdatschi: Thinly grated raw potatoes baked in deep fat. Served with apple sauce. In other regions of Germany they are called *Kartoffelpuffer*.
Hollerküchl: Elderberry blossoms dipped in pancake dough and fried.
Gugelhupf: Cake made out of yeast with raisins, nuts, almonds etc.
Dampfnudeln: Huge yeast dumplings with plums and served hot with vanilla sauce.

Württemberg/Baden
Flädelsuppe: Clear soup with pancake.
Spätzle: A kind of pasta made of flour, egg, salt and water, grated and boiled, *Spätzle* are served as a side-dish with meat and vegetables.
Maultaschen: Another form of pasta filled with minced meat and spinach. *Maultaschen* are either served as soup or as a separate dish with salad.

Hesse
Metzelsuppe: Soup with liver and *blutwurst* (blood sausage).

Handkäs mit Musik: Curd cheese served with onions.
Kasseler Rippchen: Smoked pickled loin of pork, named after a Berlin butcher named Kassel.
Zwiebelkuchen: Yeast cake (almost similar to pizza) filled with onions and bacon and usually served with a glass of young wine (*Federweisser*).
Äppelwoi: Hard cider, another very popular drink.

Rhineland
Sauerbraten: Braised pickled beef lard with bacon, usually served with potatoes and vegetables.
Hunsrücker Festessen: Sauerkraut and peas, *Hunsrücker* pudding with potatoes, horseradish and ham.
Halver Hahn: Rye bread or roll with cheese and mustard.
Kölsch: Light-coloured, surface-fermented beer.
Spekulatius, Muzenmandeln: Almond biscuits.

Westphalia
Westfälischer Schinken: Delicious ham, best when eaten with Pumpernickel bread.
Mettwurst mit Linsen: Pork or beef sausage with lentils.
Westfälischer Reibekuchen: Cakes made of grated raw potatoes and buckwheat flour.

Lower Saxony
Braunkohl mit Brägenwurst: Kale with brain sausage.
Heidschnuckenbraten: Roast lamb served with potatoes.
Braunschweiger Mumme: Very strong dark beer with a high malt content, usually mixed with ordinary beer.

North Germany-Hamburg-Bremen
Kohl mit Pinkel: Cabbage with coarse sausage and potatoes.
Labskaus: Salted meat, herring and mashed potatoes served with fried egg and beetroot.
Lübecker Schwalbennester: Veal olive filled with mashed hard boiled eggs.
Lübecker Marzipan: Favourite sweet, containing lots of almonds ground into a paste.
Rote Grütze: Pudding made from red berries – mainly raspberries – and served with fresh cream.

Berlin

Berliner Schlachtplatte: Fresh blood and liver sausage, pig's kidney and fresh-boiled pork.
Berliner Weisse mit Schuss: Wheaten beer with a shot of raspberry juice or woodruff extract.

Saxony

Sächsischer Mandelstollen: Almond cake.
Leipziger Allerlei: Mixed vegetables.
Gallertschüssel: Boiled pig's or calf's foot in aspic.
Dresdner Christstollen: Christmas cake.
Grüne Klösse: Dumplings made from ground raw potatoes.
Kirschpfanne: Pastry made of white bread, eggs, milk and butter.
Pfefferkuchen: gingerbread (from Pulsnitz).
Eierschecke: Cake with golden-yellow egg-cover, filled with sweet curd.

Brandenburg

Eberswalder Spritzkuchen: Deep-fried ring doughnuts.

Thuringia

Thüringer Klösse: Potato dumplings.
Thüringer Rostbratwurst: Grilled sausage with herbs.
Platz: Thuringian yeast cake.

Saxony-Anhalt

Halberstädter Wurst: sausage.
Salzwedeler Baumkuchen: Cake and chocolate in thin layers.

Mecklenburg-Vorpommern

Salzhering in Sahnesosse: pickled herring in sour cream.
Himmel und Erde: boiled potatoes and apples with bacon.

THINGS TO DO

TOURIST ATTRACTIONS

There is much to see and do in Germany – castles, palaces, country houses, museums, nature parks, etc. The selection listed below is restricted to castles, nature parks and adventure/amusement parks, arranged according to the principal chapters in this book.

JOURNEY ALONG THE RHINE

Castles
Schloss Biebrich, 5 km (3 miles) SE of Wiesbaden, built in the 18th century.
Schloss Gutenfels, in Kaub (12th-century).
Burg Pfalzgrafenstein, also in Kaub (14th-century).
Burg Katz, close to St Goarshausen.
Burg Thunberg (known as "Maus"), near St Goarshausen.
Burg Rheinfels, the ruins from the 13th-century throne above St Goar.
Burg Lahneck, 8 km (5 miles) SE of Koblenz.
Feste Ehrenbreitstein, above Koblenz.
Schloss Stolzenfels, 12 km (7½ miles) S of Koblenz.
Burg Stahleck, ruined castle from the 12th century in Bacharach.
Burg Sooneck, near Niederheimbach.
Burg Reichenstein, near Trechtlinghausen.

Nature parks
Nassau, via the Cologne-Frankfurt *autobahn* exits: Höhr-Grenzhausen, Montabaur, Diez, Limburg.
Rhein-Taunus, via the Cologne-Frankfurt *autobahn* or via the B260 Wiesbaden-Bad Ems, B54 Limburg-Wiesbaden.

ALONG THE MOSELLE

Castles
Burg Eltz, overlooking Moselkern was originally built in 1157.

Reichsburg Cochem, 13 km from Burg Eltz.
Burg Landshut, ruins found in Bernkastel-Kues.

THE ROAD TO COLOGNE

Castles
Ruine Hammerstein, ruins date back to the 10th century.
Burg Drachenfels, ruins lie on a hill overlooking Königswinter.
Schloss Augustusburg, castle and hunting lodge (1689), can be found in Brühl.

Nature parks
Rhein-Westerwald, Siebengebirge, Kottenforst-Ville: these three nature reserves can be reached via the Cologne-Frankfurt *autobahn* (any exit from Bonn Siegburg to Montabaur) as well as on the Cologne-Koblenz *autobahn* (any exit from Bonn-Lengsdorf to Koblenz).

Amusement park
Phantasialand Brühl, just outside Brühl, is a huge amusement centre.

HEIDELBERG

Castles
Heidelberger Schloss, Renaissance castle overlooking the river Neckar in Heidelberg.
Schloss Schwetzingen, former water castle within the beautiful garden in Schwetzingen near Heidelberg.
Kurfürstliches Schloss, the Electoral Palace in Mannheim is the grandest baroque residence in Germany.

Nature park
Bergstrasse-Odenwald, in the northeast of Heidelberg, can be reached via the Mannheim-Frankfurt and Heidelberg-Darmstadt motorways.

Adventure park
Holiday-Park nature reserve in the middle of a forest on the B39 4 km (2½ miles) West of Speyer.

A JOURNEY TO FRANCONIA

Castles
Burg Eberbach, ruins are a few miles outside the town of Eberbach.

Burg Stoltzeneck, ruins date back to 13th century and lie just outside Zwingenberg.
Burg Guttenberg, a few miles south of Hassmersheim.
Schloss Erbach, baroque castle in Erbach.
Mildenburg, built in the 15th century and situated in the middle of Miltenberg.
Wasserschloss Mespelbrunn, castle was built in the 15th century and can be found at the gates of Mespelbrunn.
Burg Löwenstein, ruins overlook the town of Wertheim.
Burg Rothfels, castle ruins overlooking the Main Valley at Marktheidenfeld.
Festung Marienberg, the old fortress is the landmark of Würzburg.
Residenz, beautiful baroque castle in the middle of Würzburg (Residenzplatz).

Nature parks
Bergstrasse Odenwald, via the Mannheim-Frankfurt and Heidelberg-Darmstadt *autobahnen*.
Naturpark Bayerischer Spessart; take any of the exits between Aschaffenburg and Marktheidenfeld on the Frankfurt-Nuremberg *autobahn*.

BAMBERG TO NUREMBERG

Castles
Schloss Weissenstein, baroque castle in Kulmbach.
Altes Schloss, landmark of Bayreuth, dating back to the 18th century.
Neues Schloss, rococo castle built during the 18th-century in Ludwigstrasse, Bayreuth.
Schloss Eremitage Burg, castle in the northeast of Bayreuth overlooking the old town of Nuremberg.

Nature parks
Naturpark Frankenhöhe, can be reached by the *autobahn* Nuremberg-Ansbach, exits: Aich-Ansbach, Ansbach-West.
Naturpark Hassberge, northwest of Bamberg.

Adventure park
Erlebnispark Schloss Thurn, adventure park and zoo, near Forchheim.

ALONG THE ROMANTIC ROAD

Castles
Kurmainzisches Schloss, castle dates back

to the 11th century and houses a museum in Tauberbischofsheim.

Schloss Bad Mergentheim, dominates the town of Bad Mergentheim.

Castle of Weikersheim, one of the most important castles of Baden-Württemberg. It is known for its beautiful interior.

Schloss Harburg, 12th-century castle overlooking the town of Harburg.

Schloss Leitheim, rococo castle near Donauwörth.

Schloss Hohenschwangau, rebuilt in the 19th century, this castle stands opposite Neuschwanstein.

Schloss Neuschwanstein, "Fairy-tale Castle" built by King Ludwig II of Bavaria. This castle and Schloss Hohenschwangau are a few miles east of Füssen.

Nature parks
Naturpark Frankenhöhe, via the Nuremberg-Ansbach *autobahn* (exits Aich, Ansbach, Ansbach-West).

Augsburg-Westliche Wälfer, on the Ulm-Munich *autobahn*; leave at Augsburg, Adelsried, Zusmarshaussen or Burgau exits.

THE GERMAN ALPINE ROAD

Castles
Schloss Linderhof, rococo castle also built by Ludwig II and lies a few miles east of Oberammergau.

Nature park
Alpenpark und Nationalpark, the national park extends around lake Königssee.

Amusement park
Märchenpark Ruhpolding, fantasyland close to Ruhpolding.

MUNICH

Castles
Schloss Herrenchiemsee, King Ludwig II built this castle on the Herreninsel, one of the three islands in the Lake Chiemsee.

Schloss Nymphenburg: The castle and various hunting lodges are in the northwest of Munich.

Residenz, lies in the heart of Munich.

Schloss Oberschleissheim, dating back to the 18th century lies some 15 km (9 miles) north of Munich.

Amusement park
Märchenwald im Isartal, fairyland near Wolfratshausen 28 km (17.5 miles) southeast of Munich.

RELAXATION IN EASTERN BAVARIA

Castles
Burg Trausnitz, a castle overlooking Landshut.

Stadtresidenz, Renaissance palace which lies in the heart of Landshut.

Nature parks
Nationalpark Bayerischer Wald, via the Passau-Regensburg motorway.

Bayerischer Wald: The Bayerischer Wald (wood) practically merges with the National Park.

LAKE CONSTANCE

Castles
Schloss Mainau, castle located on the peninsula of Mainau.

Altes Schloss, Neues Schloss: The old and the new castles are both found in the town of Meersburg.

THE BLACK FOREST

Castles
Schloss Hohentübingen, 16th-century castle overlooking Tübingen.

Neues Schloss, new castle dominates the centre of Stuttgart, the Schlossplatz.

Altes Schloss, old castle opposite the Planie (Stuttgart).

Grossherzogliches Schloss, focal point of Karlsruhe.

Neues Schloss, Renaissance castle overlooking Baden-Baden.

Nature parks
Naturpark Schönbuch, via the Stuttgart-Degerloch *autobahn* (exit: Stuttgart-Degerloch) and from the Stuttgart-Singen *autobahn* (exits: Böblingen, Herrenberg, Tübingen).

Adventure parks
Altweibermühle Tripsdrill, this huge adventure park lies 23 km (14 miles) east of Heilbronn.

ON THE TRAIL OF THE BROTHERS GRIMM

Castles

Saalburg, Roman castle which lies 7 km northwest of Bad Homburg.
Schloss Philippsruhe, 18th-century castle located in Kesselstadt, a surburb of Hanau.
Kaiserpfalz, ruins of Barbarossa's castle are in Gelnhausen.
Burg Brandenstein, castle just outside Schlüchtern.
Stadtschloss, castle was completed in 1730 and lies in the centre of Fulda.
Schloss Eisenbach, 13th-century castle lies 4 km (2½ miles) south of Lauterbach.
Schloss Hohhaus, castle dates back to the 18th century and houses the museum of Lauterbach.
Landgrafenschloss, medieval castle (13th-16th century) rises above Marburg.
Schloss Wilhelmshöhe, 287-metre (956-ft) long castle which lies on the boundaries of Kassel.

Nature parks

Hessischer Spessart, via the Frankfurt-Nuremberg *autobahn*, any exit between Aschaffenburg and Marktheidenfeld.
Hessische Röhn, park stretches E of Fulda and can be reached via the Frankfurt-Kassel *autobahn* (exits: Bad Kissingen, Bad Brückenau, Fulda-Süd/Nord, Hühnfeld).
Hoher Vogelsberg, park begins 20 km (12½ miles) SE of Lauterbach and can be reached via the Giessen-Kassel and Würzburg-Kassel *autobahnen*.

ALONG THE WESER

Castles

Welfenschloss, castle on the shore of the Werra in Münden (Hannoversch-Münden). Sababurg, castle about 20 km (12½ miles) north of Münden.
Trendelburg, castle close to the Sababurg, on B83.
Hämelschenburg, Renaissance castle close to Emmern.
Leineschloss, castle on the edge of the old town of Hanover.
Schaumburg, castle north of Rinteln.
Schloss Bückeburg, surrounded by moat, castle dates back to the 12th century in Bückeburg.

Nature parks

Naturpark Münden, stretches east of Münden. Take exit Münden-Lutterberg.
Naturpark Solling/Vogler, park can be reached via *autobahn* exits Göttingen-Nord, Nörten-Hardenberg and Northeim-West.
Weserbergland Schaumburg-Hameln: on the northern edge of the park is the Bielefeld-Hanover *autobahn*. Take exits Eilsen, Rehren, Bad Nenndorf, Lauenau.

Adventure parks

Rasti-Land, amusement park which lies 32 km (20 miles) east of Hameln.
Potts Park Minden, 10 km west of Minden.

THE NORTH SEA COAST

Castles

Schloss Oldenburg, 17th–18th century castle in the centre of Oldenburg.

Adventure park

Babyzoo Wingst, baby animal zoo. Twenty km (12½ miles) southeast of Otterndorf.

HAMBURG

Castles

Schloss Ahrensburg, the white castle of Ahrensburg lies 32 km (20 miles) northeast of the centre of Hamburg.

Nature parks

Naturpark Harburger Berge. Take the Hamburg-Bremen motorway and use exits Emsen, Nenndorf, Hittfeld.
Naturschutzpark Lüneburger Heide, west of Lüneburg; can be reached via the Hanover-Hamburg *autobahn* (exits: Behringen/Evendorf, Egestorf, Garlstorf).

FROM LÜBECK TO FLENSBURG

Castles

Schloss Eutin, 17th–18th century castle lies on the shores of the Gross Eutiner See.
Schloss Gottorf, Renaissance castle on an island in the Schlei-Bay, Schleswig.
Schloss Glücksburg, white water castle dating back to the 16th century.

Nature parks

Naturpark Aukrug, on the Hamburg-Kiel *autobahn*, Neumünster exit.

Naturpark Westensee, on the same *autobahn* further north, exit: Blumenthal-Bad Bramstedt. If you go on the Hamburg-Flensburg *autobahn*, use Warder exit.
Hüttener Berge: this northernmost park can be reached on the Hamburg-Flensburg *autobahn*, exits Rendsburg-Büdelsdorf, Owschlag, or Schleswig-Gottorf.

Adventure park
Hansaland, on the shore of the Baltic Sea, 10 km (6 miles) from Timmendorfer Strand.

DRESDEN

Castles
Augustusburg, southeast of Chemnitz, a hunting castle built in 1567 by the electoral prince Augustus I. It now houses a youth hostel, a museum and a restaurant. Famous for its strange murals in the "rabbit hall" (the world upside down: rabbits chase people).
Dresdner Zwinger, Dresden, baroque masterpiece (1711–28).
Schloss Pillnitz, 12 km up the Elbe from Dresden, surrounded by a beautiful park with a water and mountain palace and the oldest Japanese camellia in Europe (approx. 250 years).
Schloss Bad Muskau, on the border with Poland, the 16th-century building was the birthplace of Fürst Hermann von Pückler-Muskau who lent his name to the famous "Fürst-Pückler icecream". The castle burnt down in 1945 but will soon be restored to its former beauty.
Paulusschlössel, the small castle (1784) in Markneukirchen, Vogtland, on the border with Czechoslovakia, now houses a collection of musical instruments.
Schloss Moritzburg, north of Dresden, the original 16th-century hunting castle was enlarged in the 18th century and resulted in a glorious baroque castle in magnificent surroundings. The huge lake even needed a lighthouse. Some rooms in the castle contain paraphernalia of the famous artist Käthe Kollwitz.
Burg Stolpen, with the famous Coselturm was built on basalt. Approximately 20 km East of Dresden.

Nature parks
Sächsische Schweiz: Rocks of sandstone mountains south of Dresden with more than 1,000 km of well-marked footpaths criss-crossing the area through canyon-style valleys and gorges, to caves and platforms. Almost 1,000 individual peaks for mountaineers.

THE THURINGIAN FOREST

Castles
Wartburg, in Eisenach, to the east of the border with Hesse. One of the most famous castles in Germany. Where Martin Luther translated the Bible into German.
Schloss Friedensstein, first German baroque castle in Gotha, west of Erfurt. Ancestors of the royal families of Sweden, England, Belgium and Bulgaria were born here. Today, it houses several interesting museums.
Residenzschloss Weimar, northwest of Jena, built in the 16th century and rebuilt in 1618 and 1774 after two substantial fires now houses a remarkable art collection.
Grünes Schloss, another 16th-century building in Weimar contains more than 840,000 German books from the classical period.
Schloss Tiefurt, 3 km northeast of Weimar
Schloss Belvedere, 4 km south of Weimar.

Nature parks
Thüringer Wald: An area excellent for rambling and winter sports, which continues in the shape of the Rhön and the Bavarian Frankenwald. The Saale and Unstrut river valleys are fruit and wine growing areas.

BRANDENBURG TO THE BALTIC

Castles
Schloss Rheinsberg, on the Grienericksee near Neuruppin, a small water castle built in 1566 and extended by Frederick. The old tradition of musical summer festivals will soon be reinstated with a chamber opera festival.
Schloss Sanssouci, near Potsdam, surrounded by more than 290 hectares (716 acres) of gardens and parkland. The remains of the original owner, the "Old Fritz", which had been transferred to the West in 1945 will now return to the mausoleum of Sanssouci.
Schloss Branitz, near Cottbus right in the middle of the Branitzer Park. The beautiful gardens were designed by Fürst Pückler-Muskau himself.
Schloss Oranienburg, the Dutch-style cas-

tle north of Berlin housed a sulphur factory after 1814 and it was here that the history of modern dye chemistry began. The magnificent gardens were altered to a landscaped park in the 19th century.

Nature parks
The March of Brandenburg is the area that surrounds Berlin. It includes huge pine forests such as the Schorfheide and charming hilly areas such as Märkisch Switzerland (around Buckow) and Ruppin Switzerland with the Ruppin Lake and Neuruppin (northwest of Berlin).

MECKLENBURG LAKE DISTRICT

Castles
Schloss Güstrow, south of Rostock, on the F4. Most important Renaissance castle in Germany, built in 1558 as the residence of the Dukes of Mecklenburg-Güstrow. The lavender gardens give a southern flair.
Schloss Gadebusch, northwest of Schwerin, dates back to the 16th century. The beautifully divided facade shows lavish terracotta decorations.
Schloss Ludwigslust, south of Schwerin, was built in 1772–76, before the village around it had even been planned. The generous decorations are mainly made of papiermâché! The castle is surrounded by more than 330 acres of magnificent gardens.
Schloss Neustadt-Glewe, near Schloss Ludwigslust, shows features of Renaissance and baroque architecture.
Schloss Schwerin, on an island in the centre of town, was redesigned in 1843 according to plans of one of the Loire castles.

Nature parks
Mecklenburgische Seenplatte, a lake district with plenty of scope for sailors and surfers. More than 1,000 lakes are surrounded by meadows, fields and forests. The largest lake is the Schweriner See (66 sq. km).
The **Baltic Sea coast** with the islands of Rügen, Usedom and Poel combines the austere charm of the Baltic Sea with sandy beaches and modern resort life.

SACHSEN-ANHALT

Castles
Schloss Pretzsch, 6 km east of Bad Schmiedeberg on the border to Saxony. The baroque park as well as the tower and the church were designed by Daniel Pöppelmann.
Burg Anhalt, 6 km south of Ballenstedt, has been the residence of the Earls of Ballenstedt (later of Anhalt) since the 11th century.
Schloss Ballenstedt, on the southern border of the Harz mountains, was built in 18th-century baroque style on the ruins of a monastery.
Schloss Bernburg, at the lower part of the Saale river, on a sandstone rock high above the Saale. The main part of the building was erected in the 16th century but includes older buildings (Eulenspiegel tower and chapel) from the 12th century.
Schloss Dessau, in the quarter of Mosigkau in Dessau, is said to have been designed by the architect of Sanssouci, Georg Wenzeslaus von Knobelsdorff. The park features an old Japanese teahouse dating back to 1775.
Burg Falkenstein, high above the Selke valley in the Harz mountains, was built in 1120. The "Sachsenspiegel", the most famous lawbook of the German Middle Ages, was written here.
Schloss Spiegelsberge, south of Halberstadt, is a baroque hunting castle which now features a restaurant. The vaults house a wine barrel of 132,760 litres which was built in 1593-98.
Schloss Lützen, southwest of Leipzig, was build on the castle dating back to the 13th century and now houses a museum.
Rudelsburg and Saaleck, leave your car in Bad Kösen and walk up the limestone mountains by foot. The view over the Saale valley is ample reward for the effort. Both castles were erected in the 12th century to control the valley.
Schloss Wernigerode in the Harz mountains replaced the Grafenburg of the 12th century in 1862. Wernigerode is the terminal of the narrow gauge steam railway "Harzquerbahn" which has been making tracks for Nordhausen since 1899.

Nature parks
The **Harz mountains** right in the heart of Germany reach from Lower Saxony to Saxony-Anhalt. Follow the road from Göttingen to Braunlage and beyond or leave from Goslar towards Werningerode.

CULTURE PLUS

Museums and art galleries are usually open daily except Mondays.

ART GALLERIES

Listed alphabetically by town

Neue Galerie/Sammlung Ludwig
(New Gallery/Ludwig Collection)
Komphausbadstrasse 19
W-5100 Aachen
Tel: (0241) 472561

Suermondt-Ludwig Museum
Wilhelmstrasse 18
W-5100 Aachen
Tel: (0241) 472580

Staatsgalerie am Schaezler-Palais
(National Gallery at the Schaezler-Palais)
Maximilianstrasse 46
W-8900 Augsburg
Tel: (0821) 510350

Staatliche Kunsthalle
(National Art Gallery)
Lichtenthaler Allee 8a
W-7570 Baden-Baden
Tel: (07221) 23250 or 25390
(Changing exhibitions)

Brücke-Museum
Bussardsteig 9
W-1000 Berlin 33
Tel: (030) 8312029

Gemäldegalerie
(Gallery of Paintings)
Arnimallee 23/27
W-1000 Berlin 33
Tel: (030) 8301217

Nationalgalerie
(National Gallery)
Potsdamer Strasse 50
W-1000 Berlin 30
Tel: (030) 2662662

Kunsthalle
(Art Gallery)
Arthur-Ladebeck-Strasse 5
W-4800 Bielefeld
Tel: (0521) 51247980

Städtisches Kunstmuseum
(City Art Museum)
Rathausgasse 7
W-5300 Bonn 1
Tel: (0228) 773686 or 772440

Kunsthalle
(Art Gallery)
Am Wall 207
W-2800 Bremen
Tel: (0421) 324785

Herzog-Anton-Ulrich-Museum
Museumstrasse 1
W-3300 Braunschweig
Tel: (0531) 1551

Kunstgalerie Cottbus
(Cottbus Art Gallery)
Spremberger Strasse 1
O-7500 Cottbus

Gemäldegalerie Alte Meister
(Gallery of Old Masters)
Zwinger
O-8060 Dresden

Gemäldegalerie Neue Meister
(Gallery of New Masters)
Albertinum
Brühlsche Terrasse
O-8060 Dresden

Wilhelm-Lehmbruck-Museum
Düsseldorfer Strasse 51
W-4100 Duisburg 1
Tel: (0203) 28132630

Kunstmuseum Kunsthalle
(Art Museum Art Gallery)
Pempelforter Strasse 50
W-4000 Düsseldorf
Tel: (0211) 8992460

Städtische Kunsthalle
(City Art Gallery)
Grabbeplatz 4
W-4000 Düsseldorf 1
Tel: (0211) 131469

Museum Folkwang
Goethestrasse 41
W-4300 Essen
Tel: 0201/774783

**Städelsches Kunstinstitut
und Städtische Galerie**
("Stadelsches" Art Institute
and City Art Gallery)
Schaumainkai 63
W-6000 Frankfurt am Main 70
Tel: (069) 617092

Galerie Junger Künstler
(Young Artists' Gallery)
Rathaus
O-1201 Frankfurt an der Oder

Karl-Ernst-Osthaus-Museum
Hochstrasse 73
W-5800 Hagen
Tel: (023331) 207556

Staatsgalerie Moritzburg
(Moritzburg State Gallery)
F.-Bach-Platz 5
O-4020 Halle
Tel: (046) 37031

Hamburger Kunsthalle
(Hamburg Art Gallery)
Glockengiesserwall
W-2000 Hamburg 1
Tel: (040) 24825-2612

Kunstmuseum Hannover
(Hanover Art Museum)
mit Sammlung Sprengel
Kurt-Schwitters-Platz
W-3000 Hannover 1
Tel: (0511) 1684400

Landesgalerie
(State Gallery)
Im Niedersächsischen
Landesmuseum Hannover
Am Maschpark 5
W-3000 Hannover 1
Tel: (0511) 883051

Staatliche Kunsthalle
(National Art Gallery)
Hans-Thoma-Strasse 2
W-7500 Karlsruhe 1
Tel: (0721) 1351

Neue Galerie
(New Gallery)
Staatliche u. Städtische
Kunstsammlungen
Schöne Aussicht 1
W-3500 Kassel
Tel: (0561) 156266

Staatliche Kunstsammlungen
(National Art Collections)
Schloss Wilhelmshöhe
W-3500 Kassel
Tel: (0561) 36011

Kunsthalle zu Kiel
(Kiel Art Gallery)
Düsternbrooker Weg 1
W-2300 Kiel 1
Tel: (0431) 5972781

Wallraff-Richartz-Museum
Museum Ludwig
An der Rechtsschule
W-5000 Köln
Tel: (0221) 2212379

Kunsthalle Köln
(Köln Art Gallery)
Josef-Haubrich-Hof 1
W-5000 Köln
Tel: (0221) 2212335. (Changing exhibitions)

Wilhelm-Hack-Museum
Städtische Kunstgalerie
Berliner Strasse 23
W-6700 Ludwigshafen
Tel: (0621) 5043411

Städtische Kunsthalle
(City Art Gallery)
Moltkestrasse 9
W-6800 Mannheim
Tel: (0621) 5043411

Städtisches Museum
(City Museum)
Abteistrasse 9
W-4050 Mönchengladbach
Tel: (02166) 270394

Alte Pinakothek
(Old Collection of Paintings)
Barerstrasse 27
W-8000 München 2
Tel: (089) 23805216

Neue Pinakothek
(New Collection of Paintings)
Barerstrasse 29
W-8000 München 22
Tel: (089) 23805195

Schackgalerie
Prinzregentenstrasse 9
W-8000 München 22
Tel: (089) 224407

Staatsgalerie moderner Kunst
(National Gallery for Modern Art)
Haus der Kunst
Prinzregentenstrasse 1
W-8000 München 22
Tel: (089) 292710

Städtische Galerie im Lenbachhaus
(City Gallery in Lenbachhaus)
Luisenstrasse 33
W-8000 München 22
Tel: (089) 521041-3

Westfälisches Landesmuseum für Kunst und Kulturgeschichte
(Westphalian State Museum for Art and History of Art)
Domplatz 10
W-4400 Münster
Tel: (0251) 591251

Kunsthalle
(Art Gallery)
Lorenzer Strasse 32
W-8500 Nürnberg 1
Tel: (0911) 162853

Sanssouci Park mit Kunstgalerie
(Sanssonci Park and Art Gallery)
Schloss Sans Souci
O-1500 Potsdam

Saarland-Museum
Moderne Galerie
Bismarckstrasse 13
W-6600 Saarbrücken
Tel: (0681) 66361

Staatsgalerie Stuttgart
(Stuttgart National Art Gallery)
Konrad-Adenauer-Strasse 32
W-7000 Stuttgart 1
Tel: (0711) 2125108

Von-der-Heydt-Museum
Turmhof 8
W-5600 Wuppertal 1
Tel: (0202) 5636231

MUSEUMS

NON-EUROPEAN CULTURE

Listed alphabetically by town

Bode Museum
(Egyptian and Papyrus Collection)
Monbijou-Brücke
O-1000 Berlin

Pergamon Museum
(Antique Collection, Islamic Museum)
Kupfergraben
O-1000 Berlin

Ägyptisches Museum
(Egyptian Museum)
Schlosstrasse 70
W-1000 Berlin 19
Tel: (030) 3201261, 3201267

Museum für Indische Kunst
(Museum for Indian Art)
Takusstrasse 40
W-1000 Berlin 33
Tel: (030) 8301361

Museum für Islamische Kunst
(Museum for Islamic Art)
Takusstrasse 40
W-1000 Berlin 33
Tel: (030) 8301391

Museum für Ostasiatische Kunst
(Museum for East Asian Art)
Takusstrasse 40
W-1000 Berlin 33
Tel: (O30) 8301381

Kestner-Museum
Trammplatz 3
W-300 Hannover 1
Tel: (0511) 1682120

**Ägyptologische Sammlung
der Universität**
(Egyptology Collection of the University)
Marstallhof
W-6900 Heidelberg

Roemer-Pelizaeus-Museum
Am Steine 1
W-3200 Hildesheim
Tel: (05121) 1979

Museum für Ostasiatische Kunst
(Museum for East Asian Art)
Universitätsstrasse 100
W-5000 Köln
Tel: (0221) 405038

Ägyptisches Museum
(Egyptian Museum)
der Karl-Marx-Universität
Schillerstrasse 6
O-7010 Leipzig

Staatliche Sammlung Ägyptische Kunst
(National Collection of Egyptian Art)
Residenzstrasse 1
W-8000 München 2
Tel: (089) 298546

Karl-May-Museum
(American Indian Studies)
Karl-May-Strasse 15
O-8122 Radebeul

SCULPTURE & ART

Listed alphabetically by town

Kunstgewerbemuseum
(Crafts Museum)
Schloss Köpenick
O-1000 Berlin

Georg-Kolbe-Museum
Sensburger Allee 25
W-1000 Berlin 19
Tel: (030) 3042144

Skulpturengalerie
(Sculpture Gallery)
Arnimallee 23
W-1000 Berlin 33
Tel: (030) 8301252

Kunstsammlungen der Ruhr-Universität
(Ruhr University Art Collections)
Universitätsstrasse 150
W-4630 Bochum
Tel: (0234) 7004738

**Akademisches Kunstmuseum
der Universität**
(Academic Art Museum of the Universtiy)
Am Hofgarten 21
W-5300 Bonn 1
Tel: (0228) 737282

Städtische Kunstsammlungen
(City Art Collections)
Theaterplatz 1
O-9001 Chemnitz

Bauhaus Dessau
Thälmann -Allee 39
O-4500 Dessau
Tel: (047) 7051

Grünes Gewölbe
(Green Vaults)
Albertinum
O-8060 Dresden

Kupferstichkabinett
(Cabinet of Etchings)
Güntzstrasse 34
O-8060 Dresden

Porzellansammlung
(Porcelain Collection)
Zwinger
O-8060 Dresden

Historisches Museum
(History Museum)
Zwinger
O-8060 Dresden

Richard-Wagner-Museum
R.-Wagner-Str.6
O-8060 Dresden-Graupa

Liebighaus/Museum alter Plastik
(Liebighaus/Museum for
Ancient Sculptures)
Schaumainkai 71
W-6000 Frankfurt am Main 70
Tel: (069) 638907

Städtische Kunstsammlungen
(City Art Collection)
Kaisertrutz
O-8900 Görlitz

Staatliche Kunstsammlungen
(National Art Collections)
Schloss Wilhelmshöhe
W-3500 Kassel
Tel: (0561) 36011

Museum der bildenden Künste
(Museum for Fine Arts)
Georgi-Dimitroff-Platz 1
O-7010 Leipzig

Skulpturenmuseum der Stadt Marl
(Marl Museum of Sculpture)
Rathaus
W-4370 Marl 1
Tel: (02356) 105614

Schauhalle der Porzellanmanufaktur und Schauwerkstatt
(Showroom of the porcelain works and show pottery)
Leninstrasse 9
O-8250 Meissen

Glyptothek
(Sculpture Collection)
Königsplatz 3
W-8000 München 2
Tel: (089) 286100

Staatliches Museum
(National Museum)
Alter Garten 3
O-2750 Schwerin
Tel: (084) 7581

Europäischer Skulpturenpark
(European Sculpture Park)
Schloss
W-3533 Willebadessen

Schloss-Museum
(Castle Museum)
Staatsschlösser und -gärten
Oranienbaum und Luisium
O-4414 Wörlitz
Tel: (04795) 391

ETHNOLOGY

Museum für Völkerkunde
(Museum of Ethnology)
Arnimallee 23
W-1000 Berlin 33
Tel: (030) 8301-1

Übersee-Museum
(Museum of Ethnography)
Bahnhofsplatz 12
W-2800 Bremen 1
Tel: (0421) 3978357

Museum für Volkskunst
(Museum of Folk Art)
Köpckestrasse 1
O-8600 Dresden

Naturkundemuseum
(National History Museum)
Waisenhausstrassw 10
O-9200 Freiberg

Museum für Völkerkunde
(Museum of Ethnology)
Schaumainkai 29
W-6000 Frankfurt am Main 70
Tel: (069) 212-5391

Städtisches Museum
(City Museum, in the Museum of Ethnology)
Museum für Völkerkunde
Gerberau 32
W-7800 Freiburg i. Breisgau
Tel: (0761) 216-3324

Oberhessisches Museum
(Upper Hess Museum, Dept of Prehistory and Ethnology)
Abtlg. Vor-und Frühgeschichte
u. Völkerkunde
Asterweg 9
W-6300 Giessen
Tel: (064) 306-2477

Staatliches Museum für Naturkunde
(National Museum of Natural History)
Am Museum 1
O-8900 Görlitz

Halloren- und Salinenmuseum
(Museum of Salt Mines and Salt Mine Workers)

Mansfelder Str. 52
O-4020 Halle
Tel: (046) 25034

**Hamburgisches Museum
für Völkerkunde**
(Hanburg Museum of Ethnology)
Binderstrasse 14
W-2000 Hamburg 13
Tel: (040) 44195-1

**Niedersächsisches Landesmuseum
Völkerkundeabteilung**
(State Museum of Lower Saxony,
Dept of Ethnology)
Am Maschpark 5
W-3000 Hannover
Tel: (0511) 883051

Museum für Völkerkunde
(Museum of Ethnology)
der Universität Kiel
Hegewischstrasse 3
W-2300 Kiel
Tel: (0431) 5973620

**Rautenstrauch-Joest-Museum
für Völkerkunde**
(Rautenstrauch-Joest Museum of Ethnology)
Ubierring 45
W-5000 Köln 1
Tel: (0221) 311065, 311066

Museum für Völkerkunde
(Museum of Ethnology)
Johannisplatz 5-11
O-7010 Leipzig

Staatliches Museum für Völkerkunde
(National Museum of Ethnology)
Maximilianstrasse 42
W-8000 München 22
Tel: (089) 224844 oder 224846

Maritimes Museum
(Martime Museum)
August-Bebel-Str.1
O-2500 Rostock
Tel: (081) 22697 or 22698

Museum für Schiffsbau
(Museum of Shipbuilding)
Schmarl Dorf
O-2500 Rostock
Tel: (081) 71 62 02

**Mecklenburgisches Volkskunde Museum
Schwerin**
(Schwerin Museum of Folk Art
in Mechlenburg)
Schausammlung zur mecklenburgischen
Volkskultur und Volkskunst
H.-Matern-Str. 28
O-2750 Schwerin
Tel: (084) 812298

Kulturhistorisches Museum
(Art History Museum)
Mönchstr. 25-27
O-2300 Stralsund
Tel: (0821) 2180

Ozeanographisches Museum Stralsund
(Oceanographic Museum of Stralsund)
Katharinenberg 14
O-2300 Stralsund
Tel: (0821) 5135

Linden-Museum Stuttgart
(Linden-Museum Stuttgart in the
National Museum of Ethnology)
Staatliches Museum für Völkerkunde
Hegelplatz 1
W-7000 Stuttgart 1
Tel: (0711) 2050-3221

Feudalmuseum
(Feudal Museum)
Schloss
O-3700 Wernigerode
Tel: (0927) 32095

Harzmuseum
(Museum of the Harz Mountains)
Klint 10
O-3700 Wernigerode
Tel: (0927) 2856

**Museum für Naturkunde
und Völkerkunde**
(Museum of National History
and Ethnology)
Schloss
O-4600 Wittenberg
Tel: (0451) 2696

Museum für Völkerkunde
(Museum of Ethnology)
Steinstrasse 19
O-3430 Witzenhausen
Tel: (0554) 3203

SHOPPING

Germany, being a popular tourist destination, offers lots of souvenirs. The shop to look out for is the *Andenkenladen* which has anything from valuable souvenirs to all sorts of knick-knacks. Beer mugs (*Bierkrüge*) are typical gifts. You find them made out of glass, ceramics and tin, colourfully painted or plain. Especially fancy, and therefore more expensive, are mugs with tin lids. For those who do not like beer, there are typical wine glasses. White wine, for example is served in *Römer*, which are bulbous glasses.

Traditional articles of clothing in the north of Germany are the *Schiffermütze*, *Seemannspullover* and the *Friesennerz*. The *Schiffermütze* is a blue sailor's cap similar to what ex-Chancellor Helmut Schmidt wore. The *Seemannspullover* is a big blue sweater sailors wear at sea. It is very comfortable for rough winds over the North Sea coast. The *Friesennerz* is a raincoat made out of yellow rubber.

Towards the East you will find stylised figures of nutcrackers or wooden figures holding scented candles; in Meissen, watch the porcelain modellers at work.

In practically every town you will find a *Fussgängerzone* pedestrian zone with all kinds of shops, big department stores, and small specialised shops. Cigarettes, cigars and tobacco may be bought in newspaper shops which also stock postcards, writing supplies, magazines and newspapers.

SPORTS

Germans enjoy both participant and spectator sports. There is a sportsclub in every town and many athletic clubs in the cities specialising in disciplines such as wrestling, weightlifting, or boxing. The most popular sport is soccer. During the national soccer league season, millions of Germans follow the results of the games that are usually played on Saturday afternoons and shown in television excerpts at 6 p.m. Some of the main soccer clubs are Bayern München, Hamburger SV, Borussia Dortmund, Werder Bremen, Bornssia Mönchengladbach, Bayer Leverkusen, I. FC Köln.

Your hotel receptionist or the local tourist office should have information on sports activities. Since Steffi Graf, Boris Becker and Michael Stich became successful, tennis has become very popular. Other popular sports are handball, volleyball, squash, basketball, athletics, cycling, motor sports and swimming. There are parks for the dedicated jogger.

LANGUAGE

WORDS & PHRASES

Good morning
Guten Morgen
Good Afternoon
Guten Tag
Good evening
Guten Abend
Good night

Gute Nacht
Goodbye
Auf Wiedersehen
I don't understand
Ich verstehe Sie nicht
Do you speak English?
Sprechen Sie Englisch?
Could you please speak slower?
Könnten Sie bitte etwas langsamer sprechen?
What's that in English?
Was heisst das auf Englisch?
Yes/No
Ja/Nein
Please/Thank you
Bitte/Danke
Never mind
Bitte; *keine Ursache*
Turn to the right! (left)
Biegen Sie nach rechts ab! (*links*)
Go straight on!
Gehen Sie geradeaus weiter!
Above/below
oben/unten

AT THE HOTEL

Where is the next hotel?
Wo ist das nächste Hotel?
Do you have a single room?
Haben Sie ein Einzelzimmer?
Do you have a double room?
Haben Sie ein Doppelzimmer?
Do you have a room with a private bath?
Haben Sie ein Zimmer mit Bad?
How much is it?
Wieviel kostet das?
How much is a room with full board?
Wieviel kostet ein Zimmer mit Vollpension?
Please show me another room!
Bitte zeigen Sie mir ein anderes Zimmer!
We'll (I'll) be staying for one night.
Wir bleiben (Ich bleibe) eine Nacht!
When is breakfast?
Wann gibt es Frühstück?
Where is the toilet?
Wo ist die Toilette?
Where is the bathroom?
Wo ist das Badezimmer?

TRAVELLING

Is there a bus to the centre?
Gibt es einen Bus ins Stadtzentrum?
Is there a guided sightseeing tour?
Werden kommentierte Besichtigungstouren

durchgeführt?
church
Kirche
memorial
Denkmal
castle
Schloss
old part of town
Altstadtviertel
Where can I buy souvenirs?
Wo kann ich Souvenirs kaufen?
Do you know a nightclub/disco?
Kennen Sie einen Nachtklub/eine Disko?
Where is the nearest cinema?
Wo ist das nächste Kino?
What film does it show?
Was für ein Film läuft dort?
Where is the post office?
Wo ist das Postamt?
Where is the nearest bank?
Wo ist die nächste Bank?
Where can I change money?
Wo kann ich Geld wechseln?
Where is the pharmacy?
Wo ist die Apotheke?
What time do they close?
Wann schliessen sie?
open/closed
geöffnet/geschlossen
close/far
nah/weit
cheap/expensive
billig/teuer
free (of charge)
kostenlos
price
Preis
change
Wechselgeld
Have you got any change?
Können Sie wechseln?
telephone booth
Telefonzelle
Is this the way to the station?
Ist das der Weg zum Bahnhof?
Where is platform one?
Wo ist Gleis eins?
Where is the airport?
Wo ist der Flughafen?
Can you call me a taxi?
Können Sie mir ein Taxi rufen?
Can you take me to the airport?
Können Sie mich zum Flughafen fahren?
Where do I get a ticket?
Wo kann ich eine Fahrkarte kaufen?

departure/arrival	
Abfahrt/Ankunft	
When is the next flight/train to...?	
Wann geht der nächste Flug/Zug nach...?	
to change (flights/trains)	
umsteigen	
exit	
Ausgang/Ausfahrt	
entrance	
Eingang/Einfahrt	
travel agency	
Reisebüro	
picnic area	
Rastplatz	
gas (petrol) station	
Tankstelle	
bridge	
Brücke	
crossroads	
Kreuzung	
no parking	
Parken verboten	
no stopping	
Halten verboten	
one-way street	
Einbahnstrasse	
hospital	
Krankenhaus	
ferry	
Fähre	
fee	
Gebühr	
height	
Höhe	
width	
Breite	
length	
Länge	
Have you anything to declare?	
Haben Sie etwas zu ver zollen?	
customs	
Zoll	

napkin	*Serviette*
beer/wine	*Bier/Wein*
bread/cheese	*Brot/Käse*
meat	*Fleisch*
sausage	*Würstchen*
honey	*Honig*
noodles	*Nudeln*
potatoes	*Kartoffeln*
rice	*Reis*
jam	*Marmelade*
egg	*Ei*
milk	*Milch*
coffee	*Kaffee*
tea	*Tee*
sugar	*Zucker*
butter	*Butter*
Can we have the bill, please?	*Können wir bitte bezahlen?*
to pay	*bezahlen*
tip	*Trinkgeld*
to complain	*sich beschweren*

DAYS OF THE WEEK

Monday	*Montag*
Tuesday	*Dienstag*
Wednesday	*Mittwoch*
Thursday	*Donnerstag*
Friday	*Freitag*
Saturday	*Samstag, Sonnabend*
Sunday	*Sonntag*

MONTHS

January	*Januar*
February	*Februar*
March	*März*
April	*April*
May	*Mai*
June	*Juni*
July	*Juli*
August	*August*
September	*September*
October	*Oktober*
November	*November*
December	*Dezember*

IN A RESTAURANT

Do you know a good restaurant?	*Kennen Sie ein gutes Restaurant?*
Can you recommend anything?	*Können Sie etwas empfehlen?*
Could we order a meal, please?	*Können wir bitte bestellen?*
menu	*Speisekarte*
lunch	*Mittagessen*
evening meal	*Abendessen*
knife/fork/spoon	*Messer/Gabel/Löffel*

NUMBERS

0	*Null*
1	*eins*
2	*zwei*
3	*drei*
4	*vier*
5	*fünf*

6	*sechs*
7	*sieben*
8	*acht*
9	*neun*
10	*zehn*
11	*elf*
12	*zwölf*
13	*dreizehn*
14	*vierzehn*
15	*fünfzehn*
16	*sechzehn*
17	*siebzehn*
18	*achtzehn*
19	*neunzehn*
20	*zwanzig*
30	*dreissig*
40	*vierzig*
50	*fünfzig*
60	*sechzig*
70	*siebzig*
80	*achtzig*
90	*neunzig*
100	*hundert*
200	*zweihundert*
1,000	*tausend*
2,000	*zweitausend*
1,000,000	*eine Million*
1st	*erste(r)*
2nd	*zweite(r)*
3rd	*dritte(r)*
4th	*vierte(r)*
5th	*fünfte(r)*
6th	*sechste(r)*
7th	*siebte(r)*
8th	*achte(r)*
9th	*neunte(r)*
10th	*zehnte(r)*
11th	*elfte(r)*
12th	*zwölfte(r)*
13th	*dreizehnte(r)*
20th	*zwanzigste(r)*
21st	*einundzwanzigste(r)*
100th	*hundertste(r)*
1000th	*tausendste(r)*

FURTHER READING

HISTORY & SOCIETY

Bailey, George. *Germans.* (1972)
Bradley, John. *The Illustrated History of the Third Reich.* (1978)
Calleo, David. *The German Problem Reconsidered: 1860–1978.* (1980)
Craig, Gordon. *The Germans.* (1982)
Dawson, William H. *German Life in Town and Country.* (1977)
Holborn, Hajo. *A History of Modern Germany*: 1840–1945. (1969)
Jones, Brangwyn G. *Germany: An Introduction to the German Nation.* (1970)
Kirsch, Henry. *German Democratic Republic: A Profile.* (1985)
Lowie, Robert H. *Toward Understanding Germany.* (1979)
MacDonald, Ian. *Get to Know Germany.* (1975)
Marsh, David. *New Germany at the Crossroads.* (1990)

To get to know and understand the German mentality, read any of the classical works by Goethe and Schiller, Heinrich Heine and Friedrich Hölderlin, to name a few. Below is a selection of German and English/American authors:

Grass, Günter. *Headbirths*; *The Germans Are Dying Out*; and *The Flounder.*
Mann, Thomas. *Buddenbrooks.*
Mansfield, Catherine. *In A German Pension.*
Stael, Madame de. *Germany.*
Twain, Mark. *A Tramp Abroad.*

USEFUL ADDRESSES

TOURIST INFORMATION

Anywhere in Germany where tourists are expected you should find a tourist authority or information office (marked with an "i").

Write to the office of your destination for any information you require. The following overall tourist authorities in the West will give you more regional information:

Deutscher Fremdenverkehrsverband e.V.
Niebuhrstrasse 16b
W-5300 Bonn 1
Tel: (02228) 214071-73

Fremdenverkehrsverband
(Tourist Authority)
Schleswig-Holstein e.V.
Niemannsweg 31
W-2300 Kiel 1
Tel: (0431) 56302 or 561061

Fremdenverkehrsverband
Nordsee-Niedersachsen-Bremen e.V.
Gottorpstrasse 18
W-2900 Oldenburg i.O.
Tel: (0441) 14535

Fremdenverkehrsverband
Lüneburger Heide e.V.
Glockenhaus
W-2120 Lüneburg
Tel: (0413) 42006

Harzer Fremdenverkehrsverband e.V.
Marktstrasse 45
W-3380 Goslar 1
Tel: (05321) 20032

Fremdenverkehrsverband
Weserbergland-Mittelweser e.V.
Falkestrasse 2
W-3250 Hameln 1
Tel: (05151) 24566

Verkehrsverein GmbH Münster
Berliner Platz 22
W-4400 Münster
Tel: (0251) 510180

Touristik Münsterland
"Das Grüne Band"
Hohe Schule 13
W-4430 Steinfurt
Tel: (02551) 5099
Fax: (02551) 7144

Landesverkehrsverband
Westfalen e.V.
Balkenstrasse 40
W-4600 Dortmund 1
Tel: (0231) 571715

Landesverkehrsverband
Rheinland e.V.
Abraham-Lincoln-Strasse 38-43
W-6200 Wiesbaden
Tel: (0611) 73725 or 367226

Fremdenverkehrsverband
Rheinland-Pfalz e.V.
Löhrstrasse 103
W-5400 Koblenz
Tel: (0261) 31079

Fremdenverkehrsverband
Saarland e.V.
Am Stiefel 2
W-6600 Saarbrücken 3
Tel: (0681) 35376

Landesfremdenverkehrsverband
Baden-Württemberg e.V.
Bussenstrasse 23
W-7000 Stuttgart 1
Tel: (0711) 481045

Fremdenverkehrsverband
Neckarland-Schwaben e.V.
Wolhausstrasse 14
W-7100 Heilbronn
Tel: (07131) 629021 or 629062

Fremdenverkehrsverband
Schwarzwald e.V.
Bertoldstrasse 45
W-7800 Freiburg i.Br.
Tel: (0761) 31317

Fremdenverkehrsverband
Bodensee-Oberschwaben e.V.
Schützenstrasse 8
W-7750 Konstanz
Tel: (07531) 222312

Fremdenverkehrsverband
Franken e.V.
Am Plärrer 14
W-8500 Nürnberg 81
Tel: (0911) 264202 or 264204

Fremdenverkehrsverband
München-Oberbayern e.V.
Sonnenstrasse 10
W-8000 München 2
Tel: (089) 597347

Fremdenverkehrsverband
der Freien Hansestadt Bremen
Bahnhofsplatz 29
W-2800 Bremen 1
Tel: (0421) 3636 or 3631

Fremdenverkehrsverband
Allgäu/Bayerisch-Schwaben
W-8900 Augsburg 1
Tel: (0821) 33335

Fremdenverkehrsverband
Ostbayern e.V.
Landshuter Strasse 13
W-8400 Regensburg
Tel: (0941) 560260 or 520262

Verkehrsamt Berlin
Europa-Centre
W-1000 Berlin 30
Tel: (030) 21234

Hamburg-Information GmbH
Neuer Jungfernstieg 5
W-2000 Hamburg 36
Tel: (040) 351301

The tourist offices in the five new states (originally East Germany) are simply called "information". Here are some of the main offices:

Berlin-Information
Informationszentrum am Fernsehturm
O-1020 Berlin
Tel: (02) 2124675 (enquiries)
2124512 (groups)

Dresden-Information
Pragerstrasse 10/11
O-8010 Dresden
Tel: (051) 4955025

Eisenach-Information
Bahnhofstrasse 3-5
O-5900 Eisenach
Tel: (0623) 4895 or 6161

Erfurt-Information
Bahnhofstrasse 37
O-5020 Erfurt
Tel: (061) 26267

Frankfurt-Information
Karl-Marx-Strasse 8a
O-1200 Frankfurt/Oder
Tel: (030) 22249 or 24477

Gotha-Information
Hauptmarkt 2
O-5800 Gotha
Tel: (0622) 4036

Halle-Neustadt-Information
Wohnkomplex VII Block 338
O-4090 Halle-Neustadt
Tel: (046) 656398 or 656298

Jena-Information
Ernst-Thälmann-Ring 35
O-6900 Jena
Tel: (078) 24671

Leipzig-Information
Sachsenplatz 1
O-7010 Leipzig
Tel: (041) 79590 or 7959200

Magdeburg-Information
Alter Markt 9
PSF 266
O-3010 Magdeburg
Tel: (091) 31967

Potsdam-Information
Friedrich-Ebert-Strasse 5
O-1560 Potsdam
Tel: (033) 23012

Rostock-Information
Schickmannstrasse 13/14
O-2500 Rostock
Tel: (081) 22619 or 34602

Sächsische Schweiz-Information
Jakobi-Strasse 5
O-8300 Pirna
Tel: (056) 852 35

Weimar-Information
Marktstrasse 4
O-5300 Weimar
Tel: (0621) 2173 or 5690

Wittenberg-Information
Collegienstrasse 8
O-Wittenberg
Tel: (08546) 2239 or 2537

Rügen-Information
Hauptstrasse 9
O-2337 Binz auf Rügen
Tel: (082799) 81241

EMBASSIES & CONSULATES

Algeria
5300 Bonn 2, Rheinallee 32,
Tel: (0228) 356054

Argentina
5300 Bonn 1, Adenauerallee 55,
Tel: (0228) 223973

Australia
5300 Bonn 2
Godesberger Allee 107,
Tel: (0228) 81003-0

Austria
5300 Bonn, Johanniterstrasse 2,
Tel: (0228) 230051

Belgium
5300 Bonn
Kaiser-Friedrich-Strasse 7,
Tel: (0228) 212001

Bolivia
5300 Bonn 2, Konstantinstrasse 16,
Tel: (0228) 362038

Brazil
5300 Bonn 2, Kennedyallee 74,
Tel: (0228) 376976

Bulgaria
5300 Bonn 2, Auf der Hostert 6,
Tel: (0228) 363061

Burma
5300 Bonn 1, Schumannstrasse 112,
Tel: (0228) 211091

Canada
5300 Bonn 1, Friedrich-Wilhelm-Strasse 18,
Tel: (0228) 231061

Chile
5300 Bonn 2, Kronprinzenstrasse 20,
Tel: (0228) 363089

China, The People's Republic of
5300 Bonn 2, Kurfürstenallee 12,
Tel: (0228) 361095

Colombia
5300 Bonn 1, Friedrich-Wilhelm-Strasse 35,
Tel: (0228) 234565

Costa Rica
5300 Bonn 1, Borsigallee 22,
Tel: (0228) 254940

Cuba
5300 Bonn 2, Kennedyallee 22,
Tel: (0228) 309-0

Cyprus
5300 Bonn 2, Kronprinzenstrasse 58,
Tel: (0228) 363330

Czechoslovakia
5300 Bonn 3, Im Rheingarten 7,
Tel: (0228) 471277

Denmark
5300 Bonn 1, Pfälzer Strasse 14,
Tel: (0228) 72991-0

Dominican Republic
5300 Bonn 2, Burgstrasse 87,
Tel: (0228) 364956

Ecuador
5300 Bonn 2, Koblenzer Strasse 37,
Tel: (0228) 352544

Egypt
5300 Bonn 2, Uhlandstrasse 32,
Tel: (0228) 352901

Ethiopia
5300 Bonn 1, Brentanostrasse 1,
Tel: (0228) 233041

Finland
5300 Bonn 2, Friesdorfer Strasse 1,
Tel: (0228) 311033

France
5300 Bonn 2, Kapellenstrasse 1a,
Tel: (0228) 362031

Great Britain
5300 Bonn 1, Friedrich-Ebert-Allee 77,
Tel: (0228) 344061

Greece
5300 Bonn 1, Weberstrasse 83,
Tel: (0228) 215654

Guatemala
5300 Bonn 2, Zietenstrasse 1b,
Tel: (0228) 351579

Haiti
5300 Bonn 2, Schlossallee 10,
Tel: (0228) 340351

Honduras
5300 Bonn 2, Ubierstrasse 1,
Tel: (0228) 356394

Hungary
5300 Bonn 2, Turmstrasse 30,
Tel: (0228) 376794

Iceland
5300 Bonn 2, Kronprinzenstrasse 6,
Tel: (0228) 375937

India
5300 Bonn 1, Adenauerallee 264,
Tel: (0228) 5405-1

Indonesia
5300 Bonn 2, Godesberger Allee 133,
Tel: (0228) 81005-0

Iraq
5300 Bonn 2, Dürenstrasse 33,
Tel: (0228) 8203-1

Ireland, The Republic of
5300 Bonn 2, Godesberger Allee 119,
Tel: (0228) 376937

Israel
5300 Bonn 2, Simrockallee 2,
Tel: (0228) 823-1

Italy
5300 Bonn 2, Karl-Finkenburg-Strasse 49,
Tel: (0228) 82006-0

Japan
5300 Bonn 2, Bonn-Center,
Tel: (0228) 500-1

Kenya
5300 Bonn 2, Villichgasse 23,
Tel: (0228) 353066

Korea, The Republic of
5300 Bonn 2, Adenauerallee 124,
Tel: (0228) 214358

Kuwait
5300 Bonn 2, Godesberger Allee 77,
Tel: (0228) 378081

Lebanon
5300 Bonn 2, Rheinallee 27,
Tel: (0228) 352075

Liberia
5300 Bonn 2, Hohenzollernstrasse 73,
Tel: (0228) 351810

Luxembourg
5300 Bonn, Adenauerallee 110,
Tel: (0228) 214008

Malaysia
5300 Bonn 2, Mittelstrasse 23,
Tel: (0228) 351056

Malta
5300 Bonn 2, Viktoriastrasse 1,
Tel: (0228) 363017

Mexico
5300 Bonn 1, Oxfordstrasse 12,
Tel: (0228) 631226

Monaco
5300 Bonn 1, Zitelmannstrasse 16,
Tel: (0228) 232007

Morocco
5300 Bonn 2, Gotenstrasse 7,
Tel: (0228) 355040

Nepal
5300 Bonn 2, Im Hag 15,
Tel: (0228) 343097

Netherlands
5300 Bonn, Straschenweg 10,
Tel: (0228) 238091

New Zealand
5300 Bonn, Bonn-Center HI 902,
Tel: (0228) 214021

Nicaragua
5300 Bonn 2, Konstantinstrasse 41,
Tel: (0228) 355938

Nigeria
5300 Bonn 2, Goldbayweg 13,
Tel: (0228) 322071

Norway
5300 Bonn 2, Gotenstrasse 163
Tel: (0228) 374055

Oman
5300 Bonn 2, Lindenallee 11,
Tel: (0228) 357031

Pakistan
5300 Bonn 2, Rheinallee 24,
Tel: (0228) 351036

Panama
5300 Bonn 2, Lützowstrasse 1,
Tel: (0228) 351036

Paraguay
5300 Bonn 2, Plittersdorfer Strasse 121,
Tel: (0228) 356727

Peru
5300 Bonn, Mozartstrasse 34,
Tel: (0228) 638012

The Philippines
5300 Bonn 1, Argelanderstrasse 1,
Tel: (0228) 213071

Poland
5300 Köln 51, Lindenallee 7,
Tel: (0221) 380261

Portugal
5300 Bonn 2, Ubierstrasse 78,
Tel: (0228) 363011

Romania
5300 Bonn 1, Legionsweg 14,
Tel: (0228) 670001

Saudi Arabia
5300 Bonn 1, Godesberger Allee 42,
Tel: (0228) 379007

Singapore
5300 Bonn 2, Südstrasse 133,
Tel: (0228) 312007

Somalia
5300 Bonn 2, Hohenzollernstrasse 12,
Tel: 355084

South Africa
5300 Bonn 2, Auf der Hostert 3,
Tel: (0228) 8201-0

Spain
5300 Bonn, Schlosstrasse 4,
Tel: (0228) 217511

Sri Lanka
5300 Bonn 2, Rolandstrasse 52,
Tel: (0228) 332055

Sweden
5300 Bonn 1, Heussallee,
Tel: (0228) 26002-0

Switzerland
5300 Bonn 2, Gotenstrasse 156,
Tel: (0228) 376655

Tanzania
5300 Bonn 2, Theaterplatz 26,
Tel: (0228) 355065

Thailand
5300 Bonn 2, Ubierstrasse 65,
Tel: (0228) 355065

Tunisia
5300 Bonn 2, Godesberger Allee 103,
Tel: (0228) 344081

Turkey
5300 Bonn 2, Utestrasse 47,
Tel: (0228) 344081

Uruguay
5300 Bonn 2, Gotenstrasse 1,
Tel: (0228) 356570

USA
5300 Bonn 2, Deichmanns Aue,
Tel: (0228) 339-1

USSR
5300 Bonn 2, Waldstrasse 42,
Tel: (0228) 312086

Venezuela
5300 Bonn 2, Godesberger Allee 119,
Tel: (0228) 376631

Yemen, The Republic of
5300 Bonn 2, Godesberger Allee 125,
Tel: (0228) 376851

Yugoslavia
5300 Bonn 2, Schlossallee 5,
Tel: (0228) 344051

Zaire
5300 Bonn 2, An der Nesselburg 38,
Tel: (0228) 349193

Zimbabwe
5300 Bonn 2, Viktoriastrasse 28,
Tel: (0228) 356071

ART/PHOTO CREDITS

Photography by **Erhard Pansegrau**
(*unless otherwise stated*)

INDEX

439

N

O

P

Q – R

S

W